Adapting Stepl
Volume 2

Adapting Stephen King

Volume 2

Night Shift from
Short Stories to Screenplays

Joseph Maddrey

McFarland & Company, Inc., Publishers
Jefferson, North Carolina

ISBN (print) 978-1-4766-9010-0
ISBN (ebook) 978-1-4766-4821-7

LIBRARY OF CONGRESS AND BRITISH LIBRARY
CATALOGUING DATA ARE AVAILABLE

Library of Congress Control Number 2021026546

Front cover image of Stephen King
in *Creepshow*, 1982 (Warner Bros./Photofest)

Printed in the United States of America

*McFarland & Company, Inc., Publishers
Box 611, Jefferson, North Carolina 28640
www.mcfarlandpub.com*

Table of Contents

Acknowledgments

I am grateful to the many people who have helped me with my research for this volume: Richard Abate, Donald P. Borchers, Patrick Bromley, Justin Brooks, Stephen David Brooks, Adam Burkhart, Ned Comstock, Philip de Blasi, George Demick, John Esposito, Kris Etchison, Michael Felsher, Peter Filardi, George Goldsmith, Peter Hansen, Adam Charles Hart, Samson Stormcrow Hayes, Louise Hilton, David Hoffman, Del Howison, Tim Kring, Jim Kunz, Mark Lipson, Adam S. Lowenstein, Richard Christian Matheson, Tom McLoughlin, John Kenneth Muir, Lara Rosenstock, Mark Rosenthal, Ben Rubin, Jeff Schiro, Warren Silver, Fiona Subotsky, Sergei Subotsky, Doug Whipple, Harry Wiland, Byron Willinger, Gary L. Wood and John Woodward.

I must acknowledge several important libraries that have made my research possible: Browne Popular Culture Library at Bowling Green State University; Cinematic Arts Library at the University of Southern California; Internet Archive (San Francisco); Los Angeles Public Library; Margaret Herrick Library in Beverly Hills; Raymond H. Fogler Library at the University of Maine in Orono; and the Wisconsin Center for Film and Theater Research.

Last but not least: Endless thanks to my wife Liza and daughter Olivia, who put up with my geekiness.

Series Preface

To take a novel and turn it into a screenplay is sort of accepted practice. Everybody sort of understands how it's done, but I don't know if anybody really does.

—Stephen King

According to the Guinness Book of World Records, Stephen King has inspired more motion picture adaptations than any other living author. That's a strong testament to the author's popularity but most moviegoers probably still don't realize how many Stephen King film adaptations have been made. The Internet Movie Database lists more than three hundred titles, nearly fifty of which are major Hollywood feature films.

King's name is readily associated with iconic horror films like CARRIE (1976), THE SHINING (1980), THE DEAD ZONE (1983), PET SEMATARY (1989), MISERY (1990), and IT (2017–2019). The author is also associated with several infamous horror titles, like CHILDREN OF THE CORN, THE LAWNMOWER MAN, and THE MANGLER. Beyond the horror genre, his work has inspired some remarkable outliers, including STAND BY ME (1986), THE SHAWSHANK REDEMPTION (1994), THE GREEN MILE (2001), and even the Arnold Schwarzenegger vehicle THE RUNNING MAN (1986). Dig deeper and you'll find dozens more films, TV movies, sequels, spinoffs, serialized shows, anthology episodes, and "dollar babies" (short films based on stories King has licensed for $1 each). Between 2017 and 2019 alone, Hollywood studios released eight feature films and four new TV series based on King's work. As of 2022, dozens of new adaptations are in the works—which makes "adapting Stephen King" a prime topic for serious study. This book aims to bring together two unwieldy subjects: Stephen King Studies, a diffuse body of literary criticism with frequent detours into film criticism, and Adaptation Studies, a new-ish academic discipline that supersedes the fidelity criticism of traditional bibliophiles and the auteurism principles of traditional cinephiles.

King's fiction has been a subject of serious study since the early 1980s. Pioneering efforts include a pair of anthologies edited by Tim Underwood and Chuck Miller (*Fear Itself*, published in 1982; *Kingdom of Fear* in 1986) and a third by Don Herron (*Reign of Fear*, 1988), as well as standalone works by Douglas E. Winter (*Stephen King: The Art of Darkness*, 1982, revised 1986), Michael R. Collings (who published seven short books about King between 1985 and 1987), Tony Magistrale (beginning with *Landscape of Fear: Stephen King's American Gothic*, 1988), George Beahm (beginning with *The Stephen King Companion*, 1989), Tyson Blue (beginning with *The Unseen King*, 1989), and Stephen J. Spignesi (beginning with *The Shape Under the Sheet: The Complete Stephen King Encyclopedia*, 1990). King has provided additional critical fodder in his books *Danse*

1

Macabre (1981) and *On Writing* (2000), as well as dozens of essays and interviews—many of them collected in Underwood and Miller's anthologies *Bare Bones* (1988) and *Feast of Fear* (1992), and in King's own *Secret Windows* (2000). Other critics and biographers—most notably Stanley Wiater, Christopher Golden, Hans-Ake Lilja, Rocky Wood, Bev Vincent, Brian Freeman, Justin Brooks and Robin Furth—have continued to plow the field.

Over the years, an equally large volume of work has sprung up around the film adaptations of King's material. Journalists for movie magazines such as *Fangoria, Cinefantastique, Fantastic Films,* and *Starburst* led the charge in the early 1980s by conducting interviews with the author and filmmakers who were translating his work into a different medium. Today, the contributions of these writers serve as the foundation on which most studies of "Hollywood's Stephen King" are built. Michael R. Collings was the first to attempt an in-depth scholarly study; his 1986 book *The Films of Stephen King* remains a shining example of research and analysis. Jessie Horsting's *Stephen King at the Movies*, published the same year, is equally illuminating and written in a more conversational style. Following these leads, Jeff Connor conducted new primary research for his 1987 book *Stephen King Goes to Hollywood*, and Gary L. Wood did the same for a comprehensive Stephen King-themed issue of *Cinefantastique* (Vol. 21, No. 4) in 1991.

These early studies quickly became outdated, creating a market for new studies—some noteworthy and some not. Stephen Jones' *Creepshows* (2001) contributed compelling behind-the-scenes information for the newer films but could hardly do justice to the ever-expanding oeuvre within its restrictive coffee-table format. Scott Von Doviak's 2014 book *Stephen King Films FAQ* is a more comprehensive compilation of production anecdotes and critical evaluations. With the 2003 book *The Films of Stephen King*, Tony Magistrale offered the first scholarly analysis since Collings. Like his predecessor, he approached the adaptations as a student of King's literary work rather than a film scholar. As a result, his study leans toward fidelity criticism, generally assuming the preeminence of King's texts over the film adaptations and judging the films according to their faithfulness to the text. Scott Browning took the opposite approach in his books *Stephen King on the Big Screen* (2009) and *Stephen King on the Small Screen* (2011), analyzing the films through the lens of Film Studies. His approach has its limitations; Browning openly confesses to using the auteur theory—which problematically treats film directors as the primary "authors" of films—as a convenient crutch. Simon Brown tried a third approach in his 2018 book *Screening Stephen King*, which examines King adaptations within the context of horror genre history.

In recent years, other writers have chosen to focus on one adaptation at a time. The Centipede Press series Studies in the Horror Film has offered indispensable tomes on Brian De Palma's CARRIE, Tobe Hooper's SALEM'S LOT, and Stanley Kubrick's THE SHINING. Author Lee Gambin has written in-depth books about the making of Lewis Teague's CUJO and John Carpenter's CHRISTINE, both of which include a ton of new primary research. Tyson Blue has edited a critical edition of Frank Darabont's screenplays for THE SHAWSHANK REDEMPTION and THE GREEN MILE. Also, feature-length documentaries like JUST DESSERTS: THE MAKING OF CREEPSHOW (2007), UNEARTHED AND UNTOLD: THE PATH TO PET SEMATARY (2017), and PENNYWISE: THE STORY OF IT (2021) continue to provide new material for contemplation. There seems to be no end to the celebrations of Stephen King's cinematic multi-verse, and no waning of interest.

Which brings me to *Adapting Stephen King*, a prospective multi-volume series of books that will draw on the wealth of existing studies and provide additional primary research, in order to give detailed accounts of the adaptation process. The goal will be to look beyond the usual production anecdotes and focus on the ways and reasons that Stephen King's stories have been reconfigured by different storytellers for different mediums at different times.

Adaptation Studies, as an academic discipline, has come a long way over the past two decades. Leading theorist Thomas Leitch has made students acutely aware of the dichotomy between fidelity criticism, which is often organized around canonical authors like William Shakespeare and Charles Dickens, and auteurism, which is usually organized around canonical directors like Alfred Hitchcock and Stanley Kubrick. Leitch and his peers are working to bridge the gap between the two approaches. In 2011, for example, novelist Mary H. Snyder proposed a new method she termed *fidelity/infidelity analysis*, which examines "why the film was made the way it was, and why the filmmaker adapted the novel the way they did, and what about the novel was used to formulate the film." Snyder contends that such analysis should not be used to prop up *judgments* of a particular film adaptation—or to determine whether it is "better" or "worse" than the source story—but instead to illuminate the *creative process* of adaptation.

Snyder's approach presents some significant challenges. Film professor Peter Lev has pointed out that Adaptation Studies scholars often fail to consider all the steps in the process of translating a story from page to screen; they merely "content themselves with a comparison between literary source and finished film." Anyone who has worked in the film and television industry can attest that all projects go through an arduous development process involving numerous sources of creative—and, some might say, anti-creative—influence. Perhaps no critic can fully contemplate and appreciate all of the various influences. This study will focus on one crucial element of the process that should not be ignored: the screenplay. Lev points out that studying screenplays is difficult, because (1) most screenplays are unpublished and therefore relatively inaccessible, and (2) tracking changes from the source material through multiple drafts of a screenplay (not to mention treatments and production storyboards, etc.) requires painstaking research and attention to detail. Furthermore, a judicious examination of these materials demands extensive knowledge of the source story and the various storytellers, as well as some working knowledge of the film and television development process.

In confronting the latter challenge, I have taken some cues from Linda Seger's 1992 book *The Art of Adaptation*, an industry insider's practical guide to screenwriting and story development. Seger proposes that a film succeeds or fails according to the vitality of four essential elements: story (by which she seems to mean the basic plot), characterization, theme, and style. She points to Rob Reiner's film STAND BY ME—an adaptation of Stephen King's novella *The Body*—as a prime example of a good "story": *four boys on a quest to find a dead body*. She explains that the central quest gives the film a two-dimensional momentum from beginning to end, while the characters speed up and slow down the momentum and give the story depth.

Layered on top of the plot and characterizations is the element of theme, which Seger defines as a storyteller's reason for telling the story. Theme is the most difficult of the first three elements to translate into a new medium, because good storytellers have their own personal reason(s) for telling, or re-telling, a story. Stephen King has said that while good stories should function independent of theme, "there ought to be something more going on … some expression of belief" (King: "Evening" 1983). In translating a story to a new medium, plots may be augmented or streamlined and characters may be modified, but successful adaptors must go further; they must try to understand the original creator's reason for telling the story, and either channel that reason or devise a new one. In some cases, adaptors may strive for total fidelity to original storyteller's intentions. Other times, things get more complicated.

Style is an equally tricky element. In traditional film criticism, the style of a film is usually equated with the director's "vision." To be fair, style also comes from producers, screenwriters, cinematographers, production designers, actors, editors, composers, sound designers, and countless others. For the sake of this study, I will concentrate on the role of screenwriters, producers, and directors in crafting the screenplay—the vital step which is often overlooked in Adaptation Studies and Stephen King Studies.

This brings me to the difficult matter of determining a storyteller's reason(s) for telling a specific story in a particular way. Here, I defer to the writings of novelist and literary critic Dorothy L. Sayers. In her 1943 book *The Mind of the Maker*, Sayers compares the mind of a fiction writer to the mind of God, suggesting an analogous relationship between the Catholic doctrine of the Holy Trinity (the Father, the Son, and the Holy Spirit) and the threefold structure of the storytelling brain. According to Sayers, the first thing that materializes in the mind of the maker is an Idea for a story. The Idea remains with the writer "while writing it and after it is finished, just as it was at the beginning." Next comes the Energy or the work of writing the story—making the words flesh. Finally, the story manifests itself as Power, "the thing which flows back to the writer from his own activity and makes him, as it were, the reader of his own book."

Sayers maintains that no one—not even the author—can properly articulate the original idea, but Stephen King has repeatedly attempted to do so. In a 1982 essay, he declared, "Almost any writer can usually trace out the genesis of an idea that becomes a story or a novel, and it almost always resembles the conception of a child—two facts or two observations suddenly come in collision with each other and produce an offspring—a *what if?*" King added complexity to this simple statement by stipulating that "twenty different sexual encounters may result in twenty different children" (King: "On *The Shining*" 1982). King himself has occasionally tried to develop the same inciting Idea at different times in his life, producing very different stories. His aborted 1977 novel *The Cannibals*, for example, was re-imagined as the 2009 novel *Under the Dome*. Similarly, his unproduced 1983 script THE SHOTGUNNERS inspired the 1996 novel *The Regulators*.

In addition to his own reconfigurations of his fictional universe, Stephen King's ideas have been re-imagined by many different creators—perhaps I should say *co-creators*—to produce several generations of cinematic children. Rather than merely synopsize the resulting stories, my goal is to compare, contrast, and contextualize each of these adaptations as the products of their creators. This is a book about the minds of the makers.

A Note on Style

Before we get started, I should clarify that I have used an unconventional style for designating story titles. Normally, book and film titles appear in *italics*. However, because this study is about comparing and contrasting literary properties with film properties using the exact same title, I thought it important to clearly distinguish between the two. Accordingly, I have used *italics* for book titles and ALL CAPS for screenplay and film titles. For example, Stephen King's 1974 novel is identified as *Carrie*, while Lawrence D. Cohen's screenplay and Brian De Palma's film adaptation are identified as CARRIE.

When quoting previously published interviews, I have credited the author / interviewer by name after each quote. I have also indicated the year in which each quote was originally published—because memories fade, opinions change, and context matters.

Introduction

Origin Stories

Nineteen seventy-seven was a pivotal year for Stephen King. Following the success of a major film adaptation of *Carrie* and remarkably strong sales of his third novel *The Shining*, the author's back catalog of short stories—many of which had been published in magazines over the course of the previous decade—suddenly became a marketable commodity. As King's novel-in-progress *The Stand* grew to epic proportions and the author worried about meeting his publisher's delivery deadline, he proposed a short story collection to fill the void.

King had published his first short story at the age of eighteen. "I Was a Teenage Grave Robber"—a tale of a mad scientist who breeds giant, radioactive maggots—appeared in a 1965 issue of the fanzine *Comics Review*. A year later, King published a revised version of the story, now called "In a Half-World of Terror," in Marv Wolfman's fanzine *Stories of Suspense*. Soon after, the author made his first professional sale to *Startling Mystery Stories* editor Robert Lowndes, who paid $35 for "The Glass Floor," an Edgar Allan Poe pastiche about a spooky house with a deadly mirror room. Although King has dismissed both of these stories as juvenilia, they provided the necessary encouragement for him to keep writing and submitting his work for publication.

In 1968 and 1969, while he was an undergraduate at the University of Maine in Orono, King published five short stories and four poems in school literary magazines. Between 1970 and 1974, he also found an audience through the men's magazine *Cavalier*, which published ten of his stories during the lean years before *Carrie* sold. Thereafter, King continued to mine the men's magazine market, eventually getting stories published in relatively high-profile titles like *Penthouse* and *Gallery*. In 1975 and 1976, he expanded his reach to include smaller, Maine-based publications and the women's magazine *Cosmopolitan*.

When it came time to assemble the short story collection *Night Shift*, Doubleday editor Bill Thompson helped King select his best material. Thompson argued against including the short stories "The Blue Air Compressor," "It Grows on You," "The Man Who Would Not Shake Hands," "Survivor Type," and "The Wedding Reception." He also urged King not to include any poetry (Sechrest 2018). King followed his editor's advice, although he later published three of the discarded stories and one poem in the 1985 collection *Skeleton Crew*. Some other previously published stories that failed to make the first cut were "The Reaper's Image," "Here There Be Tygers," "Cain Rose Up," "Stud City," "Slade," "The Fifth Quarter," "The Revenge of Lardass Hogan," and

"Weeds." *Night Shift* compiled the best of the best: sixteen of King's hardest-hitting publications, plus four completely new stories.

The first story in the collection, "Jerusalem's Lot," is a bit of a decoy—an
old-fashioned gothic narrative told in epistolary form. Reportedly conceived by King
for a college writing assignment and later rewritten for inclusion in *Night Shift*, the
story revolves around a physical nexus of evil in an abandoned Maine village and a family cursed by their association with the place. King has said the story was inspired by
a legend about a town in upstate Vermont where the inhabitants mysteriously disappeared in 1908, but "Jerusalem's Lot" is also a conscious pastiche of Edgar Allan Poe
and H.P. Lovecraft. The young Stephen King acknowledged both writers as major influences and said he realized he needed to escape their shadows. In a 1973 essay, he advised
all his fellow horror writers to "throw away Poe and Lovecraft before you start," declaring that "most editors regard the style as outdated and bankrupt" (King: "Horror" 1973).
Why, then, did he launch *Night Shift* with a stylistic throwback like "Jerusalem's Lot"?
One possibility is that he wanted his subsequent stories to illustrate his maturation as a
writer.

With his second story, "Graveyard Shift," King makes Lovecraft's "rats in the walls"
his own, drawing on personal experience from a summer job at a mill in Lisbon Falls,
Maine, to create a modern, blue-collar milieu for the story. In his book *On Writing*,
King recalls hearing a tall tale from one of his co-workers about a cleaning expedition
in the mill's basement. The co-worker claimed he'd seen rats as big as cats down there.
King, who has a phobia of rats, took the image and ran with it. He set his story in a
dingy, dehumanizing work environment where employees are treated no better than
rats—thereby establishing the existence of "monsters" besides the rats. Years later, King
described "Graveyard Shift" as "the ultimate labor versus management story" (Beahm
1991). The underlying sociopolitical commentary distinguishes it as a modern American
horror story, as well as a distinctly Stephen King story. The author's childhood friend
Chris Chesley explains, "He was influenced by a working class, gritty little rural town.
And in that sense it made him intellectually, and literarily, an outsider. And I think a
lot of the push, a lot of the drive, a lot of the narrative force in his writing stems directly
from that—his sense of himself as being outside the mainstream, outside the American
suburban middle class ethos" (Spignesi: "Talk" 1991)

King has described the next story, "Night Surf," as a tune-up exercise for a novel
he was not yet ready to tackle (Munster 1981). Written when he was about nineteen
years old, "Night Surf" offers a brief glimpse of the post-apocalyptic world in *The
Stand*, which was partly inspired by George R. Stewart's 1949 science fiction novel *Earth
Abides*. King embraced Stewart's basic idea of a civilization decimated by an outbreak
of super-measles and made it his own. In his epic novel *The Stand*, the author populates the post-apocalyptic world with a huge, diverse cast of characters who elaborate
and elucidate King's moral worldview. In contrast, "Night Surf" is a snapshot of one isolated group of teenagers who have been wearied into indifference by the sad state of their
shared reality. A comparison of the two texts suggests that King needed a broader storytelling canvas in order to escape the initial tone of despair.

"I Am the Doorway" is another view into a dark future and a forerunner of King's
1987 novel *The Tommyknockers*. The short story, about an astronaut who makes contact
with an alien intelligence that mutates his body and infiltrates his mind, illustrates the
author's tenuous relationship with the science fiction genre. In a 1980 interview, King

said he began submitting stories to science fiction magazines when he was about twelve, even though he instinctively knew he wasn't a science fiction writer. He remembered, "Those stories had the trappings of science fiction, they were set in outer space, but they were really horror stories" (Platt 1980). This is an apt description of "I Am the Doorway," a thinly disguised Lovecraftian horror story about man's instinctive fear of the unknown.

"The Mangler" returns to the blue-collar Maine setting of "Graveyard Shift." Once again, King drew on personal experience; the setting of the story is an industrial laundromat like one where he worked after graduating from college. And again, he took some inspiration from a co-worker—a hook-handed man who had a close encounter with the laundromat's speed iron. In King's story, a demonically-possessed speed iron literally chews up and spits out the working-class characters. Combining the sociopolitical theme of "Graveyard Shift" with the supernatural horror of "Jerusalem's Lot," "The Mangler" reveals the author's distinctive voice. Burton Hatlen, King's favorite college professor, went so far as to suggest that the story's combination of "gritty social realism" and supernatural horror exemplifies the author's "unique contribution to American fiction" (Hatlen 1988).

"The Boogeyman" is more of a psychological horror story—told from a first-person perspective—but no less personal. King has said that the story originated with his habit of checking on his sleeping children late at night to make sure they were still breathing. He has also said that he sometimes writes about his worst fears so they won't come true: "If you write a novel where the boogeyman gets somebody else's children, maybe they'll never get your own children" (King: "Evening" 1983). In a 1973 essay, King elaborated, "The story takes a childhood fear and saddles an adult with it; puts him back into that dreamlike world of childhood where the monsters *don't* go away when you change the channel, but crawl out and hide under the bed" (King: "Horror" 1973). That description makes "The Boogeyman" sound like a trial run for King's 1986 novel *IT*—but there is another layer to the short story which aligns "The Boogeyman" with *The Shining*. The tale's narrator, Lester Billings, is an ill-tempered alcoholic, much like Jack Torrance in *The Shining*. King's Constant Readers might conclude that, in addition to writing about his fear of losing his children, the author was writing—probably unconsciously—about his own worst tendencies as a young husband and father, which he has described in interviews related to *The Shining*.

"Gray Matter" is a similar story. In it, one of King's down-home Maine characters makes a passing reference to the existence of a supernatural monster—a giant, cat-eating spider living beneath the streets of Bangor (another preview of *IT*?)—but the real monster in this story emerges from a can of tainted beer. It's not clear what is wrong with the beer—whether it was poisoned by the brewer or infiltrated by microbial aliens—but the stuff transforms an innocent young boy's alcoholic father into a man-eating blob. The story might be interpreted as a coded warning about alcohol addiction or simply an exercise in gross-out horror.

The next two stories, "Battleground" and "Trucks," attest to the author's fear of modern technology. In a 1983 lecture, King confessed, "Machines make me nervous. They just make me nervous. Because I live in a world that's surrounded by them. It's impossible to get away from them" (King: "Evening" 1983). In "Battleground," a professional hitman can't get away from a set of military-themed toys seeking revenge for their murdered maker. The story cleverly refutes the idea that "guns don't kill people, people kill people." In King's tale, technology is clearly in control—and playing by the rules of karmic justice. In "Trucks," sentient semi-trailers take control by surrounding and enslaving the inhabitants of a truck stop in Haven, Maine. In some ways, this story reads like a variation on Daphne du Maurier's short story "The Birds," which has been interpreted as an allegory about the dangers of taking nature for granted. King's story is an allegory about the dangers of relying too much on machines. Both "Battleground" and "Trucks" end on an apocalyptic note expressed by King in a 1993 interview: "Technology may be its own dead end" (Magistrale: *Hollywood's* 2003).

"Sometimes They Come Back" is the longest story in *Night Shift*, a tale that bridges the gap between Stephen King as short story writer and Stephen King as horror novelist. Written before King completed *Carrie*, the story—about a man returning home to confront a childhood trauma and struggling to cope with illogical manifestations of his irrational fears—seems to map out the novelist's future. Recognizable plot elements, characterizations and themes for the novels *The Shining, Christine, Pet Sematary* and *IT* appeared here first, albeit in crude form. As in *Pet Sematary*, the main character in "Sometimes They Come Back" ultimately surrenders to fear and succumbs to darkness, illustrating the author's moral worldview. King describes *Pet Sematary* as "a book about what happens when you attempt miracles without informing them with any sense of real soul. When you attempt mechanistic miracles—abracadabra, pigeon and pie, the monkey's paw—you destroy everything" (Winter 1986). "Sometimes They Come Back" tells a similar story.

"Strawberry Spring" is one of Stephen King's earliest tales, written and published while he was a student at the University of Maine. The story takes place on a college campus haunted by a mysterious figure King describes as "a cross between Jack the Ripper and a mythical stranger—like Burke and Hare" (Stewart 2/1980). In the original version of the tale, published in the UMO literary magazine *Ubris*, the killer's identity remains mysterious and the result is more of a tone poem than a plot-driven narrative. The revised *Night Shift* version builds to the revelation that the first-person narrator is actually the killer. As King pointed out in his nonfiction book *Danse Macabre*, the revised version follows the Jekyll & Hyde formula—a template he would return to for his novel *The Dark Half* and his novella *Secret Window, Secret Garden*.

"The Ledge" is a more straightforward, naturalistic revenge tale in the vein of crime writer John D. MacDonald, who wrote the introduction to King's *Night Shift* collection. It demonstrates the author's talent for descriptive storytelling and suspense building, as well as his macabre sense of humor. As critic James Van Hise has suggested, it would have made "a crackling good episode" of the TV series *Alfred Hitchcock Presents* (Van Hise 1984).

"The Lawnmower Man" reveals the influence of a very different horror writer, Arthur Machen. King has named Machen's short story "The Great God Pan" as "one of the best horror stories ever written," and "The Lawnmower Man" reads like a fever-induced tribute to Machen's tale (Grant: "I Like" 1981). In what is arguably the most disorienting story in the *Night Shift* collection, a suburban day-drinker dreams—or maybe not—about a slovenly yard-worker carrying out a pagan ritual in his backyard. The story doesn't have any elaborate explanations or obvious themes but it is nonetheless an effective mood piece.

"Quitters, Inc." is another wry tale that builds to a darkly ironic ending. Instead of depicting the horror of substance abuse, this one depicts an extreme cure for addiction.

King has talked openly and bluntly (especially in *On Writing*) about his own alcohol and drug addictions in the 1970s and 1980s, and his ability to draw on personal experience may be one reason why the story is so hard hitting. "Quitters, Inc." is also further proof that the author doesn't have to reply on supernatural bogies to terrify his readers. The story's horror revolves around a flawed but essentially decent family man who not only fails to protect his family but directly causes their suffering.

"I Know What You Need"—a story that might have been inspired by a TWILIGHT ZONE episode entitled "What You Need"—is a female-oriented narrative about paranoia, obsession and black magic. As he had with "Strawberry Spring," King revised the story for its inclusion in *Night Shift*, softening an ending in which the main character learns that her boyfriend has used occult magic to win and maintain her affections. In the story's most powerful line of dialogue, a secondary character defines the boyfriend's manipulation as "rape." King's revision leaves the rapist alive and suggests a modicum of sympathy for the emotionally desperate character.

The next two stories, "Children of the Corn" and "The Last Rung on the Ladder," share the same setting. King said he was inspired by a trip to Nebraska: "It's made a tremendous impression on me. All those wide open spaces and that big, big sky. Very strange. Very Lovecraftian" (Freff 1980). With "Children of the Corn," the author placed the mythic menace in a cornfield and built his story around two time-tested horror tropes: creepy kids and the dangers of religious fanaticism. In contrast, "The Last Rung on the Ladder" is something of an outlier in the *Night Shift* collection—a naturalistic story about a childhood trauma that haunts a brother and sister as adults. It is worth noting that Stephen King originally set out to write novels in the tradition of literary Naturalism; he only turned to writing horror stories when those early novels failed to sell. "The Last Rung on the Ladder" illustrates the author's ability to evoke subtler emotions than horror.

"The Man Who Loved Flowers" is a naturalistic and darkly ironic story about a serial killer hiding in plain sight. It has some similarities to the revised version of "Strawberry Spring," in that both stories are about killers who don't know they're killers. The two stories illustrate the author's fascination with the prospect of "going mad." As a teenager, King says he "was sure that you just went crazy all at once; you'd be walking down the road and—*pffft!*—you'd suddenly think you were a chicken or start chopping up the neighborhood kids with garden shears" (Norden 1983). King suggests that a character who can flip like this becomes "the human equivalent of a black hole" (Farren 1986). The horrific twist in this story is that nobody can see the black hole until it's too late.

"One for the Road" is a mini-sequel to King's vampire novel *'Salem's Lot*. In the early 1980s, King explained that he wrote the story while mulling over the possibility of a novel-length sequel, which would begin by revealing what happened to Father Donald Callahan after he fled the town of Jerusalem's Lot. "One for the Road" returns to the Lot during a late-night snowstorm and effectively re-establishes the aura of menace surrounding the now-abandoned town. Although it's not much more than a footnote to King's second novel, the short story conveys the intended message of King's sequel: *It's not over in 'Salem's Lot.*

"The Woman in the Room" rounds out the *Night Shift* collection. Like "The Last Rung on the Ladder," the last tale includes no hint of the supernatural. It was a deeply personal experiment for the author, who wrote it as a "cry from the heart after my mother's long, losing battle with cervical cancer had finally ended" (King: "Rita" 1996). In "The Woman in the Room," a dutiful son considers illegally ending his mother's suffering. King concludes his story and the collection on that somber note of real-world horror.

In 2020, Stephen King's specialty publisher Cemetery Dance re-issued *Night Shift* in a deluxe edition incorporating two previously uncollected stories, "The Glass Floor" and "Weeds." Thirty years earlier, King had justified his decision to republish the former story in *Weird Tales* magazine by opining that, despite its "clumsy and badly written" opening, the climax had a "genuine *frisson*" that represented the initial spark of his trailblazing career (King: "Introduction [to 'The Glass Floor']" 1990). "Weeds" serves as the opposing bookend. First published in 1976, the story was revised and republished in 1979, around which time King adapted it as a segment of the anthology film CREEPSHOW. By then, the *Night Shift* collection had become welcome fodder for filmmakers.

Cinematic Brand Stephen King

In a 1985 interview, Stephen King said, "When I sign a copy of *Night Shift*, if I'm not pressed for time, what I usually sign is, 'I hope you've enjoyed these one-reel horror movies,'—which is essentially what they are" (Grant: "Interview" 1985). Although he was eager to see his stories adapted to the screen, the author decided early on that the worst thing he could do would be to casually hand over his material to a major Hollywood studio. By 1989, nineteen of the twenty stories in *Night Shift* had been optioned for motion picture adaptations—"Jerusalem's Lot" being the only exception—but none had been developed by a major studio (Beahm 1989). Instead, many of the stories traveled a long and circuitous route to the screen.

More than half of the tales in *Night Shift* were optioned around the time the book was published in early 1978. The Production Company, which had ushered *The Shining* to Warner Bros. and Stanley Kubrick, staked its claim on "Strawberry Spring," "Battleground," and "I Know What You Need," and invited King to adapt them for a television project entitled NIGHT SHIFT. Independent British producer Milton Subotsky—well-known for anthology horror films like DR. TERROR'S HOUSE OF HORRORS (1965), THE HOUSE THAT DRIPPED BLOOD (1971), and TALES FROM THE CRYPT (1972)—optioned "Trucks," "The Mangler," "The Lawnmower Man," "The Ledge," "Quitters, Inc.," and "Sometimes They Come Back." Subotsky's plan was to produce two anthology films based on the six stories. He, too, offered King a chance to adapt his own work. The author chose instead to write a film script based on "Children of the Corn." Around the same time, King granted a pair of film students non-exclusive licenses to adapt "The Boogeyman" and "The Woman in the Room" as short films.

Not all of these projects in the first wave of *Night Shift* adaptations came to fruition and almost none of them progressed as planned. As Stephen King's brand-name value increased in subsequent years, most filmmakers concentrated on developing feature-length films from the author's work. As a result, adaptations derived from King's short stories had to compete with adaptations derived from his much weightier novels.

Obviously, the challenges of adapting a short story into a feature film are very different from the challenges of adapting a novel into a feature film. In *The Art of Adaptation*, Linda Seger sums up, "Usually a short story has fewer characters than a novel, and they are in a simple situation, sometimes one without a beginning, middle, and end. In many short stories there are few, or no, subplots to complicate the action. Working with the short story demands adding subplots, adding characters, and expanding scenes and story lines." For some filmmakers, this is a welcome challenge. Alfred Hitchcock, for example, generally preferred to adapt short stories because they provided more opportunities for stylistic embellishment. He told fellow director François Truffaut that a film "is closer to a short story, which, as a rule, sustains one idea that culminates when the action has reached the highest point of the dramatic curve. As you know, a short story is rarely put down in the middle, and in this sense it resembles a film. And it is because of this peculiarity that there must be a steady development of the plot and the creation of gripping situations which must be presented, above all, with visual skill" (Truffaut 1985).

In adapting short stories, Hitchcock's tendency was to thoroughly reimagine the plot and characters, filtering them through his own personal sensibilities and thematic obsessions. Stanley Kubrick did something similar with THE SHINING; although he kept the bare bones of Stephen King's plot, he completely reinvented the characters, themes, and tone of the story. After witnessing the result, King was eager to exert a stronger influence over future adaptations of his work.

For better or worse, however, the 1980 release of THE SHINING was followed by a dry spell for Stephen King adaptations, lasting until the latter half of 1983. During that interval, King struggled to establish his own filmmaking *bona fides* with the George Romero-directed anthology film CREEPSHOW. In his book *Screening Stephen King*, author Simon Brown observes that the film was distinctly different from Stephen King adaptations that followed in 1983. With its "strong streak of humor" and "cheerful

Actor Christopher Walken, serious and restrained in THE DEAD ZONE (Paramount, 1983).

irreverence," Brown writes, CREEPSHOW inaugurated one of two early "strands" of Stephen King adaptations, which also included CHILDREN OF THE CORN (1983), CAT'S EYE (1985), MAXIMUM OVERDRIVE (1985) and CREEPSHOW 2 (1987). The other strand included CUJO (1983), THE DEAD ZONE (1983), CHRISTINE (1983), and FIRESTARTER (1984), and Brown argues that it was this strand that established the popular "cinematic Brand Stephen King" (Brown: *Screening* 2018). In a separate book on CREEPSHOW, Brown elaborates, "Between them these films established 'A Stephen King Film' as a mid-budget studio production aimed not specifically at horror fans but at a broader, mainstream multiplex audience with an interest in horror." He concludes that "A Stephen King Film"—one celebrated by critics and scholars—is "as serious as it is restrained" (Brown: *CREEPSHOW* 2019).

It is worth noting that the films Brown labels as "cinematic Brand Stephen King" were all based on novels while the Brand X films were based on short stories. Unfortunately, CUJO, THE DEAD ZONE, CHRISTINE and FIRESTARTER were only moderate successes at the box office. Going forward, there would be no more mid-budget prestige adaptations of a Stephen King novel until 1989's PET SEMATARY resurrected the author's reputation in Hollywood. The big "Stephen King Film" success story in the early 1980s—from a financial perspective—was CHILDREN OF THE CORN. That film made less money during its theatrical release than the "cinematic Brand" films (including CARRIE and THE SHINING) but the production costs were significantly lower, yielding a much bigger profit for the filmmakers. Unfortunately, CAT'S EYE was only a moderate financial success and MAXIMUM OVERDRIVE was an unqualified disaster.

The one-two punch of PET SEMATARY and MISERY (1990)—a down-and-dirty horror movie and a more prestigious psychological thriller—resurrected both

The Creep, cheerfully irreverent in CREEPSHOW (Warner Bros., 1982).

strands and opened the floodgates to a second wave of adaptations. The heirs to PET SEMATARY's less restrained approach to genre material included GRAVEYARD SHIFT (1990), SOMETIMES THEY COME BACK (1991), THE LAWNMOWER MAN (1992), and THE MANGLER (1995)—all adaptations of *Night Shift* short stories. With the exception of THE LAWNMOWER MAN, which deviated from its source material so egregiously that King took the filmmakers to court, these films pleased neither the financiers nor (for the most part) the critics. Because the story rights had been negotiated early in Stephen King's career—at a time when the author wasn't able to hold onto any ancillary rights—three out of four titles nevertheless spawned exploitive sequels.

In fact, many of the *Night Shift* short stories have taken on expanded cinematic lives completely independent of the input of Stephen King. Perhaps that's one reason why the adaptations—even the most commercially successful ones (CHILDREN OF THE CORN and THE LAWNMOWER MAN)—have accrued bad reputations among viewers, critics and scholars. The author's disparaging comments about the films over the years are also undoubtedly a factor. Regardless, these films deserve serious study because they represent the challenge of adapting some of King's earliest, rawest, bleakest, and most irreverent stories.

It is also interesting to note how, in some cases, these cinematic re-imaginings of King's stories loom larger than their source material in the public imagination. As with Stanley Kubrick's adaptation of THE SHINING, the original creation has given way to an expanded fictional universe with many authors and no end in sight.

PART ONE

From NIGHT SHIFT
to CREEPSHOW

NIGHT SHIFT (1978 treatment)

For many years, an 88-page "first draft" of King's NIGHT SHIFT script was part of the King Literary Papers collection at the Raymond H. Fogler Library, University of Maine. Although access to the manuscript was limited, researcher Rocky Wood was able to review and synopsize it for his 2005 book *Stephen King: Uncollected, Unpublished*. Wood theorized that the script—which adapts "Strawberry Spring," "Battleground," and "I Know What You Need," and unites them via a wraparound story about a cursed Maine town—was written between 1978 and 1980. A document in the Sy Salkowitz Papers at the Wisconsin Historical Society seems to confirm this. Sometime before April 28, 1978, King delivered a 21-page treatment for NIGHT SHIFT to producer Mike Wise of The Production Company, who passed it along to Salkowitz, then-president of 20th Century–Fox Television.

The treatment establishes the small college town of Weathersfield as the new location of the three stories. King doesn't name the college but he references a building named after Harriet Beecher Stowe, so Bowdoin College in Brunswick, Maine, is the probable inspiration. According to Rocky Wood, King originally set his screen story on the campus of fictional Wiscasset College; Bowdoin is close to the town of Wiscasset. Bowdoin is also the alma mater of Nathaniel Hawthorne, writer of early American gothic fiction and a direct descendant of one of the Salem Witch Trials judges. This detail is significant because, in King's treatment, Weathersfield is afflicted by a curse related to the 1717 execution of three supposed witches in the Town Common.

Our tour guide through this anthology of thrillers is a Serling-esque fellow named Harold Davis, who breaks the fourth wall to talk with us about fear. In his treatment, King recommends deep-voiced actor Gary Merrill—best known for his performance opposite Bette Davis in ALL ABOUT EVE (1950)—for the part. Merrill was a Bowdoin alum who owned a historic lighthouse in Cape Elizabeth, Maine, from 1971 until 1983. He also ran for president in 1974. No doubt he would have brought some local color to the role.

Harold's opening monologue echoes King's foreword to *Night Shift*, which included the following passage: "The thing under my bed waiting to grab my ankle isn't real. I know that, and I also know that if I'm careful to keep my foot under the covers, it will never be able to grab my ankle" (King: "Foreword [to *Night Shift*]" 1977). Harold playfully acknowledges a similar habit, then proceeds to talk about a series of murders that took place in Weathersfield in the spring of 1968, when his grandson Richard was an undergraduate at the local college. The treatment flashes back to a segment based on "Strawberry Spring."

Originally published in 1968, "Strawberry Spring" is a first-person narrative. The narrator is not named in the story but is identified as a former student of the New Sharon Teachers College who has vivid memories of the spring semester from his senior year. He remembers reports—some accurate, some not—of four grisly murders that occurred on campus, and he also remembers some unusual weather that manifested around the time: unseasonable warmth, white drifting fog, and slow-melting snow that his roommate identified as tell-tale signs of a "strawberry spring." According to local lore, these "false" springs come around every eight years or so and foreshadow winter's harshest blows.

The narrator's descriptions of the time and place are evocative and enchanting, conveying a notion that something magical and mysterious has happened. As the story continues, the narrator's thoughts and descriptions provide subtle clues about the identity of the killer, nicknamed "Springheel Jack." The narrator theorizes that the fog became Jack's "accomplice," and further suggests that this accomplice was "female," creating a "marriage that had been consummated in blood." Reminiscing about news of the fourth murder, he theorizes that the victim went looking for her killer because "her need was as deep and ungovernable" as the killer's. The narrator also suggests that the murder itself was a "passionate romance."

An attentive reader has to wonder what kind of narrator would make such statements. By the end of the story, it became clear that the narrator himself murdered the four women—but he was not aware of his actions until now, eight years later, on the verge of another strawberry spring. The implication is that some supernatural influence caused him to kill those girls and might now cause him to kill again.

In the NIGHT SHIFT treatment, King begins the "Strawberry Spring" segment by visualizing the source story's fourth and last murder—the stabbing of Marsha Curran. In this version of the tale, Marsha becomes the first victim. Young Richard Davis writes about the murder for the campus newspaper while his roommate, Lonnie Renneker, talks about strawberry spring. As in the short story, another murder quickly follows and police prematurely arrest a suspect—the victim's boyfriend—on circumstantial evidence.

Going forward, the treatment focuses on Lonnie as the main character. He seems relieved when the first suspect is caught, then distressed when a third victim gets murdered. The following day, he has an anxious conversation with Harold Davis, the college's head of security, who tells him the place is swarming with undercover cops. This new scene helps to explain how the killer manages to avoid detection. Following the fourth murder, King adds another new scene in which Lonnie's unnamed girlfriend walks alone at night. She gets spooked but arrives safely at Lonnie's dorm—an ironic twist, since Lonnie is the killer. At this point, King imports an anecdote from the short story about a sick male student who gets mistaken for the next murder victim. It's a short bit of comic relief before the fifth and final murder, after which the killer disappears with the fog.

King's teleplay then flashes forward to present day, as Lonnie returns home from a teacher's conference in Bangor—where there was a new murder in the style of Springheel Jack. When Lonnie's wife finds the victim's body in the trunk of her husband's car,

Lonnie knifes her, too—and then (judging by later events in the teleplay) kills himself. The first anthology segment ends here and King returns to his wraparound story.

In the newspaper office, Harold and Rich wonder aloud about a possible connection between the 1968 murders and the deaths of Lonnie Renneker and his wife, ten years later. Rich doesn't believe there's any connection (other than some fog) but Harold offers an elaborate "guess" about what happened. King's teleplay visualizes the fate of Lonnie Renneker and his wife for the reader / viewer. First, the wife unwittingly stumbles upon the body of Lonnie's latest victim in the trunk of his car. Then, in a descriptive passage that evokes memories of the climax of PSYCHO, he confronts her, raises his murderous blade to a bare lightbulb and strikes. Back in the newspaper office, Harold points out that "strange" things are always happening in Weathersfield. To explain, he introduces the tale of Liz Neely and Ed Hamner—the second segment in King's anthology film.

In the *Night Shift* version of the story "I Know What You Need," Ed approaches Liz while she is studying at the UMaine Orono library (where Stephen King met his wife Tabitha, and where he later stored his literary papers) and essentially reads her mind. She likes him but she is also instinctively suspicious. When Ed helps her cheat on a final exam, Liz's roommate Alice becomes even more suspicious of Ed. She is relieved when Liz gets a boyfriend and Ed disappears.

Over the summer, however, Liz dreams her boyfriend Tony is trying to bury her alive, while Ed is trying to save her. Later, she learns that Tony has been hit by a car and killed. Around the same time, Ed mysteriously shows up to console her. It's unclear how he knows about Tony's death—or how he always seems to know exactly what to say and do to make Liz happy.

In the fall semester, Ed shows up again on Liz's doorstep and they start dating. Everything seems to be going well until Alice reveals that she has hired a private detective to investigate Ed. The detective learns that Ed is some kind of psychic, that he was probably responsible for the "accidental" death of his parents, and that he has been stalking Liz since they were in a first-grade class together. Liz goes to Ed's apartment and finds evidence that Ed has been using voodoo and black magic to win her affection—and to kill Tony. When Ed arrives, she confronts him and he bitterly complains that everything comes easy to Liz but nothing comes easy to him. She feels sorry for him but breaks the "spell" and leaves him anyway.

King's treatment adds Rich and Harold Davis to the tale and visualizes the scenes with Tony. In one completely new scene, Ed spies on Liz and Tony while they are kissing. The scene makes it clear, earlier in the story, that Ed is a vindictive stalker—which makes his character less sympathetic throughout. King also eliminated Liz's dream, arguably the most cinematic scene in the original story. At the end of the segment, Harold Davis sees Liz disposing of the evidence she collected from Ed's apartment. Despite his grandfather's alleged eyewitness account, Rich remains skeptical and the duo meanders to the Weathersfield Town Common.

Standing in front of a monument to three witches who were executed there in 1717, Harold tries one more time to convince his grandson that there are more things in heaven and earth. The *Night Shift* version of "Battleground" begins with mafia hitman John Renshaw returning to his San Francisco Bay Area apartment after murdering a toy company exec named Hans Morris. A package is waiting for him, sent from Miami by the mother of the victim. Inside, Renshaw finds a military-style footlocker, filled with toy soldiers and helicopters ... which proceed to attack him. As the small soldiers break out bigger and bigger guns, Renshaw retreats to his bedroom, bathroom, and finally the ledge surrounding his high-rise apartment. He climbs around to his living room terrace and makes a break for the living room door—only to trigger the largest weapon in the footlocker. According to a printed note that drifts down from the wreckage, the building is destroyed by a scale-model thermonuclear device.

The "Battleground" segment in King's NIGHT SHIFT treatment begins in Miami, where Renshaw watches Hans Morris die in a car explosion. In the second scene, an old woman conducts a black magic ritual to conjure a demon and asks for help avenging her son's murder. The story then returns to Weathersfield, where Renshaw checks in at a local hotel and picks up his special delivery. He goes to his hotel room and makes a phone call, then notices Hans Morris's mother standing in the Town Common across the street, staring up at him. Moments later, he is waging war against the old woman's plastic minions. The sequence of events closely follows the short story, leading up to a massive explosion that rattles the sleepy Maine town. While Rich Davis, among others, responds frantically, the old woman stands in front of the hotel and barely blinks—until she sees the note about the nuke. Satisfied, she walks away.

King follows the third story with a present-day scene at The Weathersby Café, where Harold and Rich conclude their day-long dialogue over dinner. Afterward, they part ways and Rich wanders through the Town Commons, where he notices something different about the witches monument he saw earlier. The stone faces of the three martyred woman have been replaced by the faces of three familiar men: Lonnie Rennecker, Ed Hamner, and John Renshaw. At this point, Rich breaks the fourth wall to insist that he still won't acknowledge the supernatural forces at work in Weathersfield—but he wonders if we, the viewers, will.

Unfortunately, Rich never got to pose his question to an actual audience. In his book *Danse Macabre*, Stephen King explains, "About a month after turning the script in, I got a call from an NBC munchkin at Standards and Practices (read: The Department of Censorship). The knife my killer used to commit his murders [in 'Strawberry Spring'] had to go, the munchkin said. The killer could stay but the knife had to go. Knives were too phallic." The author proposed a simple solution; he would turn the Springheel Slasher into a Springheel Strangler.

According to Rocky Wood's synopsis of the NIGHT SHIFT script formerly held in the Fogler Library, that change appeared in King's first draft of the screenplay. An interview with the author published in March 1979—in which King referred to his screenplay by the new name DAYLIGHT DEAD—indicates that he had completed two drafts. By that time, however, King was feeling less than optimistic that DAYLIGHT DEAD would ever see the light of day. In an interview published less than a year later, he said NBC had "nixed" the project because the script was "too gruesome, too violent, too intense" for network television (Stewart 2/1980).

New York–based producer Martin Poll subsequently expressed an interest in producing the script. Poll's earlier productions included THE POSSESSION OF JOEL DELANEY (1972); NIGHT WATCH (1973); and THE DAIN CURSE (1978), a TV miniseries based on a novel by Dashiell Hammett. According to author Paul Simpson, the producer hired Lee Reynolds and George P. Erengis to revise King's script in 1981. Journalist Bill Warren described the resulting script, NIGHTSHIFT, as "a perfectly dreadful" adaptation of the short story "Strawberry Spring." According to Warren, "Erengis' script is also about multiple killings on a New England campus, but he populates it with trite conflicts (newcomer vs. established athlete; East vs. California; professor and student romance), lame comedy (a college reporter straight out of Archie), and absolutely no suspense at all. The killer—or killers—are obvious from the beginning. And he throws in black magic to no good end, plus a reference to the town of Jerusalem's Lot which violates the history King created for that town" (Warren: "Movies" 1982). That seems to have been the end of the line for the proposed NIGHT SHIFT anthology.

All that remains of the aborted project is a treatment and a carefully-guarded script that illustrate the difficulties of adapting Stephen King's short stories to the screen. The treatment shows that the author was inclined to supplement the scenes in his prose stories with new action scenes—visually depicting the murders in "Strawberry Spring," Tony's death in "I Know What You Need," and the assassination of Hans Morris in "Battleground." What is lost in King's treatment are some compelling character details: the troubling thoughts of the first-person narrator (Lonnie Renneker) in "Strawberry Spring," Liz's psychologically-revealing nightmare in "I Know What You Need," and Renshaw's equally revealing worldview from the balcony of a posh San Francisco apartment ("It was better up here. Better than in the gutters.") in "Battleground."

The most significant innovation in King's treatment is the wraparound segment that unites the three pre-existing stories. The author chose to modify the settings of the short stories in order to build a mythology of a cursed Maine town. Harold's opening monologue suggests that King imagined Weathersfield as a kind of sister community to Jerusalem's Lot—a neighboring town haunted by witches instead of vampires. Late in the treatment, Harold asks Rich why a mafia hitman would choose to live in small-town Maine (instead of San Francisco). Although the question goes unanswered, King's implication is that John Renshaw was drawn to Weathersfield by supernatural forces. The final scene in the treatment seems to confirm his theory.

Had this version of NIGHT SHIFT been produced, Weathersfield might today loom as large in Stephen King's fictional universe as Jerusalem's Lot—or even Castle Rock. In early 1978, when he wrote the NIGHT SHIFT treatment, the author had already set two major works—his so-far-unpublished novella *The Body* and his soon-to-be-published novel *The Dead Zone*—in the fictional town of Castle Rock, but he had not yet depicted Castle Rock as a cursed locale. The idea of a supernatural curse on the town would first appear in *Cujo*, a novel King that started around the same time he wrote NIGHT SHIFT. Did Weathersfield—with its Springheel Slasher / Strangler, its cycle of supernatural violence, and its history of persecuting witches—serve as the prototype for King's most famous fictional setting? Describing the town of Weathersfield in 1980—shortly before he apparently abandoned it—King said, "The premise is that reality is thinner in this town, and things are weird in this one particular place. There are forces which focus on this town and cause things to happen" (Stewart 2/1980). Too bad those forces couldn't bring NIGHT SHIFT to life.

The Milton Subotsky Story

On May 25, 1978, *The Hollywood Reporter* announced that Milton Subotsky's Sword and Sorcery Productions had optioned six stories from Stephen King. It stipulated that three of the stories—"Quitters, Inc.," "The Ledge," and "Sometimes They Come Back"—would be incorporated into an anthology horror film under the working title FRIGHT NIGHT. The other three stories—"The Lawnmower Man," "The Mangler," and "Trucks"—would be combined in an anthology with the central theme of machines turning against humanity.

According to a 1988 *Starburst* interview with Subotsky, the author had visited the producer at Shepperton Studios and suggested a collaboration. If true, the meeting probably took place in the fall of 1977, while the King family was living in the south of England and King was struggling to write a follow-up novel to *The Stand*. At that time, the short story collection *Night Shift* remained in manuscript form, so King must have given Subotsky a copy of the unpublished manuscript and urged the producer to take a look.

Ultimately, Subotsky selected six stories and secured the adaptation rights to those stories from King's publisher Doubleday—which caused the author to lose control over the stories for years to come. Reflecting on the fate of his film properties in a 1992 interview, King complained that Doubleday "didn't give a shit what happened to any of those stories. They didn't make very good deals for me, because they didn't care that much about me" (Stroby 1992). Apart from his misgivings about his publisher, King says he had mixed feelings about Subotsky adapting his work. Years later, it is interesting to contemplate what might have happened if the British producer had been among the first to adapt Stephen King's work to the screen. Would it have significantly altered audience perception of the author's cinematic brand?

Initially, it seems King was enthusiastic about the possibility of having his work adapted by Subotsky—but also anxious about the prospect of linking himself to the existing Amicus brand. In 1979, the author claimed to admire the producer's shrewdness and ability to make "movies that make money." On the other hand: "He makes a lot of movies that aren't very good" (Stephen Jones: "Night" 1979). Perhaps for diplomatic reasons, King named four Subotsky productions in his 1981 book *Danse Macabre* as examples of "particularly interesting" horror films that "have contributed something of value to the genre." Those four films were DR. TERROR'S HOUSE OF HORRORS (1965), THE DEADLY BEES (1967), THE HOUSE THAT DRIPPED BLOOD (1971), and ASYLUM (1972). Three out of four were anthology horror films, the format upon which Subotsky had built his reputation. Also, three out of four were written by novelist Robert Bloch— one of Stephen King's literary idols. Bloch's association with Amicus may have been the real reason for King's enthusiasm. The rising star may have wanted to place himself at the end of a well-established tradition in cinematic horror—only to learn, from Bloch and perhaps others, that he was following a rocky road.

Milton Subotsky had first gravitated toward the horror genre in the mid–1950s when he wrote a script for a remake of Universal's FRANKENSTEIN. Subotsky and his business partner, Max J. Rosenberg, submitted the script to James Carreras at the British production company Hammer, where it was rewritten by Jimmy Sangster and became the basis for THE CURSE OF FRANKENSTEIN (1957). Subotsky received a fee for providing the concept but received no credit for his script. Hammer went on to become Britain's home of cinematic horror, while Subotsky and Rosenberg founded a rival company—initially called Vulcan Productions; later Amicus Productions. The producers' first collaboration, THE CITY OF THE DEAD (1960), a.k.a. HORROR HOTEL, was a gothic thriller about witchcraft in New England. Subotsky co-wrote the script himself.

Indulging his enthusiasm for "adult fairy tales," the producer followed up with a script for an anthology horror film in the tradition of the Ealing Studios film DEAD

OF NIGHT (1945), which consisted of five standalone stories plus a wraparound "framing sequence." Subotsky's DR. TERROR'S HOUSE OF HORRORS (1965) similarly included five stories and a wraparound segment—and incorporated the talents of three well-known Hammer stars: actors Christopher Lee and Peter Cushing, and director Freddie Francis. The film's success established Amicus as a rival "horror film company"—although Subotsky never liked that label—and the producers went on to make more horror films with director Freddie Francis at the helm.

In the mid–1960s, Subotsky recruited *Psycho* author Robert Bloch to the company's lineup. First, the producer himself adapted Bloch's short story "The Skull of the Marquis de Sade" to the screen, telling the story "in purely cinematic terms," with very little dialogue (Nutman: "Vault" 1984). Bloch liked THE SKULL (1965) enough to offer the producer adaptation rights to his unpublished story "The Psychopath." This time, Bloch wrote the script but he was disappointed when the filmmakers decided to change his ending for THE PSYCHOPATH (1966). Nevertheless, his collaboration with Subotsky continued. According to director Freddie Francis, Bloch's script for THE DEADLY BEES (1967) was inherently problematic and producer Max Rosenberg had to approve a last-minute rewrite while Subotsky was away from the studio (Palmer 1983). No one—except, apparently, Stephen King—was enthusiastic about the resulting film.

After that, Amicus returned to the anthology format that had worked so well on DR. TERROR. Robert Bloch wrote the script for TORTURE GARDEN (1967), adapting four of his early short stories and incorporating a wraparound segment conceived by Subotsky. In his 1993 autobiography, Bloch remembered, "It seemed at the time that using work already proven popular in print might help make the resultant script more foolproof, or at least director-proof. My surmise proved only half correct. Two of the stories ['Terror Over Hollywood' and 'Mr. Steinway'] remained substantially unchanged and were, I thought, fairly effective. The opening and closing items ['Enoch' and 'The Man Who Collected Poe'] had been 'improved' by some kind of cosmetic touches you might expect after turning a plastic surgeon loose on the *Mona Lisa*" (Bloch 1993).

Subotsky prided himself on his ability to "save" films in the editing room but he never underestimated the importance of finding and properly developing the right stories. In a 1969 lecture, he said, "The screenplay is the most important single item in the making of a film. It is very difficult to make a bad film out of a good script and impossible to make a good film out of a bad script" (Palmer 1983). Like RKO producer Val Lewton, he worked closely with the writers on developing screen stories. In an interview for a 1972 episode of the BBC's *Film Night* series, he outlined the collaborative process as follows: "We don't let a writer go ahead on a script unless he has done a structural outline, which may be four or five pages, but you can virtually lick a screenplay in a structural outline, because most screenplays are bad because the structure—the plotline, the story—is bad. Everything else doesn't matter. You get the dialogue right, you can get everything else right, provided your structure is right." Once the script was approved and financing secured, Subotsky generally gave his directors broad creative control over production, telling himself that "a film is very often made more in the cutting room than in the shooting" (Subotsky 1969).

Perhaps because he generally undervalued a director's storytelling contributions, the producer began using relatively inexperienced directors on his films in the early 1970s. TV director Peter Duffell, who helmed the anthology film THE HOUSE THAT DRIPPED BLOOD (1971), remembers that Subotsky "was quite happy to employ younger directors without any big track record; to give them a chance, as it were" (Callaghan 2009). The director took some bold liberties with Robert Bloch's script for that film, and remembers that Bloch was particularly unhappy with changes to his story "The Wax Museum." Bloch, however, raved enthusiastically about the changes made to one of his other stories, saying, "Due credit must be given to the director for deftly turning the final segment into a send-up of my vampire story, 'The Cloak,' and thereby improving it a hundred percent" (Bloch 1993). Subotsky entrusted the next Amicus production, I, MONSTER (1971), to another unknown director (Stephen Weeks), before returning to veteran Amicus director Freddie Francis for the most commercially successful anthology horror film Amicus made.

TALES FROM THE CRYPT (1972) drew on source material from the infamous E.C. Comics of the 1950s. Russ Jones, an associate of Subotsky, remembers that he gave the producer a reprint edition of the collected stories and that Subotsky was "a great fan of the E.C. Comics." The producer chose five stories from the collection that he thought "would lend themselves most effectively to a creative storytelling" (Alan Jones: "Tales" 1981). Subotsky then wrote the script himself, creating a wraparound segment set in … where else?

Buoyed by the film's commercial success—but dismayed by some of the director's decisions about how to shoot it—Subotsky turned to another Hammer veteran, director Roy Ward Baker, to oversee two more anthology horror films. ASYLUM (1972) was Robert Bloch's final Amicus project, and his favorite. In particular, the author praised "those portions of the film—'Lucy Comes to Stay' and 'Frozen Fear'—which were shot virtually as I'd written them, dialogue, action and camerawork" (Larson 1971). Baker claimed Subotsky was equally pleased with the film, saying, "He wanted me to direct all his films from that point on" (Swires: "Roy" 1992).

The filmmaker went on to direct THE VAULT OF HORROR—but the second E.C. Comics adaptation was not nearly as successful as TALES FROM THE CRYPT. Baker explained his failure: "I just couldn't see how to get the effect of a strip cartoon into a motion picture. The visual style of the movie owed nothing to the comic book stories. It might have worked better if it had" (Swires: "Roy" 1992). William Gaines, who owned the rights to the source stories, was also disappointed. Although there were apparently some discussions about Amicus making two additional E.C.-inspired Amicus films—announced as THE HAUNT OF FEAR and TALES FROM THE INCREDIBLE—Gaines decided to end the collaboration because he "felt they were screwing with the [source] stories" (Teitelbaum 1990).

Thus, in 1973, Subotsky was searching for new talent and new material. In an interview conducted around that time, he claimed that he read about five hundred novels a year and felt satisfied if he found two worthwhile stories. He described his criteria for a worthwhile story as follows: "What I really look for when read a book is to get underneath the dialogue, the writing, everything. Sometimes books are terribly written, poorly dialogued, and once you are underneath all that you see what the idea of the book is. […]. Now it doesn't matter if the idea isn't used well in the book as long as you know how to change it in the script and get it to work" (Knight 1973).

The following year, Amicus optioned four stories from the short story collections of British author Ronald Chetwynd-Hayes and they became the basis for the anthology film FROM BEYOND THE GRAVE (1974). The film's director, Kevin Conner, remembers that he was hired onto the project because he had recommended the source stories:

"Milton Subotsky had come across some scripts I had adapted with two friends of mine [Robin Clark and Raymond Christodoulou]—he took four of them and made them in a 'compilation film' and added a linking story—and offered me the directing job. 'But I've never directed...' I told him. 'Editors make good directors and I'll surround you with the best technicians.' And he did" (Whittington 2012). Unfortunately, it was the final anthology horror film Subotsky produced for Amicus. In the summer of 1975, he parted ways with his longtime business association Max Rosenberg and created a new production company.

Once again, Subotsky was searching for new material—but this time, he wanted to move away from the horror genre. In the early days of his Sword and Sorcery Productions, he developed an adaptation of Lin Carter's *Thongor* comic book series and tried to raise financing for a proposed film adaptation, THONGOR IN THE VALLEY OF DEMONS. When the project failed to take off, he grudgingly mounted his eighth anthology horror film. French author and anthologist (and former American International Pictures story editor) Michel Parry wrote four original stories for THE UNCANNY (1977), presumably taking some inspiration from his own 1973 book, *Beware of The Cat: Weird Tales About Cats*. Veteran actors Peter Cushing, Ray Milland, and Donald Pleasence also joined the fray but the film was a pale shadow of the Amicus anthologies of yesteryear.

In 1978, Subotsky optioned six Stephen King short stories and offered the author a chance to adapt his own work to the screen—as both screenwriter and director. In an interview conducted that spring, the producer expressed confidence that the author would in fact make his directorial debut for Sword and Sorcery. King, however, decided to proceed with caution. He might have based his decision on a candid conversation with Robert Bloch, who wrote in his autobiography that he met King sometime in the mid– to late 1970s and "tried to point out [...] some of the perils and pitfalls" of the film industry to the newbie (Bloch 1993). Bloch's war stories could have made King nervous about Subotsky's tendency to play fast and loose with an author's source material—and to supplant his directors in post-production. In interviews, however, King gave a purely practical reason for turning down the offer to write and direct a film for Milton Subotsky. In 1984, he explained, "I'd like to direct very much, but I'm scared of that—not the conceptualization or visualization, but trying to control a big crew, all of whom have forgotten more about movie-making than I'll ever know" (Lofficier 1984).

Once King turned him down, Subotsky commissioned scripts for the two King-based anthology films from the husband-and-wife team of Edward and Valerie Abraham. The British couple's previous film credits included a "story by" credit on the 1961 thriller THE TRUNK, about a new bride who falls prey to a blackmail plot involving a fake corpse and her husband's former mistress, and an original screenplay for the 1962 murder mystery SERENA. Subotsky was especially impressed with THE PIT (1962), an experimental short film that Edward Abraham had directed for the British Film Institute, based on Edgar Allan Poe's "The Pit and the Pendulum." THE PIT includes only one word of spoken dialogue and was a likely source of inspiration for Subotsky's similarly taciturn film THE SKULL.

The Abrahams went on to write an adaptation of Harold Lawlor's 1948 short story "What Beckoning Ghost?" for Subotsky—and, in 1978, the producer used that script as the basis for a new film called DOMINIQUE (Childs 1978). Subotsky subsequently hired the couple to write the anthology horror film THE MONSTER CLUB (1981), a light-hearted second foray into the fictional world of Ronald Chetwynd-Hayes, and to adapt Stephen King. Reportedly, the duo started adapting King in late 1979, before THE MONSTER CLUB went into production.

The proposed King anthologies went through many permutations over the following years. In early 1980, *Heavy Metal* magazine reported that the first film—utilizing the short stories "Quitters Inc.," "The Ledge," and "Sometimes They Come Back"—would be called NIGHT SHIFT. The second film—based on "Trucks," "The Mangler," and "The Lawnmower Man"—would be titled THE REVOLT OF THE MACHINES (Stewart 1/1980). In mid–1980, *Famous Monsters of Filmland* magazine indicated that the two films would be called FRIGHT NIGHT and TERROR BY DAYLIGHT (Anonymous: "Future" 1980). In the fall of 1980, *Variety* magazine announced that Subotsky was in pre-production on NIGHT SHIFT. Two years later, the same magazine claimed the producer was still seeking financing for the low-budget feature.

By this time, Subotsky was operating in the United States under a new company name, The Great Fantastic Picture Corporation. Within a few years, he managed to reclaim the Amicus aegis in England—but the Stephen King projects remained stalled. In a mid–1984 interview, Subotsky publicly alluded to "a non-anthology script called THE MACHINES" as well as an anthology script titled FRIGHT NIGHT, attributing both to Edward and Valerie Abrahams [sic] (Nutman: "Vault" 1984). For better or worse, neither script made it to the screen. Stephen King went on to make his own anthology horror film—taking a healthy dose of inspiration from E.C. Comics and Amicus.

CREEPSHOW (1979 screenplay)

While Milton Subotsky was in the early stages of developing his NIGHT SHIFT anthology films, Stephen King was fielding a variety of offers to create or host his own television anthology series. Just as he had shied away from Subotsky's offer to write and direct, King avoided this easy in-road to Hollywood. He went instead to Pittsburgh, to make a movie with his new friend George A. Romero.

In 1978, Warner Bros. had approached Romero and his producing partner Richard A. Rubinstein about taking the reins of the studio's troubled adaptation of 'Salem's Lot. The plan fell through, but Romero was eager to work with King. In a 1980 interview, the author remembered that the director turned up on his doorstep one day and made a straightforward proposal: "He said, 'Do you want to do a movie?' and I said, 'Can we do the movie we want to do?' and he said 'I always have'" (Peck 1980). Romero told the story a bit differently: "Actually the first time I met Steve he gave me a copy of *The Stand*, the hardback copy, and wrote in it, 'Maybe we'll get to work together some day and maybe on this'" (Gagne: *Zombies* 1987). In another interview, King elaborated, "Because I admired his work and everything, I ended up saying, 'These are the things [I've written] that are not optioned.' I just sort of put everything out and said, 'Take what you want.'" And he said, "Let's do *The Stand*'" (Thomases 1981).

Rubinstein says he and Romero decided, very quickly, to hire Stephen King to adapt his own work to the screen: "Steve had always been treated as a novelist by the studios. He got pigeon-holed like that, when he really wanted to write screenplays—and he had written some. We read some that were never used and we said to ourselves, 'Hey, Steve really knows *how* to write a screenplay'" (Crawley: "CREEPSHOW" 1982). The producer and director might have read King's screenplay adaptation of Ray Bradbury's novel *Something Wicked This Way Comes*; his early scripts for THE SHINING, NIGHT SHIFT, or CHILDREN OF THE CORN; or possibly an incomplete original screenplay about a haunted radio station that King started but quickly abandoned. Whatever the case, by the summer of 1979, Rubinstein and Romero were ready to invest in Stephen King as a screenwriter. Convincing others to invest would be more difficult.

King suggested that the team could prove itself to investors by producing a series of vignettes: "There'd be eight or nine different segments where there would not be much motivation, or where you wouldn't need any. They would be situational, like some of the old LIGHTS OUT radio shows were situational. It would almost be the equivalent to a comedy skit, only this would be horror" (Gagne: "Five" 1982). Romero proposed shooting each story in a different visual style: "One black and white 1940's-style, one 3-D— even changing the screen format from a small, squarish screen to a wide screen, really mixing it up like that" (Bob Martin 1981). Later, Romero said, "We decided that it was maybe a little too experimental, a little too radical and uncomfortable. Steve actually came up with the idea of it being a comic book and having sort of a story around it" (Gagne: "CREEPSHOW" 1982). He also came up with a title: CREEPSHOW.

Was King perhaps remembering Milton Subotsky's anthology film TALES FROM THE CRYPT? If not, he was certainly remembering the E.C. Comics of the 1950s, which had exerted a significant early influence on him as a writer. In *Danse Macabre*, King wrote that he had "cut his teeth" on books like *Tales from the Crypt, The Vault of Horror*, and *The Haunt of Fear*, stating, "Those horror comics of the fifties still sum up for me the epitome of horror, that emotion of fear that underlies terror, an emotion which is slightly less fine, because it is not entirely of the mind. Horror also invites a physical reaction by showing us something which is physically wrong." In 1979, the author and his new collaborator wanted to make what they regarded as a true "horror" movie—"a funky, flat-out, unapologetic" assault on the audience (Gagne: *Zombies* 1987). No intellectual bullshit, just guts and gusto.

Although King celebrated E.C.-style horror in a decidedly anti-intellectual context, he also championed it in a more philosophical way—as "the last gasp of a more gentle romanticism" in post–World War II America, espousing an older, "traditional American view of morality" in which "the guilty were always punished"... even if it takes a zombie to administer justice (Winter 1986, Horsting: *Stephen* 1986). Romero shared King's interest in morality plays and tales of social justice—in fact, that was what had drawn him to *The Stand*.

With THE STAND on hold, CREEPSHOW moved forward quickly. By October 1979, King had delivered a first draft of the script. Richard Rubinstein remembers, "Steve said, 'Okay, I'll write a screenplay in two months. And in two months to the day, a screenplay was there" (Crawley: "CREEPSHOW" 1982). In a later interview, King claimed he wrote the shooting script in a week and "practically" never rewrote it (Gary Wood: "Stephen" 1991). The former King Literary Papers collection at the Fogler Library included two drafts of the screenplay, as well as some "revised pages," but Romero reiterated King's claim that the changes were minimal: "Steve went in and blue-penciled a few things. But we actually worked all the way through the shoot with that very [first] copy of the script" (Crawley: "King/George" 1983).

When he set out to create his own anthology horror film, King decided not to incorporate any *Night Shift* stories. He reasoned, "With an original I felt that I could let it come out the way that it wanted to" (Nevison 1982). Three of the stories—"Father's Day," "Something to Tide You Over," and "They're Creeping Up on You"—were new, as was the wraparound segment (which concludes with a tip of the hat to Robert Bloch's "Sweets to the Sweet" segment from THE HOUSE THAT DRIPPED BLOOD). Two of the stories, however, had previously appeared in print. "The Lonesome Death of Jordy Verrill" was based on the short story "Weeds," which first appeared in the May 1976 issue of *Cavalier* magazine, and "The Crate" was based on a story of the same name published in the July 1979 issue of *Gallery* magazine.

King says the initial version of his short story "Weeds" was a 20,000-word "first chapter of a novel" (Gagne: "Interview" 1989). The published short story begins on the Fourth of July, when a meteor crash-lands on the New Hampshire farm of a "not very smart" fellow named Jordy. The lunkhead farmer competently puts out a few small fires caused by the meteor, then pours water on the meteor itself—which releases some "white flaky stuff" that looks to him like Quaker Oats. Jordy makes the mistake of feeling those Oats, which produces blisters on his fingers. He takes a few photos of the meteor, dreams of selling it to the local college, and retires for the night.

In the morning, Jordy finds green matter—"like moss"—growing out of his fingers. He revisits the meteor and realizes he can actually *hear* the "green stuff" growing around it. Later, he sees—and feels—it growing out of his own eyeball. In one of the story's most unsettling passages, Jordy contemplates ripping the moss off of his face but hesitates when he remembers that "his eye was still in there someplace." Later, he discovers the green stuff growing out of his penis, then out of his tongue. He becomes increasingly horrified by the thought that something is spreading inside him like cancer. He finally takes a cold bath to relieve the incessant itching, which triggers a major "growth-spurt."

In the evening, Jordy surveys his land and sees that alien weeds have overrun his farm and are creeping onto the property of his neighbor, Arlen McGinty. King writes that, at this point, Jordy is no longer Jordy. Instead, he's a big green humanoid whose brain is hosting "a kind of telepathy." A brief passage, reminiscent of the *Night Shift* story "I Am the Doorway," suggests that organic invaders (Triffids?) are communicating through his body, plotting their next move in a seemingly insatiable quest for food. (*"Is he the only food?"* / *"No, much food. His thoughts say so."*) The weeds actively help Jordy press a shotgun to his head and pull the trigger, then continue their march toward the nearby town of Cleaves Mills. King apparently wrote a bit more but the published version of "Weeds" ends here.

In his 1979 screenplay for CREEPSHOW, King gives Jordy more dialogue and less competence. Instead of putting out fires, Jordy breaks out a folding ruler to measure the meteor. As the character contemplates selling his discovery to the local college, King adds a fantasy scene in which Jordy dickers with a monocled professor in the "Department of Meteors." Jordy is the butt of this joke—and of all the jokes to follow. In another fantasy scene, Jordy imagines paying off a bank loan officer with his vast meteor money. His dreams are dashed when he pours water on the meteor, splitting it open and inadvertently cursing himself. King returns to the first fantasy scene, except this time the monocled professor is mocking Jordy's broken meteor. Jordy's luck continues to get worse: when he touches the meteor, he becomes infected with "meteorshit." The phrase "meteor shit" appears in the original short story but the screenplay emphasizes its comic value by reintroducing it as a compound word: *"meteorshit."*

Jordy retreats into his house and proceeds to get drunk in front of the TV, while bright green weeds sprout from the meteor crash site. Sometime later, Jordy wakes up and observes a fungoid growth on his fingers. Panicked, he picks up the phone to call his doctor—but, before he can connect, King adds another fantasy scene in which Jordy's doctor gleefully threatens to amputate the affected fingers. Jordy hangs up the phone and starts sucking his fingers—then realizes that he's probably making things worse. He rushes to the bathroom, looks in the mirror, and sees that the fungoid is now growing on his tongue, too. King juxtaposes this image with another shot of the meteor site, now completely overgrown with luminescent weeds. Jordy paces, talking to himself, quickly realizing that the "meteorshit" can grow anywhere. He finally makes the call to his doctor but receives only a recorded message, referring him to a colleague in Castle Rock. Jordy hangs up the phone and proceeds to get drunk. Just before he passes out in front of the TV for a second time, he starts to weep.

After an objective camera point of view observes the progress the weeds are making outside, King's script returns to Jordy—who is still "growing," too. He wakes up with weeds coming out of one eye socket. In response, he rushes to the bathroom and fills the tub with water. As he undresses, he discovers that the weeds have migrated to the southern half of his body. In this moment of distress, Jordy hears his father's voice—and, in a final fantasy scene, converses with the dead man via the bathroom mirror. Dad advises Jordy not to get in the water ... but Jordy can't help himself. Resigned to his dismal fate, he plunges in.

King's script cuts away again, to the lush garden outside. A proposed tracking shot follows the new growth of weeds through the house and eventually locates Jordy in the kitchen, talking to himself in a barely human voice. The screenplay describes his furry hands, fumbling with the trigger of a shotgun—then a splatter of green on the nearby stove. Outside, the weeds creep toward a road sign that identifies the nearest town as Castle Rock. The shot dissolves into a final image: the humanoid remains of Jordy Verrill, staring sadly back at us with one glazed eye.

"The Lonesome Death of Jordy Verrill" is a thoroughly audio-visual reinterpretation of "Weeds," smartly translating the inner thoughts of Jordy Verrill to the new medium while also amplifying the pathos of the source story. Most of the changes make King's story more broadly humorous—a tendency that would be amplified by the director during production, as Stephen King himself performed the role of the great green rube. King claims Romero instructed him to play Jordy as an unsubtle variation of Wile E. Coyote in the old Road Runner cartoons, which makes the character more fun. The film softens Jordy's suffering by allowing him to keep both eyes. In the end, his cinematic death seems less horrific—but no less tragic—than in the source story.

King has described the other adapted story, "The Crate," as the pivotal segment of CREEPSHOW, saying, "All of CREEPSHOW is a good-natured takeoff on *Tales from the Crypt* comics, nothing more than that—until this point" (Magistrale: "Writer" 1992). The original short story was inspired by a local news story about the discovery of an old crate at the University of Maine. The mystery about what was inside the crate rattled around in Stephen King's brain until one day he noticed his children watching *Looney Tunes* on television. Suddenly, the writer had an idea: "Suppose it was the Tasmanian Devil in that crate" (Gagne: "Interview" 1989). Seems like a reasonable companion story for The Lonesome Death of Wile E. Coyote, right?

At the outset of "The Crate" short story, Horlicks University professor Dexter

Stanley visits his colleague Henry Northrup at home and begins to tell him about a strange discovery. Dex claims that earlier that day, a janitor on campus led him to a mysterious crate hidden beneath a stairwell. When the professor went to investigate, he saw a label indicating that the crate came from an "Arctic Expedition" in 1834. Curious, the two men opened it—and encountered a hairy beast with hateful owl's eyes. The beast killed the janitor while Dex fled and bumped into a grad student, who—being understandably skeptical of the professor's crazy story—brought him back to the scene of the crime. Dex watched helplessly as the thing in the crate killed the grad student, too. Relating the story hours later, Dex is understandably hysterical. King alludes to a "central axle that binds us to the state we call sanity," and suggests that Dexter Stanley's axle is broken. Henry, however, believes his friend and promises to contact the State Police on his behalf.

Around the mid-point of the story, King's narrative leaps forward in time. Now, Henry Northrup is the primary storyteller. He explains that he gave Dex a sedative, then orchestrated the execution of his ball-busting wife Wilma—by literally feeding her to the thing under the stairs. Afterward, Dex listens in horror as his friend describes luring Wilma to the crate and laughing helplessly as she fell victim to the monster inside. Henry goes on to describe how he disposed of the crate in a nearby quarry, thereby getting rid of the evidence of all three mysterious deaths. It seems clear that Henry's axle is cracked as well.

In a 1981 introduction to the short story, King claimed he "ripped off" his characterization of Henry from Edgar Allan Poe's short story "The Tell-Tale Heart." Both tales end with the murderous narrator gone loco and laughing helplessly. In the same essay, King rhapsodized about the relationship between humor and horror, theorizing that "the horror story is the final existential development," or "one way to stay sane in a mad universe" (King: "Introduction [*Arbor House*]" 1981). In a 1992 interview, he illustrated his theory with direct references to "The Crate": "There's this scene in CREEPSHOW where the professor starts to laugh at this crate underneath the stairs. He can't control

Stephen King's crate-dwelling "Tasmanian Devil" in CREEPSHOW (Warner Bros., 1982).

Stephen King as the "great green rube" Jordy Verrill in CREEPSHOW (Warner Bros., 1982).

himself anymore. To me this is a moment of transcendence. [...] The tale transcends its genre because he actually begins to laugh. He thinks this act of murder is actually funny. He even asks the viewer to laugh along with him" (Magistrale: "Writer" 1992). King presumes that if a storyteller can succeed in getting the reader/viewer to laugh along with him, the experience can be genuinely cathartic.

This laughing-all-the-way-to-the-crypt style of humor defines CREEPSHOW. The stories King conceived specifically for the film are all revenge stories with an ironic twist. In "Father's Day" and "Something to Tide You Over," the dead return to avenge their own murders. In "They're Creeping Up on You," cockroaches terrorize a man who treats human beings like bugs. "The Lonesome Death of Jordy Verrill" is not as subversive—its moral message seems to be a simpler one, along the lines of "curiosity killed the cat"—but it manages to have fun with the idea that human existence is pathetically tragic. In each case, humor leads to what King terms "transcendence."

The author didn't have to modify "The Crate" to fit the darkly humorous tone of the film but he did make some structural changes, allowing the main events of the short story to unfold chronologically. The screen story begins with the janitor discovering the crate, then follows up with a scene at a faculty party, where we meet Dex, Henry and Wilma. Wilma is brash and boldly contemptuous of her husband, who confides in his friend Henry that he has grown to hate her. The exchange is interrupted by a phone call from the university, announcing the janitor's discovery of the crate. Dex goes to check it out and the janitor—who, in this version of the tale, is a character almost as exaggerated as Jordy Verrill—meets his gruesome fate. Afterward, Dex unwittingly leads grad student Charlie Gereson to his death, too; then rushes to Henry's house to tell him what happened.

The screen story skips ahead—using an exterior shot of Henry's neighborhood at night to indicate the passage of time—to conclude Dex's story. Henry takes a bathroom break, retrieves a bottle of pills, and stares contemplatively at his reflection in the mirror. He then drugs his friend. As soon as Dex is asleep, he writes a note to Wilma, urging her to meet him on campus to help resolve a sex scandal that Dex is supposedly involved in. He drives to the university and finds bloody evidence that his friend's story is true, then cleans up the mess and lays a trap for his wife. Meanwhile, Wilma returns home, finds the note, and gleefully reports to the school in hope of seeing Dex brought low. When she arrives, Henry cunningly lures her to her death, laughing all the while. When Henry finally sees the monster—which King describes as a furry alien with six spider-like legs (!)—he promptly stops laughing.

In the next scene, Dex wakes up and Henry explains what he's done. King's script describes a long flashback in which Henry brings the crate to Ryder's Quarry and drowns his furry accomplice. Like the short story, the screen story makes it clear that neither Dex nor Henry is inclined to tell anyone what happened; to them, it is nothing but an inside joke between friends. Unlike the short story, however, the screen story ends on a note suggesting that that the murderers will *not* get away with what they've done. At the bottom of the quarry, the monster—still alive—waits for its next meal. In classic comic book style, the final scene poses a textual question: "The End?"

The filmed version of "The Crate" incorporates two additional scenes that are not in the 1979 script: a pair of fantasies in which Henry murders Wilma at the faculty party, first by shooting her and then by strangling her. In the first scene, bystanders applaud Henry's marksmanship and he grins sheepishly. Both scenes convey Henry's thoughts while emphasizing his feeling of impotence, which makes Henry a bit more sympathetic. When Henry finally takes action to get rid of Wilma, the filmmakers linger knowingly on a brief moment when it seems like Wilma might get away from the thing in the crate. This bit of viewer manipulation illustrates Romero's prowess as a visual storyteller; like Hitchcock with PSYCHO, he wants us to dread the monster *and* cheer on the murderer at the same time.

King and Romero sought to establish their own unique blend of fun and scary, somewhere between Laff in the Dark and go for the throat. One thing they both agreed on was that old anthology horror films like the ones produced by Milton Subotsky didn't strike the right balance. King stated flatly, "Neither George Romero nor I felt the Subotsky films worked very well" (Stewart 1/1980). The author opined that Subotsky's anthologies were "kinda fun" but had "no real fire, no flash to them" (Crawley: "King/ George" 1983) At one point, he even referred to the Amicus producer as "the Hubert Humphrey of horror pictures" and "a constant Pollyanna" who wanted all of his films to have an "uplifting tone" (Stewart 3/1980). King wanted his own film to be more subversive, its dark humor more shocking and amusing. The promotional tag line for CREEP-SHOW promised, "It's the most fun you'll ever have being scared."

In a 1973 interview, Subotsky defended himself against such accusations of "prudishness" by explaining that he thought sex onscreen was "boring" and explicit violence was anticlimactic because audiences "know it's fake" (Knight 1973). King and Romero gravitated toward a bloodier brand of horror. In a 1979 interview about his film DAWN OF THE DEAD, Romero rationalized his approach: "In the same way that we've learned to live with the bomb and with the reality that we can walk down the street and get mugged, and yet we've been able to ignore that and go on with the rest of our lives hoping it doesn't happen to us, I'm kind of playing around a little bit to see if the violence can be that dominant a factor in the film and still enable the audience to get past it and experience the story line and the allegory" (Swires: "George" 1979). His goal: to transcend horror.

With its unflinching celebration of the horrific, CREEPSHOW captures the arch spirit of the E.C. Comics. King also kept the E.C. spirit alive by granting permission for illustrator Bernie Wrightson to create an actual CREEPSHOW comic book. Wrightson remembered it as "kind of a comic book adaptation of the movie," bringing the whole experiment full circle (Groth 1982). King must have been intrigued by the process of adapting his stories to yet another new medium, because around the same time he turned his short story "The Lawnmower Man" into a 23-page comic, featuring art by Walter Simonson. The result—which is even more visually bold than CREEP-SHOW—appeared in *Marvel's Bizarre Adventures* #29 in December 1981. After that, King wouldn't attempt to tell another story in comic book form for several decades—but his experience with CREEPSHOW gave him confidence to keep experimenting in film.

PART TWO

Early "Dollar Babies"

THE BOOGEYMAN (1982 short film)

After writing his screenplay for NIGHT SHIFT, Stephen King mostly avoided adaptations of his earliest short stories—creating a void that other writers were happy to fill. In the late 1970s, established Hollywood filmmakers were also avoiding the *Night Shift* collection, so several stories were ripe for the picking when a pair of untested filmmakers approached the author about turning them into short films. In response, King inaugurated an informal program through which he would grant permission for student filmmakers to produce noncommercial adaptations of his un-optioned short stories, in exchange for a $1 fee. Only King himself knows what the first "dollar baby" film was, but fans widely regard Jeffrey C. Schiro's adaptation of "The Boogeyman" and Frank Darabont's adaptation of "The Woman in the Room" as the progenitors.

When *Night Shift* was published in 1978, Bangor native Jeff Schiro was studying filmmaking at King's alma mater, the University of Maine in Orono. He had made his first 8mm horror film ("Dr. Jekyll and Ms. Hyde") at age 13 and later, as a senior in high school, won the Grand Prize at the First Annual Maine Student Film Festival in Augusta. In 1979, he transferred to New York University around the same time Stephen King moved to Bangor, to write "a very long book" called *IT* (King: "Novelist's" 1983). As it turned out, that novel harkened back to King's 1973 tale "The Boogeyman." Perhaps that's why one reason why King was open to the idea of a Bangor native giving it new life?

Schiro says "The Boogeyman" was always his favorite *Night Shift* story. He remembers, "When I read 'The Boogeyman' back in 1978 or so, there was just something about it that touched me. I suppose every kid thinks there's something lurking in his closet, and I was no different. I've always liked dramas with a psychological edge, so I found the story appealing" (Garrido 2006). Schiro was also moved by the story's "surprise ending," which reminded him of classic episodes of THE TWILIGHT ZONE TV series (Northrup 2014).

King's original short story is a third-person narrative revolving around a dialogue between 28-year-old Lester Billings and a psychiatrist named Dr. Harper. Lester says his two-year-old son Denny succumbed to "crib death" in 1967, followed by his daughter Shirl in 1971, and his son Andy "this year." Before explaining exactly what happened, he expresses nervousness about what's in Dr. Harper's closet. The doctor reassures him that there's nothing to be afraid of and Lester proceeds to say that his children were murdered by a boogeyman in their bedroom closet. Even worse, Lester confesses that he himself was an accessory to the murders.

Before Denny died, Lester explains, the boy complained about a "boogeyman" in his room. The father adopted a hardline, disciplinarian approach; he threatened to give the boy "a whack" if Denny didn't overcome his foolish fears. Later, when he found his son dead, Lester noticed that the closet door was standing open. Still, he refused to seriously consider the possibility that his son had been killed by the boogeyman. Out of stubbornness, he moved his daughter Shirl into Denny's old bedroom, and soon Shirl was complaining about a monster with claws (at least, that's how Lester interpreted her hysterical ravings). One night, Lester himself heard strange noises emanating from the closet—sounds that made him dream of slimy monsters from the old *Tales from the Crypt* comics.

After he found Shirl dead in her crib—she having swallowed her own tongue—Lester and his wife moved out of the house and had a third child. Lester tells Dr. Harper he didn't want another child at first, but that he soon grew to love Andy most of all. For a while, the family was happy but Lester's idyllic new beginning was shattered by the return of the boogeyman. Anxiously aware of the monster lurking in the shadows, Lester says he began to "snap" at his wife, "just like the old days." He also entertained nightmarish visions of his tormentor "slinking through the streets at night and maybe creeping in the sewers."

Eventually, he became convinced that childhood monsters might be real—at least, real enough to cause the deaths of two young children under mysterious circumstances. He began to encounter more and more evidence: trails of slime, broken mirrors, inhuman sounds. Ultimately, Lester's fear of a direct encounter with the boogeyman overwhelmed his fear of losing his third child, so he all but sacrificed Andy to the darkness by drunkenly ignoring his child's screams for help until it was too late. He tells Dr. Harper he saw the creature—with its "slumped shoulders" and "scarecrow head"—snap his son's neck. After that, he went to an all-night diner, drank six cups of coffee to sober up, returned home and called the police. He said nothing to the police about the boogeyman because he knew they wouldn't believe him.

After Lester concludes his narrative, King (the objective narrator) concludes the story with a scene in which the boogeyman attacks the deadbeat dad. It staggers out of Dr. Harper's closet with the psychiatrist's face—clutched like a Halloween mask—in its "rotted, spade-claw hand." "So nice," the monster coos as it moves in for one more kill.

Up until the final scene, King's story has given the reader every reason to believe that Lester Billings murdered his children. The character is a paranoid, defensive, seemingly delusional, thoroughly unsympathetic hard-ass. He admits to berating his wife and aggressively expresses an old-fashioned view of women in general. ("She still wanted to do what I told her. That's the wife's place, right?") He makes it clear that he resented his children and sometimes wanted to kill them. ("I tell you, sometimes I felt like throwing them both out the window.") Even in his happiest moments, he's tossing out casual barbs about "the hippies" and "the niggers." At his most anxious, he drinks heavily. There's no question that Lester Billings is a monster—which might lead most readers to believe that Lester Billings is, in fact, the boogeyman. King's twist ending, however, suggests that the boogeyman is real.

The ambiguity of King's story made Jeff Schiro want to adapt it as his senior production project at NYU, so he reached out to King's publisher Doubleday Books. After a long wait, he remembers getting an approval letter that specified the author's terms: "The only thing he asks for is $1, that it not be distributed commercially, and that he receives a Betamax copy when it is done" (Lealos 2015). Schiro assumed the author's generosity was a gesture of goodwill toward a fellow Bangorian. He wanted to prove himself worthy, so he got to work.

Schiro's 22-page first draft script for THE BOOGEYMAN begins with a scene of 34-year-old Lester Billings in the bathroom, undressing to take a shower. When Lester pulls back the shower curtain, he sees his daughter Shirl lying dead in the tub. In the next scene, paramedics remove the body from the house and a 40-year-old homicide investigator, Sgt. Gurland, arrives on the scene. Gurland approaches Lester in the bedroom, where Lester's wife Rita is telling him he shouldn't have "moved" the body. Gurland questions Lester, who claims he found his child dead in her crib. A pair of elderly neighbors, Mr. and Mrs. Levine, interrupt the interrogation and Gurland talks to a forensic investigator named Dave, who gives the diagnosis of "crib death" but also comments on some suspicious bruises—and notes that the Billings family lost another child under similar circumstances three months ago.

Schiro says he modified King's story in order to make it more visual, explaining, "The story works brilliantly within the confines of the office, but cinematically it would have probably been a bit boring to keep it there. So, I brought in a couple other characters and added some scenes that I thought would be visually and dramatically interesting" (Northrup 2014). The most prominent new character, Sgt. Gurland, articulates the theory that Lester murdered his kids.

The screen story moves to Dr. Harper's office, where Lester confesses that he is—sort of—responsible for the deaths of his two children. Much of the dialogue in this scene comes from King's story but the screenplay juxtaposes the doctor-patient dialogue with short flashback scenes. In the first flashback, Lester and Rita wake up to the sound of their son's screams. They rush to Denny's room and the boy tells them he saw the boogeyman. Naturally, they don't believe him. Later that same night, the parents check on their crying daughter. While Lester puts Shirl back to bed, Rita goes to check on Denny. Lester hears his wife scream and runs into Denny's room, where he sees his son lying dead in his crib.

Eager to uncover the truth about what happened to Denny, Sgt. Gurland visits Dave in the "forensic department" of the police station. Dave tells him that Ruth Billings has suffered a nervous breakdown and has been hospitalized. He also points out some similarities between the deaths of the two Billings children: both suffered fatal convulsions and both bodies showed evidence of physical abuse. Gurland proposes that the damage might have been caused by an angry father. Dave suggests it might have been an angry mother.

At the Billings house, Lester dismisses the neighbor Mrs. Levine from babysitting Andy and watches over the boy himself, while drinking beer and doing a crossword puzzle. Finally, he places Andy in his crib and goes to sleep. While he sleeps, the camera observes closed doors throughout the house. Eventually, one of the doors bursts open, awakening both Lester and Andy. The screen story jumps to an exterior shot of the Billings house as the soundtrack features Andy yelling, "No, Daddy, NO!"

Sometime later, Gurland comes knocking on the front door. Receiving no answer, he lets himself in and looks around. When he enters a darkened room, Andy's body falls at his feet. Police put out an APB on Lester as the screen story cuts back to Lester in Dr. Harper's office, as he offers an explanation straight out of Stephen King's short story: *Childhood monsters are real*. Lester says he moved Andy from his crib in order to hide him from the boogeyman. As he tells the story, Lester hears his son crying—Dr. Harper can't hear it—and covers his ears to block out the memory. The screen story flashes back to the crucial moments before Andy's murder. Lester wakes up, hears his son screaming, retrieves a baseball bat and rushes into his son's room. He approaches the closet but finds only boxes inside, so he runs out of the room, still looking for the boogeyman. Then hears his son scream again. He runs back to the boy's room but trips and falls in slow motion. The scene ends before he hits the ground; the implication is that he did not arrive in time.

Back in Harper's office, Lester concludes his story by saying he hasn't told the police yet about Andy's murder. He also explains that when he found Shirl dead in the bathtub, he moved her body to the crib because he knew police would wonder why she was in the bathtub. He claims he was trying to hide her from the boogeyman. Dr. Harper reassures Lester that everything will be fine and counsels him to make an appointment for his next session. (Not the most ethical psychiatrist, but that doesn't bother Lester....) Billings leaves the office, only to find that the doctor's receptionist is away from her desk. He returns to Dr. Harper's office and notices that the closet door is slightly open. As in the finale of King's story, the boogeyman emerges. The final image in the screen story is a close-up of the Dr. Harper face mask in the monster's spade-clawed hand.

Throughout the screen story, there is one looming question: *Did Lester Billings murder his children?* Jeff Schiro says, "I tried to do probably everything I could to lead the audience to believe that Lester Billings was indeed guilty of killing his kid" (Lealos 2015). Accordingly, he added the details about Lester moving his daughter's body and lying to police, as well as the forensic examiner's ominous conclusions, and Andy screaming, "No, Daddy, NO!" The final sequence pivots on a second question: *Has Lester's decision to go to a psychiatrist instead of going to the police led him to a worse fate than criminal prosecution?* Schiro says yes: "I took one side with the thing and believe that there really is a Boogeyman, and that would make the surprise more like a TWILIGHT ZONE ending for my film" (Lealos 2015).

The filmmaker says it took seven days to shoot THE BOOGEYMAN on 16mm film and another two years to finalize the edit. (This was back in the days when even student films were actually shot on film and edited on flatbeds—an expensive and time-consuming process.) Although King authority George Beahm claims that the short film won an award at the annual NYU Student Film Festival, THE BOOGEYMAN was not officially included in the 1982 festival. Instead, Schiro entered a two-minute, 8mm short film called "Animation Breakdown." That film reportedly won a "best in animation" award at the festival (Clavette 1982).

On November 16, 1982, THE BOOGEYMAN made its way to Jeff Schiro's—and Stephen King's—old alma mater. It was screened for an enthusiastic audience in the English-Math building on the Bangor-Augusta campus. A contemporary report in the *Maine Campus* newspaper reported that Schiro was pursuing commercial rights for King's short story in hope of selling his short film to a cable television network. The same article quoted Stephen King declaring THE BOOGEYMAN "a fine film" and suggesting that the ideal market would be HBO or Cinemax (Anonymous: "Former" 1982).

A few years later, Schiro's film appeared alongside another early "dollar baby" on a VHS release from California-based Granite Entertainment. Executive producer Gary Gray reportedly obtained the necessary rights from King's publisher, Doubleday, thereby legitimizing the first dollar baby and giving birth to TWO MINI-FEATURES FROM STEPHEN KING'S NIGHTSHIFT COLLECTION.

An Interview with Jeffrey C. Schiro (2020)

JOSEPH MADDREY: I found an article from the Bangor Daily News *in 1977, and it mentioned that you started thinking about becoming a filmmaker at age 13, when you shot an 8mm version of DR. JEKYLL AND MS. HYDE.*

JEFF SCHIRO: Right. [laughs] That was the least of them, really. I was one of those kids that ran around with the Super-8 cameras. I lived in a pretty large neighborhood of kids, so at some point we started making films. For me, it was like, Oh this is great, I know what I'm going to do with the rest of my life. [laughs]

MADDREY: Were you always interested in telling horror stories? Was that your genre?

SCHIRO: As a kid, yes. It was either that or satire. We would do spoofs of shows that already existed. We did a lot of that, but there were a few horror films. I think the better ones were the horror films.

MADDREY: The same article mentioned that when you were a senior in high school, you won an award at a student film festival in Augusta for a Claymation movie. And then you and a buddy of yours made a GODFATHER spoof.

SCHIRO: Right. When I look back on them, they're actually pretty good for just starting out. Those won at the Maine Student Film Festival. It was the first year they had this thing. Then I did a more serious film, kind of a bizarre film that won an international film festival award and was shipped around to different countries. Maybe it was only an honorable mention. That was so long ago....

MADDREY: Was that when you were at the University of Maine?
SCHIRO: Yes.

MADDREY: That's quite a bit of early recognition.
SCHIRO: Yeah, it started off great. [laughs]

MADDREY: Was there a filmmaking program at University of Maine? Which campus were you at?
SCHIRO: I was at the University of Maine in Orono.

MADDREY: So you were at King's alma mater.
SCHIRO: I was. In fact, I went to Bangor High School, which is like eight miles down the road, and they used to refer to the University of Maine in Orono as "Bangor High School Part 2," because so many kids from Bangor went to Orono. I was there for a couple years and then I transferred to NYU because at that point I knew I wanted to go into film.

MADDREY: And there was no film program at UMO?
SCHIRO: There was more of a video program. I believe I did take it at one point. But they didn't have too much equipment.

MADDREY: So if you were going to be a filmmaker, you had to go somewhere else....
SCHIRO: Exactly.

MADDREY: *My wife and I visited Bangor for the first time a few years ago. Before that, my sense of Maine came largely from Stephen King novels. I knew that King had moved his family to Bangor when he was writing IT, because he wanted to set that novel in a blue-collar, roughneck kind of town—and he thought Bangor fit the bill. When I went, that's what I was expecting, but I found Bangor to be much more bucolic. The people were very nice and the town was beautiful. In the summer, at least.*

SCHIRO: Right. In the winter, not so much. [laughs]

MADDREY: *Has it changed a lot since you grew up there?*

SCHIRO: It's changed a bit. There was a lot of urban renewal that went on. There were some streets where the buildings were so old that they were all torn down. But the downtown used to be a really vibrant downtown and it really isn't anymore. Now you have go further out to hit the Wal-Marts and the stores. But it's still a nice little town. And you do have access to the university, which is nice. They have events going on every now and then.

MADDREY: *I remember even being impressed with the cemetery. There aren't a lot of cemeteries that I would want to hang out in, but Mount Hope Cemetery....*

SCHIRO: I shot a film there, actually. That was one of my little horror films. I always loved that place too. That was right down the street from where I grew up, so I could ride my bike down there. I think it's still a nice place to hang out. Did you go to Stephen King's house?

MADDREY: *Yeah, we did the obligatory drive-by. My understanding is that the King family didn't move in there until about 1980, so Stephen King wasn't a neighbor when you were growing up.*

SCHIRO: He was not—although it's funny because in one of these films, in THE GODFATHER spoof, we filmed this house as one of the mansions. I knew the people who lived there, or my parents did.

MADDREY: *Were you aware of King's early novels when you were in high school?*

SCHIRO: I was aware of them. I don't remember when I read the other ones, but I originally read the *Night Shift* collection when I was at the University of Maine. Maybe I even had to read it for a class, I'm not sure. But I remember reading "The Boogeyman" and saying, "Someday I'm going to make this into a film. I don't know when or how...." It just grabbed me.

MADDREY: *And you were enterprising enough to write to his publisher and ask for the rights to do an adaptation.*

SCHIRO: But it took a while. I think I heard back, like, two years later. Then I said, all right, I'm gonna attempt to do this.

MADDREY: *You ended up making THE BOOGEYMAN as your senior project at NYU, so you must have requested permission pretty soon after you started there.*

SCHIRO: I'm not sure exactly when I wrote to them. I couldn't find the letter—but the return letter is dated February 6, 1980.

MADDREY: *When you asked for permission, were you already thinking of making THE BOOGEYMAN as your senior project? Or that's just how things turned out because they took so long to get back to you?*

SCHIRO: That may have been how it turned out. As time went on, I probably thought, well, I'm going to be getting free equipment and some free film. So I probably realized at some point that I should do this as a senior thesis, and that's what I ended up doing—although it took me two years to make. I think I was already out of school by the time I finished it.

MADDREY: I found an itinerary for the 1982 NYU Student Film Festival, and it looks like you had two films in the festival that year, ANIMATION BREAKDOWN and THE BOOGEYMAN. The festival was in February, and I've also read that THE BOOGEYMAN was also shown on campus at the University of Maine in November 1982.

SCHIRO: I set that up for friends and family. I actually left an invitation for Stephen King and he showed up to my little screening. He had some great things to say and he was really helpful. He gave me a big bear hug and told me how much he liked it.

MADDREY: He was quoted in an article about that screening, talking about how to get the film commercially distributed.

SCHIRO: The [initial] deal was that I wasn't supposed to sell it commercially. Shortly afterwards, this guy named Frank Darabont made "The Woman in the Room," so those two films were put together [and released on VHS]. Stephen King agreed to let that happen. He gave it his blessing.

MADDREY: You've said it was the psychological edge of the story that originally attracted you, so I'm wondering what sort of horror movies you liked at the time. It occurs to me that you made this film at a time when most horror movies were slasher movies—right after the success of HALLOWEEN and FRIDAY THE 13TH—but you decided to make a different kind of horror film. Did you have any specific horror films you wanted to emulate?

SCHIRO: That's a good question. I did find the psychological aspect really appealing. At that point, I think I wasn't into slasher films. I wanted it to be much more of a psychological journey. I always liked courtroom dramas. I kind of saw this as a courtroom drama as well. That's what really interested me. And to ask that ultimate question: "Did he do it or did he not do it?" I'm trying to think of the type of … you know, I grew up on DARK SHADOWS, so I suppose that influenced me a little bit.

MADDREY: That makes sense. When I compared King's story to your script, I noticed that you added a completely new storyline about a criminal investigation. You added an objective point of view on the events in the original story.

SCHIRO: Right. I found that fascinating. I didn't want it to be a slasher. I didn't want there to be a lot of blood. I think there's only one drop of blood in the whole thing. Maybe two drops. [laughs]

MADDREY: I think that shows how you filtered the story through your own sensibilities. King's original story has several passages in which the main character imagines the boogeyman as a slimy monster out of the old Tales from the Crypt comics. Potentially, you could have latched onto that aspect of the story and adapted it to the screen as a monster movie— and made something more like CREEPSHOW. That's one interpretation, but you focused instead on the psychological horror.

SCHIRO: That's just what appealed to me about the story. That and spending many moons as a kid, looking at my closet, wondering if there was anything inside.

MADDREY: *Did you ever think about showing the boogeyman at the end? Or did you always think that would diminish the power of the film?*

SCHIRO: I had hired somebody to make a monster mask that we could use, but it was absolutely horrid. [laughs] I said I can't do this because I really don't have enough money to make a great-looking, Hollywood-type mask, so the idea was to do something a little more abstract. And quick. Although I think some people would love to see that big monster with the glowing red eyes, it wasn't practical for me at the time.

MADDREY: *In King's story, he describes the boogeyman as having a scarecrow head.*

SCHIRO: That's right.

MADDREY: *The reveal in your film is very impressionistic, but it almost looked like you had a mask made out of spider webs.*

SCHIRO: That is pretty much it. He was wearing a black hood and we put a spiderweb-like material over that. We did make a mask of his face, but….

MADDREY: *You cut away before we see it.*

SCHIRO: It was tough because that was cut on film, so it was frame-by-frame. I wonder what it would be like if we'd had the digital equipment to make that. Maybe it would be a very different film.

MADDREY: *You've certainly got more experience now, and your sensibilities have probably changed in terms of what you would pull out of the story.*

SCHIRO: Oh yeah. There are parts of this that make me cringe. I say, "Why did I do that?" But that's to be expected, I think.

MADDREY: *When I read King's original story, I can't help relating it to* The Shining. *In my mind, Lester Billings is a less sympathetic Jack Torrance. He's clearly an alcoholic, he seems like a misogynist, he admits being borderline abusive to his children. I feel like you softened that character a bit in your film. The things he says in your script and your film aren't quite as reprehensible. You make him a little easier to sympathize with. At the same time, by adding the criminal investigation story, you make him look just as guilty in a different way.*

SCHIRO: I did read the *Night Shift* story last night, and I agree completely that he was not the most likeable guy. [laughs] I think I probably did try to soften it by taking out some of the lines that he had.

MADDREY: *You also opened up the story visually by adding the scene in the bathroom, where Lester finds one of his kids dead in the bathtub. Did you add the bathroom because you wanted more variety in shooting locations?*

SCHIRO: I think that was part of it. I also thought I had to do that to make the story make sense. I remember when I was trying to come up with it, it got a little confusing with the three kids. I thought I had to show one of them die at the beginning, so at least I could get one out of the way. Some of the other stuff, I look at now—like the whole thing with the neighbor, Mrs. Levine. The only thing I can think of is I must have just tried to write anything just to get those characters on paper, and then see where I could take them from there.

MADDREY: *There's more of the neighbors in the script than in the finished film.*

SCHIRO: Oh yeah, a lot more.

MADDREY: Reading the script, I was thinking these neighbors are wildly enabling this potential child murderer.

SCHIRO: [laughs] That's funny. But you're right. I don't even remember writing that. I don't know where it came from. All I can think of is it's just part of the process.

MADDREY: You added a lot of new characters, so maybe you were thinking, "I know who can play this part. Aunt Sally wants to be the neighbor."

SCHIRO: [laughs] It could be. Absolutely. You'd know better, as a writer.

MADDREY: It's interesting comparing adaptations of King's novels to adaptations of his short stories. Usually with the novels, the screenwriter has to trim the story, whereas the short stories often have to be expanded. You did expand "The Boogeyman." King's story is basically one scene, one long monologue. You took it out of the psychiatrist's office and gave it a B-story. The temptation must have been to use the scene in the psychiatrist's office as a framing story and then do the rest in flashbacks, but you didn't do that. You expanded the story and made it your own. You also condensed the time frame of the story, from something like ten years to a few months. Was that a practical decision, to reduce locations and wardrobe changes?

SCHIRO: I didn't remember that until you just said that, but I think that was a practical concern for sure. You'd have to age all these people and move them to another house.

MADDREY: Right, because in King's story the boogeyman follows the family to another house. Lester imagines him slithering through the streets and sewers—which in my mind connects the story to IT. Both stories tackle the idea that a rational adult couldn't possibly cope with the existence of mythical monsters. Did that idea influence your final shot in the film? To me, it seems like Lester dies of fright.

SCHIRO: Could be. I think people get frustrated because whenever they ask me about that, I say, "Well, whatever you think it is." But I'm quite sure that was his demise. Whether he died of fright or whether he fell to the ground and got *mawed*, I'm not really sure.

MADDREY: One way or another, the boogeyman is real for him and causes his death.

SCHIRO: Right. Exactly.

MADDREY: What about changing the last line of dialogue. In your script and your film, the boogeyman says, "It's only a game." At the end of King's story, he says, "So nice." Do you remember the thought process behind that change?

SCHIRO: I think it was basically that I wasn't sure people would understand the last line. Especially coming from a cobweb-headed boogeyman. I'm not sure I could have done it justice enough that people would have understood it. Whereas the whole "game" thing I could tie in earlier. When he's on the floor and he says, "What am I gonna tell the cops? That the boogeyman is playing games with me?"

MADDREY: That works well with your B-story, because the boogeyman is playing a game with the investigators, making Lester look guilty.

SCHIRO: That's what I was going for. Luckily, King didn't have any problems with the change. For the book, you can mull it over and you can think about it. For the film, if somebody misses those last words—"What did he say again?"—I was afraid that a lot would have been lost. I didn't think it ["So nice."] was as appropriate for the film as it was for the book.

MADDREY: *I understand you hand-delivered the finished film to Stephen King's house.*

SCHIRO: I did. Somebody who knew him—or knew the family—said, "You should just go over and drop it off. That's the kind of people they are."

MADDREY: *Once upon a time.*

SCHIRO: Once upon a time. Exactly right. So I did. It was, I think, the middle of winter and I went over with my Betamax copy. I knocked on the door and he answered the door. I gave him the tape and I gave him a flyer for the screening I was going to have the University of Maine. As it turns out, he showed up for the screening.

MADDREY: *So he was very supportive of you. I heard that he later recommended you to direct an episode of the TV show TALES FROM THE DARKSIDE.*

SCHIRO: Yeah, he recommended me for that and for a Ramones music video. It was called "Time Has Come Today," a remake of an old Chambers Brothers song. It was in the early days of MTV and I still had a lot to learn.

MADDREY: *On TALES FROM THE DARKSIDE, weren't you originally going to do "Sorry, Right Number," the episode Stephen King wrote?*

SCHIRO: Yes, I was.

MADDREY: *That was a big vote of confidence from Stephen King.*

SCHIRO: Yeah, but [the producers] wouldn't let me do it. I mean, they gave me a pretty good episode—a comedic one. I think they thought the other one was going to be too complicated, but I think the one they gave me was more complicated, to tell you the truth.

MADDREY: *The episode you directed ["The Grave Robber"] seems like it would have been more of a tonal challenge, because it shifts from a horror story to a comedy. When I first saw it, I thought the mummy was supposed to be a guy that was dressed up to trick the treasure-hunters. I didn't realize he was actually supposed to be a mummy—until the episode turned comedic.*

SCHIRO: The mummy was this guy named Arnold Stang, who was an old-time actor. He was the voice of Top Cat [in the 1961–62 TV series TOP CAT] and he was really well known in the old days.

MADDREY: *The episode would have played differently for me if I had known that.*

SCHIRO: I just remember walking around for a couple days with a knot in my stomach the size of Texas.

MADDREY: *Were you nervous about doing comedy?*

SCHIRO: No, I liked doing comedy. They chose the script for me. I didn't really have a choice. But it was a real learning experience.

MADDREY: *It was a chance to show your range as a director.*

SCHIRO: Yeah. Getting directing work in New York was difficult, especially being 22 or whatever. So I came out to Los Angeles. It was about the same time that the non-linear editing systems were coming out, and that was a love of mine—editing—so I got into that.

MADDREY: *Have you been to any of the Dollar Baby Film Festivals?*

SCHIRO: I have. I did one out here [in Los Angeles], at the old Cinefamily theater on Fairfax [in 2010].

MADDREY: You must have been a major celebrity at that, because you're the guy who kicked off the "dollar baby" program—you and Frank Darabont. Did they pull you up on stage and say "This is all your fault"?

    SCHIRO: [laughs] Exactly.

MADDREY: Is it exciting that your name comes up whenever someone makes a new dollar baby film?

    SCHIRO: Yeah, it's kind of fun.

MADDREY: I'm sure you've heard the rumor that there might be a feature-length adaptation of "The Boogeyman" coming soon.

    SCHIRO: I heard that. I heard it was [being developed by] the guys who did STRANGER THINGS.

MADDREY: I'd be curious to see how they expand the original story, which is basically one scene. To have to string that out to feature film length is daunting. Would you want to take that on? What would be your approach to that?

    SCHIRO: Well, as you mentioned, the original story takes place over ten years.... I think it would be a tough story to adapt.

MADDREY: I think that what you did—adding a B-story about the investigation—would make sense for a feature film. There would be plenty of time to develop the investigator as a character who doesn't want to see this guy get away with murder but has to keep watching the kids die over the course of ten years.

    SCHIRO: I'll be interested to see if they make it, to see what they do with it.

THE WOMAN IN THE ROOM (1983 short film)

    Around the time Jeff Schiro graduated from Bangor High School in 1977, Frank Darabont graduated from Hollywood High School and became a professional factotum. For the future Oscar-winner, 1977 to 1986 were "lean years" during which he took several odd jobs—including busboy, theater usher, telephone operator, and forklift operator—while trying to gain a foothold in the film industry (Argent 2016). Darabont got his first break in late 1980, when he took a job as a production assistant on the slasher film HELL NIGHT, starring Linda Blair. He remembers, "I made $150 a week, which was horrible pay even back then. But it was my entry into the film business, and began my association with Chuck Russell" (Lilja 2007). After working for six years as a freelance set dresser on non-union shows, commercials and low-budget movies (including Ken Russell's CRIMES OF PASSION and Charles Band's TRANCERS), Chuck Russell hired Darabont to co-write A NIGHTMARE ON ELM STREET 3: DREAM WARRIORS for New Line Cinema. The rest, as they say, is history.

    Darabont went on to write and direct THE SHAWSHANK REDEMPTION, which is widely regarded as one of the best Stephen King adaptations—as well as one of the greatest films ever made. The project probably wouldn't have come to fruition if Darabont hadn't established an early rapport with King by making a short film out of the author's story "The Woman in the Room." Darabont remembers how it came about: "My friends and I—the same friends that worked with me on [HELL NIGHT]—thought we should make a film. We should make a short film, not a Super-8 mm film like we made in high school. (That was back in the days when 8mm actually meant film. Now it means something else.) But we thought we should make a real 16mm movie with real actors in it" (Emery 2003). Darabont had read King's short story and thought it would make a great subject for adaptation—precisely because it wasn't the obvious "Stephen King–type" horror story (Argent 2016). He wrote a script and mailed it to the author—never dreaming, he says, that King would give him the rights to make it.

King's original short story is an omniscient third-person narrative with frequent first-person digressions. The main character, Johnny, spends much of the story agonizing over the slow death of his cancer-ridden mother, who has been immobilized by a botched surgical procedure. He pays an early-winter visit to the hospital in Lewiston, Maine, and contemplates ending her misery by administering a fatal dosage of prescription pain pills. As he approaches the room, he wonders if his plan will work and whether or not his mother will go along with it. Inside the room, he hesitates—despite having numbed his own anxiousness with plenty of alcohol (five beers on the way to the hospital and another one when he goes outside to urinate in the snow). All he offers his mother is a cigarette and a cup of water.

The dialogue between the mother and son is filled with desperation and self-pity. For Johnny, the heartbreak of seeing his mother on her deathbed is compounded by vivid memories of a time when she was young and strong. He recalls a specific day when he was an impetuous twelve-year-old and his mother swatted him with his dying grandmother's soiled diaper. The author doesn't explain why this particular memory occurs to Johnny at this particular moment. Johnny later remembers finding his grandmother dead, so the reader might assume that he is anticipating a repeat of that traumatic childhood experience.

After leaving the hospital, Johnny visits his brother Kevin, whose seemingly blasé attitude about their mother's final days frustrates Johnny. He returns to the hospital and talks to his mother's doctor, who offers no hope of relief. Exasperated, Johnny once again contemplates ending his mother's suffering—as well as his own. Sitting in the hospital room, he mentions to her that he has brought some stronger pain pills from home. His mother urges him not to let the doctors and nurses see them, then proceeds to chew the pills, one by one. The mother and son do not discuss what they are doing, but Johnny thinks, "It is many too many, even she must know that." Johnny's mother tells him he's a good son, then casually goes to sleep. Johnny kisses her goodbye and leaves the scene of the crime. With the deed done, King writes that Johnny "feels no different, either good or bad." The ending suggests a kind of relief, but also a dehumanizing numbness. Johnny goes home and waits—soberly—for the inevitable phone call.

Since Darabont submitted a script to Stephen King before securing permission to adapt his story, it is reasonable to assume that the completed short film adheres closely to the script. The screen story begins with a tracking shot through a woman's bedroom, then cuts to an introductory scene of Johnny in the bathroom. He retrieves a bottle of pills from the medicine cabinet and stares at himself in the mirror for a few moments. In the next scene, Johnny exits an elevator and walks down a hallway to his mother's hospital room. Much of the subsequent dialogue between the mother and son is taken from the short story but one exchange is more pointed than anything in King's original. Johnny's mother says, "I wish it were over." Johnny tells her not to say that. Afterward, he leaves the room to get her some water and removes the bottle of pills from his pocket. He looks at himself in the mirror again, obviously contemplating whether or not to give the pills to his mother. The silent interrogation of his mirror image visualizes the first line and central question of King's story: "Can he do it?" When Johnny returns to the room, he gives his mother a cigarette and leaves. Back at home, Johnny calls his brother Kevin. The film presents only one side of the brief conversation, illustrating Johnny's inner desperation at a minimum production cost. (No additional actor or shooting location are needed.)

Next, Darabont essentially replaces Johnny's conversation with his mother's doctor with a more revealing dialogue. King's story doesn't bother to identify Johnny's occupation but Darabont identifies him as a lawyer. In the completely new scene, he meets with a client—a murderer on death row. Darabont remembers that he "needed a forum for presenting the main character's thoughts and conflict in simple cinematic terms. King, of course, can simply tell us what the guy's thinking and feeling by stating it outright. Since one loses that ability with the camera, one must find other ways" (Collings 1986). Instead of interrogating his mirror image, Johnny questions The Prisoner, who the writer/director characterizes as Johnny's dark half, explaining, "It was a summit meeting, so to speak, between a man's finer instincts and his baser ones, in which compromises had to be reached" (Collings 1986).

After a brief discussion of The Prisoner's legal case, Johnny confesses that he hasn't been sleeping lately due to anxiety over his mother's cordotomy. The Prisoner volunteers that he had a buddy in 'Nam who underwent the same procedure. He remembers that it "short-circuited his pain" and "short-circuited just about everything else along with it." Since they're on the subject of death, Johnny asks The Prisoner what it "feels like" to kill. The Prisoner coldly replies that he "never felt one way or the other about it"—except when he euthanized the buddy who had the cordotomy. Although Stephen King opined that The Prisoner character was "a bit clichéd," the added exchange communicates two important ideas: (1) that a mercy-killing is more emotionally difficult than killing in the line of duty, and (2) that the son's duty may not be so different from a soldier's job (Collings 1986). At the end of King's story, Johnny feels nothing. Darabont's adaptation goes a different way.

First, the writer/director invented a new dream sequence, in which Johnny gets chased down a hospital hallway by a patient in a wheelchair. The patient's identity is concealed behind a body bag. Johnny escapes into an elevator, only to find his pursuer in the elevator with him. He unzips the body bag and sees his mother's ghostly face, benevolently smiling back at him. Relieved, he leans forward to hug her—and the face transforms into that of a desiccated corpse. The dream sequence ends as Johnny wakes up in horror.

Darabont has offered a couple of explanations for the added dream sequence. In a 1986 interview, he reflected that he was—perhaps in a moment of weakness—playing to the author's reputation and fan base. It is worth noting that the author did something similar in his short story, making several allusions to horror fiction. At one point, Johnny compares the hospital patients to the zombies in George Romero's NIGHT OF THE LIVING DEAD. He also describes a set of hanging IV bags as "a Salvador Dali dream of tits." If that's not an invitation for a horrific dream sequence, what is?

In a 2008 interview, Darabont offered an alternative explanation for the dream sequence, saying, "I wanted to keep the film from being a talking-head movie" (Rausch: Fifty 2008). The dream sequence added action, suspense, and visual style to the short film. In the new scene, Darabont also paid homage to his own horror movie background, as he explained in a 2007 interview: "That corpse [in the elevator] originally appeared in HELL NIGHT. If I remember correctly, Linda Blair stumbles into a room at one point where a bunch of corpses are propped around a table—it was a male corpse, but in my short I passed him off as a woman" (Lilja 2007).

Darabont's film concludes with a scene in which Johnny gives the pills to his mother. Compared to King's final scene, Darabont's is more intimate. In the short story, Johnny's only specific memory of his mother is when she walloped him with his grandmother's dirty diaper, shocking his twelve-year-old self into submission. In the final scene of the film, Johnny reminisces aloud about a blissful day when his mother took him to an amusement park. At the same time, he's feeding her the pills that will end her life. Although there is no discussion about euthanasia, Johnny asks his mother—with a directness that is absent from King's story—"Do you want another one?" She answers, "Yes. Please." He proceeds to give her the entire bottle, one pill at a time. Afterward, he thanks her for "that day in the park" and she drifts off to sleep. Darabont's screen story ends with a shot of the mother sleeping rather than a scene of the son at home waiting. The film offers a greater sense of closure and peace.

One might reasonably wonder if the filmmaker's softer ending provided some peace and closure for the author himself. King's "The Woman in the Room" is a hard-hitting story of unbearable heartache and helplessness. Although the main character overcomes his feelings of helplessness, the triumph provides no relief. In terms of tone, Darabont's THE WOMAN IN THE ROOM is equally poignant but not nearly as despairing. The author's bleak Maine winter setting gives way to a sunnier southern California setting. In the final scene, a warm glow fills the death room. With such changes, Darabont delivers a sophisticated reinvention of the source story rather than a straightforward adaptation.

In a 1995 essay, Stephen King described his initial reaction as follows: "Frank sent me a videocassette of his film, and I watched it in slack-jawed amazement. I also felt a little sting of tears. THE WOMAN IN THE ROOM remains, twelve years later, on my short list of favorite film adaptations" (King: "Rita" 1995). A 1985 ad in *Variety* magazine also quoted King as saying, "THE WOMAN IN THE ROOM is clearly the best of the short films made from my stuff." When Granite Entertainment Group paired Darabont's film with Jeff Schiro's THE BOOGEYMAN on a home video release titled TWO MINI-FEATURES FROM STEPHEN KING'S NIGHT SHIFT COLLECTION, the cover art prominently featured the quote.

Unfortunately, although the VHS release introduced the two short films to a generation of horror fans, it didn't make Schiro or Darabont any money. According to Darabont, the two filmmakers "got equally screwed" by the Granite producers (Lilja 2007). Their reward was an ongoing relationship with Stephen King, who later granted Darabont a $1 limited license to adapt the novella *Rita Hayworth and the Shawshank Redemption*. At some point before he made THE SHAWSHANK REDEMPTION, Darabont also concocted a plan to adapt King's short story "The Monkey" for Granite Entertainment. He was still thinking about the adaptation (minus any association with Granite Entertainment) in the early 2000s, and also contemplating an adaptation of King's novella *The Mist*.

Having now directed three of the most successful Stephen King adaptations of all time—THE SHAWSHANK REDEMPTION (1994), THE GREEN MILE (1999), and THE MIST (2007)—Darabont is apparently not as enthusiastic about THE WOMAN

IN THE ROOM. In a 2007 interview, he dismissed his first film as "creaky" and "slow" (Lilja 2007). Stephen King and Darabont's fellow "dollar baby" filmmakers beg to differ.

DISCIPLES OF THE CROW (1983 short film)

Although largely forgotten, another early "dollar baby" film was released commercially by the opportunists at Granite Entertainment. John R. Woodward's DISCIPLES OF THE CROW—based on Stephen King's short story "Children of the Corn"—has probably fallen into obscurity because it was immediately eclipsed by the 1984 feature film. Nonetheless, DISCIPLES (a.k.a. THE NIGHT OF THE CROW) was the first film adaptation of what has become the most famous story in Stephen King's *Night Shift* collection.

DISCIPLES was made over a period of nineteen months in 1981 and 1982, by writer/producer/director/editor John R. Woodward. At the time, Woodward was a student at the University of Texas at Austin and he shot his thesis film on back roads and small towns north of the city. To accommodate the filming locations, he changed the nominal setting of King's story from the fictional town of Gatlin, Nebraska, to the real town of Jonah, Oklahoma. Today, Jonah is a ghost town situated near the north end of the city of Enid, the purported "Wheat Capital of the United States." As its name suggests, Jonah is a predominantly Christian community—but built on historic tribal lands of the Plains Indians. The local Native American traditions may have been a source of additional inspiration for the short film.

In Stephen King's short story, the "children" of Gatlin worship a Lovecraftian god dubbed He Who Walks Behind the Rows. In John Woodward's adaptation, the children instead worship "sacred" crows. The opening scene in the short film shows a young boy, Billy, kneeling and apparently praying to the crows in the trees above him. Later, Billy secretly leads a group of children through prayer and offerings as they prepare for a ritual sacrifice. In the next scene, the children attend Sunday morning service at the local Mercy Baptist Church with their parents, and exchange conspiratorial glances as the preacher sermonizes about indecency and immorality while Billy's mother flirts openly with her lover. That night, the kids murder the adults in their sleep.

The screen story then flashes forward twelve years, to 1983, and picks up where King's short story began. In both versions, a teenage boy flees through a cornfield to a main road and a bickering couple accidentally hits him with their car. DISCIPLES appropriates some dialogue from King's story but offers no hint of Burt and Vicky's backstory. King's story establishes that the couple is married and that Burt is a Vietnam vet, but the only thing we know for sure about the couple in the film is that they're driving a car with Texas license plates … and Vicky is eager to get out of Oklahoma.

A point-of-view shot, accompanied by the sound of heavy breathing, indicates that someone is watching them from inside the cornfield. Finding an ornamental knife in the dead boy's body, Burt realizes they are in danger and urges Vicky to get his shotgun. He then checks the boy's pockets and finds a pouch filled with dried corn and a mummified crow's foot. These discoveries are original to Woodward's adaptation. As in the short story, Burt puts the boy's body in the trunk and the couple drives away.

The middle section of DISCIPLES OF THE CROW consists of a series of short, moody scenes, juxtaposing Burt and Vicky's experiences with the local children's actions. In one scene, teenage Billy tends to a captured rabbit and hears a crow cawing. He seems to interpret the sound as a meaningful message. In a subsequent scene, Burt and Vicky hear a message through the radio: a preacher castigating "the defiler of corn." Vicky turns off the radio and the couple starts bickering again, failing to heed the ominous warning. The film then circles back to Billy's rabbit, now dead and hanging like a sacrifice above a pile of corn. Vicky continues to see warnings, including a series of roadside signs declaring that the "defiler" will be vomited out, but the film's viewer sees more than she does. The sequence ends with a shot of a human skeleton hanging in the corn like a scarecrow, followed by a shot of a road sign announcing the couple's arrival in Jonah, and a cryptic scene of a young girl feeding corn and red liquid to a "drinking bird" toy.

On the desolate streets of Jonah, Vicky suddenly decides to heed the warnings and pleads with Burt to keep driving. As in King's story, Burt is too stubborn to listen to her. Instead of leaving town, he takes them to the Jonah Bar and Grill, where they hear the laughter of children. They also find a framed photo of President Richard Nixon (standing in for the LBJ photo in King's story), outdated prices on the menu, and a calendar dated October 1971. Despite the laughter, Vicky concludes that "there hasn't been a living soul in this town for years." The scene ends with an ominous refutation from the drinking bird, still in motion.

Unlike King's story, in which the threat remains vague until the very end, the filmmaker has structured the screen story to ensure the viewer knows the town is populated by murderous children. In the short story, the children eventually surround Vicky in the car while Burt is inside the town church. In the short film, the two parallel narratives also collide at the church. While Burt is discovering evidence of a crow-worshipping cult in Jonah, Vicky remains in the car—oblivious to the crows gathering in the tree-tops around her. One cannot help but think of a similar scene in Hitchcock's film THE BIRDS. Woodward expands on the familiar scenario by revealing that the children of Jonah are also quietly closing in. The viewer sees them coming but Vicky does not, heightening the tension.

Instead of breaking the tension by having Vicky lean on the car horn—as she does in King's story—Woodward breaks the tension in the parallel scene in the church, then juxtaposes the two scenes as they play out. Billy confronts Burt while he is reading the cult's handwritten bible, and hisses, "How dare you?" A moment later, one of the other children smashes the car window beside Vicky's head. The attack on the couple is driven by rapid-fire cross-cutting and a cacophony of high-pitched string music (another nod to Hitchcock?). The suspense is amplified by a new beat in which Burt throws the keys to Vicky; the keys fall short, landing on the hood of the car, and Vicky almost loses an arm trying to retrieve them. She barely manages to get away from two teenage boys who are trying to pull her through the window. Another new beat makes it seem as if Vicky is going to leave Burt for dead. Luckily for him, she remembers to stop for him and they successfully flee Jonah together.

As the couple drives off into the sunset, it seems as if DISCIPLES OF THE CROW is going to have a much happier ending than Stephen King's short story—in which the couple is killed. But the filmmaker adds one more wrinkle a close-up shot of the dashboard reveals that the car's engine is running hot. Oblivious, Burt asks, "How could this thing go on all these years? Why didn't somebody know about it? Unless that god they worship approves...." An exterior shot of a corncob knife embedded in the car's hissing radiator serves as a vague suggestion that fate is on the side of the killers. The short film ends with a shot of the blazing sun as hordes of birds cross the sky—headed in the same direction that Burt and Vicky are traveling.

The 1983 Student Academy Awards acknowledged the deftness of Woodward's cinematic storytelling; both he and his producer/cinematographer Johnny Stevens received a Dramatic Merit Award. The other Merit Award winner that year was NYU student Spike Lee (for his short film JOE'S BED-STUY BARBERSHOP: WE CUT HEADS). DISCIPLES later went on to win a Gold Hugo Award at the Chicago Film Festival. For Woodward—as well as for Stephen King's "Children of the Corn"—it was an auspicious beginning.

An Interview with John R. Woodward (2020)

JOSEPH MADDREY: Is DISCIPLES OF THE CROW an official "dollar baby"? From what I gather, Stephen King sold the rights to adapt "Children of the Corn" to a Maine-based production company around 1978/9, but did he also grant you a license to make your film in 1981?

JOHN R. WOODWARD: 1981 sounds right. Maybe 1982. I finished the film in January 1983. At the time, there was no designation of "dollar baby," but Mr. King did grant written permission for the film to be made. I have a letter from him somewhere.

MADDREY: I understand you made DISCIPLES as your thesis film at the University of Texas at Austin. Were you in a film program there? Studying to be a director?

WOODWARD: DISCIPLES OF THE CROW was my thesis film at UT Austin for an M.A. in Film Production. I was personally focused on studying to be a director, but the program included classes in editing, writing, production, as well as directing.

MADDREY: Why did you pick Stephen King's story as the basis for your film? Were you specifically interested in making a horror film? What aspect(s) of the story appealed to you personally?

WOODWARD: I read King's *Night Shift* collection at about the time I was making the decision on subject matter for my thesis film. I couldn't put down the book. I recall reading it while working as an intern for an industrial filmmaker. We were in a van driving to a distant location. The boss was irked that I was reading the book, and he said I'd never get the rights from Stephen King and I'd never be a filmmaker. I believe the story was 13 pages in the paperback version and I felt that I could bring the elements together to make the film. A couple faculty members thought it was too ambitious for students to pull off. They were concerned about someone getting hurt and liability related to that. However, I received a great deal of encouragement to proceed from several professors, especially Loren Bivens. Loren was the UT faculty member who was most instrumental in the development of my thinking about making movies.

MADDREY: Do you still have a copy of the script? Did the script change at all as you were filming or did you follow the script closely?

WOODWARD: I couldn't find a copy of the script, but I think I have it. My script was much closer to the King story than other versions [the 1983 and 2009 feature film adaptations CHILDREN OF THE CORN] were. I mostly made changes to accommodate the budget. In 1982, we had neither money nor expertise for special effects. We also made changes to take advantage of filming locations. For example, we were filming on an isolated road in a cornfield and someone noticed a dead rabbit alongside the road. We set up a shot that used the rabbit as an item the children had sacrificed to their God. Later, I purchased a live rabbit to film it being caught for the sacrifice.

MADDREY: Why did you decide to move the actions of King's short story from the fictional town of Gatlin, Nebraska, to the real town of Jonah, Oklahoma?

WOODWARD: We were filming in and around Austin, Texas, and I thought we might not be able to make all the locations seem like Nebraska. King's premise was that the children got too literal about the religious teaching they received in an isolated Bible Belt town. Texas and Oklahoma were also known for plenty of isolated Bible Belt towns. Consequently, I didn't think the change mattered to the story. We also made the change from Nebraska to Oklahoma based on the intense Texas/Oklahoma football rivalry. When the lead characters Bert and his wife Vicky drive by a series of threatening religious roadside signs, Vicky begins to laugh at the signs. Bert asks her, "Are you all right?" She responds, "I will be, just as soon as we're out of Oklahoma." I thought the UT students in the thesis night screening would respond. They did with thunderous laughter.

MADDREY: I've read that you filmed DISCIPLES in the Texas towns of Bartlett and Jarrell, outside of Austin. Is that accurate? Why did you pick those locations?

WOODWARD: I don't remember all the names of the towns. Bartlett sounds right. We selected one town because, at the time, it looked abandoned. We only had to ask a couple of people to move their cars for it to look completely abandoned. We selected another town because it had a church we liked, and others for their cornfields.

MADDREY: King's short story is a limited point-of-view narrative that follows Burt and Vicky to a seemingly abandoned town, where they get attacked. Neither the characters nor the reader find out what happened in the town twelve years ago until near the end of the story. Why did you decide to structure your adaptation differently, putting the town history (the children murdering the adults) at the front of the story?

WOODWARD: I was drawn to the story based on the limited point-of-view narrative. It made it feasible to shoot the film on a shoestring. We thought the earlier time period scenes would function as a hook without eliminating the mystery that Vicky and Burt navigate.

MADDREY: In King's story, all of the kids are named after books of the Old Testament. In the final scene, King develops them a little bit as distinct characters. Why did you decide to name only one of the children (Billy) and to avoid developing the others as distinct characters?

WOODWARD: For me, the kids functioned like the birds in Hitchcock's THE BIRDS. I didn't think the children needed individual personalities. Logistics for a nineteen-minute student film required scaling back. The kids as distinct characters seemed like something we could cut without affecting the power of the narrative.

MADDREY: Perhaps the biggest change you made was having the children worship "sacred" crows rather than the invisible cornfield god in King's story. Why crows?

WOODWARD: I thought the crows were a visual way to create mystery, tension, and eventually suspense. We tried to teach the audience that nastiness ensued when the crows started to arrive. I was trying to tell the story as visually as possible. Also, at the time, the University of Texas at Austin had synch sound equipment, but it had to serve the department's entire student population. Time with synch sound equipment was limited for any single student project.

MADDREY: One of the most impressive scenes in the short film is the one where the children surround Vicky in the car. In King's short story, the reader shares Burt's POV in this scene—so we don't realize what's going on until Burt hears Vicky blow the horn, then looks out the window and sees her being attacked. Your adaptation is more suspenseful: You show the kids approaching the car, allowing the viewer to anticipate the attack before Vicky does. Did you conceive scenes like this as opportunities to exercise your technique as a visual storyteller?

WOODWARD: Absolutely. We wanted the audience to feel an extended build up to the attack. The car she was in was mine. Most of the blows to the car were done on a matching car that we shot in a junkyard, but one kid accidentally smashed my car with an axe.

MADDREY: Were you influenced by any specific films or filmmakers?

WOODWARD: Many filmmakers influenced me. At that time, for this film, I studied films by Hitchcock, Kubrick, Spielberg, and Ridley Scott. When I made my film VICE [2000], aka TEXAS TALIBAN, one critic wrote, "VICE does for victimless crime what DR. STRANGELOVE did for nuclear war."

MADDREY: In King's story, the characters never make it out of Gatlin and the author implies that there is a legitimate supernatural force keeping them there. In your adaptation, the couple seems to escape and Burt essentially wonders aloud if the "god" of the murderous children is real. You then reveal that Burt and Vicky's car has a damaged radiator, which suggests that they will not escape ... and that maybe that the children's god is real? It seems like a more ambiguous take on the supernatural. Was that your intention?

WOODWARD: There is ambiguity. I think I used King's dialogue as he wrote it when Burt wonders aloud, "How could this go on so long? Why doesn't anybody know about it? Unless that God they worship approves...." I wanted the images of the radiator overheating and the hot light blinking to imply Burt and Vicky would not get away. I wanted the visual of the massive flock of crows pursuing Burt and Vicky to suggest they were doomed, but it's ambiguous enough for audience members who want to believe the couple gets away to have a bit of wiggle room to believe that.

MADDREY: DISCIPLES OF THE CROW received a Dramatic Merit Award at the 1983 Student Academy Awards, alongside Spike Lee's short film JOE'S BED-STUY BARBER-SHOP: WE CUT HEADS. Did you win the Gold Hugo Award at the Chicago Film Festival the same year? Did those awards help launch your career as a filmmaker?

WOODWARD: I did receive the Gold Hugo Award at the Chicago Film Festival the same year, along with my producing partner Johnny Stevens. Had I moved immediately to Los Angeles, the awards may have helped more. I stayed in Austin because of opportunities I had there. I wanted to learn more about helping actors with interpretation, motivation, and performance. While developing THE CELLAR [1989], I took several acting classes in the Austin community. I gained experience and confidence about what I could do as a director to help actors. In fact, because of my interest in acting from the POV of a director, my mentor Loren Bivens asked me to take over the class he taught when he pursued an opportunity to make a feature film [TRESPASSES]. It was a tremendous learning opportunity. Director Richard Linklater was a student in one of my acting classes, and I recall one evening during a break he described a film he wanted to make. It became his first feature, SLACKERS.

MADDREY: *Less than a year after you completed your short film, the feature film CHILDREN OF THE CORN appeared in theaters. Did that help or hinder your film and career?*

WOODWARD: I don't know if it helped or hindered my career. The people who made that film asked us to change the name from CHILDREN OF THE CORN. That's why it's called DISCIPLES OF THE CROW.

MADDREY: *How did Karl James Associates and Simitar Entertainment end up distributing DISCIPLES on VHS?*

WOODWARD: One of the owners at Karl James Associates contacted us. He had already had success distributing another group of Stephen King horror shorts.

MADDREY: *I'm curious about your first feature film credit, THE CELLAR. How and why did you decide to adapt David H. Keller's short story "The Thing in the Cellar"? Were you chasing a career as a horror filmmaker at that time?*

WOODWARD: At the time, I figured I had success with DISCIPLES OF THE CROW, a horror short that I could point to when trying to get another project off the ground. I thought pitching another horror film was a viable way to attach myself as director. I looked for a successful horror story to option and adapted it for the screen. I dealt with David H. Keller's son or grandson to acquire the rights. Obviously, getting a green light, or funding feature films for unknown directors is difficult. Following the success of DISCIPLES OF THE CROW with a project in the same genre seemed like a way to minimize producer/investor objections to the project or to me as the director.

MADDREY: *How do you feel about DISCIPLES OF THE CROW today? Any desire to re-visit Stephen King's cinematic universe?*

WOODWARD: I'm very proud of DISCIPLES OF THE CROW. It was a labor of love and learning, and I built some wonderful relationships. I'm really proud of all the many students, friends, and others who worked so hard for so long to make the film. I still love Stephen King's work. I'd be more than happy to re-visit. I wrote a horror screenplay called FATAL PREJUDICE with an immortal racist as the villain. It's perfect for the times. I'm also trying to produce a femme fatale thriller I wrote in the vein of BODY HEAT.

PART THREE

CHILDREN OF THE CORN

Development Hell (Oral History)

STEPHEN KING: I did a screenplay based on "Children of the Corn" from *Night Shift*. I did it not because I thought a movie would come of it but mostly because I needed some practice. (Chute 1979)

STEPHEN KING: I shopped it around—[to] Dan Curtis [creator of the TV series DARK SHADOWS and director of THE NIGHT STRANGLER, TRILOGY OF TERROR and BURNT OFFERINGS] and some other people… (Stewart 2/1980)

In the winter of 1978–79, a pair of Maine-based documentarians—David Hoffman and Harry Wiland—reached out to the author about collaborating on a feature film project.

HARRY WILAND: I said, "Stephen, I live in Maine and you live in Maine. We're both sort of outcasts. Nevertheless, we're both successful in show business. How about getting together and seeing if we can do a project together?" (Gagne: "Stephen" 1980)

STEPHEN KING: They sent me some scripts that were terrible, and I sent them CHILDREN OF THE CORN, saying I thought it would make a great movie. (Horsting: *Stephen* 1986)

DAVID HOFFMAN: Our idea was to make a low budget feature film in a documentary style, which was a popular style at that time. Still is, to some extent. The idea of making fiction look real is my specialty as a filmmaker. My first feature film, which was made in 1969, was called KING, MURRAY. It won the Critics Award at the Cannes Film Festival. It was a documentary but some of the material in it was reenacted, which at the time was extremely controversial. "Is the documentary real or was it a reenactment?" That was what the press chose to focus on, so I had some reputation at making that kind of film. And Stephen liked that film. (2020 interview with the author)

STEPHEN KING: For years, I've desperately wanted to get a film crew into Maine. […] Wiland came along with production facilities on call and got the rights for a song— as Laurel did for CREEPSHOW and THE STAND. (Conner 1987)

HARRY WILAND: He had written an earlier draft [of a screenplay for CHILDREN OF THE CORN] and he gave it to me and he said, "What do you think?" I gave him notes and he said, "I like your notes." We got along and so we wrote together. He would come over on his motorcycle, from Bangor to Rockport. As I remember, I did most of the rewriting. We'd have a meeting and he'd say, "Yeah, I agree with this," "I don't agree with that," "How about this?" Two weeks later, I'd send it to him and he'd mark it up again. (2020 interview with the author)

STEPHEN KING: I did two drafts of the screenplay; they kept insisting I add some kind of Vietnam metaphor. (Horsting: *Stephen* 1986)

HARRY WILAND: I was in the Army reserves for five and a half years and it was in the Seventies. I remember being what they called "Section Ten." I was a bad boy. So [the Vietnam suggestion] could have been mine. (2020 interview with the author)

Wiland is not the only person who has interpreted King's short story as a Vietnam allegory. At the Fifth International Conference on the Fantastic in the Arts in March 1984, author Tony Magistrale presented an essay entitled "Stephen King's Viet Nam Allegory: An Interpretation of 'Children of the Corn.'" Stephen King was in the audience, and he spoke to Magistrale afterwards.

TONY MAGISTRALE: He told me there was no way in hell he intended that story to be an allegory for Vietnam. [...] To me, there were so many things that stood out in the story: the guy was a medic in Vietnam, kids were getting killed at eighteen, the land had become tainted and polluted, and the high school was named after JFK. Steve didn't concede my point, but we just chalked it up and laughed. (Rogak 2009)

King did, however, incorporate the idea into the Second Draft of his CHILDREN OF THE CORN screenplay.

CHILDREN OF THE CORN (Undated Second Draft)

King's second draft of CHILDREN OF THE CORN was probably written in 1979 or early 1980. The title page indicates that the project was being developed by Harry Wiland of Amesbury Hill Productions, who had some very specific ideas about how to modify the story. A one-page prologue sets the main action in 1980, backdating the inciting incident in the town of Gatlin to 1968. In the *Night Shift* version of King's short story, the children of Gatlin murder their parents in August 1964 and attack Burt and Vicky Robeson twelve years later, in the summer of 1976. Wiland probably wanted to modify the dates for two reasons—(1) to contemporize the story and (2) to set up a Vietnam allegory. The script prologue establishes that the crisis in Gatlin began in 1968, suggesting that it is a local manifestation of the widespread social chaos of that year. Wiland remembers, "That was the year the whole country went mad. It's kind of poetic license to say that in Gatlin, they went even madder" (Gagne: "Stephen" 1980).

The addition of the Vietnam subtext altered King's plot, characters and theme in significant ways. First, the basic plot was expanded. The original story revolves almost entirely around Burt and Vicky, who seek help in the town of Gatlin after hitting a child with their car. When they get to Gatlin, they experience a vague sense of dread about what has happened to the town—and about what might happen to them if they stay there. By the time the children attack them, the story is practically over. King's short story is a slow-build to that violent turn of events and the author caps off his tale with a brief denouement revolving around the children's worship of their pagan god. King's second draft screenplay follows essentially the same slow-build formula but adds new details and dialogue about Burt and Vicky's background. The screenplay also elaborates the children's story as a parallel narrative instead of saving it for a climactic reveal. Throughout the script, the screenwriter juxtaposes the two parallel narratives.

The opening scene, in which Burt and Vicky hit a child with their car, is preceded by a new scene of that child (Joseph) fleeing through the corn. His pursuers, a vindictive pair of children named Malachai and Isaac, spy on Burt and Vicky after the accident. As in the story, the couple drives on to Gatlin—but, first, King adds a stop at a Mobil gas station, where they converse with an old coot who warns them to steer clear of the sleepy, creepy town. Amusingly, the man advises them to go to Hemingford (the home of saintly Mother Abigail in King's novel *The Stand*) instead. The added scene—including specifics of the dialogue—is remarkably similar to a scene in Wes Craven's 1977 film THE HILLS HAVE EYES. Like the city slickers in Craven's film, Burt and Vicky fail to heed the prophetic warning to stay on the main road.

The couple's arrival in Gatlin is juxtaposed with a parallel sequence in which the children brutally murder the gas station owner who has betrayed them. Then, once the threat has been clearly established, the screenwriter plays the couple's dread-filled exploration of the town for maximum suspense—avoiding the murderous children altogether and forcing the reader / viewer to wonder where they are and what they're doing (and when they'll attack). This section of the screen story closely follows King's source story.

The script returns to the cross-cutting / dual narrative formula by separating the two protagonists. Burt searches for answers in Gatlin's Town Hall, while Vicky waits alone in the car. As he discovers evidence of the town's horrifying history, the children sneak up on Vicky. At this point, the screenwriter allows the reader (and prospective viewer) to know more than the author allowed readers to know at the same point in the short story. The story of the couple and the story of the children finally collide when Vicky gets attacked in the car. She hits the car horn and Burt races to her rescue—but, as in the short story, he arrives too late. He watches the children murder his wife, then manages to escape into the cornfield. Instead of following him, as in the short story, the children halt their pursuit and wait.

The screenwriter prolongs the tale by once again telling dual narratives. While Burt hides in the corn and contemplates his next move, the children gather and discuss theirs. In a new ending, both fates are decided by a third party—a Lovecraftian god called He Who Walks Behind the Rows.

By stretching out the overall plot, the screenwriter has also fleshed out the characters. As in the short story, Burt and Vicky have a very contentious relationship, but the screenplay does a better job of explaining why. Dialogue in the first scene of the script defines Burt as a brash and sarcastic man, not unlike Jack Torrance in *The Shining*. The same scene sets up Vicky as a high-maintenance sex bomb—the screenwriter compares her to model and actress Tuesday Weld, who was best known at the time for starring roles in PRETTY POISON (1968) and PLAY IT AS IT LAYS (1972)—and specifies that the tension between the two characters is sexually-tinged. Again, like the tension between Jack and Wendy Torrance in *The Shining*.

As the story progresses, the screenwriter reveals that Burt is a Marine who served in Special Forces during the Vietnam War; a new line of dialogue specifies that he participated in a total of sixty-two "patrols." An accusatory line of dialogue from Vicky also suggests that he may have participated in the My Lai massacre or a similar atrocity. Then again, Vicky might be trying to rankle her husband with the hideous accusation. In the short story as well as in the screenplay, Burt snidely refers to her as the ex-Prom Queen, mocking her for her narrower range of personal experience. The screenplay also includes some new lines of dialogue indicating that she is either a student or a teacher in an American People class, as well as a member of some kind of "consciousness-raising" group. The overall implication is that Vicky is (or acts) younger and more liberal-minded than her husband. Their differences are taking a toll on the marriage.

When the couple encounters the children in Gatlin, those differences are amplified with tragic results. Burt instinctively responds to the threat as a soldier—becoming hyper-vigilant, laser-focused, and adrenalized. Vicky responds by becoming hysterical and urging Burt to steer them away from the threat. When he refuses, she becomes frightened and frustrated by his stubborn refusal to listen to her. Vicky's reaction turns out to be the more sensible one. As in the short story, Burt's stubbornness dooms them both.

The screenplay also establishes a pair of bickering antagonists named Isaac and Malachai. The short story identifies Isaac as a child prophet whose visions prompt several of the older children—including Malachai, who is said to be eighteen years old—to sacrifice themselves to He Who Walks Behind the Rows. The screenplay develops the two characters further and sets up a power struggle between them, by establishing Isaac as the spiritual leader of the children and Malachai as more of a physical leader. Isaac tells them all what they should do and why. Malachai commits acts of violence that the younger boy might not be capable of. For example, he leads the attack on Vicky and personally confronts Burt afterward.

Burt fights back—in a proposed SLOW MOTION sequence that showcases the ex-Marine's martial arts abilities—then verbally challenges the established dynamic of the children's cult, trying to rationalize with his attackers. He speaks down to the children like a disciplining adult in a scene that the screenwriter explicitly compares to William Golding's novel *Lord of the Flies*. That novel—about a group of children who

Spiritual leader Isaac (John Franklin) and physical leader Malachai (Courtney Gains) in CHILDREN OF THE CORN (New World, 1984).

become stranded on a desert island and form a primitive, cutthroat society—ends when an adult arrives on the island and shames the children for their violent behavior, effectively destroying their mini-society. In CHILDREN OF THE CORN, Burt's admonishment initially has the same effect; even Malachai suddenly hesitates. Isaac, however, recognizes the threat to his power and quickly reasserts his authority by throwing a knife at Burt. With this act, Isaac restores the children's "faith" in the social order of the cult and firmly establishes himself as their true leader.

The power struggle between the two leaders ends in the final act of the screen story, as Isaac accuses Malachai of breaking the congregation's covenant with their god by killing one of their own in the cornfield at the beginning of the story. He claims the unholy murder made their congregation vulnerable and asserts that the infidels (Burt and Vicky) represent a test of their collective faith in He Who Walks Behind the Rows. Isaac's solution is to restore the covenant with the god by offering Malachai—as well as the other 18-year-olds in the congregation—as a sacrifice. Like a good cult leader, he knows he can restore his authority with a display of power over the older, and physically stronger, members of the group. It also doesn't hurt that he has an eldritch corn god on his side.

The final-act appearance of He Who Walks Behind the Rows—described by the screenwriter as a huge black manta ray with green eyes and a fiery red maw—descends on Burt and restores Malachai's faith. Later, we see that the children have crucified Burt and Vicky. The screenplay concludes with a scene in which Isaac's second-in-command enters the cornfield to sacrifice himself. Before he goes, Malachai has a brief conversation with a young woman named Ruth, who is pregnant with his child. She vocalizes her contempt for the corn god, but Malachai urges her to be obedient and to raise their child according to the rules of the cult. She promises she will. The implication is that Ruth—and others like her—will remain trapped in their cruel, insular society. No adults are coming to their rescue.

With the final scene in the script, Stephen King highlights the apparent theme of his original short story. At the outset of the *Night Shift* version of the tale, Burt and Vicky heard a radio evangelist spouting fundamentalist rhetoric about the corrupting influence of "the world," and warning listeners to renounce fornication, covetousness, homosexuality, and "defilement" of the corn. In the same scene, Vicky recalls being raised in a religious group that held tent meetings and salvation events where children were indoctrinated and encouraged to evangelize. Vicky is clearly horrified by her childhood experiences and King's story suggests that her horror is justified; the cult in Gatlin crucifies Vicky, gouges out her eyes, and shoves corn silk into the empty sockets.

In his screenplay, King slightly modifies the details of Vicky's childhood experience. Instead of talking about "tent meetings," Vicky specifies that she was brought up in the Catholic Church. This change suggests that perhaps the screenwriter is targeting Christian dogma in general, not just cultish fundamentalism. Another minor but noteworthy change is the absence of a scene from the short story in which Burt finds a Bible with the entire New Testament torn out. The implication of that scene in the short story is that He Who Walks Behind the Rows is a vengeful Old Testament god—demanding obedience and retributive justice, instead of preaching love and forgiveness. In the script, the corn god becomes more nebulous.

Significantly, neither version of the story dismisses the children's belief in He Who Walks Behind the Rows as a delusion or ruse. Perhaps in his effort to emulate

H.P. Lovecraft—who, according to King, was at his best when writing about "stupendous, Cyclopean evil"—the short story writer reveals He Who Walks Behind the Rows as "something huge, bulking up to the sky … something green with terrible red eyes the size of footballs" (King: *Danse* 1981). With this climactic revelation, the horror of encountering a murderous cult that brainwashes children is overshadowed by the fact that their bloodthirsty god actually exists.

The addition of the Vietnam allegory to the screen story aligns the short story's bloodthirsty cult leaders with the "God-fearing" warmongers of the U.S. military who sent "children" to die in the jungles and fields of Vietnam. In interviews over the years, Stephen King has gingerly discussed his mistrust of organized religion, but he has been more outspoken in his criticisms of U.S. involvement in the Vietnam War—probably because he experienced a dramatic "conversion" on the latter issue.

In a 2016 essay, the author confessed that he held a pro-war stance during his first three semesters of college. In the spring of 1967, he even wrote an editorial for the school newspaper, excoriating "intellectual peaceniks" as draft-dodging "yellow-bellies" and asserting his own resolve to do "the right thing" if drafted (King: "Yellow-bellies" 1967). Later that year, he wrote a second editorial shaming "mealy-mouthed" opponents of the war—but hedged his criticism by saying he did not regard Vietnam as an "honorable war" (King: "Opinion" 1967). Sometime in 1968 and 1969, his opinions changed more dramatically. By the spring of 1970, King described himself as "extremely radical," claiming that recent events—including the assassinations of Martin Luther King, Jr., Robert Kennedy, and Fred Hampton; the student killings at Kent State and Jackson College; and the My Lai Massacre in Vietnam—had transformed his political perspective (King: "King's" 1970). Ten years—and six published books—later, King told an interviewer that his novels "taken together, form an allegory for a nation that feels it's in a crunch and things are out of control" (Peck 1980). Many of the short stories collected in *Night Shift*, all of which were written during the 1970s, reflect the same sociopolitical turmoil.

Although King says he did not conceive "Children of the Corn" as a Vietnam allegory, the short story explicitly references the war. In the beginning, King writes that Burt and Vicky's road trip is an attempt to save their marriage the same way "grunts went about saving villages in the war." The comparison echoes a famous Vietnam War dispatch from the Battle of Ben Tre: "It became necessary to destroy the village in order to save it." The phrase sets up Burt—who, according to the short story, served as a "medical orderly" in Vietnam—as a dedicated soldier. When the couple arrives in the "hick" town of Gatlin, they confront an army of children devoted to a "decidedly unchristian" god. The children attack the outsiders with crude weapons and eventually drive Burt into a vast cornfield that comes alive around him. The implication is that, by sacrificing Burt to their pagan god, the children are protecting their land. King makes this implication even more explicit in the screen story by referencing "fertility rituals."

In his 1988 essay on "Children of the Corn," critic Tony Magistrale insisted that "the reader with any sense of history will recall the violation of the land in Vietnam by such toxic chemicals as Agent Orange" and conclude that the land in Gatlin has been similarly tainted. Magistrale writes, "If we place the events of this story in such a context, it becomes possible to understand why all the adults past the (draft) age of nineteen are sacrificed. These are the individuals who were most responsible for the war." As a result, Gatlin's version of a Revolutionary Youth Movement sacrifices Burt and Vicky because they are "adult representatives of fallen, post–Vietnam America" (Magistrale: *Landscape* 1988). In a cruelly ironic twist, the children must also sacrifice themselves as soon as they reach the age of maturity. Like drafted American soldiers going to war, they submit themselves to the deadly cornfield on their eighteenth birthdays.

King's CHILDREN OF THE CORN screenplay amplifies this allegorical interpretation of the tale and makes it explicit. In addition to setting the backstory in 1968—the year of Stephen King's "conversion"—the script adds specific verbal references to the Vietnam War, as well as some visual references to anti-war culture. For example, in the scene where the children attack Vicky, they flip over her car and set it on fire—a familiar image from violent protests in major American cities throughout 1968. In the later part of the story, Burt escapes into the cornfield and King specifically compares it to a "jungle." When the former soldier gets lost among the corn, the screenwriter specifies that he is re-living his experience in Vietnam and classifies him as "Section Eight" (in military terms: mentally unfit for service).

Interestingly, the Vietnam allegory does not lend itself to a single, simple interpretation. One is left wondering whether the children are the victimizers or the victims. Like the children in *Lord of the Flies*, most seem capable of guilt and remorse—but they are also afraid to disobey. Although he is the main protagonist, Burt acts more sadistic than most of his tormentors. He is—like the American leaders who perpetuated the war in Vietnam—overconfident in his physical superiority, haughtily warning the children that they are messing with the wrong guy, and then refusing to retreat or surrender. In a brief but significant exchange, Burt accuses Isaac of enjoying the act of murder. Isaac, a true believer if not a total sadist, replies that his god wants him to enjoy it. If, in this version of the tale, He Who Walks Behind the Rows is an allegorical representation of Burt's Uncle Sam, then this version of the story expresses a distinctly American gothic horror in which the sins of the fathers are visited upon ... well ... everyone.

CHILDREN OF THE CORN (Revised: 6/80)

In an interview published in the summer of 1980, producer/director Harry Wiland said his collaboration with Stephen King was ongoing: "Stephen has given us a re-write, and I've incorporated things into the revision that flesh out the story more" (Gagne: "Stephen" 1980). The title page on a revision dated 6/80 suggests that Wiland may have also incorporated input from credited producer Joseph Masefield. Furthermore, novelist Dennis Etchison gave King some editorial notes to be incorporated into a "final draft" (Etchison 1988). Etchison's handwritten notes on two drafts of the script can be found in the University of Pittsburgh Library System's Archives & Special Collections, along with notes related to producer meetings on May 30 and April 30, 1980.

Many of the changes between King's Second Draft and the shorter Revised 6/80 draft are logistical; scenes have been re-numbered, combined, and broken into shots. Suggested camera angles have been removed from scene descriptions, presumably to avoid alienating prospective directors. There are also quite a few changes in scene descriptions and dialogue. For example, references to Burt's Special Forces background and details about his experiences in Vietnam have been removed, along with references to Vicky's American People class and consciousness-raising group. The couple's bickering is not as intense or ugly, and there are now occasional moments of tenderness between them. The filmmakers obviously wanted to make the protagonists more relatable.

The 6/80 draft also modifies the antagonists' story. In the scene where Isaac and Malachai appear for the first time—lurking in the corn, watching Burt and Vicky—Isaac admonishes Malachai for killing Joseph. This provides an earlier setup for the subplot about the congregation's need to restore their covenant with He Who Walks Behind the Rows. Later, when Isaac addresses his followers, the 6/80 draft intercuts flashback scenes of the 1968 murders that established the covenant. In the Second Draft, the same flashback scenes were intercut with Burt's discovery of the town's dark history—suggesting that he was privately imagining the horrific events. By instead contextualizing the 1968 backstory as part of Isaac and the other children's collective memory, the 6/80 draft makes the horrific events seem more factual and the children more clearly motivated.

When Burt and Vicky arrive in Gatlin, their exploration of the town follows a different route and pauses in different locations—which is probably a result of writing to specific prospective filming locations. A July 5, 1980, article in the *Des Moines Register* reported that CHILDREN OF THE CORN producer Joseph Masefield had recently abandoned plans to shoot the film in central Iowa—because the cornfields near Adel and Prairie City weren't "flat enough and large enough." Masefield said he was planning to base the production in central Illinois, near the towns of Pawnee and Divernon, instead (Associated: "Hilly" 1980). In a separate article published that summer, journalist Paul R. Gagne indicated that the filmmakers intended to shoot in Kansas. The screenwriters could have been picturing any number of towns.

In the 6/80 draft, Burt and Vicky stop at the Gatlin Town Hall and find a series of news clippings about the crises of 1968—including an essay about the rise of new religious cults in America. Instead of imagining what actually happened there, the couple concludes that something must have scared away the residents of Gatlin. The possibility almost scares them away too. They go back to their car, but then Burt decides to return—alone—to Town Hall, to research Hemingford Home as their alternative destination.

The writers added a few other details to amplify the suspense in subsequent scenes where the Gatlin children sneak up on Burt and Vicky. When Vicky realizes that she is being surrounded in the car, she hits the car horn—only to realize that the horn won't work because the engine is turned off. By the time Burt realizes that Vicky is under attack, the children have engaged a safety bolt on the nearest exterior door of the Town Hall, preventing his quick escape and dooming Vicky.

Among other significant changes is a re-think of the third act twist involving the appearance of He Who Walks Behind the Rows. Unlike the short story and the Second Draft script, the 6/80 draft does not describe the corn god in visual terms. Burt sees the monster but the script reader only "sees" a dark shadow—and Burt screaming. After that encounter, Burt disappears from the story and the children speculate that Burt was killed by their god. Their assumption is disproven by a new ending in which Malachai fakes his own death in the cornfield. The older boy is presumably planning to overthrow Isaac but he doesn't get the chance. Burt—having gone mad and essentially becoming a physical manifestation of He Who Walks Behind the Rows—reappears and kills Malachai. The 6/80 draft ends on a proposed high angle shot of the cornfield, showing how close Burt was to the highway when he succumbed to madness. The new ending reinforces the Vietnam allegory by replacing the bloodthirsty god with the Vietnam vet.

Development Hell (Oral History)

The first major road bump for the CHILDREN OF THE CORN film project was a parting of ways between producers David Hoffman and Harry Wiland.

STEPHEN KING: One of the conditions of the split was that each of them would have a year to get the project off the ground. One of them tried and didn't make it; the second guy tried, and United Artists almost produced it. (Horsting: *Stephen* 1986)

According to journalist Bill Warren, United Artists and Filmplan of Canada both expressed an "early interest."

DAVID HOFFMAN: I think I still have those letters of interest [from United Artists and Filmplan of Canada] in my file. But "interested," we learned later, doesn't mean anything in Hollywood. Even taking an option doesn't mean anything. We were going different ways at the time; I was beginning to do major television documentaries and Harry was more interested in Hollywood. I was pretty much done with Hollywood. I never understood it. It's a different world. I never got involved with Hollywood. When he and I split, which I believe was in 1980, he kept on trying to find a way to pay for that movie. (2020 interview with the author)

In his book Stephen King Goes to Hollywood, *Jeff Conner writes that 20th Century–Fox and HBO eventually agreed to co-finance the film on a budget of $2.75 million. Actor Lance Kerwin, who played the character Mark Petrie in the SALEM'S LOT miniseries, was reportedly cast in a starring role.*

HARRY WILAND: I remember going to Iowa with the team, selecting locations in the cornfields, and feeling like this was really happening. I came back [to Los Angeles] and Sherry Lansing, who was head of [production at] the studio, had gotten into an argument with [head of distribution] Norman Levy. And the film became part of the argument. Before Christmas break [1980], Sherry Lansing said to me, "Why don't you go home"—at that time, I was living in New York—"and right after New Year's, we'll set everything up." New Year's came and I got a terse note saying they had put the film in turnaround. (2020 interview with the author)

In his book Creepshows: The Illustrated Stephen King Movie Guide, *Stephen Jones claims that HBO had contributed $750,000 to the film's budget. When 20th Century–Fox pulled out, director Harry Wiland and his producing partner Joseph Masefield had to make up the $2 million budget shortfall.*

HARRY WILAND: I had the right to buy them [20th Century–Fox] out. I had, I think, four more months of the legal option [on Stephen King's story]. I was on the phone trying to raise money and I couldn't. I remember an independent group of financiers—from Cleveland, of all places—said they were interested. There was only a week left of the option and I said, "You have to sign paperwork. Otherwise I'm going to lose the option." They said yeah yeah yeah. They said they'd come to Los Angeles. I remember having a meeting set up in L.A. and they never showed up. I could never reach them on the phone again. I lost track of [the rights] after that. (2020 interview with the author)

DAVID HOFFMAN: Stephen realized we weren't going to pull it off and he still believed in it. For Stephen, it was not a matter of money. It was a matter of creativity. (2020 interview with the author)

On July 29, 1982, Variety *magazine reported that Hal Roach Studios had optioned an "original script" by Stephen King, titled CHILDREN OF THE CORN. It was eventually rewritten by screenwriter George Goldsmith.*

GEORGE GOLDSMITH: The problem I felt Stephen had with his script was that it was not cinematic, it was not visual. It was a great story but the first 35 minutes was two people in a car in the rain in a cornfield, hating each other. And I just didn't think that was gonna be appealing to audiences. [...] I created these two characters, Jobie and Sarah, to be the eyes through which [...] we could experience the story. (Felsher: "Field" 2017)

Lacking investment money, Hal Roach Studios sought a production partner. Roger Corman's New World Pictures was an obvious prospect ... but Corman had recently sold his company.

ROGER CORMAN: When I sold New World, all I sold was the name "New World" and our distribution arm. Three motion picture lawyers—Harry E. Sloan, Larry Kupin and Larry A. Thompson—had done some dealing with us and realized how profitable all of this was, and they wanted to get into the business. Our name had become somewhat powerful. (Armstrong 2020)

DONALD P. BORCHERS: I had been recently named to the position of executive in charge of worldwide production for the New World studios, and I had asked to be able to hire someone that I had known from an experience that I had had in Indiana, whose name was David Simkins. (Felsher: "Stephen" 2009)

DAVID SIMKINS: I walk down this hallway in Roger Corman's old offices and I open this closet door and all this stuff falls out, and one of the things that hits the floor is this script for CHILDREN OF THE CORN, written by George Goldsmith. [...] The thing that really intrigued me was, this thing could be made—not literally, but—this thing could be made for like a quarter and shot in a cornfield. (Holwill 2016)

Outsiders on the inside: Job (Robby Kiger) and Sarah (AnneMarie McEvoy) in CHILDREN OF THE CORN (New World, 1984).

DONALD P. BORCHERS: When I read the script, I thought to myself, "Hmmm, it's mostly what I want to do, but I would like to do this, this and this differently." [...] I was real interested in examining the idea of dogma, the idea of blind faith, faith without questioning, and the consequences of all this. [...] I asked our legal department to enter into negotiation. We were successful and that became literally the second picture that we produced after the acquisition of the studio from Roger Corman. (Felsher: "Stephen" 2009)

On September 12, 1983, Variety *magazine reported that Hal Roach Studios had sold the distribution rights for CHILDREN OF THE CORN to New World Pictures. One month later,* Variety *reported that George Goldsmith had written a new script.*

George Goldsmith's CHILDREN OF THE CORN (Second Revision 8/5/83)

George Goldsmith's first full draft of CHILDREN OF THE CORN is dated August 5, 1983. The screenwriter apparently made multiple revisions the same day and the longest extant draft of CHILDREN OF THE CORN is the Second Revision, which runs 120 pages. Subsequent drafts collected at the Margaret Herrick Library in Beverly Hills—a 107-page draft dated August 23 and a 110-page draft dated August 29—probably reflect changes made during the production of the film. On October 25, 1983, producer Mark Lipson also submitted an unspecified draft, which credited both George Goldsmith and Stephen King as screenwriters, to the Writers Guild. Goldsmith contested the shared credit and King decided not to respond, so the former has sole screenwriting credit on the final film. For purely commercial reasons, however, the film was released as STEPHEN KING'S CHILDREN OF THE CORN.

Goldsmith's Second Revision is structurally similar to Stephen King's drafts but features new characters, new dialogue, new locations, and a different theme. Instead of starting the story with Burt and Vicky in the car, Goldsmith begins with five-year-old Job's memory of the mass murders in Gatlin—which, in this version of the story, took place three years before the main action of the story. The flashback, described in voiceover narration by Job, connects the Gatlin children's rebellion to a devastating local drought and the arrival of a 12-year-old preacher named Isaac. The new opening also introduces Job's sister, 4-year-old Sarah, as a clairvoyant whose crayon drawings show that she was aware of the massacre before it happened. On the fateful day, Job witnessed several children, led by teenaged Malachai, attack the adults—including his father—while Isaac looked on, like a miniature Charles Manson. After the bloodletting, the script segues into an opening credit sequence featuring Sarah's tableaus of the murders. In one image, a preacher hangs from a church bell tower.

Goldsmith kicks off the present-day story in Burt and Vicky's hotel room, where the camera sneaks up on Burt sleeping. The proposed POV shot seems like a stylistic nod to the slasher movie subgenre—a style repeated ad nauseum by countless low-budget filmmakers in the early 1980s. Subgenre progenitors HALLOWEEN and FRIDAY THE 13TH both began with scenes in which the camera stalks and kills the story's first victim before the narratives flash forward to a "new" string of murders. CHILDREN OF THE CORN follows the same basic structure but in the opening scene the "stalker" turns out to be Vicky, surprising her husband with a happy birthday song.

By 1984, slasher movies had become unpopular—to the point that the CHILDREN OF THE CORN filmmakers wanted to distance themselves from the subgenre. Donald Borchers says he was drawn to Goldsmith's script because it stood apart from the standard horror movie plots of the day. The producer also hired a director, Fritz Kiersch, who was equally disenchanted by "all the recent splatter-squiring offerings" (Alan Jones: "CHILDREN" 1984). Sharing these sentiments, Goldsmith gets the hack-and-slash clichés out of the way early, then proceeds to tell a horror story that does not rely entirely on murder set pieces.

The screenwriter sets up Joseph's desperate escape through the cornfield in a new scene that also features Job and Sarah, thereby establishing them as "outsiders" among Gatlin's children of the corn. Following the accident, he incorporates King's gas station scene, giving the curmudgeonly attendant a name (Chester Diehl) and a dog (Sarge). He then proceeds to a new sequence in which Burt and Vicky literally drive around in circles, only to arrive at the exact spot where Burt hit Joseph with the car. In an interesting twist, the couple notices that the formerly green cornfield has turned brown near the site of the accident. When they return to the gas station to call for help, they find the attendant murdered.

The couple drives on to Gatlin and searches the town, becoming separated there. In the short story, Burt went into the local church and left Vicky alone in the car. In King's script(s), Vicky stayed in the car while Burt explored the Town Hall. Goldsmith has Burt and Vicky visit a local farmhouse, where they encounter the clairvoyant child Sarah. Burt foolishly decides to keep looking for local authorities but Vicky's maternal instincts prompt her to stay with the little girl. While Burt examines newspaper records in the town's municipal center, Malachai and his cronies attack and abduct Vicky. Back at the Town Hall, Burt sees an image of the Virgin Mary being attacked by a dragon and somehow senses that Vicky is in danger. He rushes back to the farmhouse, only to learn—from Job and Sarah—that the other children of Gatlin have taken Vicky into the cornfield to sacrifice her.

Burt rushes into the field but the corn attacks him. He escapes to a nearby barn where he discovers the town's main source of fuel: huge vats of "gasohol" (part gasoline, part corn ethanol). At this point in the screenplay, the writer interjects a flashback scene in which the former police chief of Gatlin visits the same barn three years prior. Chief Hotchkiss discovers a page torn from a Bible, then gets jumped by a group of teenage boys. It is not the first flashback in the script but it is perhaps the most narratively significant, setting up the circumstances of the film's final fight. The barn sequence ends with Burt fleeing to the local church, where the screenwriter interjects a second flashback scene of Isaac ripping a page out of a Bible. The two flashbacks suggest—to the reader/viewer—that the missing page is narratively important. Unfortunately, Burt doesn't know that yet.

In the church, Burt witnesses a religious ceremony involving blood-drinking and ritual sacrifice. He confronts a teenage priestess named Rachel Deigan, who is in the process of sacrificing her older brother on his 19th birthday. (The brother and sister are based on two names from Stephen King's short story: Rachel Stigman and Amos Deigan.) As in King's script, Burt tries to admonish the children for their uncivilized behavior and they respond by attacking him. In this version, it is Rachel—instead of Isaac—who stabs Burt, then summons Malachai to finish the job. The cult's main enforcer and his so-called "Huns" chase Burt through the town, until Burt finds refuge in an underground bomb shelter with Job and Sarah.

One of the biggest differences between King's story / script and Goldsmith's script is the characterizations of Burt and Vicky. In Goldsmith's script, Burt is not a former military man but a former med student, bound for an internship in California. For the most part, his profession doesn't affect the narrative—although, in one gruesome scene, he uses his knowledge of human anatomy to reconfigure a pile of dead bodies as a *cheval de frise*. When his pursuers fall into the deadly trap, Burt jokes with one of the weaponized corpses, "Thanks for the hand." (Hey, it was the '80s.... Jokes like this were almost obligatory in genre films.)

In Goldsmith's version of the tale, the couple is not yet married. Vicky Baxter wants to become Vicky Stanton but Burt is not ready to commit and "settle down." Whereas King's couple had already grown apart before the story started, Goldsmith's couple grows closer as the story progresses. They become surrogate parents to Job and Sarah, and Burt eventually warms to the idea of being a protective husband and father. In the end, after the threat has been vanquished, he invites the two tykes to come live with them, establishing an instant nuclear family for the happy ending.

Like King's script, Goldsmith's screen story also features a secondary "family conflict"—featuring Isaac and Malachai and their cadre of killer kids. Goldsmith makes it abundantly clear that Malachai is the more physically aggressive leader while Isaac is the more manipulative of the two. When Burt escapes into the bomb shelter, Malachai and Isaac spar over whether or not to use Vicky as bait to lure Burt out of hiding. In a departure from King's story, Malachai physically restrains Isaac and urges the other children to crucify him. Isaac warns that He Who Walks Behind the Rows will punish them for the betrayal but Malachai shrugs off the warning. Meanwhile, Burt urges Job and Sarah to escape to the nearby town of Hemingford while he goes to rescue Vicky.

In the climax of the screen story, He Who Walks Behind the Rows manifests as a force of nature: hurricane-strength wind emanating from an immense shadow in a (slightly less?) black sky. The shadow overtakes Isaac, apparently killing him, while Burt takes advantage of the distraction to rescue Vicky and do battle with Malachai in hand-to-hand combat. Burt ultimately spares Malachai's life, attempting to use this display of mercy as a way to win over the other children—but his plans are thwarted by the return of Isaac in demonic form. Goldsmith describes the new "demon Isaac" as a half-eaten corpse with green skin, huge eyes, and corny hair. After he kills Malachai, the demon incarnate uses hurricane-force winds to attack the other children and destroy the town.

Burt consults Job and Sarah, who tell him that Police Chief Hotchkiss confronted the same "monster" three years ago—by reciting a specific page torn from the Bible. Luckily for everyone, Job saved the page, which reads: "And the devil that deceived them was cast into the lake of fire and brimstone, where the beast and the false prophet are, and shall be tormented day and night for ever and ever" (Revelation 20:10). The passage reminds Burt about the gasohol stills in the barn and he quickly surmises that Hotchkiss intended to use the gasohol to burn the cornfield—creating a literal "lake of fire." In an elaborately detailed action sequence, Burt tries to carry out the police chief's plan while the shadow god assaults him and his family with dead corn and dead bodies. After a few false starts, Job finally manages to light the fire as the family flees the devastation. Hesitating on the edge of town, they look back and see—instead of a dark shadow set against a black sky—a bright light set against orange flames. The final image in Goldsmith's Second Revision is a close-up of the page that was torn from the Book of Revelation.

The "instant nuclear family," led by Burt (Peter Horton) and Vicky (Linda Hamilton), in CHILDREN OF THE CORN (New World, 1984).

Goldsmith explains that the Biblical allusions were important to him because he regarded the screen story as an allegory about the dangers of religious extremism. In one scene in the script, the screenwriter refers to Isaac as the children's "Ayatollah." In a 2017 interview, he explained that his adaptation was based on the 1979 Iran hostage crisis; he essentially recast Burt and Vicky as the American hostages, Isaac as Ayatollah Khomeini, Malachai as the Revolutionary Guard, and the doomed gas station owner as the American oil companies (Felsher: "Field" 2017). In this allegorical reading of the tale, the children represent the Iranian college students who stormed the U.S. embassy in Tehran on November 4, 1979, and held fifty-two American hostages there for more than a year. Most Iranians regarded the hostage crisis as a protest of the U.S. government's support of the Shah of Iran, a deposed leader who had been replaced by the theocratic ruler Ayatollah Khomeini. Most Americans regarded it as an act of terrorism.

Goldsmith sensibly avoids an excessively close reading of the story through this interpretive lens, claiming that CHILDREN OF THE CORN is also a "universal" story about any regime where the leader claims to speak for God and uses a "divine mandate" to subjugate followers (Felsher: "Field" 2017). In Goldsmith's Second Revision, the screenwriter also compares the children of the corn to robots, religious fundamentalists, and future members of the "Moral Majority." The latter comparison aligns the fictional killer kids with followers of Jerry Falwell, who forged a political coalition of conservative Christians and right-wing Republicans in 1979. Since the fictional children of the corn are, after all, Americans, this allegorical interpretation is arguably more insightful.

The style of Goldsmith's Second Revision is comparable to King's first draft. Suspense scenes are similarly broken down into shots, with camera angles spelled out on the page. For example, in the early scene after Burt and Vicky hit Joseph on the road, Malachai creeps into the road, unseen by the characters but obvious to the camera. Vicky eventually looks at the spot where Malachai is / was standing, but by then he is gone. Goldsmith takes the sequence one step further. In a subsequent shot, Vicky looks back and sees that Malachai has returned—delivering a moment of shock. Goldsmith delivers another shock a few moments later, as Vicky approaches the body of Joseph on the road—and Joseph abruptly sits up, startling her. In the script, it's unclear whether this actually happens or Vicky simply imagines it. Either way, the shock leaves the reader / prospective viewer with a lingering sense of unease about what might happen next. Later, when Burt and Vicky arrive in Gatlin, Goldsmith recommends POV shots of various children spying on the couple—again prompting the reader / viewer to wonder when they will attack. The stylistic influence of slasher movies, which rely heavily on killer POV shots, is apparent.

Goldsmith's visual storytelling style is also on display in several flashback sequences. The flashbacks are brief and violent and intercut with present-day scenes that take place in the same physical setting. The juxtaposition of past and present suggests a kind of psychic "reading" of events, as if the people in each scene—or perhaps the places themselves—are remembering or intuiting what has happened there. The screenwriter's most ambitious visual set piece is unquestionably the climactic battle with He Who Walks Behind the Rows. Goldsmith calls for nothing less than a god-like storm and a massive lake of fire, and throws everything but the kitchen sink at his protagonists in a bravura finale.

According to producers Donald Borchers and Mark Lipson, the film was rushed into production. Borchers says he initially wanted to hire Sam Raimi (hot off of THE EVIL DEAD) to direct, but Raimi balked at the production schedule (Holwill 2016). Borchers turned instead to director Fritz Kiersch and his producing partner Terrence Kirby, who were accustomed to much more aggressive production schedules on TV commercials. Kiersch remembers, "It had to be shot before the corn turned golden" (Alan Jones: "CHILDREN" 1984). Nineteen eighty-three turned out to be a major drought year in Iowa—and so the race against the corn began.

During the following weeks, Goldsmith's screen story was streamlined; dialogue was truncated, flashbacks were eliminated, and action was simplified. The story remained essentially the same until the climax, when Burt explicitly articulates the theme of the film in a confrontation with the children. "Any religion without compassion is a lie," he tells them. Malachai attacks but Burt quickly gets the upper hand and the other children throw down their weapons. It seems like the indoctrination has worn off and Burt has won the day—but then "demon Isaac" appears, illustrating that the corn god is real. Isaac kills Malachai on the spot and Burt and Vicky confront He Who Walks Behind the Rows in an effort to save all the misguided children from His wrath.

By the end of the shoot, it seems the filmmakers were wildly improvising. Instead of a giant shadow in the sky, He Who Walks Behind the Rows somehow became an underground monster. Director Fritz Kiersch remembers how they created the monster on a budget of only $100: "We decided [...] we would build a ditch and build a wooden track in that ditch, take the wheelbarrow, turn it upside down and run it on this track, pulled by cable which was pulled by the tractor. Over the top of the ditch would be a canvas, on top of which would be some vermiculate and loose soil. And as the tractor moved, it would pull the wheelbarrow on the track, which would push the canvas up" (Perry

Martin 2004). The filmmakers also improvised a new ending, ostensibly to resolve the question of what happened to all the children of the corn—but perhaps also to satisfy horror movie audiences that were accustomed to one last scare before the credits rolled. As the heroic family prepares to leave Gatlin and walk to nearby Hemingford, Rachel Deigan jumps out of the back seat of their car—and Burt unceremoniously coldcocks her. The director opines that the improvised ending plays like "an homage to all those 50s B-movies that ran out of money" (Alan Jones: "CHILDREN" 1984). CARRIE, it ain't.

Reflections on the Film (Oral History)

CHILDREN OF THE CORN was released into U.S. theaters on March 9, 1984—following in the wake of three other Stephen King film adaptations: CUJO (released August 12, 1983), THE DEAD ZONE (October 21, 1983), and CHRISTINE (December 9, 1983). Critics were mostly snarky.

VINCENT CANBY (movie reviewer for *New York Times*): For those who take Mr. King seriously, this is high-proof King corn, which is to say it has a kick to it even though it hasn't much taste. (Canby 1984)

KYLE COUNTS (movie reviewer for *Cinefantastique* magazine): [Director Fritz Kiersch] is sabotaged at every turn by a script that is predictable, clumsy and utterly confusing. [...] For those of us who like a little logic with their hokum, there are those nagging, unanswered questions: why does little [Robby] Kiger [who plays Job] seem so unaffected by the slaughter he witnessed at the diner? Just how has pipsqueak [John] Franklin [who plays Isaac] managed to brainwash so many kids? Did he spike their Kool-Aid? (Counts 1984)

BILL WARREN (in his 1988 essay "The Movies and Mr. King, Part II"): Running from murderous children, Burt immediately accepts Joby as a friend: Why? He leaves Sarah and Vicky behind in the house, although he knows a murderer is at large: Why? How can Burt so easily talk the kids into giving up their religion? (Warren: "Movies, Part II" 1988)

ANN LLOYD (author of *The Films of Stephen King*, 1993): Why don't Burt and Vicky high-tail it out of there? How come the absence of the entire adult population of Gatlin has gone unnoticed in the outside world for more than three years? For those wishing answers to those questions, CHILDREN OF THE CORN is the wrong film. If you can suspend disbelief—it's a treasure trove. (Lloyd 1993)

JOE BOB BRIGGS (movie reviewer for *Dallas Times Herald*): Better than CUJO, not quite DEAD ZONE, but what the hey? Steve delivers, right? [...] A little too much plot getting in the way of the movie, but a decent drive-in flick anyhow. (Briggs 1987)

TONY CRAWLEY (movie reviewer for *Halls of Horror* magazine): Although there are one or three good moments when it pays to have taken your girl to see it with you, the feature is short on real style, suspense, special effects and supernaturalism feelings. (Crawley: "Media" 1984)

ROGER EBERT (movie reviewer for *Chicago Sun Times*): CHILDREN OF THE CORN is a movie about a thing that lives behind the rows of corn. I am not sure if the thing is a god, a spirit, or John Deere crossed with a mole. [...] When I first saw this thing, whatever it is, I knew it was time to abandon all hope for CHILDREN OF THE CORN. (Ebert 1984)

FRITZ KIERSCH: The effects at the ending really do suck. [...] But we did very well for the amount of money this film cost as it does come across as a more expensive production, knowing the size and scope of it. It works well on certain levels. (Alan Jones: "CHILDREN" 1984)

DONALD P. BORCHERS: I'm delighted that we had the opportunity to take that wonderful story, truly a tale of nihilism and the enormity of evil, and supply a happy ending. We would have had to keep the finale very nihilistic and kill the heroes to be completely faithful to King. I don't believe then and I still don't think that that's commercial filmmaking. (Crow: "Terror" 1997)

GEORGE GOLDSMITH: CHILDREN OF THE CORN was, needless to say, a hit, and after it came out I saw Stephen on a TV talk show. He was asked what he thought of it. He hesitated for a moment and then very thoughtfully and deliberately said, "I think it's the work of people who are going to do better." I really chuckled at that. I like to think he learned from me just as I learned from him. (Borseti 2016)

In a 1985 article in his official fan newsletter Castle Rock, *Stephen King declared* CHILDREN OF THE CORN *one of the ten worst movies of all time—alongside BLOOD FEAST (1963), PLAN 9 FROM OUTER SPACE (1959), TEENAGE MONSTER (1957), OLD YELLER (1957) and the Chuck Norris vehicle MISSING IN ACTION (1984).*

STEPHEN KING: My feeling for most [film adaptations of his work] is like a guy who sends his daughter off to college. You hope she'll do well. You hope that she won't fall in with the wrong people. You hope she won't be raped at a fraternity party, which is really close to what happened to "Children of the Corn," in a metaphoric sense. (Modderno 1985)

As CHILDREN OF THE CORN has grown into something of a cult classic, King's opinion seems to have softened. Or maybe the original film just looks better when compared to the endless stream of sequels that followed.

STEPHEN KING: Awwww, c'mon ... it's not s'bad. To me, it had a WICKER MAN-ish feel. (Rogak 2009)

STEPHEN KING: I actually liked the original pretty well. I thought they did a pretty good job on that. (Fleming: "Stephen" 2016)

An Interview with George Goldsmith (2020)

JOSEPH MADDREY: First, I'm curious to know about your writing experience prior to CHILDREN OF THE CORN.

GEORGE GOLDSMITH: I became a professional investigative journalist when I was 14. I lived in Oyster Bay, Long Island, and I got the local slumlord thrown into jail for substandard housing that was dangerous. I finished high school when I was 16 and went to Syracuse University's Newhouse School of Public Communications, where I majored in journalism and minored in film. I finished college right after I turned 20 and I went out to L.A. because I thought I might want to make movies and change the world.

MADDREY: According to IMDB, the martial arts movie FORCE: FIVE (1981) was your first produced screenplay. Is that right?

GOLDSMITH: That was my first produced screenplay and second produced credit. When I got out to L.A. in 1975 I was already a martial artist. I was a high-level brown belt in a couple of different styles and I bodyguarded Joan Jett and The Runaways when they played in the L.A. area. I really liked Joan. She was really down to earth, not full of herself, and really nice. I also bodyguarded acts like Eddie Money and a bunch of other music stars. I also taught at the Beverly Hills Karate Academy, which was right next to the Troubadour. And I wrote.

Around that time, I moved to Sweetzer Avenue, right off of Melrose. That was back in the days when Orson Welles would hold court at Ma Maison on Melrose, right around the corner from me. This was in, like, 1977. I became really good friends with a guy named Steve Axelrod, who was George Axelrod's son. George Axelrod wrote THE MANCHURIAN CANDIDATE (1962), THE SEVEN YEAR ITCH (1955), BREAK-FAST AT TIFFANY'S (1961)—so Steve grew up with old time film stars and filmmakers like "Uncle Billy Wilder." We became really good friends. We were young writers, so I opened up my apartment—which was on the second floor at 736½ North Sweetzer—every Thursday night for a writer/artist open house.

Steve and I would invite two or three hundred employed and unemployed actors and actresses over. They'd show up at different times, rotate in and out, and we'd give them sides and they'd do a cold reading on our works in progress. It was good for the writers, because we could see whether or not our stuff really worked. Sometimes the actors would give me a different perspective. I might have heard something in my head but when an actor gave a different interpretation, I'd maybe modify the dialogue and the character. That went on for almost a year, and we had a blast.

Around that time, I wrote a story called MOMENT OF RAGE and MGM optioned it. This was back in the Freddie Silverman days, when Freddie was at ABC [1975–1978], Dan Travanti signed on to play the lead. It was a really good story. We had Travanti, and Freddie Silverman liked it, but for some reason at the last minute they kiboshed it. I was shocked and disappointed.

MADDREY: Mark Lipson said that when he hired you, you were more of a playwright than a screenwriter....
GOLDSMITH: [Laughs] Not at all. I was a screenwriter from day one.

MADDREY: But you and Lipson didn't know each other personally, right? You were connected by a mutual friend?
GOLDSMITH: There was a guy named John Solomon, whose parents owned the Holly Solomon Art Gallery, a pretty famous art gallery at that time in New York City. John was a [script] reader and he had read a couple of my scripts and he called me in for a meeting. We became good friends. So when Lipson was looking for someone who could do CHILDREN OF THE CORN, Solomon recommended me and Mark called me in.

MADDREY: Were you initially hired to adapt Stephen King's short story or to rewrite his script?
GOLDSMITH: Stephen had already written one draft of a script based on his book. Mark sent me over the script that Stephen had written. I read the short story, then I read Stephen's script, then I called Mark up and I said, "I can tell you exactly what the problem is. The problem is that Stephen isn't realizing that literature is internal, intellectual where the reader supplies the visuals out of his or her imagination, and cinema is external, visual, and supplies those things to the viewer." I used exactly those words. I said, "It's a visual, external medium." The first 35 pages of Stephen's script—literally—was

Burt and Vicky in the car, arguing as they're driving through the cornfield in the rain. And the windshield wipers are slapping back and forth. I said, "Mark, you can shoot that if you want, but nobody's going to go watch it. It's going to be a dog." He said, "I agree with you. How would you fix it?" I said, "Give me a couple of days."

We took another meeting and I came in and I said, "The fix is this: I'm gonna create these two little pack rats, Job and Sarah"—who were not in the short story or in Stephen's script. "We're going to see the movie through their eyes. We're going to put them in danger, which is a bit predictable, but it's the way to do it…." He said, "I like it. I'd like to get Steve's buy-in."

I came into the office another day, not long after. I forget whether I wrote a draft and then we had the phone call or we had the phone call and then I wrote the draft…. I think what happened was I wrote a draft and Mark showed it to Steve and then we had a phone call. Stephen said, "You don't understand the horror genre. The horror genre is about the imagination. It's about the images you conjure up in your mind." I said, "Steve, respectfully, you don't understand cinema. You're right for literature, absolutely, but not for a screenplay." We had a bit of a testy phone call. I just held my ground. I was respectful. He was respectful.

MADDREY: Had you read any of Stephen King's other short stories or novels before you wrote CHILDREN OF THE CORN?

GOLDSMITH: I read a number of the stories in the anthology [*Night Shift*] but not any of his novels at that point.

MADDREY: Do you remember when you completed your first draft of CHILDREN OF THE CORN?

GOLDSMITH: I have the first draft here. I pulled it because I knew I was going to be talking to you. [The cover page reads:] "Based on a story by Stephen King. First draft for New World Pictures. 8/5/83."

MADDREY: That's the same date as the version I've read, which is labeled "Second Revision."

GOLDSMITH: I wrote seven drafts total, including the shooting script, but it didn't change much between my first draft and the shooting script. There were some minor revisions but I nailed it on the first one.

MADDREY: Is the date the same because you never wrote a Second Draft, only revised the First Draft?

GOLDSMITH: Probably what happened is I delivered the script in the morning, Mark read it, gave me some thoughts, then I went home and, in two hours, wrote five pages and delivered them on the same day. I write very fast.

MADDREY: I understand you approached the story as an allegory for the oil embargo and the Iran hostage crisis….

GOLDSMITH: Yes, I modeled the entire script on the taking of the American hostages in Iran. It doesn't take a genius to figure out that "Children of the Corn" was about the dangers of religious fundamentalism and cults and things like that. We were fresh off the hostage crisis, and I just said, "Isaac and Malachai are Ayatollah Khomeini and the Revolutionary Guard. Burt and Vicky are the American hostages. The old guy running the gas station is the oil companies." I said, "I can write a story about the dangers of religious extremism—and how it becomes political—and masquerade it as this little horror film." And that's what I did.

MADDREY: *It seems like there was a desire among the producers to make sure CHILDREN OF THE CORN was not a slasher movie. Do you remember any specific discussions about that?*

GOLDSMITH: I don't remember a specific discussion about that. It certainly could have been said. I can tell you I had no interest in writing a slasher movie. If they had asked me to do that, I probably would have just dropped out and said, "I'm not your guy." Because all those slasher movies, I thought, were very violent toward women—and I wasn't gonna be a part of that. I just felt it was misogynistic. I'm not highly political—I'm very apolitical—but I'm a humanist and I just didn't like that stuff.

MADDREY: *Was it your idea to soften the Burt and Vicky characters in the film? They're pretty nasty to each other in the short story....*

GOLDSMITH: I definitely did not like that element [of the short story]. I thought it was too hostile. I mean, I never care about characters that are assholes. Well, sometimes. There's a Nic Cage movie [BAD LIEUTENANT: PORT OF NEW ORLEANS] where he's kind of an asshole but he does something great. He was down in Louisiana and he played a prosecutor who had gotten fired because he was drinking and making bad choices, but he was onto some big political corruption case and he just couldn't let it go. At one point, he turns around and says, "Look, I know I'm an asshole, but I'm right about this." And I thought: You *are* an asshole and you *are* right about it. I would back his play. If that was real life, I'd back his play.

MADDREY: *Because of his strength of character?*

GOLDSMITH: Yeah. Strength of character rather than.... Burt and Vicky were just obnoxious. I didn't give a shit about those people. I mean, why are they together? And why is he gonna turn himself inside out to rescue her, or vice versa?

MADDREY: *In King's story, he doesn't rescue her. His stubbornness ends up killing them both.*

GOLDSMITH: Right. Exactly. I was thinking maybe I should just have him say, "Sorry, honey, luck of the draw," and drive off to California or wherever they were going.

MADDREY: *Did your script have a happy ending from day one?*

GOLDSMITH: Day one. I definitely made a choice right from the outset. That was one of the things that was wrong with King's story, in my view. It was too dark. I get why he did it, as a film noir kind of thing. Everybody's waiting for a happy ending and, in a good film noir, there's no happy ending. That's Jean-Paul Sartre and existentialism. But in this case, with a low-budget movie, you want to get people in the theaters. I didn't want it to be a bummer.

MADDREY: *It seems like you were reading the pulse of the times. Audiences were not very receptive to bleak horror films in 1982. They hated John Carpenter's THE THING, which is now regarded as a classic.*

GOLDSMITH: I'll tell you something.... I was very sickly as a child. And I watched a lot of television. I didn't go to school a lot. I did two things. I read incessantly and I watched horror movies: THE CRAWLING EYE, THE CREATURE FROM THE BLACK LAGOON, THE BLOB, THE THING, PLAN 9 FROM OUTER SPACE—even stupid things like that. I watched them all and I loved them. And I loved science fiction: Robert Silverberg, Isaac Asimov, Harlan Ellison, all those guys. I just devoured that stuff. And I devoured mythology. I love Greek, Roman, and Norse mythology. That stuff shaped my perspective on the heroic, the noble, the chivalrous.

MADDREY: *The hero's journey.*

GOLDSMITH: The hero's journey—but sometimes the journey goes from being a bum to being a hero. I love those stories of redemption. Like SEVEN SAMURAI. I'm such a Kurosawa fan. I've seen every Kurosawa film about ten times.

MADDREY: *It's interesting that you bring up Kurosawa, because screenwriter Lawrence Cohen said Kurosawa's THRONE OF BLOOD inspired the impalement scene in CAR-RIE. I'm curious to know what inspired your "lake of fire" ending in CHILDREN OF THE CORN? That's not in the short story....*

GOLDSMITH: It comes from the Bible, the Book of Revelation.

MADDREY: *Right, but why did you add it to the story?*

GOLDSMITH: It's a story about religious extremism or religious fundamentalism. Religion has always fascinated me. I'm a deeply religious person. Some people would call my religion "spiritualism." I'm Jewish but I don't conform to classical thinking. I study Kabbalah. Not Madonna bullshit but real Kabbalah. Gershom Scholem and guys like that. I read a lot of Christian literature and Christian history. I'm very, very interested in that. I think the Bible is an amazing piece of work, so my writing is imbued with all of that stuff.

I wrote a script that was never made called THE NATURE OF THE BEAST, and the fundamental question at the core of the script—and the reason I wrote it—is I came to believe that there's a universal desire to transcend. That desire exists on a macro level, across all of humanity, and it exists on a micro level, within every individual. It turns some people into Al Capone and some people into Mother Theresa, but there is a universal desire to transcend. I think religion addresses that. It also helps us to understand the natural world and the mysteries of the natural world, which are so far beyond us.

I've been to many spiritual places in the world and I can feel their energy. I don't profess to really understand it but I sense it and I'm in awe of it. I'm inspired by it. There are mysteries out there—and it's okay that they're mysteries. All of that kind of comes together in this mix when I'm writing. I try to reduce it to its simplest formula. As Oscar Wilde said, "Simplicity is the last refuge of the complex mind."

MADDREY: *What you just say about the mysteries of nature is interesting because, in your script for CHILDREN OF THE CORN, the god worshipped by the children manifests as an abstract force of nature. Given the special effects in the final film, that doesn't really come across onscreen....*

GOLDSMITH: No, not at all.

MADDREY: *The last twenty pages or so of the script is pretty epic. Burt fights to the death with Malachai. He Who Walks Behind the Rows is literally throwing dead bodies at them. Then Burt and Job light the cornfield on fire. The finale of the film is comparatively underwhelming.*

GOLDSMITH: The lake of fire is there, because Burt quickly got it. His response to Isaac and Malachai was: "You want religion? I'll give you religion. Here's some fire and brimstone, you son of a bitch!"

MADDREY: *It's funny that the "lake of fire" extends your oil embargo allegory—Burt is using the children's home-grown gasohol (instead of foreign oil) to destroy everything.*

GOLDSMITH: Ethanol wasn't really a big thing in the consciousness back then, but the gasohol…. Yeah.

MADDREY: *Did you make changes to the script during production?*

GOLDSMITH: The first time I sat down with Fritz Kiersch, the director—a great guy—and Linda Hamilton and Peter Horton [who played Burt and Vicky in the film], I just said, "Let's go through it, and if there's any dialogue that is awkward for you to say or you want to say it a different way, tell me and I'll write it so that we have it on paper. I'll write it the way you feel comfortable saying it." Fritz said, "That's really cool, man, thank you for that." Linda and Peter were also surprised and appreciative I respected their artistic input. I said, "We're all artists here. It's a collaboration and I want it to work the best it possibly can." That was my attitude.

During shooting, one night we had a green cornfield and there was an early frost. I got this frantic call and Fritz said, "We're shooting this scene tomorrow in the cornfield, which is supposed to be green. It's been green for all the other scenes so we can't do an exterior. We have to do something interior." It was around 10 o'clock at night. I said, "Send a messenger to my house at 6 a.m."—and that was my apartment on Sweetzer, I was still living in that place—"and there'll be new sides under the mat. Don't ring the doorbell, I'll be sleeping." We didn't even talk about it. He just said, "Write me an interior scene," and I did. I don't even remember what the scene was, but I changed an exterior green cornfield scene to an interior scene.

MADDREY: *Do you remember getting any script notes from Mark Lipson or Donald Borchers?*

GOLDSMITH: I got no notes from anyone. I had a couple of rehearsals with Fritz and Linda and Peter, and then on the set a couple of times I talked to John Franklin [who played Isaac] and Courtney Gains [who played Malachai]. I really liked Courtney. He was a good guy. Little bit of a wild man, which was why I liked him. And John Franklin was so fucking weird, I loved him. We got along great. I said the same thing to them: "If there's anything that doesn't work for you, or you have any ideas, we can always write it in." They liked that.

Terry Kirby was the producer, as I recall, but I barely talked to Terry. Don Borchers might say some stuff to me, but I'd just completely ignore him. I had almost nothing to do with Borchers. Once New World got involved…. I don't have any bad feelings about this film, other than the fact that New World tried to give King the [screenwriting] credit and make me the second writer. I just said, "I'm sorry, that ain't happening. This is my script." I later became a longtime credit arbiter for the Writer's Guild and I always remembered what these guys tried to do to me. I always tried to protect the writer whose work it really was.

After the movie came out, I saw Stephen King on a talk show. The interviewer said, "What do you think of CHILDREN OF THE CORN?" He was quiet for a few seconds and then he said, "I think it's the work of people who are going to do better." I thought that was so gracious, because I knew he hated that script. He hated what we did to his book, but he was still a gentleman and gracious, and I really appreciated that.

MADDREY: *He has said some pretty harsh things about the film but he seems to have warmed up to it over time.*

GOLDSMITH: He's an artist. You're a writer, so you understand—you get very pro-prietary about your original stuff. My attitude in Hollywood always was, "Look, I might disagree with the direction you want me to take this script, but your name is on my check…." That was always my attitude.

MADDREY: *Why do you think Stephen King didn't like your addition of the characters Job and Sarah? It seems to me that they're a lot like the children in some of his novels. They're innocent and victimized by adults [like Danny Torrance in* The Shining *or Charlie McGee in* Firestarter*]. And Sarah has a hidden supernatural power….*

GOLDSMITH: "And a child shall lead them," right? And "child is the father of the man"? All of that was very organic to me—that Job and Sarah were us. They were the audience. They were our innocence about everything that was going on, and therefore they were in danger and trying to figure things out and trying to make sense of it all. When I came up with them, it was just one of those things where you know in your bones that it's right. I said, "This is the only way that this story can be told well, through their eyes."

MADDREY: *It seems to me that you turned a very bleak short story into a story that's closer in spirit to Stephen King's humanistic novels. You made CHILDREN OF THE CORN a story of Good versus Evil—and you established that dichotomy right at the outset by establishing Sarah and Job as counterpoints to the other children. Sarah's visions seem to be a supernatural force for Good, which does not exist in the original short story….*

GOLDSMITH: I believe in a force that's much bigger than us, that's all around us all the time. There are good manifestations and bad manifestations of that force. It's very simple logic: If the Devil exists, then God exists. If demons exist, angels exist. You can't have one without the other. In the *Tao Te Ching*, the high is built upon the low, the dark upon the light. There's always a duality in the universe—Good and Evil. I try to resonate with Good—with the forces of Light—and I like my characters to have those qualities.

MADDREY: *It sounds like you and Stephen King have similar philosophies—but maybe he hadn't quite worked out his philosophy yet when he wrote "Children of the Corn." Or maybe he just had a different objective when he was writing short stories, as opposed to novels. A lot of the* Night Shift *stories build to dark twist endings. The novels are closer to morality plays.*

GOLDSMITH: I think he became more like me as he matured as a writer. Not that he wasn't a mature writer or greater than me—but I think the reason he eventually liked CHILDREN OF THE CORN is because he recognized impulses in it that he agreed with.

MADDREY: *How did CHILDREN OF THE CORN affect your career as a screenwriter?*

GOLDSMITH: For years, I made a good living as a ghost or as a [script] doctor. My name's not on a lot of scripts that I'm responsible for getting shot. People would come to me because I write fast. Writing just comes naturally to me. But I walked away from the business. I was pretty successful but I was more interested in living than writing, so I kind of walked away from it.

And then my life took a different turn that was more interesting. I spent 30+ years in the intelligence arena as a contractor, traveling the world, working for different governments and entities. I traipsed around Africa over a period of 30-some years and I wrote what was, at the time and for a long while, the highest-rated series ever on South African television. I did lots of crazy things around the world and then I invented the private sector asset recovery business in America—because all of the criminals and terrorists and assholes I was chasing around the world were all funded by financial crime. I got sick and tired of governments and their bullshit, so I started doing financial crime investigation and asset recovery from the private sector, beholden to no one but myself and my own ethics. I invented that business in the U.S., the first one to do it who was not a lawyer or any other kind of business professional. There's others that do it now but I was the first to commercialize it. I used my intel background and my relationships to hunt down financial criminals and narco-terrorists and money launderers and human traffickers—and sort them out.

People always say, "How did you go from being an investigative journalist to a TV and movie writer and then an intel guy?" To me, it's like being a doctor. You go to a doctor and say "My stomach hurts," and then the doctor has to become a detective. Investigating and researching, that's a lot of what we all do. You're conducting an investigation right now. You're questioning me. You've got your theories and your hypotheses. You know some of the answers to the questions you're asking me. You're seeing if the answers fit. That's the process.

To me, it was all a very clear through-line. I love to research. I'm a maniac for research. I find out things about people and then I learn about people. I see the difference between the façade we present to the public or even to our spouses. It could have made me a cynic, but instead it made me more of a humanist. I think you probably understand that.... We're all fragile. We're all frail. We all want to transcend. We all want to be more than we were.

MADDREY: I think humanists find it easy to love and respect individuals, but hard to love and respect groups of people. Stephen King has said he is a pessimistic about humanity as a whole, but he obviously still loves individuals. He obviously loves the characters in his novels, despite their flaws. Or maybe because of them. That's his strength as a writer.

GOLDSMITH: It's so funny. I feel exactly the same way. Anytime you have two people who agree on the same thing, you have the roots of fascism. It's the danger of group mentality.

MADDREY: It turns into "us and them" thinking, which creates a lot of problems. There's a great line in your CHILDREN OF THE CORN script where Burt and Job are down in the bomb shelter and Burt says, "The Communists aren't going to get us, Job. We're going to get us."

GOLDSMITH: Right, right. That was an echo. There was a very famous comic strip in the 1950s called *Pogo*. It was about this little insect character, walking around, spouting off these lines of wisdom. One of his most famous lines was "We have met the enemy and he is us." It's a very famous line. I wish it was one of mine.

MADDREY: There's another interesting line in your script where Sarah is talking to Job about Isaac and Job says, "I wish Isaac had never come here." And Sarah says, "He's always been here." It's a throwaway line but it was obviously a line that was important to you as a writer.

GOLDSMITH: Thank you. It really makes me feel good that you're noticing these things.

A while back, I wrote a script called FIRE IN THE LAKE, based on a book by Francis Fitzgerald. It's about the Vietnam War and "fire in the lake" is from the *I Ching*. It's the symbol for revolution. I have some great throwaway lines in there. One guy says to the hero of the story, "If memory serves me correctly, you did this." And the hero, Johnny, looks at him and says, "Memory serves no one correctly." [laughs] Sorry, I love my own lines. [laughs]

MADDREY: "Outlander, we have your woman!" is another fan favorite. What do you think of the fact that CHILDREN OF THE CORN has become such a cult classic and spawned, to date, eight sequels and two remakes?

GOLDSMITH: It really bothers me that I was not hired to write a single one of them. In my mind, that was 100 percent a financial decision. They didn't want to pay me what I was obviously worth, given the success of CHILDREN OF THE CORN, and that was a dumb decision, based on greed. I would have made them—and myself—a bunch more money, and created a real interesting family of CHILDREN OF THE CORN films, because I'm a serious writer and would have increasingly given them substance and style.

Legacy (Sequels, Sequels, Sequels)

The new New World Pictures got off to a strong start with the commercial success of its first theatrical releases. In early 1984, the $3 million-dollar sexploitation movie ANGEL grossed a total of $17.5 million at the domestic box office. Soon after that, CHILDREN OF THE CORN grossed $14.5 million on a rumored budget under $3 million. ANGEL quickly spawned a sequel (AVENGING ANGEL, 1985) so it was perhaps inevitable that CHILDREN OF THE CORN would have its own progeny. For the next several years, however, the rights-holders avoided an immediate return to Stephen King Country.

The stock market crash in October 1987, combined with a string of less successful films, spelled doom for New World. Amid rumors that producers Bob and Harvey Weinstein were bidding on the company, CEO Robert Rehme publicly conceded that the production company—which also operated as a distributor for its films—had grown "too big too fast" (Kathryn Harris 1988). In 1990, an investment group acquired the flailing company. Soon after, Larry Kupin and Harry E. Sloan—the former heads of New World—formed Trans Atlantic Pictures and promptly reacquired New World's film and home video assets, which included franchise rights for CHILDREN OF THE CORN as well as Clive Barker's HELLRAISER. This time, Kupin and Sloan didn't waste any time exploiting their properties but they learned from their mistakes at New World and minimized their financial risk by allying themselves with multiple production and distribution partners.

Screenwriting partners Gilbert Adler and Alan Katz were working on the TV series FREDDY'S NIGHTMARES (1988–1990) when "some friends" approached them about writing and producing a sequel to CHILDREN OF THE CORN. Presumably, the friends were Scott A. Stone, David G. Stanley, and/or Bill Froelich, all of whom had worked with Adler and Katz on FREDDY'S NIGHTMARES. In association with Lawrence Mortoroff's Fifth Avenue Entertainment, Stone, Stanley and Froelich went on to develop CHILDREN OF THE CORN 2, using Katz and Adler's script (Newton: "BORDELLO" 1996).

At some point, Froehlich approached David Price—who had helmed the low-budget vampire movie SON OF DARKNESS: TO DIE FOR 2 (1991)—to direct the sequel. Price was nervous because he knew Stephen King hadn't exactly turned cartwheels for the first film, but he was enthusiastic about the sequel script, originally titled DEADLY HARVEST. He told one interviewer, "There's more of a story now. It's not so much of a run-and-chase. It's fleshed out a little more. There are some great characters, which didn't happen in the first one, because the townspeople were all dead" (Biodrowski 1992).

In the finished film, the people of Hemingford, Nebraska, provide refuge to the surviving children of Gatlin. When one of the children (Micah) becomes possessed by He Who Walks Behind the Rows, the others start killing the adults in Hemingford, one by one. A disgraced New York reporter and his estranged son provide an outsider perspective on events, which follow the standard slasher movie formula and revolve around a series of imaginative murder set pieces. In one scene, a cranky old witch gets crushed under a house and dies squawking, "What a world, what a world!" At least the film has a sense of humor.

The screenwriters convey a vague eco-horror theme through an ancillary Native American character who offers two possible explanations for the murders. Red Bear invokes the Hopi Indian word Koyaanisqatsi to suggest that Mother Earth is taking revenge for man's habitual disrespect and exploitation of the natural world. According to director David Price, the basic idea was that "she's decided to recall the adults, and these children will take over" (Biodrowski 1992). On the other hand, Red Bear blames a real-world chemical called Aflatoxin for driving the local kids crazy. All roads lead back to the mysterious Gatlin god, who once again burrows His way into the final act.

Once the film was shot and edited, Kupin and Sloan turned to the Weinstein brothers to distribute the film. Around the turn of the decade the Weinsteins had distributed several low-budget horror films—including RETURN OF SWAMP THING (1989), EDGE OF SANITY (1989), STEPFATHER 2 (1989), and HARDWARE (1990)—under the banner Millimeter Films. Within a few short years, however, they achieved greater success with their company Miramax Films and promptly rebranded their "genre films" division Dimension Films. Among the first films released by the new division were CHILDREN OF THE CORN 2: THE FINAL SACRIFICE and HELLRAISER 3: HELL ON EARTH, which had been shot back-to-back.

The following year, Disney bought Miramax while the Weinsteins focused on building Dimension. The breakout success of the dark supernatural action film THE CROW (1994) proved to be a boon for the company and the producers quickly invested in sequel rights for the popular HALLOWEEN franchise. A year later, Dimension had another hit with Robert Rodriguez and Quentin Tarantino's action-horror hybrid FROM DUSK TILL DAWN, followed by Wes Craven and Kevin Williamson's groundbreaking SCREAM, which solidified the company's reputation as Hollywood's premiere home for horror. For every gold-plated franchise, however, Dimension fostered a red-headed stepchild. Between 1995 and 2001, the Weinsteins continued to send new CHILDREN OF THE CORN movies out into the field.

Screenwriter Dode B. Levenson wrote the script for CHILDREN OF THE CORN 3: URBAN HARVEST (1995), which became a co-production of Trans Atlantic Entertainment and Park Avenue Productions. Levenson, the son of a Conservative Jewish rabbi, had become a screenwriter in order to financially support his first love: journalism. He studiously analyzed a collection of successful screenplays and promptly sold his first spec script. The script didn't get produced but it did lead to his first paid screenwriting assignment, on Trans Atlantic's ANGEL 4: UNDERCOVER (1994). At first, Levenson didn't want to write low-budget exploitation movies but he quickly realized it was a great way to focus his storytelling and learn the craft of filmmaking. Of URBAN HARVEST, he says, "Making a vegetable menacing was quite challenging, but I was just happy writing movies, I didn't care what kind" (Brinn 2015). Soon after, Levenson decided he was more comfortable writing comedy, which could explain why URBAN HARVEST is the most overtly humorous entry in the franchise—although some of the humor might have been added by screenwriter Matt Greenberg, who reportedly did an uncredited rewrite of the script. The humor could explain why Stephen King "actually liked" this sequel (Warren: "King" 1997).

The conceit behind URBAN HARVEST is simple; one critic aptly described it as CHILDREN OF THE CORN meets BOYZ N THE HOOD. No doubt the film was inspired by the success of contemporary "urban horror" films like Wes Craven's THE PEOPLE UNDER THE STAIRS and the Clive Barker-produced CANDYMAN (both 1992), and it fit in well with other 1995 releases like Craven's VAMPIRE IN BROOKLYN, CANDYMAN: FAREWELL TO THE FLESH, and TALES FROM THE HOOD. Much like those films, URBAN HARVEST delivers pointed messages about the corrupting power of capitalism and the horrors of socioeconomic stratification, through its formulaic fish-out-of-water plot. The story revolves around two brothers from Gatlin who are sent to live with yuppie foster parents in Chicago. Older brother Joshua gets schooled by the "urban" (black) neighbors while Eli creates his own village of the damned. The goth kids end up worshipping He Who Walks Behind the Rows in a magical warehouse filled with supernaturally modified corn. When Eli's foster father learns about the crop, he makes plans to get rich off of the stuff. Eli coolly advises, "You reap what you sow." Josh eventually intervenes and destroys Eli's Bible—which is, somehow, the source of his strength—in order to save the world. Or does he? A final twist reveals that a shipment of Eli's special corn has made it all the way to Germany, where He Who Walks Behind the Rows will presumably attempt world domination in the next movie.

For better or worse, Dimension brought the CHILDREN OF THE CORN franchise in-house with the next film. Trans Atlantic Entertainment / Park Avenue Entertainment apparently handed off the sequel rights but (according to a 2017 Complaint for Declaratory Relief in the case *Donald P. Borchers vs. The Weinstein Company*) retained the rights to characters from the first three films, prompting the Weinsteins to abandon the existing storylines from those films. Film critic Bradley Schauer has suggested that Dimension also abandoned the idea of making true sequels and instead employed the old notion of a "cycle" of films—like the monster movies produced by Val Lewton for RKO in the 1940s or Roger Corman's adaptations of Edgar Allan Poe for AIP in the early 1960s—which "are similar in content but contain no recurring characters or continued storylines" (Schauer 2017).

Around the same time Dimension began churning out CHILDREN OF THE CORN movies, the studio also acquired sequel rights for the HELLRAISER franchise, allowing the Weinsteins to exercise creative control over the production of HELLRAISER: BLOODLINE (1996). According to contemporary reports, the producers released the film's director after the principal photography, then brought on a new writer—Rand Ravich—and a new director to prepare extensive reshoots and craft a completely new version of the HELLRAISER film (Hughes 1995, Ferrante 1996). Perhaps not coincidentally, Rand Ravich's writing partner Stephen Berger co-write the script for

CHILDREN OF THE CORN: THE GATHERING (1996). What is not clear is whether Berger was commissioned to write a script for the series, or whether THE GATHERING was a pre-existing spec script that was modified to fit the CHILDREN OF THE CORN "cycle." Actor Doug Bradley, star of the HELLRAISER series, claims that the three HELLRAISER films produced after BLOODLINE were all based on "pre-existing screenplays that were given a spin to turn them into HELLRAISER movies" (Grosso 2010). The Weinsteins might have approached the CHILDREN OF THE CORN series in the same way.

CHILDREN OF THE CORN: THE GATHERING revolves around a young med student who returns to her hometown of Grand Island (a place mentioned briefly in Stephen King's short story) to support her agoraphobic mother. She takes a job as a nurse at the same time the local kids begin suffering from an undefined illness that gives them high fevers and zombie-like stares. The film itself is plagued by dream sequences reminiscent of the NIGHTMARE ON ELM STREET films. The eventual explanation for the mysterious illness also harkens back to the more famous franchise. It turns out that the children of Grand Island are being haunted / possessed by the ghost of a dead child evangelist named Josiah, who was exploited, corrupted, and burned alive by the town's authority figures many years ago.

Like some of the NIGHTMARE ON ELM STREET sequels and many of that franchise's imitators, THE GATHERING is an exercise in cinematic style over storytelling sense, featuring a series of wildly inventive but loosely connected murder set pieces. In one scene, for example, a character is bisected by a hospital gurney with a retractable guillotine blade; it's unclear who took the time to design and create such an elaborate torture device. In another scene, Margaret White's crucifixion in CARRIE is re-created using farm equipment. Aside from creepy kids and corn, the film doesn't have much else in common with Stephen King's story or with any other films in the series.

Writer/director Ethan Wiley, a guiding creative force behind the first two HOUSE films for New World Pictures, took the reins on the fifth CHILDREN OF THE CORN film. In 1998, he summed up the franchise as follows: "There hasn't been a continuity, so to speak, with one writer or another director like you had with SCREAM or even with myself with the first HOUSE movies, where you kind of had someone with a connected vision between the different movies. Here it's really been different filmmakers doing their own thing each time" (Beeler: "CHILDREN" 1998). Accordingly, Wiley did his own thing. The working title for his film, FIELD OF SCREAMS, suggests that it could have been an ironic take on horror movie tropes in the style of SCREAM, but the final product—re-subtitled FIELDS OF TERROR—is a more predictable affair.

The film introduces a new child prophet, Ezekiel, who serves a mysterious green "eternal fire" housed in a grain silo in a sleepy town called Divinity Falls. When a quartet of impertinent teenagers pass through, they run afoul of Ezekiel's cult and its undead adult "savior," Luke. The characters briefly acknowledge the real-world horror of cults and brainwashing, but the film mostly focuses on slasher-movie kills. The most audacious murder set piece revolves around a confrontation between veteran actors David Carradine (as Luke) and Richard Roundtree (who plays the town sheriff). The film ends with a scene indicating that a newborn baby has somehow inherited / internalized the "eternal flame," thereby setting the stage for another sequel.

Of course, the next sequel ignores its predecessor entirely. Instead, it revolves around a character from the original CHILDREN OF THE CORN film—while blatantly ignoring the ending of that film too. The original film's child prophet Isaac returns to the franchise because actor John Franklin, who played Isaac, wanted to get back to his roots. Franklin remembers, "My writing partner [Tim Sulka] and I wanted to write a sequel since 1984 when the first CORN came out. [...] My acting manager had a connection to Dimension / Miramax. We set up a meeting and pitched ISAAC'S RETURN and they were, 'Great! We were running out of ideas!'" (Trembath 2016).

Like FIELDS OF TERROR, ISAAC'S RETURN starts with a young woman returning to her hometown—in this case, the town of Gatlin. Hannah has a couple of ominous hallucinations, then finds Isaac asleep in a hospital bed. According to the film, he's been there for nineteen years—but now he wakes up and starts killing again. One of the supporting characters explains, "Jim Jones. David Koresh. Hitler. They all came at the right time. Why not Isaac?" What makes this the right time? Isaac said it himself: the producers were running out of ideas.

The central idea in the story is that Hannah's return has fulfilled an old prophecy; Isaac's firstborn is supposed to mate with her and thereby produce a new cult leader who will replace Isaac. The story gets increasingly convoluted from there. The final gloomy shot of a sunset, accompanied by voiceover narration assuring us that "the seed has already been sown," is a typically ambiguous ending for a CHILDREN OF THE CORN sequel. According to John Franklin, ISAAC'S RETURN was intended as the series finale but it "made too much money," so the producers "kept cranking them out" (Trembath 2016).

Around that time, Stephen King reflected on the unnaturally long tenure of the series, bluntly saying, "Get a life, you guys. There are thousands of good scripts, there are thousands of good screenwriters out there, but their work is going begging because people are so intellectually bankrupt that they have to do CARRIE 2 or CHILDREN OF THE CORN 6" (Stephen Jones: *Creepshows* 2002). Dimension responded with CHILDREN OF THE CORN: REVELATION (2001), a threadbare story—even by CHILDREN OF THE CORN standards—involving creepy kids in a creepy apartment building in a creepy cornfield. When in doubt: add a dream sequence.

Seven movies on, many viewers and reviewers feel obliged to ask why anyone would continue to follow this disjointed series. What exactly is the enduring appeal of the CHILDREN OF THE CORN franchise? One answer lies in the simple fact of its endurance. Dimension kept making sequels and horror fans kept watching them, as if to test their endurance. In the Internet age, a new generation of fans seems to take perverse pride in watching and ranking all of the films. The original 1984 CHILDREN OF THE CORN and URBAN HARVEST usually rank near the top while FIELDS OF TERROR and REVELATION rank near the bottom. For a while, at least, it seemed like the series might have run its course—but, as every horror fan knows, true evil never dies.

Donald P. Borchers' CHILDREN OF THE CORN (2009)

Twenty-five years and six sequels later, producer Donald Borchers returned to Gatlin. The filmmaker says he got the idea to remake CHILDREN OF THE CORN after seeing the ratings success of the 1997 TV miniseries THE SHINING, which Stephen King had promoted as a more faithful adaptation of his famous novel. Borchers surmised that "there are two audiences for Stephen King product"—one of which is the author's

Constant Readers, who "don't want you to change" the stories they know (Holwill 2016). Concluding that there might also be an audience for a more faithful adaptation of "Children of the Corn," the producer revisited Stephen King's source story as well as King's original script for the CHILDREN OF THE CORN movie—and decided that King's script was "the better script than the one we had used," and the short story "the better story than the story that we had told." Borchers then renounced his own "Hollywood-ized" version of the story and set out to remake CHILDREN OF THE CORN "in the spirit of what Stephen King had originally written" (Waddell 2011).

The first order of business was acquiring the remake rights, which proved to be no small feat. Borchers says he charted the legal chain of title through a series of rights holders, then delivered his research to 20th Century–Fox, where he ultimately set up the new project as a made-for-television movie. Next, he revised Stephen King's script from 1980, updating the time frame of the story and adding a few new flourishes. To make sure the vision of the final film was true to the script, he decided to direct it himself.

Borchers initially deviated from King's script (and short story) by including a prologue that sets up the character of Isaac and establishes his influence over the children of Gatlin. In King's *Night Shift* tale, the nature of the threat to Burt and Vicky is not revealed until very late in the story; the narrative unfolds like the pilot episode of the original TWILIGHT ZONE TV series "Where is Everybody?" For a first-time reader, Burt and Vicky's discovery of a twelve-year old calendar and twelve-year old prices in the Gatlin diner might suggest that the townsfolk have been supernaturally abducted … or worse. Perhaps they experienced a fate similar to the residents of Jerusalem's Lot? If so, what exactly happened to the "children of the corn"? By adding a prologue about Isaac, Borchers answers the question before it is asked.

In the first scene of the 2009 TV movie, Isaac evangelizes to the children at a tent revival meeting, saying, "There's no rain for our corn. And why is that? Because of all the adults in our world." In this version of the tale, Isaac invokes "the God of the Old testament, the God of sacrifice" and urges his followers to "sacrifice the sinners to protect ourselves from the outside world." The children sacrifice a pig on the spot, making it clear that there is more bloodletting to come.

Borchers' film then jumps ahead twelve years, from 1963 to 1975, and picks up where King's script began—with Burt and Vicky in the car, bickering their way through Middle America. Borchers says he wanted to faithfully reproduce King's characters, "two people at the bitter end of a terrible marriage, who would like to see each other dead" (Waddell 2011). Much of the dialogue in the 2009 movie comes directly from Stephen King's 1980 screenplay, although the revision gets to the fateful car accident much sooner. After that, Borchers continues to utilize big chunks of King's dialogue and even some of King's suggested camera blocking—although he freely rearranges scenes and dialogue exchanges within the scenes. As the story progresses, he continues to make minor but important changes.

First, Borchers truncates King's gas station scene. Burt and Vicky stop at the gas station but find no one there, and an omniscient camera shot reveals that the gas station attendant was killed long ago. Burt and Vicky don't see the dead man's skeleton, so they receive no "warning" about the town of Gatlin. The change makes their stop in Gatlin seem less foolhardy.

As in King's short story (but not his script), Burt visits the local church and leaves Vicky alone in the car without keys. Inside, he finds a Bible from which the

New Testament has been removed—but Borchers does not visualize Burt's imaginings about what happened years ago in Gatlin. Instead, the writer/director keeps the story grounded in present day action. Simultaneous to Burt's exploration of the church, the children surround Vicky in the car. In this version of the story she does more than blow the horn; she retrieves Burt's shotgun from the backseat and shoots one of the killer kids off the hood of the car. Isaac, standing on a nearby rooftop and conducting his followers like an orchestra, gives a gameshow-worthy thumbs-down gesture, his way of ordering the others to kill her.

Afterward, Burt confronts the children and, as in King's script, embraces an opportunity to exact revenge. The 2009 movie doesn't indulge the author's slow-motion chop-socky idea, but it does feature a scene of hand-to-hand combat. Burt snaps a teenage boy's arm, giving him a horrific compound fracture. Isaac responds by throwing a dagger at Burt, injuring him, then Burt retaliates by fatally stabbing another boy in the throat. The kids are shocked—and so, presumably, is the viewer. Neither King's short story nor the 1984 film adaptation featured the graphic murder of children by adults, perhaps because that scenario seemed taboo. Borchers, however, had a very specific reason for making the change; he wanted to establish that Burt and Vicky are *not* heroic characters. The writer/director's perspective was that "as a protagonist faces an enormous challenge by evil itself—with no particular way to conquer it—that they must simply be good. And to the extent that they fail doing that, they fail" (Borchers: "The Shining" 2016).

The rest of the 2009 screen story is as bleak as Stephen King's original short story. Burt flees into the cornfield and the children follow, hunting him. Borchers incorporates a short scene from King's screenplay in which two male children talk in the

Unheroic Burt prepares to fight back in CHILDREN OF THE CORN (20th Television, 2009).

cornfield and one claims to have seen He Who Walks Behind the Rows. In King's script, the boys are undistinguished characters named Peter and Daniel. In the Borchers film, the younger boy—the one who claims to have seen He Who Walks Behind the Rows— is rechristened Nahum, after a minor prophet from the Old Testament. The older boy— who suggests that Nahum might be the "next prophet," Isaac's successor—is Malachai. The revised scene gives Malachai a concrete reason to rebel against Isaac.

Toward the end of the chase sequence, Burt hallucinates U.S. soldiers fighting alongside him in the corn. King's script didn't carry the Vietnam allegory quite so far, but Borchers didn't want to leave the main character's psychic disintegration to the viewer's imagination. In thrall to flashback, Burt murders two more children, including Nahum. The new twist seems to partly explain the sudden appearance of He Who Walks Behind the Rows. As the children retreat, leaving the fields to their god (who reputedly hunts by night), Burt sits down and munches on some sacred corn—no doubt breaking another taboo.

Speaking of breaking taboos, the next segment of the 2009 movie includes its most shocking scene. Seemingly inspired by a flashback in an early draft of King's script, in which a couple of older teenagers have sex as part of a fertility ritual, Borchers incorporates a scene in which a group of younger children leer at two older children having sex. Whereas King's scripted scene ended with the children's horrified reaction to the sudden appearance of He Who Walks Behind the Rows, the scene in the 2009 movie ends with the children gleefully moaning and jouncing in a frenzied imitation of the couple's climax. As shot, it is a tasteless bit of exploitation filmmaking.

Burt wakes up from an equally frenzied dream of death and destruction, only to be physically attacked by the corn. He manages to escape into a clearing where he finds Vicky crucified with cornstalks in her eye sockets. In another hallucinatory moment, Vicky turns her head and speaks to him, cooing, "It's not so bad. Join me." Instead of a climactic encounter with He Who Walks Behind the Rows, this encounter becomes the climactic moment of the Borchers version—one in which Burt and Vicky meet their hellish fate. The filmmaker implies that they deserve it because they could not "simply be good." They have proven themselves to be exactly the type of adults that Isaac warned his followers about at the start of the film—the type of adults that must be sacrificed in order to protect children "from the outside world."

The 2009 movie does not visualize Burt's death. Instead, Borchers jumps from Burt's hallucination to a scene of the children feeding a funeral pyre as they prepare to sacrifice the oldest members of their group. The scene ends with a shot revealing that Burt has been crucified and strung up nearby, like an eyeless scarecrow. As in King's script, Isaac hisses the word "scarecrow" at him before following his tribe away from the site.

The 2009 movie also includes a brief post-credits scene in which Ruth and Malachai talk about Malachai's decision to willingly sacrifice himself to the corn god. The dialogue comes from King's script, but Borchers adds a brief vision of Ruth standing in front of the cornfield on fire. As Malachai disappears into the cornfield for the last time, Isaac glares at Ruth. The scene could be interpreted as a nod to the 1984 film, in which the cornfield burns at the end, or perhaps a setup for a new sequel, in which Ruth challenges Isaac's leadership. Either way, the postscript mitigates Stephen King's ultra-bleak ending.

Borchers says he never expected to get good reviews on his film—because he knew that King's script did not follow the traditional "hero's journey" at the heart of so many

Hollywood movies. He did, however, hope that the "hardcore Stephen King fans" would embrace the new film (Borchers: "SyFy" 2016). He also wanted to please the author, and proudly reported that although King wanted nothing to do with the production of the film, he "elected to keep his name in the credits" as co-screenwriter (Burke 2009).

An Interview with Donald P. Borchers (2020)

JOSEPH MADDREY: I understand you went to business school and started out in the entertainment industry doing accounting and preparing budgets. Did you always plan to become a producer?

    DONALD P. BORCHERS: I went to business school because I wanted to be a producer. What happened was I was in a youth organization in New York. It was called Junior Achievement. It's like Boy Scouts for business instead of nature; kids start a company and everything. I was an ace achiever and I got solicited to do this fundraising gig during my senior year in high school. I had kind of a peculiar year because you couldn't graduate early in 1974 but all I had to do was take English, so all I did was take English. I enrolled, non-matriculated at St. John's University and spent a fair amount of time in Manhattan at the Junior Achievement national headquarters and got solicited into doing this fundraising gig at the Biltmore Hotel, where about eight or ten of us kids acted out what it's like [starting a company]: gonna sell stock, gotta select the product, figure out who's gonna be in charge. It was like a little play and we all had a role to play.

    I met a producer—a woman who was an off-Broadway producer. Out of every job I had ever seen in my life, there was just something about this one that rang a bell in my head. The more I talked to her and the more I asked her about what she did, the more I liked it. She said her biggest regret was that she was not good with money and she always went over budget. I said, I think what I'll do is I'll take care of that first, so I enlisted in all these business classes at St. John's University, then I went to University of Notre Dame to get a degree in business.

    Father Durbin, my freshman year studies counselor, said, "Mr. Borchers, what would you like to be when you grow up?" I said, "Oh, I want to produce movies, Father." He said, "*Seriously*, Donald, what do you want to do when you grow up? We have to select which college to send you to." I said, "Oh, I'm going to the College of Business." "And how do you know that?" "Because I worked with this producer in New York...." He said, "What you need, Donald, is an angel. And I mean that in more ways than one." [laughs] I didn't know at the time that "angel" also referred to an investor. For a movie producer, an "angel" is the guy putting up the dough for the movie.

MADDREY: Also, one of your breakthrough films at New World Pictures was titled ANGEL....

    BORCHERS: Completely separate story. The ANGEL [1984] story is as follows: I'm dating this beautiful woman in the accounting department, three years my junior. I'm 26 years old and I'm thinking I've met my mate. But I'm dealing with the fact that she keeps saying she's going to quit smoking—the smell just turns my stomach. But she's even willing to take showers after she smokes. She wants to make it work but she doesn't want to quit smoking. And I'm willing to listen to country and western music, even though I hate country and western music. We get into this huge argument about when our kids are born. I think they should go to Notre Dame and she doesn't know if Catholic University is right for her kids. I say, "They can pick for themselves." And she says, "But they can't, because of their religion. They're going to be Jewish." I'm thinking, well, you know, if you're going to be well-practiced Jews—more than I'm well-practiced as a Catholic—that might be great for them. Then she says, "And if we have a son, I'm going to name him Angel." I said, "That's a hooker's name." She says, "No, it's a beautiful name. It's Mexican." I say, "Neither of us are Mexican. You're a Jewish girl from the Valley and I'm a Catholic boy from Brooklyn. I'm telling you: Angel is a hooker's name. Watch any Humphrey Bogart movie." So we're having this hellacious argument.

Around that time, [my mentor, film producer] Sandy Howard calls me and says, "Kid, I just read this keeper by Bob O'Neil. It's called HOLLYWOOD STARR. It's about this girl who lost her parents, there's a stalker on the loose, and she's trying to make grades in school while making it on her own on Hollywood Boulevard." So I looked my girlfriend straight in the eye and I said, "If you call it ANGEL, I'm in." [laughs] Sandy goes, "Oh, I love that title." From that phone call, her name [of the main character in the script] changed to Angel. That had nothing to do with school. That had to do with me breaking up with my girlfriend.

MADDREY: That explains how ANGEL fell in your lap, so what about CHILDREN OF THE CORN? David Simkins has said that when you moved into Roger Corman's old offices at New World, he opened a door and a bunch of scripts fell out, and one of those scripts was CHILDREN OF THE CORN.

BORCHERS: Yes, the only thing left was the scripts in the closet. There was not a stitch of furniture. I had just ordered a desk and I'm making forms—literally, I've got a T-square out and I'm making budget forms so I can take them to a printer and do budgets for our pictures. Simkins walks in and he says, "You know we have a CHILDREN OF THE CORN screenplay here?" I said, "Good to know." Didn't think much of it because we didn't have any money. We had spent all the money buying the company. We had to make some foreign sales. So what I'm doing is I'm thinking who's gonna be on my staff, the furniture, the forms we're gonna use—this is what's on my mind. I'm not looking for projects yet because then people are gonna start to ask me if we're gonna make those movies, and I'm gonna have to say, "We don't have any money."

One day, Harry Sloan calls me up and says, "I just had a meeting with Judy over at HBO. She's willing to do some deals with us. They'll give us, like, half a million dollars against HBO rights and we can release the film theatrically first. I want to pick up a horror film I can do for, like, a million dollars. Maybe a million-two, maybe a million-four." He didn't say a million-five, right? He says, "So I picked THE HOWLING 2 as my first one." [Author's note: HOWLING 2: YOUR SISTER IS A WEREWOLF (1985) was developed by producer John Daly at Hemdale Film Corporation.]

Having done the original budget on THE TERMINATOR (1984), having done the original budget on MIRACLE MILE (1988), having done a dozen budgets for John Daly, I said, "Guys, you don't want to do this." They said, "Well, find us a better franchise." The bell goes off: David Simkins, 48 hours ago. I said, "How about CHILDREN OF THE CORN?"

Now, mind you, the day I said this, here's what we knew: We knew that the release date would fall somewhere between an $8 million CUJO picture, an $8 million PET SEMATARY picture, and an $8 million DEAD ZONE picture. A million-and-a-half dollar CHILDREN OF THE CORN picture inside that Stephen King traffic made all the sense in the world—except, from their point of view, "Who's ever heard of 'Children of the Corn'"? Those other books were famous. The $8 million movies were based on bestsellers.

The only reason we knew about "Children of the Corn" at all was because, at the time, Stephen King was known to answer all his fan mail. Certainly, he answered all of David Simkins' letters. So, when Simkins came across that CHILDREN OF THE CORN script in the closet, he wrote to King. King wrote and told him that after he wrote the story for *Penthouse* magazine, Doubleday and he re-acquired the rights and sold his story to Hal Roach Studios. Hal Roach's granddaughter's husband had read [the short story] in *Penthouse* magazine, and on behalf of Hal Roach Studios, he bought the "Children of the Corn" movie rights.

Getting back to the point: "Who's ever heard of 'Children of the Corn'?" I said, "Look at the deal we just found at Hal Roach. Read Exhibit A, paragraph 5." Exhibit A, paragraph 5 is the most "fuck you" standard studio language you could ever give to an artist. It says the studio has complete control over your name, complete control over licensing and products, can use it to sell soap, can use it on TV, can do anything we want, fuck you. So … the name of the movie became "STEPHEN KING'S CHILDREN OF THE CORN." And they went, "Oh, brilliant."

MADDREY: I understand George Goldsmith originally wrote the CHILDREN OF THE CORN script for Hal Roach, so is that the version you saw?

BORCHERS: That's right. When David handed me the script, it was not the draft that Stephen King had written. The first time I ever got the draft Stephen King wrote was after I had finished photography on the movie. I didn't even possess that script until after I finished shooting the movie. I only had Goldsmith's script. George Goldsmith's major contribution was inventing those adorable munchkins, Job and Sarah. Those are all purely invented by him. I inherited that to start. I added a happy ending, a CARRIE twist, and I cut George Goldsmith's 123-page script down to well under 100 pages.

It came to me as something that was too expensive to shoot, for the money we had available for the budget. If we had shot everything George had written, the movie would have been a good 20, 25 minutes longer, and repetitive. "Oh, now he's going to go back into the cornfield and walk around some more?" That kind of stuff. So I had a meeting with [director] Fritz [Kiersch] and George at my home in Sherman Oaks. I went to Staples and got a box full of Scotch tape rolls, a pair of scissors, and three reams of paper, and I printed out nine copies of the script. Handed three scripts to each of us, to cut up. I said, "Okay, here we go, guys. We're going to spend the weekend here—it's a three-bedroom house—and we're not leaving until we have a shooting script that's close to something we can shoot in twenty-four days." I figured, magnanimously, we could shoot four pages a day, so I said, "I really don't want to shoot more than 96 pages." We cut and pasted the shooting script and I swear to God the stuff we cut was completely redundant. That's how I knew to cut it out. George was milking the terror of being in the corn. First, there was the tease before they get to the gas station. Then, the tease after the gas station. And this is just in the part of the script with the car! None of that stuff made the cut.

MADDREY: Once you learned about the Stephen King script, what did you think of it?

BORCHERS: After I read the script, it made me want to read the short story, so I read the short story. Mind you, the only thing I was doing at the time, in greenlighting and making CHILDREN OF THE CORN, was getting a movie made that was not THE HOWLING 2. Before I got CHILDREN OF THE CORN made, [several producers] had taken serious runs at all the studios with the George Goldsmith draft on behalf of Hal Roach. *Serious* runs. They turned up no interest. Nobody bought it. Nobody connected with it on any level—and I know why that is. Most people don't understand the most essential thing of every successful horror film—and, yes, I'll say that again: *every* successful horror film.

There's a professor at the University of Utah named Jan Harold Brunvand, who writes about apocryphal stories. An apocryphal story is a story that, when I tell it to you, you don't feel the need to do any research or check any facts. As soon as you hear it, you know it's true. You're so sure it's true that when you repeat it to the next person, you now add a false validation: "I saw it myself." "This happened to my cousin." "I read it in the paper." An example of an apocryphal story is "The Mexican Pet." A lady goes to Tijuana and picks up this cute little dog, but it turns out to be a Mexican sewer rat. You tell that story to someone and they'll repeat it because they know that happened. PEE WEE'S BIG ADVENTURE (1985) uses the story of "The Vanishing Hitchhiker": Large Marge. HALLOWEEN (1978) uses "The Hook," the story of the guy who escapes the mental institution and goes on a killing spree. What's another one?

MADDREY: WHEN A STRANGER CALLS [1979]?

BORCHERS: Right! The person who's hiding upstairs in the attic. They're really no-brainers. They're about fears that will always exist in society. Look at the Mexican folk story that just recently became a movie, THE CURSE OF LA LLORONA [2019]. It's a natural. "Don't go in the river bed because it's haunted." They made up a story about a woman who married a prince, then there was an infidelity, and she drowned her sons because they were his. Now she mourns their death and haunts the river bed and takes the lives of any children she sees. What does that mean, kids? That means "don't play in the river bed." That's what makes it an effective horror story—it expresses a natural fear.

MADDREY: And the "Children of the Corn" short story has the same kind of simplicity....

BORCHERS: What CHILDREN OF THE CORN had—right out of the gate—is kids killing their parents. That is the scariest fucking thing you could think of. This is why THE OMEN [1976] works. This is why THE EXORCIST [1973] works. The devil-child. So I'm thinking to myself: I get Jan Harold Brunvand, I get why OMEN works, I get why EXORCIST works, so with CHILDREN OF THE CORN—if we shoot anything close, we've got a hit.

I've also got to give [film editor] Harry Keramidas credit. Harry was in between gigs and Fritz's business partner Terry [Kirby] knew a lot of commercial people and they knew that a high-end film editor was currently unemployed and looking. Harry Keramidas had no business working on our movie. He cut his rate drastically because of two things: (1) the start date. We had something he could literally start on Monday, so he could get a paycheck next week and that means something to some people. Number two: he had been making a long commute to work and his mentor owned a bungalow across from the Hollywood Police Station. He said if we rented that bungalow from her—which had a movie editing suite in it—that would cut his commute down so much that it would be worth it. That's how we got Harry on board.

Fritz put together the first assembly and Harry comes to me and says, "You've got a problem." I said, "What's wrong?" He said, "You need to shoot pickup shots so I can cut a scary sequence where the kid sits up in the road." I said, "Could you make a list of shots?" He says, "Funny you should say that." He had been working with Fritz, but Fritz was too afraid to ask me because he knew I'd say no.

The first time I met Fritz, I was an assistant director on a commercial he was doing for Lamy pens. He shot a pen for like eight hours. He shot something like ten thousand feet of film for a thirty second spot. It took us two days just to watch the dailies. I know Fritz—he'll just keep shooting. "Oh, I've got an idea for a shot." "Here's a good idea...." So he knew that if he asked me to do a pickup shoot [for CHILDREN OF THE CORN], I'd say no. So he sent Harry with the list. Harry said, "We know what we need." He convinced me they were not fucking around.

I had met Harry originally on GOLDENGIRL [1979] when I was at Avco-Embassy Pictures, and he went on to cut BACK TO THE FUTURE. The point is he was an A-list guy. So, when he came to me and said, "These are the shots you're missing. If you gave them to me, I'll cut them into the picture and you'll have a hit," I was thinking—with everything I had studied about corn—we were fucked. But I came to find out that there's actually a spring [corn] crop in California. We could go up to Bakersfield and make it work! For the purpose of these inserts—and that's where we got all the stuff like the reflection in the mirror and the knife behind behind her—I went back to Harry [Sloan] and Larry [Kuppin] to get a few bucks.

This was Harry's point: If you establish the kid in the road and she thinks he's dead, it's going to scare the bejesus out of people when he sits up. It's gonna work because we think there's somebody behind her who's going to kill her. You insinuate this [with the pickup shots]. Harry said, "I want to build the montage. I want to build the threat. I want to make it credible. I want to make it close enough so that when the kid sits up in the road, we think it's the guy behind her is stabbing her in the back."

MADDREY: *It's that old Hitchcockian art of misdirection. Manipulating the audience.*

BORCHERS: I hired Harry Keramidas and I believed the man. He told me that, considering the script that was approved, this is the best version of the film that's ever going to be cut. He said, "You don't need to waste any money trying to do it any better than this. The director got everything the script asked him to get, and with the three days of pickup shots, we have put the icing on the cake." All we needed then was the score and I was introduced to Jonathan Elias by my producing partner, Terry Kirby. Terry and I both went to grade school in Garden City, Long Island, New York. Jonathan Elias had been working with John Barry, who was his mentor. John Barry had had him do something on BLADE RUNNER (1982). I got to hear it and it was fucking awesome. So I sat him down and told him my whole theory about the John Carpenter theme and the sound of [kids chanting]. He put those two thoughts together with everything he'd been trained to do by John Barry and we got a classic score.

MADDREY: *I'm curious to know how you came around to the idea of remaking CHILDREN OF THE CORN.*

BORCHERS: That was a no-brainer. The year is 2005. I'm looking around at a remake of THE TEXAS CHAINSAW MASSACRE, a remake of LAST HOUSE ON THE LEFT... The list goes on. I said, "Fuck it. I'm remaking CHILDREN OF THE CORN."

MADDREY: *Was the plan always to go back to the Stephen King script?*

BORCHERS: Back in '97, I remembered the script. I had no claim on any rights to it; I just remembered the script. I thought, I might have the only existing copy of that script and I thought somebody might want to shoot it, so I called up Rena Ronson, who was the head of foreign distribution at New World Pictures, and I said, "You're over at New World. I'm assuming you have the rights to do another CHILDREN OF THE CORN movie…." At the time, she affirmed that she did. Later, these rights went to Larry Kuppin. The chain of title went like this: New World to Trans Atlantic distributors, to Oceana, to Lakeshore, to Fifth Avenue, to Park Avenue, to Graphic Novel, to me. That's how I ended up being the rights holder.

Then I said, I'm going to take this [Stephen King] script and I'm going to set up a file. Then I'm going to take the short story and set up another file. Then I'm going to put the two files back-to-back. Now I'm going to take [the advice of screenwriting guru] Syd Field and make a 5-point structure. Everything I need, I'm going to pull up from the short story or the script, and we'll see what's left over. I did that and then I looked at the stuff that was left over and I said, "This might work here. That might work there." Then I looked at more stuff that was left over and I said, "That doesn't work at all." Looked at more stuff that was left over and reworked it. Finally, I didn't have any stuff left over. By then, the script was standing up on its own and I just looked at it and said: Pretend this script was submitted to me and I wanted to fix it. I read it that way and I did everything I would to fix it. Then I sent it to three writers who had worked for me in the past and I said, "I'd like your notes." They gave me notes and I addressed their notes and then I was done.

MADDREY: You're obviously re-telling a story that was already well known, so how did you make decisions about what to keep and what to change? Did you want to make the story seem new to people who had seen the original film?

BORCHERS: Let me put it this way: When I made the original movie, I was in a hellacious argument with Fritz Kiersch, George Goldsmith, and—even though he didn't have conviction to back up his partner—Terry Kirby. Now, remember, this was my movie. I could do whatever I wanted. I had carte blanche. I didn't have a boss, particularly. Harry and Larry were out there running and gunning, but I ran production. That's what I was hired to do and I was doing it. I was producing this movie. So: "Oh, let me check with the studio. Okay, I just talked to myself and this is what the studio says."

They wanted to go with George's ending. I said, "No, I am going to require Vicky to look at Burt, before he goes off on a mission to die, and say, 'I love you, Burt.' And then Burt's gonna look at Vicky and say, 'I love you, Vicky.'" George says, "I won't write it." I say, "Then I'll get a writer who will." Fritz says, "I won't direct it." I say, "Then I'll get a director who will." They both looked at each other and went, "I guess that's what they're going to say." I stuck to my guns and I made them do it.

MADDREY: But wasn't there a consensus among all of you about making the two main characters more empathetic and creating a more uplifting ending?

BORCHERS: You just said two things. There was never a discussion on empathy. I don't recall ever having that discussion. I recall reading George Goldsmith's script and saying…. I like British humor. I remember watching Monty Python skits when I was in college. I remember Peter Cooke and Dudley Moore did this one skit [from an Easter 1970 special episode of the sketch show IT'S MARTY] about two extraordinarily bored airline pilots on a transcontinental flight. It has one of them saying, "I spy with my little eye something that begins with the letter C." The other guy looks at him and says, "Clouds." So I said, "Guys, you've got to use the line 'I spy with my little eye something that begins with the letter C.' 'What?' 'Corn.'" That had to be in the movie. I said, "I saw it on TV. It's brilliant. It works. You've got to use it." That was as much empathy discussion as I remember having.

MADDREY: *What about the ending?*

BORCHERS: What happened was, on the ending, we didn't really have it. I recall wanting to do the "not really dead" thing with the girlfriend [Rachel] and making them put that in. That wasn't in the script. That was what I was getting out of CARRIE—that the audience wants one more scare at the end. So the pregnant girlfriend comes back and tries to attack them and Burt knocks her out and then worries about whether or not she's alive. I had that for the end.

At New World, we greenlit THE PHILADELPHIA EXPERIMENT [1984] as a studio. [Visual effects designer] Max Anderson calls me up—and I had met him in the past on some John Carpenter stuff—and Max said, "I really want this movie. What do I have to do to get it?" I said, "Well, it's a numbers game, Max." He said, "Help me with my numbers." I went over and I looked at how he was spending his fixed cost and his overhead and how many people he was hiring and what his work days should look like and his hours and how he could run his shop. Based on that, he put in a number of $750,000 for THE PHILADELPHIA EXPERIMENT. Then I said, "I can come up with the better part of $100,000 [for visual effects on CHILDREN OF THE CORN], but I need like a quarter of a million dollars' worth of roto[scope] work." He said, "I'll split the difference. I'll have the PHILADELPHIA shop do it. I'll take your money and I'll hire a couple of extra people to do it. But it's going be less than a B effort on my part." I'm thinking that I have recently seen Larry Cohen movies like IT'S ALIVE [1974] and liked them— and liked the numbers. I had my eyes wide open when I said, "Perfectly acceptable. As long as I can see that there's actually a face of a monster and I can resolve that that spirit is now in anguish, and then gone. Poof." He said, "Yeah, we can get that done."

MADDREY: *I think one of the boldest things about the remake is the decision to have Burt and Vicky fight back and kill some of the kids, which obviously doesn't happen in the 1984 movie.*

BORCHERS: Which kid gets killed?

MADDREY: *Vicky shoots a shotgun at one of the kids through the windshield of the car....*

BORCHERS: That was intentionally ambiguous. I never showed the corpse. All I showed was her blasting—but, I mean, she couldn't miss at that range. [laughs] And you don't see him in any more scenes after that.

MADDREY: *Later, when Burt gets cornered in the alley, he breaks a kid's arm—gives him a compound fracture....*

BORCHERS: I set up the Chuck Norris movie AN EYE FOR AN EYE (1981) when I was at Avco-Embassy, and I had this movie I wanted to do with Chuck that we never did. There were two scenes that I wanted in the movie and this was one of them. I said, "I've always wanted to see somebody take someone's arm and just break it across their knee like it's a two by four." So I did that in CHILDREN OF THE CORN. I knew that was going to be effective. I'd been wanting to do that for thirty years.

MADDREY: *From a story point, you also made a decision that this guy—who has been in combat in Vietnam—would defend himself. Even if attacked by kids, he would use violence to defend himself. The earlier film didn't go there.*

BORCHERS: You couldn't. The CHILDREN OF THE CORN film that got the R rating, MPAA originally gave that film an X rating. We had to argue and hire lawyers and fight and I had to go before the board and make arguments. They thought the idea of children killing their parents—the idea itself—was an X-rated idea. That's what we were up against.

MADDREY: By 2009, you could get away with much more—even on television.

BORCHERS: Oh fuck yeah. Not a problem. I actually made two versions. I submitted both versions—the R rated version and the TV version—to SyFy Channel, and SyFy Channel made me take stuff from the R rated version, like that [scene where Burt breaks the kid's arm], and put it in the TV version. That was not in my TV cut. It was supposed to be a special bonus for [home video distributor] Anchor Bay. But Anchor Bay was happy enough to get [actress] Zita Vass naked.

MADDREY: I didn't see it when it originally aired on SyFy, so I'm only familiar with the longer DVD cut. Was the "fertility ritual" scene in the TV version as well?

BORCHERS: It's in there but no nudity. I don't remember if the tag is in the TV version or not—the scene after the end credits.

MADDREY: I was wondering about that, because the scene revolves around a character from the short story and it feels like a setup for a sequel that tells Ruth's story. I recently watched CHILDREN OF THE CORN: RUNAWAY, which follows that Ruth character. When I saw that, I said, "Oh, it's a sequel to the 2009 remake...."

BORCHERS: Yeah, you know how that happened? In the spring of 2009, I still had an ambition to release CHILDREN OF THE CORN theatrically, so I called up Mark Berg and I go, "Mark, I don't know Bob Weinstein, but I want to see if he wants to buy this movie." He goes, "I'll give him a call." Fifteen minutes later, I answer my phone and hear, "I have Bob Weinstein for you." I told Bob, "I've got CHILDREN OF THE CORN in the can." It was Wednesday and he says, "Can you get on a plane today?" I said, "No, I can't even get the film out of the lab today." He says, "Well then, get on a plane tomorrow and we'll watch it Friday."

So I'm off to the London Hotel in New York, showing him the film. He watches it and says, "I'm going to develop a film myself. I want to put more production value in it. I'm going to spend $20 or $30 million on marketing, so I want a $20 or $30 million movie." Which, in everyday language, means $10 million. Mine was clearly $3 million, so he had to pass. But I had featured a character that was not in the first film—Malachai's girlfriend. The pregnant character in the first film [CHILDREN OF THE CORN, 1984] is Isaac's girlfriend, not Malachai's. At the end of the 2009 remake, Ruth lights the cornfield on fire—and for good reason. Because [actress Alexa Nikolas, who plays Ruth] wanted to be in this movie.

She called me and asked me to be in it. I said, "I'm only going to spend money for two names, Burt and Vicky. Everybody else is scale." She goes, "I don't have anything going on and I want to be in the movie." I said, "I'm happy to put you in this movie but your agent will never close the deal because you're the star of a Nickelodeon series [ZOEY 101]." I called the agent up and they were pissed. They knew she wanted to do it and they knew I wasn't going to pay anything. I said, "Sign the papers or I'm going to recast it." They signed the papers and she was in it. That's why the part is so good. I got somebody who never should have been in that part. She's the only one in the picture that had a series. Everybody else was *in* a series but she *had* a series. She was a major star. She should have a much bigger career than she has right now.

MADDREY: I want to go back to Burt and Vicky becoming violent with the children, because I think that's what really distinguishes the remake from the original film. When they make the decision to kill the kids, I think it changes the characters and gives the story an edge that the 1984 version doesn't have. Was that your intention?

BORCHERS: I want to say I got that from the short story. I can't swear to it; I'd have to re-read the short story. The breaking-the-arm thing is just something I wanted to do for thirty years. The shooting the shotgun thing: I want to say that that was in the script that King wrote. I don't think that was my idea. It makes sense if you understand what prompted King to write the short story. Stephen King watched the Spanish picture WHO CAN KILL A CHILD? [1976], and after that he wrote "Children of the Corn."

On the remake [CHILDREN OF THE CORN, 2009], my intention was: [Burt and Vicky] die in the short story, they're going to die in this movie. This is going to be a tragic ending. All I had to do was just tell the short story, because the short story was compelling—and then fluff it up with stuff from the screenplay that nobody knew about. There was stuff that was in the shooting script that wasn't in the movie because I went over schedule and, in order to get back on schedule, I did the old John Ford thing: I cut out four pages. The four pages I took out was a chase scene after Burt runs out of the alley, before he runs into the cornfield. In the script, the alley connects with the school and there's a chase through the school and out the other side, into the cornfield. That's not in the movie.

MADDREY: I read a 2017 interview in which you said you were going to make a CHIL-DREN OF THE CORN miniseries, set in a future world where children hunt adults....

BORCHERS: That's still going to happen. I'm 64 years old and it'll happen by the time I'm 70, but most probably as a European-based TV Series. Did you ever see the French series THE RETURNED [2012]? It had a short life as a U.S. import around 2013 or 2014. What happens is, like five years before the TV series starts, a school bus full of children and a couple of adult supervisors goes off the road and everybody dies. This is in a town that has a mysterious nuclear power plant or something like that. It's a STRANGER THINGS kind of setup. In fact, I promise you the STRANGER THINGS guys watched THE RETURNED. So what happens is, five years later, somebody walks in who was on the bus. And they haven't aged. And they reveal themselves to their parents, who know their child when they see them. It's one of the best series I've ever watched.

MADDREY: It sounds like what you were talking about earlier: an apocryphal story.

BORCHERS: Here's my log line for the CHILDREN OF THE CORN TV series: "In a dystopian future, children rule the world and adults are a hunted and endangered species." I wrote a first act—the fifteen to twenty minutes that gets you hooked. It's set in a cornfield and there's a ceremony and all these kids get eaten by the corn and turned into fertilizer—except one girl who wants to run. She runs and there's a chase and—oh my god—there's a helicopter flying above her. We pull out and see that this cornfield is in Central Park. We're in Manhattan. That's the first act break.

The idea is that whatever happened to the kids [in Gatlin] happened everywhere. If you pit kids against adults, who's going to win? The adults. Kids can't win. But if the adults win, that's genocide. The adults have a real problem on their hands, so what do the adults do? It's the ESCAPE FROM NEW YORK solution: "We're going to stick them all in Manhattan until we figure this out."

MADDREY: Maybe I shouldn't quote you on all this. I don't want to give away your story before you have a chance to make it.

BORCHERS: It's no secret. I don't think that people are going to watch it or not watch it based on…. Let me put it this way: When you see a Stephen King movie, you already know the book. That's my take on this. So what happens is that the girl who ran explains everything to us in the first act, because she's also a schoolteacher. She explains that Mother Nature started to really hurt. There's images of oil spills, forest fires—you get the idea. We see everything that man's doing that's corrupting the environment that we live in. Father Earth got mad—and I wrote this over a year ago [before the coronavirus pandemic]—and sent a virus to the Earth, to get rid of everyone over the age of 18. Because children have to be taught to hate. They have to be taught to pollute. They have to be taught to be greedy. None of this comes natural to children. The adults teaching them is the problem. A year later, the story is: We've been here for a year now and everything they indicted the adults for—being corrupt and abusive—the kids running the city are now doing the same things.

MADDREY: One thing that's interesting about the story you're telling is that it doesn't include He Who Walks Behind the Rows. Neither does the 2009 remake. In King's story and script, Burt comes face to face with the kids' god. In the 2009 remake, he finds Vicky crucified….

BORCHERS: In my mind, in the original picture, there absolutely is a He Who Walks Behind the Rows, and He gets killed at the end. On the [forthcoming] TV series, there is absolutely a manifestation of Earth itself—not unlike what James Cameron was doing with AVATAR [2009], the way the planet itself is sentient. That's where I'm going. But with the 2009 remake, if you ask me, the monster did not exist. Ever. All that happened was the megalomania amongst children. And that's what [writer/director of the 2020 film CHILDREN OF THE CORN] Kurt Wimmer responded to the most. Not Stephen King's idea of He Who Walks Behind the Rows, but the idea of megalomania. Remember what Lee Iacocca said? "In life, you lead, follow, or get out of the way."

Reset

In 2011, Dimension Films attempted to reboot the CHILDREN OF THE CORN franchise with a new film subtitled GENESIS. The reboot was written and directed by Joel Soisson, a veteran low-budget filmmaker who had previously written and directed several direct-to-video titles for the Weinsteins—including THE PROPHECY: UPRISING (2005), THE PROPHECY: FORSAKEN (2005), PULSE 2: AFTERLIFE (2008), and PULSE 3 (2008). Soisson had also written and produced some later sequels in Dimension's HELLRAISER and DRACULA 2000 series, so he brought plenty of low-budget filmmaking experience to the CHILDREN franchise—although he probably didn't have any particular interest in the series.

In a 2002 interview, Soisson described his filmmaking goals as follows: "I'm locked into making low budget movies that are not meant to be permanent. They are not meant to be revisited in ten years. They are not meant to be paragons of art or social commentary. They are just meant to entertain somebody for 90 minutes and then they go on about their day." In the same interview, he quoted screenwriter William Goldman as saying that "sequels are whores' movies," and conceded, "I don't think any producer in history has done as many sequels as I have" (Ford 2002). To clarify, Goldman maintained that sequels are never of "similar quality" to the original film because the "pulse" for a sequel is always financial, never creative (Goldman 2000). This seems like a fair assessment of Dimension's pulse for horror movie sequels.

Around the same time CHILDREN OF THE CORN was being rebooted, the Weinsteins also produced and distributed a ninth film in the HELLRAISER franchise (subtitled REVELATIONS). Actor Doug Bradley, the long-time star of that series, declined to participate in the new film and publicly speculated that the producers were rushing a cheap, shoddy sequel into production in order to retain their franchise rights. In a 2017 interview, he said, "The key to this [theory] is that Dimension bought into the HELLRAISER franchise at exactly the same time they bought into the CHILDREN OF THE CORN franchise. [...] Exactly the same time REVELATIONS was being made, a CHILDREN OF THE CORN was made." A few years later: "At exactly the same time HELLRAISER: JUDGMENT was being made they were making another CHILDREN OF THE CORN movie" (Paul 2017).

CHILDREN OF THE CORN: GENESIS (2011) revolves around a young couple who foolishly wander off the main road in California's Mojave Desert and encounter an old hermit, a Russian mail-order bride, and a feral child locked up in a barn. It turns out the old hermit is a former resident of Gatlin who believes that his child is cursed by the "evil" that destroyed that town. At the very least, the child demonstrates wide-ranging psychic and psychokinetic powers, which prompt the travelers to speculate endlessly about what's real and what's not. At a loss for concrete answers, one of them concludes, "We can sit here and run through every pop culture explanation you want, but that is not gonna help us." Once the possibility of concrete answers has been thrown out the window, the narrative builds to a relatively elaborate action sequence and the final revelation that a new generation of cursed children is being bred in the desert.

In 2016, Joel Soisson wrote the script for another sequel, CHILDREN OF THE CORN: RUNAWAY, to be directed by John Gulager. That story revolves around the character Ruth, Malachai's pregnant partner in Stephen King's short story. According to RUNAWAY—which echoes the ending of the 2009 remake of CHILDREN OF THE CORN—Ruth burned the cornfield to save her unborn child, then fled the town of Gatlin. Thirteen years later, she and her son become stranded in the town of Luther, Oklahoma, where Ruth has guilty flashbacks to the Gatlin massacre and ominous encounters with a savage local girl. The central question for the viewer is whether Ruth is a savvy heroine—Linda Hamilton in TERMINATOR 2—or a delusional psychopath. Taken together, Soisson's CHILDREN OF THE CORN films seem like an attempt to reboot the franchise as a series of loosely connected tales about haunted ex-Gatliners.

By the time RUNAWAY escaped, however, the legal rights to the CHILDREN OF THE CORN franchise appeared to be in limbo. Following a series of high-profile allegations against Harvey Weinstein, The Weinstein Company declared bankruptcy in July 2018 and Lantern Entertainment acquired the company's assets, which ostensibly included the CHILDREN OF THE CORN franchise. Prior to that, producer Donald Borchers had sued the Weinsteins, maintaining that he—rather than Dimension—held the sequel and "spinoff" rights for the series. Borchers requested a judicial ruling that would free him to make his own spinoff movie. Although he dropped the lawsuit in 2018, he eventually moved forward with the spinoff.

On April 3, 2020, *Daily Mail Australia* reported that a new CHILDREN OF THE CORN movie was being shot on the outskirts of Sydney, in spite of government-mandated laws about social distancing related to the coronavirus pandemic. Production continued and the film wrapped in either May or June, at which point *Deadline* reported that the "reboot" had been written and directed by Kurt Wimmer and that it revolved around "the events leading up to the infamous massacre of the adults of a small town in Nebraska by their children" (Grater 2020). In late October, the prequel/reboot premiered without much fanfare at a pair of theaters in Sarasota, Florida.

Like the Weinsteins before him, producer Donald Borchers seems to have been chasing a deadline to secure his legal right to "spinoff" Stephen King's story. In 2016, King initiated attempts to reclaim all of his rights related to the "Children of the Corn" short story, using Section 203 of the U.S. Copyright Code. According to the official website of the U.S. Copyright Office, Section 203 permits authors to "terminate grants of copyright assignments and licenses that were made on or after January 1, 1978, when certain conditions have been met." One condition is the passage of 35 years since the execution of the grant. King delivered notices of termination to 21st Century-Fox in 2016, to Dimension Films / The Weinstein Company in 2017, to the Walt Disney companies in 2018, and to Donald P. Borchers in 2018. The termination date on King's notice to Borchers was October 31, 2020—a few days after the new CHILDREN OF THE CORN premiered.

As of Halloween 2020, it would seem that the U.S. adaptation rights for "Children of the Corn" have reverted back to the author. If so, one wonders what he will do with them. Will he try to redeem the franchise or will he give the children of Gatlin a long-deserved rest?

PART FOUR

From CAT'S EYE
to SOMETIMES THEY COME BACK

Development Hell (Oral History)

MILTON SUBOTSKY: Edward and Valerie Abraham and I worked out a very nice script called FRIGHT NIGHT, based on three stories: "Sometimes They Come Back," "Quitters Inc." and "The Ledge." [...] I couldn't get it financed and then I had a call from Dino De Laurentiis. He wanted to buy these three stories and take an option on the others. (Brosnan 1988)

MARTHA DE LAURENTIIS: Stephen actually recommended to Dino some stories from the book *Night Shift* that he had sold to Milton Subotsky. (Blake Harris 2015)

STEPHEN KING: I wanted to see some of those things made and I thought that if Subotsky made them it would actually be worse than if they were never made at all. I don't like to root for my things not to be made, *but!* (Hewitt: "CAT'S" 1985)

In July 1984, Screen International magazine reported that Milton Subotsky had sold the NIGHT SHIFT / FRIGHT NIGHT script to producer Dino De Laurentiis, who reportedly agreed to use it as the basis for an upcoming film and to consult Subotsky on the production. In the end, Subotsky said he had nothing to do with the development of the resulting project, CAT'S EYE.

LEWIS TEAGUE: Dino said, "Lewis, we make another movie! I want to make a movie with you, Stephen King, and Drew Barrymore! What do you think we do?" He went out and bought a collection of Stephen King stories, something like *Night Shift*. So CAT'S EYE used two short stories from *Night Shift*, and Stephen King wrote a new original short story ["The General"], and we tied it all together with this silly device of the cat trying to return home to save Drew Barrymore from the troll. (Muir: *1980s* 2007)

STEPHEN KING: Dino was very taken with the concept of the little girl and the cat, and he thought that the cat would make a wonderful device to bind the three stories together. He said, "Stephen, can you put the cat in all three stories?" (Conner 1987)

STEPHEN KING: I had a story in mind [...] about a little boy whose cat is falsely accused of trying to kill him by stealing his breath. I switched the sex [...] and turned the story into a little film script. (King: "Foreword [*Silver Bullet*]" 1985)

LEWIS TEAGUE: I think the script overcame any perceived difficulty with the format. [...] In TWILIGHT ZONE [THE MOVIE, 1983], for instance, there were four completely different stories, written by different writers, directed by different directors. Each story was dissimilar in style and content [...] But in CAT'S EYE, there was only a qualitative difference; they took place in the same time period, the same "universe." They're written by the same man, directed by one director with a similarity of tone and style for each segment. (Horsting: "CUJO" 1983)

LEWIS TEAGUE: The last two pictures I had done—FIGHTING BACK [1982] and CUJO [1983]— were more on the gruesome side— serious, grim, suspenseful. They really weren't what I enjoy doing as much as my other movies, ALLI-GATOR [1980] and LADY IN RED [1979], which were more light-hearted and exciting. The script for CAT'S EYE is vastly different from ALLIGATOR but it has a lot of the same wry sense of humor in it, while being suspenseful as well. (Everitt: "To Direct" 1985)

CAT'S EYE (May 14, 1984, screenplay)

The May 14, 1984, draft of Stephen King's script opens on a Little Girl lying lifeless in her bed and a cat meowing at a mysterious bell sound in the bedroom. After being

Actress Drew Barrymore cuddles her heroic co-star in CAT'S EYE (MGM/UA, 1985).

chased out of the house by the girl's cat-hating, Uzi-wielding (!) mother, the cat becomes the focus of the film as it follows visions of the girl through a series of loosely connected vignettes. Early close encounters with an angry St. Bernard, a red 1958 Plymouth, and a ten-wheel truck ground the story in Stephen King's fictional universe. The cat eventually ends up in Atlantic City, where it sees the Little Girl on a TV screen in a store window. The ghost girl urges the clever feline to "find" something but at this point the four-legged hero's mission is unclear. Like Odysseus on a circuitous return to Ithaca, the cat takes the long way home and gets waylaid by a series of misadventures.

The first of the three CAT'S EYE vignettes is based on King's *Night Shift* short story "The Ledge," a darkly humorous tale set in a seedy criminal underworld. The author advertises his literary influences in the script by naming a casino building "Westlake Towers." Donald E. Westlake wrote a series of hardboiled crime novels under the moniker Richard Stark, and King has also paid tribute to Westlake's alter ego by adopting the name Richard as the first half of his own pseudonym, Richard Bachman, and giving the name Stark to the villain in his 1989 novel *The Dark Half.* In the CAT'S EYE script, King's sadistic villain Cressner also uses the phrase "the girl, the gold watch, and every-thing"—the title of a sci-fi novel by John D. MacDonald. It is easy to imagine that when King adapted "The Ledge," he was thinking of MacDonald's contributions to the TV series THRILLER or perhaps THE ALFRED HITCHCOCK HOUR. CAT'S EYE is similar in tone.

In the short story "The Ledge," Cressner—an "Organization overlord" and "A-number-one, 500-carat, dyed-in-the-wool son of a bitch"—ensnares a middle-aged tennis bum named Norris, who is having an affair with Cressner's wife Marcia. In the first scene, Cressner holds Norris at gunpoint in a swanky penthouse apartment while one of his goons plants a package of heroin in the hapless lover boy's car. Then Cressner treats his victim like a caged animal, challenging Norris to walk a narrow ledge around the 43-floor building in order to earn his freedom. Norris endures cold air, cruel crosswinds, and a sadistic pigeon as he methodically navigates the challenge.

King's first-person narrative conveys Norris's initial determination and increasing desperation. Once he returns to the (relative) safety of Cressner's penthouse apartment, Cressner tells him that his lover Marcia is dead and the narrative takes another emotional turn. Norris disarms Cressner's gun-wielding goon Tony (a character that King compares to square-jawed actor Rondo Hatton), then sadistically forces Cressner himself to walk the ledge. In the final passage, Norris sits alone inside Cressner's apartment, listening eagerly for the sound of his tormentor's scream.

King's adaptation of "The Ledge" starts earlier and sets up the two main characters while also "opening up" the setting of the story. From outside the casino building, Cressner observes the film's hero cat trying to cross a busy street and coldly bets on whether or not he'll make it. The scene establishes Cressner's immorality and foreshadows his equally cold treatment of Norris, who is already on the run from Cressner's goons. Marcia, the cheating wife, is only a name in the short story but she makes a brief appearance in a new scene in Norris's car. In spite of their precarious situation, the couple takes time to canoodle and the scene establishes Norris as a decent, caring guy. Soon after Marcia gets out of the car, Norris gets nabbed by Cressner's goons and ushered at gunpoint to the penthouse apartment, where the rest of the story takes place. In the apartment, Norris is bolder and more physically aggressive than the character in the short story, but his theatrics do him no good. While the hero cat looks on, Norris accepts Cressner's bet and steps out onto the ledge.

Unable to move the screen story forward by focusing on Norris's private thoughts, King embellishes the visual and aural details of Cressner and Norris's cat-and-mouse game. At one point, Cressner breaks Norris's concentration by honking a comically-loud air horn at him. Later, he sprays Norris with a fire hose. The sadistic pigeon in King's story has no new action but King has some fun with the smallest cast member, referring to him in the script as "Yasser Arafat" and "Dracula." Through some equally snappy dialogue, King amplifies the humor of the tale while maintaining suspense through a careful sequencing of shots. Scripted scenes are numbered according to specified changes in camera perspective, indicating that King was very focused on the change of medium. As in the short story, repeated shots of a nearby bank clock serves as a constant reminder of the passage of time—vaguely suggesting a countdown to death.

King also adds a few gruesome details to the story's conclusion. When Norris confronts Cressner, he kicks his "reward" for surviving the challenge—ostensibly, a bag of cash—and watches as his lover's decapitated head rolls across the floor. In that shocking moment, the hero cat trips Cressner's goon and allows Norris to subdue the murderous husband. The cat flees the building and Norris gets his revenge—but this time, the storyteller doesn't leave us waiting for Cressner's scream. The pigeon returns for an encore performance and Cressner's fall is punctuated by the sound of a cartoonishly-loud air horn. In King's script, the hero cat gets spattered with blood as it runs toward the second vignette.

In a brief interlude between stories, the author/screenwriter repeats the gag of referencing his own fiction; the cat passes through the "Jersey Pine Barrens" (an allusion to *IT*) and the Lincoln Tunnel (an allusion to *The Stand*) on his way to Manhattan, where he sees Drew Barrymore's face on a department store mannequin. The mannequin urges the cat to return to Westport, Connecticut, to "help" the Little Girl fight "it." Before the cat has a chance to redirect, however, a stranger scoops him up and throws him into a station wagon, delivering the tenacious kitty to his next shocking ordeal.

The second vignette is based on the *Night Shift* story "Quitters, Inc.," which opens with a chance encounter in New York's Kennedy Airport between chain smoker Dicky Morrison and reformed smoker Jimmy McCann. McCann tells Morrison about a mysterious outfit that helped him quit—but he doesn't offer any details, just a card with the address for Quitters Incorporated. A month later, Morrison pays a visit to the office. Initially, he is pessimistic—even downright snarky—about the prospect of a miracle cure, but his no-nonsense sponsor Vic Donatti demands a serious effort. Donatti shows Morrison a torture chamber where he administers volts of electricity to an innocent rabbit. If Morrison doesn't quit smoking, the new sponsor promises, he will do the same thing to Morrison's wife and young son. After that, Morrison has trouble sleeping; he imagines one of Donatti's men is hiding in the bedroom closet, waiting for him to fall off the wagon. The scene reads a bit like a humorous riff on King's story "The Boogeyman."

Next, the short story breezes through a literary montage of "scenes from the life of Richard Morrison, October to November," in which the author articulates the perverse theme of his story: *unemotional pragmatism is the only way to cure an addict.* The sequence ends when Morrison stumbles upon a forgotten pack of cigarettes in the glovebox of his car and succumbs to temptation. When he arrives home, his wife is missing and Vic Donatti calls to schedule an appointment for "aversion therapy." At Quitters, Inc., Morrison watches in horror as Donatti electrocutes his wife. Afterward, Morrison tells her why—and is stunned when she responds with compassion and gratitude. In the long run, "aversion therapy" cures him but Donatti adds one more condition to their deal: If Morrison gains too much weight as a result of quitting, his wife will lose a finger.

The final scene in "Quitters, Inc." seems to take some inspiration from a 1960 episode of ALFRED HITCHCOCK PRESENTS titled "Man from the South." Based on a story by Roald Dahl, it revolves around a contest between a compulsive gambler and a man whose faith in his cigarette lighter is so great that he is willing to gamble his own fingers as collateral. Everything is going well until a woman interrupts the game and the gambler notices that she is missing three fingers. King's story ends on a similarly grim note. In the final scene, Morrison crosses paths again with his old buddy Jimmy McCann, and notices that McCann's wife is missing a finger.

King's CAT'S EYE script makes a series of minor adjustments to the story: in the first scene, McCann leads Morrison to the front doorstep of Quitters, Inc., then leaves nervously; Morrison has a daughter instead of a son; Donatti zaps a cat (the film's hero cat) instead of a rabbit, and later proposes a much stricter aversion therapy program. (Third strike is someone rapes your wife!) Morrison also physically tries to confront the "boogeyman" in the closet. Although he doesn't find anyone, he discovers evidence the following morning that someone was definitely in there. King also adds a completely new scene in which Morrison visits his daughter (a Drew Barrymore lookalike) in a school for mentally-challenged children. This scene humanizes the character while also demonstrating to Donatti that Morrison can be manipulated through his family. Finally, King replaces the short story's literary montage with a cocktail party scene in which Morrison sees cigarettes everywhere. One party guest has cigarettes dangling—literally—from every visible orifice! The writer proposes that the scene should be set to the tune of The Police hit "Every Breath You Take." As in his adaptation of "The Ledge," King is obviously keen to play up the humor.

Unfortunately for Dicky Morrison, it's not all fun and games. He sneaks a smoke while stuck in traffic, and gets caught. Soon after, he is forced to watch his wife dance to the tune of "96 Tears" in Vic Donatti's "juice room." Like Norris in "The Ledge," Morrison puts up more of a fight in the script than he does in the short story, even slugging Donatti at one point. The hero cat joins the melee and manages to escape in the midst of the chaos. The remainder of the story unfolds the same way. Instead of hearing Morrison's confession to his wife, King chooses to focus on a conversation between Donatti and a goon named Junk. They place bets on whether Cindy will hug him or slug him. King caps off the story with the "Man of the South" ending and follows the hero cat to Westport, Connecticut, for the final segment.

"The General," an original screen story, resolves a conflict that was set up in the opening scene of CAT'S EYE—between the heroic housecat and a life-sucking troll that lives inside the Little Girl's bedroom wall. A family-friendly supernatural story—and not particularly humorous—it seems like an odd pairing with "The Ledge" and "Quitters, Inc." But King obviously liked it, as he eventually published the original screenplay in Richard Chizmar's 1997 book *Screamplays*.

One is left to wonder how CAT'S EYE might have ended if King hadn't contributed the new story. How would the story "Sometimes They Come Back" have played next to "The Ledge" and "Quitters, Inc." in the proposed FRIGHT NIGHT anthology? Like "The General," it would have represented a tonal shift into supernatural horror. Perhaps an alternative story would have fit the anthology better? King might have suggested "The Fifth Quarter," "The Cat from Hell," or "Man with a Belly"—uncollected stories published in *Cavalier* magazine in the 1970s—as replacements. If he had, CAT'S EYE would have become an anthology of darkly humorous stories that all involved small-time criminals (and cats). Instead, "The Cat from Hell" was adapted to the screen in TALES FROM THE DARKSIDE: THE MOVIE (1989) and "The Fifth Quarter" became an episode of the 2006 TV series NIGHTMARES & DREAMSCAPES. "Man with a Belly" remains uncollected and unadapted.

CAT'S EYE entered the world as a somewhat disjointed, off-brand Stephen King movie. It didn't help that the film was re-conceived during post-production. According to King, the head of MGM (the studio that distributed CAT'S EYE) eliminated the film's prologue, thereby eliminating the "cat hero" narrative as a linking device. In a 1985 interview, the author himself characterized the truncated film as "a maligned Disney picture," acknowledging that it was a tough sell to Disney fans and horror fans alike (Wiater: "Horror" 1985). He was perhaps thinking of recent "dark phase" Disney fare such as THE WATCHER IN THE WOODS (1980), SOMETHING WICKED THIS WAY COMES (1983), and RETURN TO OZ (1985). Reflecting more broadly on CREEPSHOW and CAT'S EYE, the author theorized that his limited success as a screenwriter might be related to inherent problems of the anthology film format. He would have plenty of upcoming opportunities to test his theory.

THE MACHINES / BEWARE THE GREEN GOD

Just as the moderate box office returns of CREEPSHOW undermined George Romero's attempts to turn *The Stand* into a feature film, the lukewarm response to CAT'S EYE seems to have thwarted Milton Subotsky's attempts to make his anthology film THE MACHINES. In a 1986 interview, the producer said he had tried and failed to convince MGM to finance his Stephen King project. At that point, Subotsky offered the rights to King's short stories "Trucks," "The Lawnmower Man," and "The Mangler" to producer Dino De Laurentiis. Ultimately, De Laurentiis purchased only "Trucks," which became the basis for King's directorial debut MAXIMUM OVERDRIVE (1986). King wrote the script himself, but Subotsky noted that MAXIMUM OVERDRIVE bore some resemblance to the script he had commissioned for THE MACHINES, explaining, "The trouble was that the original deal included them taking a look at my own Edward and Valerie Abraham script for THE MACHINES, and what ended up in MAXIMUM OVERDRIVE are ideas from the other two stories that they didn't option." To be fair to the author, Subotsky stipulated that he did not believe King ever read THE MACHINES (Alan Jones: "Subotsky" 1986).

For decades, THE MACHINES has languished in the late producer's private archives. In 2020, Milton Subotsky's son Sergei unearthed a draft featuring a title page that credits The Great Fantastic Picture Corporation as the production company, which suggests the script was printed sometime between 1981 and early 1984. This undated draft of THE MACHINES is set in a sleepy southwestern U.S. town—possibly Oakville, California. It begins with a scene in which a retired salesman named Castonmeyer observes his neighbor struggling to start a lawnmower. The neighbor is Harold Parkette, the main character in King's short story "The Lawnmower Man." The first fifteen pages of the 91-page, 107-scene script streamlines but closely follows the plot of that short story.

Harold goes inside his house and calls a lawn care service, then gets drunk and passes out. Sometime later, Mr. Castonmeyer witnesses the arrival of an unusual yard worker and Harold awakens to the sight of a morbidly obese, alarmingly eccentric lawnmower man. As in King's story, Harold goes along to get along with the strange man— until he wakes up from a second nap and sees the lawnmower man naked on all fours, eating grass trimmings and a dead cat. (In the short story, the dead animal is a mole.) Harold faints and wakes up a third time to some perplexing dialogue about the lawnmower man's "boss"—the Greek god Pan. Harold realizes that his insane visitor has cloven feet, so he quietly goes back inside to call the police. Before the cavalry can respond, however, the pagan gardener sics his "mechanical familiar" (the lawnmower) on Harold, who runs into the front yard. Mr. Castonmeyer witnesses his neighbor's gory demise.

It is hard to believe that Milton Subotsky, whose horror films were never very graphic, intended to produce this portion of the script as written. Then again, Stephen King adaptations were big business in the early 1980s and the author was a vocal critic of adaptations that strayed too far from his source material. As it happened, King himself had already written a faithful adaptation of "The Lawnmower Man" for the 1981 comic book *Marvel's Bizarre Adventures*. That adaptation hewed closely to the details of the short story while amplifying its darkly humorous tone. King dubbed the title character "Karras" and artist Walter Simonson visually depicted him as a towering blob. Exaggeration was the key element in that re-telling, which ended the same way as the source story—with a pair of police officers surveying the gruesome crime scene and one of them making a groan-worthy joke about a "Norse of a different color."

THE MACHINES adaptation dispenses with the final joke as well as the humorous tone. In the Subotsky-commissioned version of the tale, Harold is unable to cut his grass because his lawnmower is broken (rather than because he's a drunken lout). After the professional lawnmower man admonishes Harold for letting the yard go to seed, solemnly suggesting that he has failed in his sacred duty to nature, he repairs Harold's old lawnmower (instead of providing his own "mechanical familiar") and goes to work. When Harold witnesses the gardener's pagan ritual (not to mention his naked bum), he phones the police and complains to a Sergeant Hall—but gets cut off by the lawnmower man, who laughs maniacally as the machines claim their first victim. At this point, "The Lawnmower Man" adaptation transitions into a 38-page adaptation of "The Mangler."

King's short story "The Mangler" begins with Officer John Hunton's arrival at the Blue Ribbon Laundry, following the accidental death of an employee named Adelle Frawley. Hunton talks briefly to foreman George Stanner, who points the investigator toward the grisly remains of the victim—and the blood-soaked machine that tore her apart. Later, Hunton discusses the apparent accident with his friend Mark Jackson, a college lit professor who has some working knowledge of "the mangler" and its safety features. The two men conclude that the accident must have been caused by a malfunctioning safety bar on the machine. When Hunton meets with safety inspector Roger Martin, however, Martin assures him that the mangler is in perfect working order. He suggests an alternative theory: "It's a spook." The inspector recounts a tragedy that occurred in the nearby town of Milton; multiple animals and a small child were found dead in an abandoned icebox at the town dump. When a dump worker got too close, the icebox door inexplicably closed on his arm—like a spring-loaded trap. Hunton relates the story to Mark Jackson and, following a second unexplained accident at the Blue Ribbon Laundry, Jackson concludes that the mangler is indeed haunted.

Taking some inspiration from *The Golden Bough*, a classic study of primitive religion, Jackson theorizes that the machine is possessed by some kind of demonic spirit— *maybe the Greek god Pan?* The two friends investigate further and learn that "accidents" have been happening at the laundry ever since a young woman named Sherry Oulette cut her hand on the mangler and bled into the machine. Virgin's blood, Jackson explains, is a key ingredient in certain "hex formulas." After the mangler claims yet another victim (foreman George Stanner), Hunton and Jackson awkwardly confirm that Sherry is a virgin, then sneak into the laundry to exorcise the demonic spirit from the machine. There's only one problem—which Stephen King reveals to the reader in a wicked narrative aside; they misidentify the spirit and use the wrong ritual to dispel it. Instead of removing the ghost from the machine, the exorcism turns the device into a monstrous mutation of fire and steel. King describes the machine pulling itself out of the concrete "like a dinosaur trying to escape a tar pit" and escaping the building. Hunton runs to Roger Martin for help—but when he hears the sound of the demonically-possessed mangler running wild in the streets, he knows it's too late to stop what he has started.

In the Edward and Valerie Abrahams version of "The Mangler," we meet police chief John Hunton as he is responding to the mysterious death of Harold Parkette. Hunton talks to officer Chester Martins, then to Harold's neighbor who asserts that Harold's killer was a naked man with green skin. In a scene that is completely original to the script, Hunton and Chester consult a medical doctor who assures them that the witness is not delusional. Hunton then consults his friend Charlie Jackson (a professor of anthropology and comparative religion) about other possibilities. Jackson alludes not only to *The Golden Bough*, but to psychologist Carl Jung's writings about the collective unconscious, explaining to his friend that the "green man" is a recurring figure in ancient myths and fertility cults. This speech sets up the central idea that unites King's three source stories ("The Lawnmower Man," "The Mangler," and "Trucks") into the single narrative of THE MACHINES—the idea that a mysterious green god is responsible for turning machines against humanity.

For the time being, Hunton remains pragmatic and skeptical. He sends Harold Parkette's lawnmower to a police lab for forensic processing but the investigation yields no helpful results and the lawnmower simply gathers dust in an evidence storeroom … until the Green God telepathically summons it. The screenwriters describe an elaborate panning and tracking sequence which illustrates that the machine is receiving musical "vibrations" from somewhere outside the storeroom. In a subsequent sequence, the writers reveal that machines all over town are receiving the same vibrations—including a mammoth steam ironer at the local laundromat, affectionately known as "the mangler." Sometime after it has received its coded message from the green god, the mangler obediently mangles Adelle Frawley.

Hunton responds to the scene of that accident and talks to foreman George Stanner as well as safety inspector Taylor. Much of the dialogue in this section of the script is taken from King's short story, up until Hunton's exchange with Taylor is interrupted by a phone call. The caller summons Hunton to the scene of yet another mysterious death—a dog suffocated in an old refrigerator. Transforming the inspector's anecdote from the short story into a new scene gives Hunton a more active role to play; he drives to the local dump to check out the murderous refrigerator. Afterward, he ponders the incident with the lawnmower and begins to wonder if there might be some kind of connection. Around the same time, a vagrant takes refuge from a thunderstorm inside the haunted refrigerator—and is eaten alive.

Hunton returns to the laundromat and talks to an employee named Gillian, who remembers that a young co-worker named Consuela once cut her hand on the mangler. Hunton has a follow-up conversation with Stanner, who reveals that Adelle Frawley was taking cold pills when she died. The police chief notices that the pills include a drug called atropine … which will be important later. Elsewhere, a hapless dump attendant discovers the dead vagrant inside the refrigerator. When he attempts to remove the door, a haunted crane drops a car on him.

Hunton is baffled by yet another inexplicable death—but Jackson isn't. He presents his "hex formula" theory to Hunton and identifies atropine as the most dangerous ingredient in the most powerful hex. Unlike Stephen King, who presented this detail in an omniscient aside, the screenwriters allow the main character to connect the dots. That, in theory, gives Hunton a fighting chance against the mangler. Ever the rationalist, however, he orchestrates a routine safety inspection of the machine rather than an exorcism. A state examiner named Carter takes the mangler apart but finds nothing mechanically wrong with it. After he gives it a clean bill of health, the machine attacks George Stanner, tearing off the foreman's arm while Hunton tries in vain to shut it down. By making the protagonist a witness to this attack, the screenwriters motivate his future actions. The filmmaker's version of an omniscient aside reveals that Harold Parkette's lawnmower, still confined to the evidence store room, is humming in approval.

Carter shuts down the laundromat while Hunton and Jackson visit Consuela Lopez and verify that she is a virgin. Afterward, Jackson outlines his plan for an exorcism and the two men get on with it. As in the short story, the mangler taunts them at first, by operating itself independently and then shutting itself down. Jackson delivers a more elaborate rite of exorcism than in the short story, but the added verbiage doesn't help their cause. The mangler morphs in front of his eyes, then kills the amateur exorcist and escapes—like a dinosaur from a tar pit—as Hunton looks on helplessly. The police chief tries to escape in his car but quickly learns that relying on another machine won't help; the car refuses to start. The hulking steel dinosaur bursts through the brick wall of the laundromat and crushes Hunton's car, then the shell-shocked investigator runs off into the night.

At this point, THE MACHINES script runs amok for about ten pages that don't correspond to any specific passage in King's prose fiction. The gonzo sequence perhaps owes its greatest debt to the third act of Alfred Hitchcock's film THE BIRDS, in which we see a town torn apart by an unlikely army of attackers. In THE MACHINES, Harold Parkette's lawnmower escapes from the police store room and mows down several officers before being destroyed by Officer Chester. Chester leads the human resistance against the machines until a telephone launches itself into the side of his head, leaving him helplessly disoriented. Hunton arrives as machines literally explode from the building and the man vs. metal melee spills out into the streets. In homes throughout the town, dishwashers, electric carving knives, and cars turn violently against their owners. Hunton and Chester eventually make their way to the hospital, where the now-mad Mr. Castonmeyer reiterates that the "green man" is responsible for the revolt of the machines. Meanwhile, an anesthesia machine quietly kills Officer Chester. Others chase Hunton back outside, where he witnesses the massive explosion of a nearby gas station. Finally, a wrecking crane demolishes the local fire station, dashing any hopes of a large-scale rescue. One citizen fights back with a fire extinguisher—but the fire extinguisher explodes in his hands. A not-too-bright looter attempts to take advantage of the chaos and steal some electronics; his story doesn't end well either.

At the end of this grand action sequence, Hunton and a group of other survivors flee the town center. Hunton takes refuge in a motel parking lot, where he sees the lawnmower man / green god laughing maniacally as trucks run down the hotel's inhabitants. When Hunton makes eye contact with the master of disaster, the green man sics one of the trucks on the police chief, who runs into the woods and reemerges on the side of a freeway. There, he encounters a young couple, Linda and Jerry, who help him escape to a nearby truck stop and diner—setting up the third short story adaptation in THE MACHINES.

On the page, King's short story "Trucks" begins *in medias res*, with a motley group of characters trapped in a truck stop that has come under siege by self-driving trucks. In much the way that filmmaker George Romero reimagined Hitchcock's THE BIRDS with zombies, King reimagines NIGHT OF THE LIVING DEAD with trucks. At the outset of the author's short story, several characters have been driven mad already by the absurdity of the events they've witnessed. They are grasping desperately for an explanation: "Electrical storms in the atmosphere? Nuclear Testing? What?" One character suggests that the trucks are angry for the way they've been treated by humans. Although it's an outrageous premise, King treats it with the utmost seriousness in the short story, establishing a tone of apocalyptic dread. By the end of the tale, the first-person narrator has been enslaved by the trucks, forced to pump fuel into their tanks until he drops dead or is exterminated. Despondent, the narrator ruminates on the "stink that the dinosaurs must have died smelling as they went down into the tar pits." This reminder of a line in "The Mangler" might have been what prompted Milton Subotsky to tie the stories together in the first place.

The third and final act of THE MACHINES dramatizes much of the action from the short story "Trucks," beginning with the foolish behavior of a man named Snodgrass, who bolts from the diner and becomes roadkill, and ending with the main character (in the screen story: Hunton) enslaved by trucks. Although earlier scenes in THE MACHINES script established that *all* machines are capable of rebelling, the characters in this section inexplicably find themselves only in conflict with the trucks, which seem to have overpowered even the green god. In the end, Hunton observes that the earth now belongs to the machines—and that the green man has turned asphalt gray. The script ends on a final image of a long line of fuel-hungry trucks, viewed from high above the truck stop—an image that would eventually appear in MAXIMUM OVERDRIVE.

After Dino De Laurentiis purchased the rights to the short story "Trucks," THE MACHINES became an unproduceable script. Subotsky tried to salvage the project by eliminating the "Trucks" passage and adding a new ending. A revised draft, attributed to Edward and Valerie Abraham and assigned to Subotsky's revitalized Amicus Productions (sometime after 1984), is titled BEWARE THE GREEN GOD. Until page 64, the script is identical to THE MACHINES. After that, the story veers toward a hasty ending. After John Hunton gets rescued by a young couple (renamed Jane and Carl) in a Land Rover, he flees to another devastated town. There, the Land Rover revolts and tries to kill its occupants by driving them off a cliff. Hunton escapes for a final battle with the green / gray man in a burning wheat field. The titular villain utilizes a trio of off-road vehicles ("Reapers") to kill his nemesis and end the story on a decidedly grim note. For better or worse, the Green God never got his Hollywood close-up.

Development Hell (Oral History)

According to Stephen King, the first screenwriter to take a crack at adapting "Trucks" for Dino De Laurentiis was novelist John Farris. Neither King nor De Laurentiis liked Farris's treatment, so the producer asked King to write the script himself. Initially, the author refused.

STEPHEN KING: The thing with Dino is that he's almost telepathic. He knows when the ideas have started to sink in. (Horsting: "Stephen" 1986)

STEPHEN KING: I had had an idea that was to expand the story beyond trucks running by themselves, to everything running by itself; which is something that is inherent in the story anyway. (Farren 1986)

STEPHEN KING: I started thinking about—Jesus Christ—think about these kids getting run down by their own radio-controlled toys. Think about people getting electrocuted by hairdryers. Think about—oh, video games—and all this stuff… (Berrong 1986)

STEPHEN KING: I got this idea of doing a sort of mechanical BIRDS. […] Then I said, what would cause that? (Hewitt: "OVERDRIVE" 1986)

STEPHEN KING: You have to give people a reason […] so, I said it's a comet. Halley's Comet is coming around in 1985 and '86, so it's a comet. (Farren 1986)

STEPHEN KING: Dino […] asked me one more time to do the screenplay. I immediately said yes, because by then, I had a very clear picture of the plot and found myself wanting to go ahead with the adaptation. (Horsting: "Stephen" 1986)

STEPHEN KING: For me, writing movie scripts, particularly adaptations, always felt like overpacking a suitcase and then kinda like sitting on it to make it shut and make it latch. There's always that feeling of having to cram things in or get rid of things. (King: "Inside" 2021)

STEPHEN KING: It isn't an *anti*-creative act, but it isn't creative either. It's just trying to take out everything that you can from the original work in order to fit a mold. (Cadigan 1982)

STEPHEN KING: The problem [with turning the short story "Trucks" into a feature film property] was fleshing it out—that's a problem that I love to have. (Farren 1986)

STEPHEN KING: Giorgio [Postiglione, production designer for Dino De Laurentiis] said to me, "Stephen, you must direct this picture," and I said, "No, I couldn't do that." And he said, "But you must. For anyone else, Dino say, 'ees too much.' For you, anything." (Hewitt: "OVERDRIVE" 1986)

Stephen King promises to "scare the hell out of you" in a teaser trailer for MAXIMUM OVERDRIVE (DEG, 1986).

STEPHEN KING: When CREEPSHOW happened, my wife Tabitha understood that I was not simply there to see that no one mutilated my baby. I was there largely to study under Romero; she knew that I wanted to direct. I was gone for the whole summer, and she said, "This is kind of hard on the family" [...] Now the kids are older; I think it was last winter [1984–1985] sometime she said, "If you want it, go for it." (R.H. Martin 1985)

MARTHA DE LAURENTIIS: Stephen later said to Dino, "I want to direct." And Dino said to Stephen, "Why not? You should." (Blake Harris 2015)

STEPHEN KING: I think that it would be fun to direct a horror film, and I'd feel that sense of narration that I don't get when I'm writing a film script, because I feel now like I'm doing a blueprint instead of a picture. (Wiater: "Horror" 1985)

STEPHEN KING: In the case of MAXIMUM OVERDRIVE, what I'm doing is seeing whether or not I can take whatever it is that makes people like the books, and buy the books in big numbers, over into the film and see if people will really like it. (Herndon 1985)

STEPHEN KING: A lot of people have directed Stephen King novels and stories. And I finally decided if you want something done right, you ought to do it yourself. (1986 teaser trailer for MAXIMUM OVERDRIVE)

TRUCKS / OVERDRIVE / MAXIMUM OVERDRIVE

Three different drafts of Stephen King's adaptation of "Trucks" circulate among King fans and collectors. The first, titled TRUCKS, is dated February 8, 1985; it runs 100 pages and includes 545 numbered shots. The second, titled OVERDRIVE, is dated May 22, 1985; it runs 96 pages and includes 529 shots. The third draft, MAXIMUM OVERDRIVE, is dated May 29, 1985, and includes minor revision notes (mostly related to the removal of brand names such as Toys R Us and Pepsi) dated 6/27; the page and scene count is the same as the previous draft. The film went into production on July 14, 1985.

The first script appears to have been written—at least partially—before King took on the role of the film's director, as it includes a line deferring to the director's expertise on how to stage a particular action sequence. A similar line appears in King's original script for CREEPSHOW, indicating that the writer did not (yet) perceive himself as a potential director. As he said in contemporary interviews, however, the author was interested in directing one day, so he intently observed director George Romero's creative process. On CREEPSHOW, he remembered that Romero translated the script into a "writing person's storyboard," visualizing the original script's scenes in methodical detail: "It would say in my original screenplay 'The thing in the crate gets the janitor—the director will know how to shoot this.' [...] And so George had broken this thing down." The shot breakdown, King reflected, is "the essence of what the director does to create suspense" (Crawley: "King/George" 1983). It was a vital trick of the trade that he needed to learn.

King also studied—from a more distant vantage point—Alfred Hitchcock's creative process. The Master of Suspense famously said that, for him, shooting a film was anti-climactic because by the time he was on set he'd already pre-visualized the entire movie in storyboards. King explained that he followed Hitchcock's lead on MAXIMUM OVERDRIVE by planning "shot-for-shot, literally angle-for-angle, everything I wanted in the movie" (Gary Wood: "To Direct" 1991). He then asked Dino De Laurentiis how many camera setups were typical for an action movie and the producer reportedly told him "anywhere from eight hundred to a thousand" (Wiater: "Stephen" 1986). With this number in mind, the writer-turned-director filled a production binder with 1,175 "shot cards" so he could make his movie the Hitchcock way: no surprises.

The first draft (2/8/85) of TRUCKS has half as many shots because the writer's emphasis is on scenes rather than shots. The big challenge, at that point, was expanding the source story and fitting it into the traditional three-act mold of a Hollywood feature film. In his assessment of King's screenplay, author Rocky Wood opines that MAXI-MUM OVERDRIVE is actually *not* an adaptation of "Trucks," because "the stories have no real connection other than the base idea of trucks becoming sentient and attacking humans" (Rocky Wood 2010). This is an overstatement. All three drafts of King's screen-play are structured similarly, expanding the screen story into three distinct acts. In the first (and longest) act, machines become sentient and the main characters in the story become barricaded inside the Dixie Boy truck stop in Wilmington, North Carolina. In the second act, the characters fight the machines and plan their escape to nearby Haven Island. This section replicates the action in the short story (which was set in Haven, Maine). In the third and shortest act, the surviving characters escape the truck stop and wage one final battle with the machines on Haven Island.

King has said he does not enjoy the process of adapting his novels to the screen because it inevitably means trimming the source story. He prefers expanding shorter stories (CHILDREN OF THE CORN, CREEPSHOW, CAT'S EYE) or creating origi-nal screen stories (SLEEPWALKERS, GOLDEN YEARS, STORM OF THE CENTURY, ROSE RED, KINGDOM HOSPITAL). After writing unused screenplays for THE SHIN-ING, THE DEAD ZONE, and CUJO, King hesitantly agreed to adapt SILVER BULLET. In a foreword to the published screenplay for that film, he explained that he had con-ceded only because he saw an opportunity to repair a broken source story. The source story, *Cycle of the Werewolf*, was conceived as a calendar project with twelve interrelated vignettes accompanied by original illustrations. King found that he hated the limita-tions of the proposed form and he struggled to write the short-short stories—until he discovered the character of Marty Coslaw, a wheelchair-bound kid who encounters the beastly terror of Tarker's Mills over the 4th of July holiday. After that, King says, "I could see ahead of what I was writing to all the things I *would* write, and I could see backward to all the things I would fix up" (King: "Foreword [*Silver Bullet*]" 1985).

When he was asked to adapt *Cycle of the Werewolf* to the screen, he had a similar eureka moment. While watching the 1962 film adaptation of Harper Lee's novel *To Kill a Mockingbird*, he became enchanted by the film's voiceover narration. Afterward, he decided to apply "that elegiac, retrospective, and rather gentle form of narration" to his own story (King: "Foreword [*Silver Bullet*]" 1985). No such narrative voice had existed in *Cycle of the Werewolf*, so King invented one and SILVER BULLET became Marty Coslaw's story as told by his sister Jane. King says it was the act of recreating the story that appealed to him and that the screen story did "what should have been done with it to begin with, which is to take this character, the little boy in the wheelchair and to use him as the unifying character to turn it into, well, in this case a movie, what would have been a novel if it had ever been fleshed out" (Hewitt: "Stephen" 1986). "Trucks" has a similar relationship to MAXIMUM OVERDRIVE; the script re-develops the story around a central character and also changes the tone of the tale.

In all three drafts of the script, the opening sequence introduces the threat.

Onscreen text explains that Earth is passing into the tail of a rogue comet named Rhea-M and the following scenes illustrate the results. The Cape Fear River drawbridge in Wilmington opens itself, a bank clock broadcasts obscenities, and an ATM machine spits cash at a customer. King may have taken some inspiration from his unfinished 1978 screenplay about a haunted radio station which the author has outlined as follows: "One of the deejays commits suicide, and after that the machine starts to take over. It's saying things like, 'And now the latest from, and *blah, blah, blah*, and fuck you, you're going to die; I'm going to kill you'" (Chute 1979). The bank clock in TRUCKS doesn't go quite that far … but the ATM machine in the final film musters the nerve to call Stephen King an asshole. The director's goal, it seems, was to not take himself (or his writing) too seriously.

The main story begins at the Dixie Boy truck stop where radios, video games, and electric knives are on the fritz. The sequence introduces several characters, giving them names and backstories that don't exist in the source story. King may have intended for the lack of proper names in the short story to convey a sense of dehumanization, but he does not go for that effect in the screenplay. Instead, he combines the short story's first-person male narrator with an unnamed short-order cook to produce the film's hero, a relatable everyman named Bill Robertson. King replaces other unnamed characters in the short story with a high-strung waitress named Wanda June, a skeevy employer named Hendershot, and a gas pump jockey named Duncan Keller—who becomes the first victim of the machines.

In promotional interviews for the film, King described Duncan's first scene as a nod to Hitchcock. The Master of Suspense famously explained his method for building suspense with an allusion to a scene in the 1936 film SABOTAGE, in which a young boy is delivering a bomb wrapped in packing paper. Hitchcock made sure his audience knew what was inside the package, even though the boy did not. As the bomb ticked toward explosion, the audience had to wait anxiously while the boy remained blissfully unaware of the increasing danger. In King's film, the audience knows—because of the opening sequence—that machines are going rogue, attacking their creators. Duncan Keller does not. King explains, "We have a guy [Duncan] outside pumping gas, and all of a sudden the pumps stop. He cuts off the automatic device and looks at it, then digs around with his finger, trying to get the dirt out of the line. Then he looks into the nozzle. We all know *what's* going to happen—he's going to get sprayed with gasoline—but we don't know when" (Blue 1986). In the script, Duncan gets doused right away. In the final film, the director pauses for effect. Afterward, all hell breaks loose in the Dixie Boy diner—the electric carving knife attacks Wanda June and a spastic arcade game (Atari's *Space Invaders*) electrocutes a patron with a burst of alien blue flame.

At this point in the TRUCKS script, King cuts away to a suburban backyard, where a drunken lout is watching a baseball game on a handheld TV… and unknowingly being stalked by his lawnmower, which is also spurting blue flame. King's stock character faces the same fate as Harold Parkette in "The Lawnmower Man," which might explain why this scene was cut from subsequent drafts of the script. (At the time, Milton Subotsky still owned the adaptation rights for "The Lawnmower Man.")

The script then transitions to a shot of a dark blue Plymouth Fury rolling down a two-lane highway. King's Constant Readers might assume it's Christine (the haunted car in his novel of the same name), but in fact this Fury is a docile one. In a promotional interview for the film, King explained that when he reconceived "Trucks" as a story about the revolt of *all* machines, he decided to cast the cars as "friendlies" (Strauss 1986). As a result, the blue Fury safely delivers two new characters—a crass salesman named Camp Loman and an attractive female hitchhiker named Brett Brooks—to the Dixie Boy, where a gas pump jockey named Joe is refueling a sinister-looking eighteen-wheel tractor trailer with a Toys "R" Us logo on the side. The script indicates that the truck is watching the humans through a ghostly green filter. A moment later, it charges Camp and Brett, who narrowly escape into the diner.

Back on the highway, a couple of young newlyweds—the script names them Curt and Connie—flee from a driver-less truck. In the short story and in subsequent drafts of the script, the couple drives a Plymouth Fury, but in this draft they drive an Aries K, another "friendly." When they make their way into the Dixie Boy diner, they complete the roster of characters trapped there, attracting a horde of driver-less trucks to the parking lot.

The next sequence—one that did not make it into subsequent drafts of the script or the final film—revolves around the possibility of a Lee Marvin cameo. The sequence takes place on a movie set overseen by MAXIMUM OVERDRIVE producers Dino De Laurentiis and Martha Schumacher, as well as an unnamed but comically exasperated director. The movie in production is a remake of the 1962 western THE MAN WHO SHOT LIBERTY VALANCE. The set goes haywire when a renegade Pepsi machine starts shooting cans at the cast and crew, killing several of them. Only a child actor named Deke Jacobs manages to escape, but he's chased by Martha Schumacher's golf cart.

One can only speculate about why this film-within-a-film sequence was nixed from MAXIMUM OVERDRIVE, but the screenwriter repurposed the soda machine attack in his subsequent draft. In OVERDRIVE, the scene takes place on a baseball field where coaches and their kids, including Deke, come under fire. Instead of ending with a golf cart chase, the baseball sequence ends with a chase involving a runaway steamroller.

The TRUCKS draft includes one more extraneous set piece, this one taking place at a regional airport where a pilot's private plane decapitates him. Perhaps King was trying to invent scenarios that could utilize resources available to his producer; in his foreword to the published screenplay for SILVER BULLET, the author remembers that Dino De Laurentiis owned a private Learjet. Whatever the case, the airport scene disappeared from the next draft and the story picks up with Deke as he rides his bike down the same suburban street where we saw the shitfaced homeowner get killed by his lawnmower. Deke hides from a blood-spattered ice cream truck, then gets chased away by the blood-spattered lawnmower.

Meanwhile, runaway trucks claim two more victims at the Dixie Boy diner. Duncan's near-blindness makes him an easy target and Camp Loman gets knocked into a drainage ditch. (In the short story, the drainage ditch victim was a man named Snodgrass.) Soon after, all of the trucks fall in line behind a designated leader: the Toys "R" Us semi. The machines literally circle their wagons around the Dixie Boy to prevent the arrival of Curt and Connie but the newlyweds find a way through. Deke also finds a way in, by crawling through an underground drainage pipe. When he arrives in the cellar of the Dixie Boy, the heroes learn that Hendershot has a stash of illegal weapons down there.

In the next scene, Bill and Brett have a post-coital (!) conversation about their surreal predicament. Bill theorizes that the machines have been brought to life by the

Rhea-M comet and he concludes that all they have to do is wait until Earth moves out of the comet's tail in seven days. His simple plan gets dashed when the power goes out.

Up to this point, Stephen King's screenplay has been more of a prequel to "Trucks" than an adaptation of the short story. Going forward, however, the screen story replicates some of the main action of the source story. In "Trucks," the Dixie Boy survivors hear Snodgrass calling for help from the drainage ditch, but they don't help because Bill is convinced it's a suicide mission. In TRUCKS, the more heroic Bill leads a rescue mission, but finds the man (Camp Loman) dead in the ditch. He and Curtis barely make it back to the Dixie Boy; they are saved by Hendershot, who fires a bazooka at one of their pursuers. Hours later, the machines retaliate by enlisting the help of an Army truck equipped with a machine gun, plus a bulldozer that starts ramming the building. Hendershot wages war against the machines but is quickly gunned down. Wanda Jane freaks out, shouting "*We made you!*," before she too is gunned down. This section of the story ends in a ceasefire as Deke realizes that the trucks are trying to communicate via Morse code. The message is simple: *Feed us or die.* Bill starts pumping gas.

King's original short story ends here on an ambiguous note, posing the question of whether or not humans are fated to become enslaved by the machines they created. The screen story continues. Bill speculates that the revolt of the machines is only the beginning of the end—a house-cleaning exercise to prepare the way for a full-scale alien colonization of the planet Earth. He further speculates that their only chance of survival is to escape from the Dixie Boy, so the remaining characters raid the weapons cache and make a break for it. Amidst a volley of flying grenades, they dodge the wrath of the circling trucks and abscond to a Wilmington marina. Bill's plan is to sail to the nearby island of Haven, where all the electricity can be shut off with one swift action—by bombing the local power plant.

In the marina, the group does battle with a chain hoist, some not-so-friendly cars (storytelling logic be damned) and a Coast Guard boat equipped with a machine gun. Two minor characters get killed, but not before firing Hendershot's bazooka one last time. At this point, King's screenplay highlights an image of Bill, Brett, and Deke, which seems to suggest that they are well on their way to becoming a reconstituted family.

Once the larger group arrives on Haven Island, they settle into an idyllic beach house. Bill and Brett go for a walk on the beach and contemplate their uncertain future. In the same moment, Stephen King springs one last scare—a "CARRIE ending"?—on the lovers. A mercenary dune buggy attacks them, but the trusty bazooka saves them again. This beat was eliminated from the subsequent draft of the script, but both scripts end on a quieter scene in which the new step-parents vow to keep fighting the machines in hopes of building a better future for their adopted son.

Stephen King's second draft, OVERDRIVE, is a slightly shorter version of TRUCKS with added emphasis on the three lead characters. According to author Simon Brown, King had handwritten the following message on the first page of TRUCKS: "Basic philosophy. It's about trucks going bazonka, not people and their problems" (Brown: *Screening* 2018). The author-turned-filmmaker apparently changed his tune after receiving some conflicting advice on the first draft from his producers. In a 1986 interview, he said, "One of the few really sensible things that anybody said at the story conference [was] that if the characters don't stand out and this is just a movie about machines, it'll be a bad picture. Their solution was to suggest that a lot of dialogue and scenes between the major characters be added for character and texture" (Horsting: *Stephen* 1986).

In OVERDRIVE, King added a few short scenes and some playful dialogue to amplify the romance between Bill and Brett. He also added new dialogue to flesh out their backstories; Brett reveals that she escaped a bad relationship in Texas with the help of a razorblade, and Hendershot reveals that Bill served time in prison for an inept 7–11 robbery. The new draft also reveals that the late Duncan Loman was Deke's biological father, giving Bill a more personal reason to protect the boy. When Hendershot tells Deke that his father was killed by the trucks, Brett displays her protective instincts by punching Hendershot in the face. Later, in the confrontation with the Coast Guard boat, Bill literally throws himself on top of Brett to shield her from machine gun fire. Taken together, these additions amplify the "new family" dynamic, which now serves as the emotional core of the story.

In the end, however, the added character beats didn't make it to the silver screen; they were shot but edited out of the movie. King explains, "You could only take so much of these people looking soulfully into each other's eyes and discussing their past history, how they happened to be on the road while all the machines in the world are going crazy around them, before you start looking for Leslie Nielsen to walk in out of AIRPLANE." The director decided he did not want to graft "a soap opera onto what's basically a trash 'em and bash 'em" (Gary Wood: "Stephen" 1991).

King ultimately decided that the best way to capture the spirit of his short story— and the *Stephen King-ness* of his work in general—was to craft MAXIMUM OVER-DRIVE the way he'd always crafted his books. *Not* by methodically planning out the details, but by plowing ahead with his foot on the gas, taking risks, and making discoveries. In the end, it seems he scrapped his goal of emulating Hitchcock and went instead for the bronze. As he explained in his book *Danse Macabre*, "I recognize terror as the finest emotion and so I will try to terrorize the reader. But if I find

Bill (Emilio Estevez) and Brett (Laura Harrington) are the new parents of a "reconstituted family" in MAXIMUM OVERDRIVE (DEG, 1986).

that I cannot terrify, I will try to horrify, and if I find that I cannot horrify, I'll go for the gross-out" (King: *Danse* 1981). Some of the most memorable scenes in MAXIMUM OVERDRIVE are gross-out moments, revolving around bodily functions, blood and carnage, and set to the dulcet tones of AC/DC. The medal winner is probably the shot in which a little leaguer's head gets crushed—or, to be perfectly accurate, *popped*—by a steamroller. (The "popping" effect was removed from the final film in order to avoid an X rating.) Such scenes were obviously intended to generate a visceral reaction from viewers. The scenes also generated a predictable reaction from film critics who looked through a series of plot holes and saw only juvenile antics.

When it came time to face the reviews, King took the unusual approach of promoting his directorial debut as a lark. In press junkets, he boasted that he had intentionally made a "moron movie" and practically dared critics to like it. In the years since, the author has been much more somber about his directorial debut—describing MAXIMUM OVERDRIVE as "just terrible" (Gary Wood: "To Direct" 1991) and "a stinker" (King: *On Writing* 2000)—even as repeat viewers have warmed up to it.

Reflections on the Film (Oral History)

STEPHEN KING: This is a moron movie, like SPLASH! You check your brains at the box office and you come out 96 minutes later and pick them up again. People say, "How'd you like the movie?" and you can't say much. (AP August 3, 1986)

STEPHEN KING: BACK TO THE FUTURE is a moron movie, RAMBO is a moron movie, I loved 'em both. I went in there and I made a picture and there are a lot of people shooting at each other and there's some passable characterization, but I was more interested in pace than I was in character. (Horsting: *Stephen* 1986)

STEPHEN KING: People who have seen it in the advance screenings say the picture seems like it's only ten minutes long, because of the suicidal pacing. And that's what I wanted, that's what comes across. (Wiater: "Stephen" 1986)

STEPHEN KING: I think the people who don't like my written stuff, who find it vulgar and tasteless, will find this vulgar and tasteless, gross and grizzly, unpleasant and possibly boring, awkward, stereotypical and all the rest. And people who do like my stuff, are gonna find it vulgar, tasteless, but they're going to see the spirit behind it, which is a combination of Monty Python and Jack the Ripper. (Strauss 1986)

STEPHEN KING: We've made a good, fun picture—but I'm not rehearsing my Academy Award speech. (Gross 1986)

JOHN PARELES (movie reviewer for the *New York Times*): For the most part, [King] has taken a promising notion—our dependence on our machines—and turned it into one long car-crunch movie, wheezing from setups to crackups. (Parales 1986)

PATRICK GOLDSTEIN (movie reviewer for the *Los Angeles Times*): As long as King is tinkering with his crazed machines, the film sustains a certain amount of ominous tension, but as soon as the author turns his attention to his actors, the movie's slender storyline goes limp. (Patrick Goldstein 1986)

DANN GIRE (movie reviewer for the *Chicago Daily Herald*): King has only himself to blame for the stripped gears in the suspense-less OVERDRIVE. King the writer saddled King the director with a mechanized script, faulty characters and a preposterous premise. (Gire 1986)

RON BASE (movie reviewer for the *Toronto Star*): The irony here is self-evident, but nonetheless rather sad: Stephen King, the author dissatisfied with what the movies did to his books, has made the worst Stephen King movie ever. (Base 1986)

STEPHEN KING: I think a measure of my success at doing what I wanted to do was that the *New York Daily News* said they would give it zero stars, and furthermore, there was a bathroom scene that is vulgar beyond description, and I thought damn, I've succeeded! Once you get outside the big cities the reviews improved drastically, because I think people seemed to understand that what I was doing was in a spirit of fun. (Fletcher 1987)

JOE BOB BRIGGS (movie reviewer for the *Orlando Sentinel*): We got the maniac cigarette machine, the attack diesel pump, the leapin' electric carving knife, video game electrocutions, a little kid on his bike getting' Aunt Jemimaed by a steamroller, Coke-can brain surgery, various forms of deranged lawn-care equipment, exploding 18-wheeler aliens, and, of course, Pat Hingle runnin' around shootin' off a bazooka he happens to keep in the basement of his truck stop. Great stuff. Great flick. (Briggs 1986)

MARTHA DE LAURENTIIS: Did we do the wrong tone? Maybe. But that's the sensibility that Stephen wanted to translate at the time of telling that story. And I think he delivered what he wanted to make. (Blake Harris 2015)

JOHN FALLON (movie reviewer for *ArrowintheHead.com*): Now if you want to be a jerk-off, you can bitch and moan about the plot holes [...] but if you actually stop for a second and think: THIS IS A MOVIE ABOUT KILLER TRUCKS THAT DRIVE BY THEMSELVES AND SQUASH PEOPLE, then maybe you'll do the smart thing and let that shit go! (Fallon: "MAXIMUM" 2001)

CHRIS CHAKA (movie reviewer for *VHSRevival.com*): The brilliance of MAXIMUM OVERDRIVE is that it hits you with so much concentrated nonsense that it is too exhausting to even try to understand. The best advice I can give you is to just let it go and let it flow over you. Like Zen, but for horseshit. (Chaka 2019)

Whatever its long-term appeal as a cult movie, MAXIMUM OVERDRIVE made less than $7.5 million in theatrical release, failing to recoup its reported $9 to $10 million budget. As Simon Brown has noted in his book Screening Stephen King, *this commercial failure sullied King's cinematic brand for years to come.*

SCOTT VON DOVIAK (in his book *Stephen King Films FAQ*): It's true that lowbrow humor and gross-out sequences have always been tools in his kit, but they represent a very thin sliver of what we think of as the Stephen King experience. [...] His relatable, all-too-human characters; his facility for building credible communities, particularly rural and working-class ones; and most of all, the relatable, down-to-earth voice [...] these are the qualities that typify the best of his written works, and they're nowhere to be found in MAXIMUM OVERDRIVE. (Von Doviak 2014)

STEPHEN KING: The problem with [MAXIMUM OVERDRIVE] is that I was coked out of my mind all through its production, and I really didn't know what I was doing. (Magistrale: *Hollywood's* 2003)

Brian Taggert's TRUCKS (1997)

On August 16, 1988, De Laurentiis Entertainment Group Inc. filed for bankruptcy, a move that eventually threw the film adaptation rights to several Stephen King stories into limbo. Around the same time, VHS distributor Vidmark Entertainment ventured into film production under the banner of Trimark Pictures and began carving out a spot in the niche market for low-budget horror films. Over the next few years, they bolstered their brand with franchise-spawning titles like WARLOCK (1989), LEPRECHAUN (1993), and THE DENTIST (1996). In 1991, Vidmark also distributed Dino De Laurentiis's latest Stephen King adaptation, SOMETIMES THEY COME BACK, which paved the way for Trimark Pictures to make SOMETIMES THEY COME BACK … AGAIN (1996) and SOMETIMES THEY COME BACK … FOR MORE (1998). Between sequels, execs also decided to develop a new adaptation of "Trucks" and hired veteran screenwriter Brian Taggert to write it.

Taggert, a Los Angeles native, launched his career in the early 1970s by writing episodic television as well as the 1974 TV movie THE MARK OF ZORRO. In 1976, he debuted a play entitled When Last I Saw the Lemmings, synopsized by one L.A. critic as a "comedy of fear" about "self-destruction within our over snobbish society" (Dan Goldstein 1976). The writer himself has described his theater work as "sort of acerbic, Noel Coward meet Edward Albee," which might make him seem an unlikely scribe for a low-budget horror movie (Leicht 2014).

Around the same time, however, Taggert also wrote a spec screenplay entitled SHE'S … DIFFERENT, based on memories of his "weird" sister, who had "the appearance of special powers" and may have been "psychic" (Leicht 2014). The screenplay generated some interest at Columbia Pictures and seemed to be on a fast track to becoming a feature film, but plans changed abruptly on November 3, 1976, when Brian DePalma's film CARRIE was released. According to the screenwriter, SHE'S … DIFFERENT was promptly "reduced to an NBC movie called THE SPELL" (Petkovich 2019). Taggert claimed he was unaware of Stephen King's story when he wrote his spec script, but he was certainly aware of CARRIE when he delivered the November 12, 1976, shooting script for THE SPELL. Although it's unclear what changes were made between the spec script and the shooting script, critics dismissed THE SPELL as a low-rent CARRIE knockoff.

Taggert went on to write the 1978 TV movie NIGHT CRIES, a psychological thriller about a woman haunted by the dreams of her stillborn baby, after which he was asked to write a slasher movie for Canadian producer Pierre David. According to the screenwriter, David's associate Denise DiNovi had attended WHEN LAST I SAW THE LEMMINGS and explained to him, "You have a very twisted sense of humor, and in horror you need that every seven minutes or so to leaven the horror. I think it'll sell the picture" (Petkovich 2019). Taggert took the job, and the success of VISITING HOURS (1982) secured his reputation as a horror filmmaker. Most of his subsequent projects within the genre were adaptations, sequels, and remakes—including OF UNKNOWN ORIGIN (1983), WANTED: DEAD OR ALIVE (1986), POLTERGEIST 3 (1988), OMEN 4: THE AWAKENING (1991), WHAT EVER HAPPENED TO BABY JANE? (1991), and TRUCKS (1997).

By the time Trimark execs approached Taggert about adapting Stephen King, he had no qualms about writing a low-budget horror movie—but he wasn't sure he wanted to remake a film directed by the undisputed Master of Horror. To him, that seemed like an exercise in arrogance. After reading the short story "Trucks," however, he saw an opportunity to create his own variation on King's theme, which he articulated as follows: "It's really what Einstein said, isn't it? He said, 'The generation that relies totally on machines will beget a next generation [that] will become idiots.' And I kind of used that as my guide" (Leicht 2014). According to Snopes.com, Albert Einstein never actually made this statement, but the sentiment is nonetheless relevant—and became the basis for the 1997 telefilm on the USA network.

Although the telefilm TRUCKS purports to be "based on a short story by Stephen King," it might be more aptly described as "inspired by" King's short story—as well as the popular TV series THE X-FILES. Taggert's version of the tale features an entirely new roster of characters and a distinctly new setting in the fictional town of Lunar, New Mexico. The story begins in a desolate salvage yard, where a slovenly old man gets mauled by a self-driving junker. At a nearby gas station/diner/motel—advertised as "the last stop before Roswell"—an attractive middle-aged (and newly divorced) woman named Hope has a testy encounter with a local redneck who leaves and becomes the second victim of the film's mechanical monsters. Later, Hope takes a trio of Area 51 tourists—an estranged father and daughter, plus a conspiracy-spouting new ager—on a "lunar expedition" into the desert. They find the dead redneck and get attacked by another driver-less truck. Gas station owner (and newly widowed nice guy) Ray, along with his teenage son Logan, comes to their rescue and the motley crew ends up stranded together in the diner, along with Ray's terminally-ill father and a pair of acerbic nymphomaniacs.

A scene involving a drainage pipe and a scene in which Ray realizes that the trucks "want fuel" serve as reminders that this screen story is actually based on King's short story, but Taggert generates entirely new dialogue for his characters, offering variations on familiar themes. The most vocal character in the film is conspiracy-guy Jack, who insists that the trucks are "making a statement." He pontificates, "I always knew the industrial age would end in chaos. It's our fault. We don't deserve this planet, the way we misuse it." Later, Jack echoes MAXIMUM OVERDRIVE by suggesting that a "recent comet shower" might have "bombarded our atmosphere with alien particles which somehow interfered with our energy signals, affecting radio waves, electricity, all that stuff." Another character poses an obvious follow-up question: *Why trucks?* Stephen King couldn't answer that question and neither can Taggert, who quickly moves on to more conspiracy theories. A not-too-bright trucker suggests the people of Lunar have become "little white mice" in some "government experiment." He blames Area 51. Another character, an ex-soldier who was once stationed at Area 51, alludes to SETI and Project Phoenix before Jack circles back to King's ideas, saying, "What if this is just the beginning? Inanimate objects able to think. They could make us their slaves."

With Ray's assertion that, no matter what, "*we act together*," Taggert shifts the focus of his narrative to character dynamics and essentially re-establishes Stephen King's MAXIMUM OVERDRIVE story of a "new family" in the making. Ray and Hope are both newly single; both recovering from traumatic pasts; both outsiders who have recently settled (or resettled) in Lunar. For the experienced movie viewer, there can be no question about whether or not they will end up together. It is equally obvious that the two teenage characters, both emotionally estranged from their fathers, will make a connection as well. Oddly, these character dynamics not only echo MAXIMUM OVERDRIVE but also A RETURN TO SALEM'S LOT (about an estranged father and son who move to a small town and find love amidst strange circumstances), CHILDREN OF THE CORN 2 (about an estranged father and son who move to a small town and find love amidst strange circumstances), and PET SEMATARY 2 (about an estranged father and son who move to a small town and find ... well, mostly, strange circumstances).

At the end of TRUCKS, the four main characters escape to apparent safety—but they don't remain safe for long. Taggert remembered, "What got the audience was a very unique twist at the end, which they loved and which really buttonholed the picture" (Petkovich 2019). The new family takes to the skies in a government helicopter, only to realize that there's no one piloting. Stephen King claims that this twist ending was supposed to be a launch point for an ongoing TV series that would have elaborated on Ray's prophecy about "a world covered in rust" and Taggert's generation of idiots (Stephen Jones: *Creepshows* 2002).

Instead, Trimark added three new scenes to the existing movie and released it on home video. In the first scene, a postal worker trips over a remote-controlled toy truck. When he hits the ground, the truck starts ramming his skull into a concrete curb—repeating the action until the man's head resembles a busted watermelon. In the second scene, a Hazmat suit self-inflates and attacks a pair of (Area 51?) workers with an axe. The results are equally gruesome. A third scene, involving an electrician who gets fried to an elevated transformer, was probably also shot for the VHS release.

It seems safe to assume that these scenes were aimed at the gore-oriented contingent of Stephen King fans. It also seems safe to assume that screenwriter Brian Taggert had nothing to do with them. In a 2014 interview, the screenwriter confessed that he had never seen the "whole" movie. He also said he had trouble finding work after TRUCKS, because he hadn't been willing to "throw guts at the screen" (Leicht 2014). Sadly, just as the screenwriter began his moviemaking career in the shadow of Stephen King's CARRIE, he ended his career in the shadow of TRUCKS.

As for Stephen King, he admitted that he watched the TV movie "with some trepidation," fearful that Taggert and director Chris Thomson might succeed where he failed. He was both relieved and dismayed to find that TRUCKS was "worse" than MAXIMUM OVERDRIVE—"and that's hard to do" (Stephen Jones: *Creepshows* 2002). The critics—those who bothered to watch the TV movie at all—generally agreed that TRUCKS, which takes itself far more seriously than King's coke-fueled film odyssey, was unnecessary.

In spite of this apparent dead end, King's son (and fellow novelist) Joe Hill suggested in 2020 that he'd like to follow in dad's footsteps as a filmmaker. He told interviewer Mick Garris, "If someone offered me the chance to write and direct a relaunch of MAXIMUM OVERDRIVE, I'd jump at that in a second." In his proposed version of the tale—conceived in the midst of the COVID-19 pandemic—the revolt of the machines is caused by a virus (Garris 2020).

SOMETIMES THEY COME BACK (First Draft, c. 1987)

According to Stephen Jones's book *Creepshows*, producer Dino De Laurentiis announced plans to make SOMETIMES THEY COME BACK as early as 1984, while he was working on FIRESTARTER. Around 1987, the producer hired screenwriting duo Lawrence Konner and Mark Rosenthal—whose previous credits included THE LEGEND OF BILLIE JEAN (1985), THE JEWEL OF THE NILE (1985), and SUPERMAN IV: THE QUEST FOR PEACE (1987)—to write a first draft script for his latest Stephen King

project. The writers had previously written a remake of the 1955 film noir THE DES-
PERATE HOURS for DeLaurentiis, and Rosenthal says they were eager to work with the
producer again. They were also excited about the prospect of making a horror movie,
which was a new genre for them as professional writers.

"Sometimes They Come Back," arguably the most cinematic story in the *Night Shift*
collection, revolves around an anxious schoolteacher named Jim Norman. At the outset of the tale, Jim arrives home to his wife Sally after a job interview, but he doesn't tell
her much about how it went. Later, Jim wakes up from an old, familiar nightmare and
King presents an omniscient flashback to the job interview with a pair of officious fellows named Fenton and Simmons. The scene prefigures a similar opening scene in *The
Shining*, where Overlook manager Stuart Ullman questions Jack Torrance about a violent run-in with a former student. Jim Norman has had a similar run-in but, in contrast
with Jack's explosive attack, Jim fainted. The comparatively timid teacher explains to the
interviewers that he was under a lot of pressure at the time, due to his mother's recent
death and a hit-and-run accident that had nearly killed his wife. Simmons assures Jim
that he has the job if he wants it.

King hints that maybe Jim shouldn't take the job; after hours, the new school seems
haunted to him. Jim thinks he can "almost hear it breathing." It's unclear at this point
whether the author is writing about a haunted building or a haunted person, or both.
King later reveals that Jim is hiding a deep, dark secret from his wife, something related
to a childhood encounter with a bully. During his waking hours, Jim manages to sup-
press his secret—but in a Period 7 literature class, where he is antagonized by "slow
learners," his wounded psyche starts to come unraveled. When Jim stands up to an
aggressive jock named Chip Osway, the author reveals the details of the teacher's childhood trauma and recurring nightmares.

In a dream, 9-year-old Jim and his 12-year-old brother Wayne are walking down
Broad Street in their hometown of West Stratford, Connecticut, on the way to the
library. In real life, Stephen King and his older brother David spent several formative
years living in an apartment on West Broad Street in Stratford, and the layout of the
local library inspired the Derry Library in King's novel *IT*. In "Sometimes They Come
Back," the boys never make it to the library; they are waylaid by four "local losers" that
are bumming around underneath a railroad overpass. Wayne confronts the goons and
gets stabbed to death. Jim urinates in his pants and runs away, only to wake up in the
dark decades later.

At the start of his second semester at the new school, Jim learns that one of his
Period 7 students was killed in a hit-and-run accident over the Christmas holiday—by
an old Ford sedan with the phrase "Snake Eyes" scrawled on the side. At the same time,
he inherits a new student—a juvenile delinquent named Robert Lawson, who has supposedly transferred from a school called Milford. Jim notices that Lawson looks exactly
like one of the goons that killed his brother. Apparently believing that he can't trust
his own senses or judgment, the teacher decides not to tell his wife about the new student, or his nightmares. When Lawson antagonizes him, however, the teacher briefly
acquires an ally in a female student named Kathy Slavin—who promptly dies under
mysterious circumstances. Jim reads about her fatal fall in the newspaper. Later, another
familiar-looking hooligan named David Garcia takes her place in class.

Chip Osway visits Jim at home and warns him that the new students are gunning
for him. Soon after, Chip disappears mysteriously (his stepfather claims he "ran off")

and his spot in the class is taken by Vinnie, who boldly asks Jim how his brother is doing. Jim reacts by tracking down Officer Nell, an old-timer who used to chat up him and his brother at a Stratford diner when they were kids. Jim calls Officer Nell from a pay phone booth and asks if his brother's killers were ever caught. Nell gives an unsurprising answer: they weren't. When the officer asks why Jim suddenly wants to know about the killers, Jim reveals his fatal flaw; he can't trust anyone because he's afraid they'll think him "crazy." When he gets off the phone, Jim is startled by the sight of Vinnie's face pressed against the phone booth glass. It's a cinematic "jump gag," underscoring King's penchant for cinematic storytelling.

King transitions to the next scene with an equally cinematic shorthand: "Class again." This time, Jim asks Vinnie about the fourth goon—a fellow nicknamed Bleach—and comes to a realization: Bleach hasn't joined the class because, unlike the other three goons, Bleach is still alive. Vinnie seems rattled by this truth and threatens to murder Jim's wife. When Jim threatens to kill Vinnie first, the cool ghoul quips, "Kill me? Man, I thought you knew, I'm already dead." His suspicions confirmed, Jim concludes that he's dealing with the supernatural—and that he's going to have to fight fire with fire. Although Sally practically begs him to talk to her, Jim keeps his secrets and turns his attention to a book called *Raising Demons*. He plans to banish his childhood ghosts by conjuring a demon to drag them to Hell.

Before he can execute his plan, Jim receives a follow-up call from Officer Nell, who tells him that three out of the four delinquents who killed his brother subsequently died in a car crash—in the exact same Ford sedan that ran down Kathy Slavin and attempted to run down Jim's wife. The fourth delinquent, Charlie Sponder, is still alive—but Nell won't provide his contact information until Jim explains the sudden interest in a decades-old crime. Jim refuses, sealing his own fate as well as his wife's. King transitions to the next scene in a jarring fashion, by offering no initial context for a scene in which the teacher is racing to his wife's hospital bedside. When he gets there, a nurse delivers the bad news with cold precision: "She died at 9:04 p.m." Jim faints.

The author describes a hallucinatory montage of faces and fragments of dialogue as Jim drifts through his wife's funeral. Afterward, Vinnie calls him on the phone, awakening him from another nightmare. Jim challenges the lead goon to a confrontation at the school. Later, the teacher enacts a sinister plan and King's climax unfolds beat-by-beat. First, Jim enters the seemingly haunted school alone at night. He stops into the faculty lounge and retrieves a portable stereo and a sound-effects record. He sets up the stereo in his classroom and plays a train whistle cue to help re-create the environment of his brother's death. Then he opens his Satanic self-help book to a chapter entitled "Malefic Spirits and How to Call Them." Following the directions in the book, he cuts off his index fingers and throws them into a pentagram that he has chalked on the floor. The least cinematic moment in the story is a cryptic avoidance of the words Jim speaks here. Presumably, the author doesn't want the reader to know exactly what his character is conjuring.

We learn the details later, when the undead delinquents arrive boisterously and make their way to Jim's classroom, taunting him as they approach. In the moment of confrontation, King writes that the classroom walls become "misty, insubstantial," and a figure resembling Jim's dead brother rises out of the pentagram. Jim, the three goons, and the "Wayne-Thing" reenact their struggle beneath the train trestle, but this time the events play out differently. When Vinnie attacks Wayne, the ghost's face collapses and bursts into flames. The human-faced demon then dispatches the other two visitors and coldly promises Jim that he will "come back." In the final scene of King's short story, Jim quietly leaves the school. On his way out, he senses the presence of something evil hidden in the darkness and remembers a specific passage from the book *Raising Demons*: "You could perhaps summon them, perhaps cause them to do your work. You could even get rid of them. But sometimes they come back." The conclusion of King's story is Jim's realization that he has conquered his childhood fears but damned himself in the process.

Screenwriter Mark Rosenthal remembers that his main goal in adapting the story was "to try and make it more, for lack of a better word, *literary*. To give it more sense of ambiguity, so you're not sure if [the undead goons] are really there or if he's just seeing things. We wanted to make sure that you had to question whether this guy was having a nervous breakdown or not. But regardless of whether [the supernatural threat] is real or not, the physical toll that takes place is real." The screenwriter, who boasts a strong background in English literature, alludes to Nathaniel Hawthorne's short story "Young Goodman Brown" as a storytelling model: "The question is, *Did [Goodman Brown] really see really see the witches and the devil in the woods?* The reply is, *What's the difference?* People kill people over these things, whether it's real or not."

Rosenthal says that, for him, King's story is about the human inability to forget pain and humiliation. He elaborates, "The notion of repressed memory is not accepted by most academics in the field of psychology. In fact, it's the opposite. It's not that we repress them, it's that we can't get rid of them. Most people, while they might forget something wonderful that happened to them when they were seven or 15 or 22, will in most cases remember who insulted them when they did something embarrassing, or when they farted accidentally [and felt humiliated]. The human mind remembers the bad stuff so we won't repeat it. It's probably an evolutionary strategy: 'Oh, when I went down that path, a snake bit me or some guy attacked me, so I'm not going down that path again.' We're hard-wired for this stuff. We might avoid talking about it, the way Holocaust survivors avoided talking to their families about what happened, but we don't ever forget it." Rosenthal remembers a particular line from his script that articulated his theme: "We collect our humiliations the way kids hold onto baseball cards."

This reading certainly suggests that Jim's demons exist only in his mind, but Rosenthal says he felt compelled to incorporate the supernatural into the final act. Although he eliminated some "specifics" of the demon-summoning ritual because he felt that the scene in the short story was "a little ham-handed," the screenwriter added one big supernatural element to the classroom encounter: "At the end of the short story, [Jim] played a recording of a freight train as part of his ritual, so we had an actual freight train come—almost like [in *The Polar Express*] by Chris Van Allsburg—at midnight. We felt like we needed that interstitial between the Now and the Beyond." As for the ending of the story, Rosenthal reflects, "What great horror and ghost stories are all about is the human need to reconcile loss, because you're inevitably going to lose everything and everyone you love. So how do you make sense of life? That's what these movies ask." He says his goal was to craft a cathartic ending that offered closure as well as an abiding sense of grief and melancholy: "I'm certain there was a sense of 'it's not over' but I don't remember the details."

In January 1988, SOMETIMES THEY COME BACK went into limbo along with every other project in development at the De Laurentiis Entertainment Group (DEG).

As the production company careened toward bankruptcy later that year, De Laurentiis resigned from the studio that shared his name but somehow managed to retain the rights to the King property. He later struck a deal with CBS executive Jeff Sagansky to make SOMETIMES THEY COME BACK for network television. At that point, Rosenthal and Konner bowed out—mainly due to their lack of interest in making a TV movie. Rosenthal says that, from that point forward, he had "no relationship" with the project. To date, he has not seen the film that evolved from his script—and he discarded his version of the script many years ago.

SOMETIMES THEY COME BACK
(Fourth Draft—August 31, 1990)

In 1989, Dino De Laurentiis turned to director Tom McLoughlin, who had previously written and directed the feature film DATE WITH AN ANGEL (1987) for DEG, to shepherd SOMETIMES THEY COME BACK to the screen. McLoughlin says he and De Laurentiis were both dissatisfied with the existing script by Konner and Rosenthal. According to the director, "[It] lacked the deeper family dynamic and a haunting and emotional tone that I felt was needed in a King tale. Dino agreed and liked the ideas I proposed for the changes" (McLoughlin 2021). In an interview conducted around the time the film was made, McLoughlin summarized his changes as follows: "We eliminated Jim's wife's death and the ritual at the end where Jim cuts off his fingers. We also had Jim return to the town where his brother was killed rather than just any town, and we fleshed out the relationship between Jim and his wife and gave the spirit of [Jim's brother] Wayne a bigger role in the proceedings" (Shapiro: "Master" 1991). In a separate interview, he added, "There's more of a classic cathartic feel to the movie's ending. The goal in the movie is not to just get rid of the punks, it's to stop running. The other major change is that we've added a character. We've given [Jim] a son, and he's been desperately trying to recreate his relationship with his brother more than twenty years later with his son." McLoughlin's summary of the changes, which he says were intended to create a film "much closer to STAND BY ME and THE DEAD ZONE than PET SEMATARY"— seems to indicate that Konner and Rosenthal's first draft hewed more closely to the plot of Stephen King's short story (Dawidziak 1991). McLoughlin knew that he had to soften King's story for the small screen, and the major changes between the short story and the McLoughlin-approved shooting script reflect that.

Because the director was committed to other projects while SOMETIMES THEY COME BACK was racing toward a production deadline, Dino De Laurentiis hired screenwriter Tim Kring to revise the script based on McLoughlin's ideas. Kring's recent work on BAY COVE, an NBC TV movie about a coven of WASP-y witches, might have made him seem like a good match for the material. The Fourth Draft shooting script— dated August 31, 1990—is attributed to Lawrence Konner and Mark Rosenthal, but McLoughlin says it is Kring's uncredited rewrite.

The 108-page, seven-act script begins with a heavenly descent into the idyllic town of Berlin, New Hampshire, accompanied by a voiceover that sets a wistful tone. The voice belongs to Jim Norman, who clarifies that he is returning to his hometown—the place where his brother died—for a teaching job and a chance to rid himself of old fears. The first time we see him, he's standing in front of his new house alongside his wife Sally and their 9-year-old son Scott. As he passes through the front door for the first time, Scott startles him—an obligatory horror movie jump scare. Later, Jim and Sally christen the new house with a late-night roll in the hay.

The screen story overlaps with the source story for the first time as Jim enters the classroom. In the script, he is more down to earth than King's character—and less timid. Chip Conway recounts a rumor that the new teacher once threw a student out a window, but Jim Norman seems to be a model of quiet contemplation and restraint. A history teacher rather than a composition instructor, he advises his students that those who do not learn history are doomed to repeat it, while those who learn from historical patterns can exert some control over their present-day lives. His own story becomes an object lesson. Luckily, the screen story's Jim Norman is a more effective communicator and much better at coping with psychological trauma than the short story's version of the character; he talks to his wife about the sources of stress in his life and he relieves stress by playing catch with his son. At night, however, he is haunted by something he doesn't talk about.

Instead of waking up from a nightmare, the screenwriter's version of the character seems to dream while awake. He hears the faint sound of a child crying and goes to comfort his son, only to find that his son is not the one crying. Instead, Jim has a waking vision of himself as a 9-year-old boy being comforted by his older brother Wayne. The "waking dream" scene suggests that Jim's childhood memories are essentially "alive" in the new house. The dream-walking adult follows the vision out of the house, to the scene of the crime that ended his brother's life. Beneath a railroad bridge, a Black Chevy Malibu SS 396 (a more intimidating-looking car than a Ford sedan) pulls up behind the two young brothers. Four hoodlums get out and accost them but the confrontation doesn't play out the same way it does in King's short story. The screenwriter adds a crucial new detail: a key chain with a red rabbit's foot on it. When the hoods notice the sound of an oncoming train and realize that their car is parked on the tracks, they scramble to find the distinctive key chain while Jim seizes the opportunity to get away. As soon as the train makes impact, adult Jim "wakes up" in his front yard at night. Sally finds him there and he struggles to make sense of what has just happened; has he been sleepwalking or has he experienced something more profound?

Back at school, Jim gets into an argument with Chip Conway over a bad grade. Chip kicks his teacher's car but Jim manages to deescalate the situation, thanks partly to the intervention of another student named Billy Stearns. As suspicious Principal Simmons looks on, Billy unknowingly drops his wallet, and Jim retrieves it and goes after him. In what seems like another waking dream, he then wanders into a confrontation between Chip and the hoods who killed his brother decades ago. For reasons that are not clear—and which heighten the ambiguity of Jim's experiences—only Billy can see his attackers. Jim simply sees his student drive off a cliff, then senses a chill as he remembers (or actually *hears*?) his dead brother's voice urge him to run away. The scene concludes Act 1.

At the start of Act 2, Principal Simmons introduces a new student to Jim's class: a transfer named Robert Lawson. The new blood and news of Billy's death immediately put the teacher on edge. When Chip antagonizes him, Jim reacts aggressively. Principal Simmons observes it all. The screenwriter seems to be setting up the teacher to take the blame for the deaths of his students. In the meantime, Jim slowly becomes aware of a *physical* superimposition of his childhood fears into his adult life. First, he finds a pair of familiar old-fashioned sneakers in his backyard. Then, following a trip to the local video store, he sees home movie footage of himself and Wayne spliced into a Jimi Hendrix concert. He goes back to the video store, gets spooked by a cardboard cutout of a zombie, then tells the clerk about his discovery. The clerk casually suggests that VHS technology can record ghosts. (Perhaps he's remembering the urban legend about the dead kid in THREE MEN AND A BABY?) He also advises his customer to see a psychiatrist. After leaving the video store, Jim bumps into one of his students, a young woman named Kate, then he hallucinates a vision of his younger self running away from the four hoods and hears Kate scream. Before he can run to her rescue, Jim abruptly wakes up in his own bed at the conclusion of Act 2.

At the top of Act 3, Jim reads in the morning newspaper that Kate is "missing." From this point forward, the screenwriter plays fast and loose with the internal logic of the story. It seems as if a supernatural threat is targeting Jim Norman's students. Less clear is Jim's role as an observer / participant in the events leading to death or disappearance. If he can see and hear the ghostly hoodlums while he's awake, then why couldn't / didn't he help Kate? Did he black out and sleepwalk home? Are we, the reader/viewer, meant to assume that Jim might be responsible for her death? There are some similarities here to Stephen King's 1989 novel *The Dark Half*, about a novelist whose pseudonym develops a physical life of its own and begins killing people close to the novelist, thereby framing him.

Jim certainly doesn't believe that he's responsible for Kate's death and so he joins a police search for her, led by Chief George Pappas. While searching in the woods, he hears Kate's voice calling for help. Unwisely, he tells the other searchers that he knows where she is and then leads them right to the dead girl's body. The scene makes him look guilty to the other characters (although, for some reason, Chief Pappas doesn't immediately question him as a suspect) while the reader/viewer is led to assume that he is capable of seeing and hearing ghosts. Maybe he's a Johnny Smith brand of psychic?

After an unrevealing exchange with the school psychiatrist, Jim returns to his classroom and finds some answers in the form of a dark-haired goon named Vincent. Just to make sure we're following the story, Jim verbally accuses Vincent and his goons of killing his students so they can make room for themselves in the class. This, of course, makes Jim look crazy—and perhaps guilty—in the eyes of the other students. Vincent plays to the audience, suggesting that good ol' Mr. Norman has gone around the bend. Later, Jim sees Vinnie's black Chevy in the school parking lot, which solidifies his belief that his brother's killers really have "come back."

In the next scene, Jim receives a house call from Chip, who clarifies that he's *not* in cahoots with the crazies from class. Before Jim can redirect the conversation, he sees his student get pulled into a familiar black Chevy by "pale arms." His response is to tell Sally to pack her bags; they're leaving town. Chief Pappas turns out to be one step ahead and brings Jim to the police station for interrogation. Jim pleads his innocence while the undead hoods torture Chip in their car. In the first scene that doesn't rely on Jim's narrative point of view, Lawson and Vinnie are joined by North. When they pull up next to a cop car, the cop can't see or hear them. It seems only Jim Norman and his students can see these particular ghouls who promptly rip off their faces to terrify Chip. As Act 3 comes to a close, they literally tear him apart and throw his dismembered body parts into a river.

Act 4 begins as Jim returns home from the police station—and stubbornly refuses to tell his wife Sally what is going on. As in King's short story, he merely advises her to

Back from the grave and ready to party: (from left) actors Nicholas Sadler, Robert Rusler, and Bentley Mitchum in SOMETIMES THEY COME BACK (CBS, 1991).

be careful. In the next scene, Jim learns about Chip's murder and North threatens to finish what was started decades ago. Making good on the threat, the goons stalk Jim's son Scott, following him home from school. Chief Pappas subsequently interviews the boy as well as Sally, who acknowledges that her husband has been acting strange lately. At night, Jim puts his son to bed and then finally comes clean, telling his wife that the creeps who murdered his brother have come back for him and his family. Sally offers a rational response: "But they're dead." Jim sets out to prove otherwise, by tracking down Bob Nell, a policeman who witnessed the aftermath of his brother's murder. There's only one problem; according to Chief Pappas, Bob Nell was critically wounded a few days earlier in a hit-and-run accident.

When Jim visits Nell in the ICU ward of the local hospital, the officer conveys a written message: "794 OAK." The message leads Jim to a nearby cemetery, where he discovers the graves of Robert Lawson (1950–1969), Paul Vincent (1951–1969), and David North (1950–1969). The experience jogs his memory and Jim remembers the name of the fourth goon: Karl Mueller. At this point, the screenwriter makes use of a loose thread from King's short story: Jim searches the phone book and learns that Mueller still lives in town. Act 4 concludes as Jim pays Mueller a visit.

The remaining three acts of the screen story deviate significantly from Stephen King's source story. In Act 5, Jim and Mueller visit the railroad bridge together. Although it's unclear what they are trying to accomplish there, the field trip runs parallel to an attack on Jim's wife and son. Sally protects her son until Jim fortuitously shows up and shoots Vincent. This time, the hero asserts, he won't be running away from the ghosts. As police approach, the ghosts run while Jim and his family flee through the woods to Elm Street (a nod to filmmaker Wes Craven?) and take refuge in a church. Sally now believes her husband's story about undead teenagers, but she's not sure what to do about it. Jim theorizes that the ghosts want revenge but he's not sure why—in spite of scripted memory flashes that hint at the answer. Once Jim remembers the red rabbit's foot, he tells his wife and son to stay in the church while he goes out to fight his literal demons.

Jim returns to Mueller's house and the duo takes another trip down memory lane, returning to Jim's childhood home so he can retrieve the rabbit's foot—and the car keys attached to it—from a secret hiding place. For some reason, he still can't remember what happened all those years ago, but intermittent flashbacks of the encounter beneath the railroad trestle indicate that the story is about to come full circle. On cue, the ghosts show up and kidnap Mueller, then leave Jim stranded without a car as they go after his family. Jim rushes to his wife and son's rescue but gets waylaid by police who believe he's the real murderer. He manages to escape into a cemetery, where he pleads for his dead brother's help. Act 5 ends with an effects-heavy display of natural and supernatural power: a mini-earthquake, a lot of wind, and a flood of "inner light" herald Wayne's return from the grave.

At the top of Act 6, Jim and ghost-Wayne talk. It is apparent that this Wayne is not the lookalike demon from Stephen King's short story; instead, it is a self-professedly "weak" but willing entity. The reunited brothers head to the church, where the undead hoodlums are being held at bay by an unanticipated supernatural force; if they cross the threshold of the church, they will burst into flames. The new development offers some clarification about the nature of the undead monsters. Although they are only visible to certain humans at certain times, they appear to be flesh-and-blood creatures that can be destroyed through physical means. Armed with that knowledge, Jim and Wayne lead them away from the church, toward the railroad bridge. There, the various players ritualistically reenact the original tragedy. Jim tells the undead goons that Wayne has "tricked" them by luring them to the one place that can make them "alive" and vulnerable. Theoretically, all the hero has to do is shoot them—but this simple plan is thwarted by Chief Pappas, who shows up and shoots Jim, thereby giving Lawson an opportunity to kill Wayne (again). When the goons turn their ire toward Pappas instead, Wayne reminds his brother about what happened the first time. As a train approaches, Jim completes the reenactment ritual by hiding the keys … just as he did all those years ago. Act 7 ends with an explosive collision as the train crushes the black Chevy.

Act 8 is an extended denouement in which Wayne visits the church and mistakes Scott for 9-year-old Jim, then tries to take Scott with him into the "incandescent glow" of the afterlife. In a scene that is reminiscent of the finale of Steven Spielberg's films CLOSE ENCOUNTERS OF THE THIRD KIND and E.T.: THE EXTRA-TERRESTRIAL, Jim confronts his brother's ghost on the edge of the woods and pleads with him to leave Scott alone, promising to go in his son's stead. Sally protests, then Jim threatens to shoot his undead brother. Ultimately, he embraces him instead. In the spirit of love, Wayne goes willingly into the light alone—without making any promises to "come back." Jim gives his son the "lucky" lunch money that the goons were trying to steal from him and Wayne all those years ago, and the film fades out on a shot of the happy family.

The denouement is a radical departure—in terms of plot, characterization, theme, and tone—from Stephen King's short story, but it is arguably faithful to the author's more mature work, which frequently emphasizes familial love as an antidote to horror.

In a 1985 interview, King denounced his novel *Pet Sematary*, saying that it misrepresented his personal beliefs: "It just spirals down into darkness. It seems to be saying nothing works and nothing is worth it, and I don't really believe that" (Modderno 1985). He might as well have been talking about "Sometimes They Come Back," which ends on a similarly defeatist note, or any number of other *Night Shift* short stories. It seems, however, that King has always held his short stories to a different standard than his novels; the former are often bleak while the latter rarely are. Film adaptations of King's work—whether the source material is a novel or a short story—seem to satisfy critics and audiences more often when they end on a lighter note. When *Cujo* was adapted to the screen in the early 1980s, the novel's downbeat ending was changed to a relatively happy one. When *Pet Sematary* was adapted to the screen in the late 1980s, the filmmakers adopted a more playfully irreverent tone for the admittedly horrific ending (set to the tune of a new song by The Ramones). The success of those films is one reason why Tom McLoughlin decided to re-imagine "Sometimes They Come Back" as a more wistful, family-oriented story with a more cathartic ending—and why he wishes, in hindsight, he also could have added more humor to the tale.

An Interview with Tom McLoughlin (2011)

This interview was originally published in The Modest Proposal *e-journal in March 2011. It was later incorporated into the 2014 book* A Strange Idea of Entertainment: Conversations with Tom McLoughlin.

JOSEPH MADDREY: In 1990, you adapted Stephen King's short story "Sometimes They Come Back" to the screen. Are you a Stephen King fan?

TOM McLOUGHLIN: I'm a huge Stephen King fan. Obviously he saw the same TWILIGHT ZONEs we all saw, the same OUTER LIMITS, the same Corman movies—he loved that stuff—and because of his writing talent he was able to take those basic ideas and stories and fill them with the thoughts of his characters. That's his brilliance. He shows us our dreams and our nightmares in [his characters'] thoughts, which allows his readers to have a personal relationship with the stories.

In my opinion, most of the Stephen King movies don't work. You can't get that same experience [of the characters' thoughts], so the filmmakers usually substitute something else. The movies that really succeeded were the ones that had stronger characters—CARRIE, THE DEAD ZONE, THE STAND. But a lot of the other ones didn't quite get there for me, because you're trying to condense something that's so rich in the books into 90 minutes of screen time. You can sell a title and you can sell the idea but it's got to be fleshed out differently.

I think that's what SOMETIMES THEY COME BACK suffered from—it wasn't fleshed out properly. The writers had to expand a short story, so they put a lot of "the best of Stephen King" moments into it. Like the evil car [from CHRISTINE]... a lot of things like that were borrowed from other works to flesh out the story.

MADDREY: I have to admit that when I watched SOMETIMES THEY COME BACK, I was confused about the nature of the monsters. Are they ghosts or are they the living dead? Do they exist in the flesh or only in the main character's imagination? What are the rules?

McLOUGHLIN: When Dino De Laurentiis offered the project to me, I remember saying to him, "This really doesn't work." The writers had moved on because they were not going to do another rewrite without being paid a fortune, so Dino brought in Tim Kring, the future creator of HEROES. Tim is a great guy and very smart, and we saw eye to eye right away. But whenever you deal with Dino, there are a lot of stipulations—"don't lose this, don't lose that, because I like that…." So we were trying to Frankenstein things together.

Eventually the main question was whether or not the audience would accept that we're in this realm where anything can happen. I think if you're a horror aficionado, you know that there needs to be—like you said—rules that are very clear and show an understanding of the genre. For most people, it's either creepy because it's surreal or it just doesn't work.

MADDREY: In the short story, the threat is a group of teenagers who are possessed by the spirits of the dead. In the movie, I wasn't sure if the teenagers were possessed or reincarnated or just ageless monsters. At first, I thought they only existed in the head of the main character, because he's so tormented by his past—but then his wife and son are able to see them too and be hurt by them….

McLOUGHLIN: The way I approached it was that these guys have *literally* come back—they are solid ghosts. They are ghosts walking around in human form, in the same way that I believe angels and demons walk around in totally human form. These guys to me really were flesh and blood and could hurt other people.

I saw a lot of those kinds of teenagers [violent '50s greasers] when I was growing up—they picked on guys like me with the long hair. Those guys in real life were scary enough. Now to say that they can come back from the dead, hurt other people in your life, and do things that nobody else would believe they can do—my God! I mean, they can tear off their own faces!—and if you get into a car crash with them, they're going to walk away and you're not. They were solid when they needed to be solid but they could disappear when they needed to not be there.

MADDREY: So there really were no rules for them as monsters…. That's what makes them scary.

McLOUGHLIN: Yeah, maybe so. The old cop was the only one that gave Tim's character any kind of explanation. There really was no mythology outside of that.

MADDREY: Maybe that's even what Stephen King was thinking. Maybe he sat down to write the story and asked himself what he was really scared of in his life. He thought of kids like that who acted as if the rules didn't apply to them, and then he took it to the next level—where the scientific laws about life and death and the passage of time—didn't apply to them. How scary would they be then?

McLOUGHLIN: It's not a figment of the character's imagination that they are back. They are literally back. Where do they live? Do they eat? You can dismiss all those rational questions because, when you see them, they're back simply to torment you and harm people you know. That's why they exist.

[At this point, our conversation is fortuitously interrupted by the sound of a distant train horn.]

McLOUGHLIN: To this day, I can't hear a train horn and not think of SOMETIMES THEY COME BACK, because that's something that I purposely put in the film. Tim Matheson hears that sound the second he gets back to his hometown, and it has a haunting quality to it. When I was growing up, that was a reassuring sound—it meant somebody was going somewhere and life was going on. My idea was to take that sound and make it part of a dark memory—make it really horrific because it's associated with his brother's death. One of the cool things about movies is to be able to take things like that and turn them into something else.

To me, that's something that a good movie does—or good music, painting, sculpture, whatever. It mixes with life. People say, "I cannot go into the water because every time I try, I think of JAWS." Or, "I can't take a shower when I'm home alone because I think of PSYCHO." Powerful horror movies really can make a lifelong impression and it's wonderfully cool to be able to do that.

I have learned, after many years and many films, that I can personalize a lot of things because of my love of the genre or because I have had some experience in my life that connects me to the world in the story. I can take somebody else's material and somehow fuse it with my own thoughts. In fact, I often feel that it's more interesting to take on other people's material and try to find my own way into that universe, as opposed to drawing exclusively from my own experiences and trying to create things that way.

Then of course you need the same level of participation from the actors, the cameraman, the editor … all these other people. You've got to get everybody thinking and feeling in the same direction.

MADDREY: *Which seems like it would never work. But there must be something universal about certain patterns and symbols that makes good stories resonate for a lot of different people with different backgrounds and experiences. Like the train horn—maybe the sound is comforting to a lot of people because it's a subconscious cue that life goes on. I feel that way about airports—all the coming and going….*

McLOUGHLIN: Yeah, airports are a hotbed of emotion. Having spent so much time in them over the years, I can say that I get energized in environments like that. It helps me to focus—just like being on a movie set. I love working in situations where I'm surrounded by a lot of people. For some people, it's distracting, but not for me.

MADDREY: *You like being in the eye of the hurricane….*

McLOUGHLIN: I don't like focusing on doing things solely for myself. I love being part of something bigger. Whenever I've gone into states of depression, it's mentally and physically debilitating. That's the worst kind of death—you're alive but you can't do anything. To me, that's scarier than anything else—the idea of being on this planet and not being an active part of the world around you. I really learned this lesson again when I had children. I found I wanted to make sacrifices to see them happy, to see them light up.

It's the same thing when I'm working as a director. When I do something that allows an actor to shine, I stand back and go, "God, I'm so happy that I was able to help make that moment happen." Maybe I was the one who said yes to casting them in the picture. Maybe I was the one who said, "What would happen if you were saying that to your father instead of your boyfriend?" Sometimes I don't even know where the idea came from but the result is amazing. The other person gets it and runs with it. To have that level participation—to help create something that goes beyond my individual life— is amazing. My greatest dream is that certain films I've worked on in my life might have a lasting effect on people after I'm gone.

IT'S A WONDERFUL LIFE was absolutely life-changing for me. So was ROCKY, because it came out during a period in my life when I felt like I was never going to be able to direct, and was never going to achieve any of my dreams. Seeing [Rocky] pull himself up on the ropes—that image stayed in my mind every time I got rejected, every time somebody said, "No, we don't like your idea. No, we're not going to hire you for that." Sometimes I felt so defeated, and then I remembered that image. It's not that it's the greatest movie ever made but that image of the down-and-out guy trying his best just to get through—and the fact that he is still standing at the end—really was a powerful influence on me. As a filmmaker, you can make a difference if you focus your work on the things that not only entertain, but inspire.

MADDREY: ROCKY is a story about survival in a tough, gritty, depressing and often debilitating world. In contrast, Stephen King's short story ended on a very dark note—the main character summons the spirit of his dead brother in order to survive, and after that he is forever cursed. The movie, on the other hand, gives the lead character a choice about his future—he can go to heaven with his brother or stay with his wife and son in an imperfect, painful world. How much of that ending was your idea and how much was already in the script? I can't help noting that, when you made that movie, you were a pretty young father....

McLOUGHLIN: What was going on in my life was actually very important. In 1990, my dad was dying. We knew he was going to die; it was just a matter of time. My daughter was born during that same time period, so I had this conflict between birth and death going on.

At the same time, I was working on my friend Steven Banks's show, HOME ENTERTAINMENT CENTER, which was going to be a pilot for Disney. That was fulfilling a childhood dream for both of us; we both wanted to work at Disney. Then Universal gave me [as co-producer] an order for twenty episodes of a TV series called THEY CAME FROM OUTER SPACE and twenty episodes of SHE-WOLF OF LONDON. So I was trying to get directors and writers for those episodes while creating the pilots. I ended up kind of letting go of both of them, and never was happy with the end results.

And then Dino offered me SOMETIMES THEY COME BACK, so that was being prepped during the same time period. I've never had that much on my plate at the same time—life, death, two TV series, a four-camera pilot at Disney, and a feature film. The thing that was of primary importance was my wife and unborn daughter—making sure that the pregnancy was okay and that I was a part of that.

When I was told about my dad's illness, it was this horrible situation. I was in a hospital, standing in a hallway with a doctor and other family members, hearing that his cancer had spread throughout his brain and that there was nothing that could be done. I'm standing there with the doctor—and I can't even believe I did this—but I said, "No, I've directed this scene. There *is* something you can do. There is *always* something that can be done." And he said, "In the movies, maybe … but this is reality. I'm sorry." And I'm still going, "No, we're going to figure out something." He said, "You can get another opinion, but I'm telling you—this is just the way it is." I went home and cried because I couldn't figure out what I could do about it. I wanted to control the situation like a director. I had so much that I *was* controlling at that time … but how do you save your father from dying?

My father was very quiet and shy and I know he was scared about what might be on the other side, but he wouldn't really talk about it. He wouldn't talk about how much pain he was in. I was trying to do whatever I could, knowing that the clock was ticking.

We did a lot together. I took him to see a David Copperfield show.... I did anything that I could to make him feel loved. The fact that I was so busy and couldn't spend all of my time with him made me feel very guilty. There was so much I wanted to learn from him about his life. I had so many questions and I knew it was just a matter of time, a very short amount of time, before he'd be gone.

I had to emotionally pull myself away from the two TV shows, because you can't suffer over something that seems meaningless compared to life and death in your own family. But Steven Banks is my best friend and I wanted to be there 200 percent for him on his show. So that was a challenge.

Then the script for SOMETIMES THEY COME BACK didn't quite work. Dino didn't think it was emotional enough and I agreed. So he brought in Tim Kring and we forged these emotional connections between Tim Matheson's character and his son and his brother. We set up the idea that he'd lost his brother when he was the same age that his son is now, and that set up the ending.

Finally, my lovely daughter Hannah was born. I made sure that my dad got a chance to hold her. Then, in the middle of rehearsals for Steven's show, I got the phone call saying that my dad had died. Unfortunately, the funeral was on the day we were supposed to tape the show. I was lucky to have a very cool assistant director who did the rehearsal blocking for me so that I could go to the funeral, but then I had to return to the studio for the shoot.

I was feeling guilty the whole time because I wasn't with my family, but thankfully they understood. And I knew that my father would be telling me not to sit there and be miserable over him. "Go to work—you're lucky—you're fortunate." I knew that's exactly what he would say. I somehow managed to get through Steven's show, and I believe it was literally the next day that I had to get on a plane to Kansas to start shooting SOME-TIMES THEY COME BACK. There was no time to mourn or grieve. So this is a huge, long story to say that all of that baggage is what I walked into this movie with....

Now, if ever a movie was cursed, this was it. I'm not exaggerating. Every day, something went wrong ... and not small things. I'm talking about major things—people falling down on set, ambulances showing up, the entire transportation department walking off, leaving all the trucks at the last location.... Every lighting setup took two or three hours instead of the hour that was budgeted.... And it was one of the coldest winters they'd ever had in Kansas. When we were shooting that scene in the railroad tunnel, it was so cold that we were all in pain.

One day, Tim Matheson was doing a scene in there. He was sitting down on the ground and, just as he got up, a boulder—probably two feet by two feet—fell down from the top of the cave and landed right where his head had been a minute before. It was a miracle he didn't get hit.... On another day, Brooke Adams fell and twisted her ankle, so we were shut down because of that.... Then we had an actor who had a heart attack—the old cop who says "Sometimes they come back."

He'd had a heart attack in L.A. just before the shoot but he begged and pleaded with us not to replace him because he hadn't worked in so many years. I couldn't say no. So he came and, sadly, had a really tough time remembering his lines. We had to use huge cue cards and shoot the scene in sections. He was very embarrassed about that but we kept going. And then when the footage came back the next day, we found out that the camera department had exposed the film for the wrong stock, so the whole thing was purple and grainy. This movie was just one horrible thing after another.

At the end of the production, some local asked, "How's your movie going?" And I said, "Well it's been a little rough—we're eight days over schedule." Which for a low-budget movie like that is absurd. Thank God Dino is a producer from the good old days and he would just call me and say, "So are you giving me a goddamn good picture?" I'd say, "Yessir." He just dealt with the overages because he understood it wasn't anything I was doing [that was causing the problems]. We were victims of one bad circumstance after another. Then this local person says, "You realize you are shooting on Indian burial ground." I said, "Oh bullshit." He said, "You can look it up." So I did, and sure enough that railroad tunnel was not supposed to have been built. They literally dug up an Indian burial ground to create that tunnel.

Director Tom McLoughlin is "cursed" with actor Robert Rusler on the set of SOMETIMES THEY COME BACK (CBS, 1991) (courtesy Tom McLoughlin).

So was the movie cursed? Who knows? I was willing to accept any explanation at that point because anything that could go wrong had gone wrong—starting on day one, when it snowed six inches during a time of year when it never snows. From that first day, we were way behind schedule.

MADDREY: *Did you tell Stephen King about all of this?*
McLOUGHLIN: Never did. Should have.

MADDREY: *Sounds like something he would have written into the story....*
McLOUGHLIN: And I'm just giving you the tip of the iceberg. There were personality conflicts.... The production crew had been pulled from places across the United States and everybody hated each other. The [working] climate was like: "Can we just get this fucking thing done and over with?" Departments were sabotaging each other.

I have this unbelievable story from the cemetery shoot. We had a soundman who was overly intense about his job. If anything messed up the sound, he really took it into his own hands to get into people's faces—because to him, sound was everything. We had these huge lights that had these balustrade things that were buzzing, and he thought it was a problem. It's three o'clock in the morning in a cemetery, so even the crickets are quiet, and these things had a buzz that only the soundman could hear but he kept asking for the gaffers to move the balustrades. And they wouldn't do it. I don't know if they were just being difficult or if it really wasn't possible. But this guy decided he was going to do it on his own. He started moving things, a cord came loose and hit something, and [simulates the sound of an electrical shock] all the lights in the entire cemetery went out.

We were moments away from doing a huge emotional scene with Tim and then we had to wait for someone to fix the generator. I don't remember how long it took, but I remember we were chasing the dark. I was terrified that the sun was going to come up before we could finish the scene. We just barely made it…. All because some sound guy was pissed off about hearing a buzz that we could have easily fixed in post. That just epitomizes the experience of making this movie. We were lucky to get this thing finished at all. I'm amazed that the film works on *any* level.

One thing that I'm incredibly proud of is the score by Terry Plumeri. He hadn't done a lot of movies but I took a chance on him because he had such passion. We had very little money and he was going to find a way to make this score work. And he created a fabulous orchestral score that was much better than the usual synth score you have to do on a film like this. I remember that [the editor] Charles Bornstein and I were temping our early cut with a very haunting music by Georges Delerue from THE ESCAPE ARTIST. I didn't want Terry to rip that off, but I wanted something that was like that. I spent a lot of time with him, plucking out notes—making him keep rewriting. I was obsessed. He finally came up with two wonderful themes that we kept repeating throughout the film. I felt like he really gave the movie its soul.

And Tim [Matheson] did an amazing job. That was one of the best casting choices in my life. I was so blessed to have him. He's the kind of person I would like to be in an ideal world. I was just really impressed with his manner, the way he handled things, how charismatic and funny—he just has all the qualities I wish I had. And because I identified with him so closely, that movie did become much more of a personal journey for me.

I was also very fortunate to get Brooke Adams, who I've admired since DAYS OF HEAVEN. And the boy, Robert Gorman [who plays Matheson's son in the film], was amazing. He came in for the casting session and was the only one who played the scene as if all the props were in the room with him. Most child actors will just read the lines of the character but he acted it out with imaginary props—as if he had a real belief that he was looking at those things or looking at someone else in the room who wasn't there.

So I was really lucky in these ways but it was still very difficult to put all the pieces together and make that movie. I always say there are two kinds of movies. There are the movies that you make and there are movies that you survive. Thank God I do the second kind very, very seldom. But that was a survival movie. I just tied myself to the helm and said, "I'm going to get to shore or go down with the ship."

MADDREY: I assumed that you must have had much more creative control over that film because the ending seems so personal. In the final scene, Tim's character chooses the future over the past—he lets go of his brother and chooses his wife and son—and at the same time you were letting go of your father and embracing your new daughter. That final scene also seems to be about choosing reality over fantasy … and, as it turned out, this was your last fantasy-oriented film for a while….

McLOUGHLIN: It's about love—losing somebody that you really love. And now that I think about it, the older brother really was like a father-figure to the young Tim Matheson character. I wasn't conscious of that at all at the time but maybe because of all the emotional stuff that was going on, I had some sort of personal connection to the end of the movie.

In most ghost stories, you've got to somehow resolve the spirit's conflicts so that they can move on. Once they move on, you know you're never going to see them again. I *was* choosing life over death.

Anytime I've had dreams of my father or my mother, I'm aware in the dream that they are dead and I'm dreaming. I don't want the dream to end because I've got an opportunity to be with them in that realm for a certain amount of time and it's wonderful. It's such a bizarre thing to sit here and talk about it or intellectualize it, because in a dream you're not supposed to be aware that you're dreaming. How does that work? I really do feel the same emotions that I would in life if I saw them again. If they suddenly walk through the door, I'm like, "Don't leave yet.... I have so much that I want to ask you." It's interesting how the mind works.

I guess I think of my dreams as "movies." Some of them have a great ending and some of them have a horrible ending. Sometimes the film breaks and you don't get to the end.

Legacy (... AGAIN ... FOR MORE...)

When there's money to be made, they almost always come back. Tom McLoughlin's telefilm of SOMETIMES THEY COME BACK aired on CBS on May 7, 1991, to disappointing ratings and mixed reviews. A gorier cut played theatrically overseas and premiered domestically on home video in April 1993. Apparently, that release performed well enough to prompt a sequel from Trimark Entertainment. In a 1996 interview, producer Michael Meltzer claimed that SOMETIMES THEY COME BACK ... AGAIN would be "based more on the characters" in King's story and "remain true to the theme and the morality of the original" (Beeler: "SOMETIMES" 1996). Despite that claim, the screen story by Guy Riedel and director Adam Grossman follows a completely new set of characters, including a demonic villain modeled after occultist Aleister Crowley.

The main character is Jon Porter, a psychotherapist who returns to his hometown with his teenage daughter Michelle following the death of his mother. Jon eventually learns that his mother was murdered by an ageless Satanist named Tony Reno, who also murdered Jon's sister when he was a teenager and now wants to sacrifice Michelle. The plot is reminiscent of CHILDREN OF THE CORN 2, embracing the tried-and-true slasher movie formula—stock "crazy prophet" character, endlessly quipping villain, dead teenager parade—while paying homage to Stephen King's larger fictional universe by introducing a clairvoyant teenage "witch" and a mentally-challenged lawnmower man who gets *literally* mowed down. (Never mind that King's original "lawnmower man" wasn't mentally-challenged; the filmmakers seem to be more familiar with the in-name-only film adaptation than the short story.) In the end, dad saves daughter from demons and the final scene reiterates the "message" of SOMETIMES THEY COME BACK: we overcome our fears by recognizing and facing them.

Perhaps the most interesting thing about the sequel is that it utilizes the black magic idea from Stephen King's story to explain the return of Tony Reno and his death-less goons. SOMETIMES THEY COME BACK … FOR MORE follows that thread (sort of) but relocates its Satanists to an arctic military outpost in an apparent homage to THE THING. The screen story by Adam Grossman and Darryl Sollerh is another tale of two brothers, one of whom faces his demons while the other conjures them to kill people. Director Daniel Berk sums up the theme: "To be a man, to really grow, you have to deal with personal obstacles. You can't just ignore them. They come back to haunt you and prevent you from moving ahead in your life" (Crow: "Screaming" 1998). After the poor performance of the second sequel, the filmmakers at Trimark decided to move on.

Still … it is hard to imagine that we've seen the last of this title. In a 2021 interview, at the height of a surge of Stephen King film and television adaptations, CHAPEL-WAITE co-creator Peter Filardi indicated that he'd like to tackle a new adaptation of the short story, saying, "I know it's been adapted, but…" (Ryan 2021).

PART FIVE

From GRAVEYARD SHIFT
to THE MANGLER

Development Hell (Oral History)

STEPHEN KING: I sold "Graveyard Shift" from *Night Shift* to this total unknown from Pittsburgh for I think $75 or something like that because he seemed interested in it and he seemed bright and most of all he seemed to have the right sense of humor—and maybe he can bankroll it and we'll have something that will be really outrageous like EVIL DEAD. (Horsting: "Interview" 1986)

The "total unknown" was 21-year-old Pittsburgh native George Demick, who had previously worked as an apprentice to filmmaker George Romero on KNIGHTRIDERS (1981). An aspiring filmmaker, Demick was a frequent visitor to Romero's Laurel Entertainment offices. One day, he got lucky.

GEORGE DEMICK: I saw George and mentioned I was going down to South Carolina to watch a wrestling card. He suggested I stop by and meet Steve [King] at Dino De Laurentiis's studio. I was 21 at the time. (Tilley 2014)

GEORGE DEMICK: When I get down there, he's prepping MAXIMUM OVERDRIVE. I remember he was wearing a Venus fly trap t-shirt that had a rubber fly on the shoulder. And he was like, "Hey, nice to meet you, man. George has said some nice things about you." I honestly don't know what George thought when he sent me down to meet Steve. I don't know if he had an inkling that I would ask for something. Actually, it was [Romero's cinematographer] Mike Gornick who was like, "Well, you know, he's let other people option his short stories for very little money. Why don't you look at some of his stories and see if there's anything…?" So I looked, and the ones I liked were "Graveyard Shift" and "Gray Matter." In my memory, the conversation went like this: "Could you sign my copy of *Danse Macabre*?" "Oh, absolutely." He signed it and then I go, "I was wondering, does anybody have the rights to 'Graveyard Shift'?" "No." "Well, is there any way I could get them because I'd like to make a feature film…" "You're talking about a *feature* film?" "Yeah." And he literally picked up the phone and called [his literary agent] Kirby McCauley. I remember him saying, "Give this guy the rights. I have faith in him." I was blown away. […] I initially asked Mike Gornick if he would be interested in directing. He goes, "Yeah, of course. However, I have no track record of directing. You need to get somebody attached to it who has a name value." I didn't want to approach George Romero. So Mike goes, "What about Tom Savini?" (2021 phone interview with the author)

TOM SAVINI: I am up to direct it. […] Legally, they have to get an approved script by a certain date or they have to pay something. Pennies. That's a token gesture from Steve King. George [Demick] is looking for the backing. The screenwriter is John Esposito, who I recommended to him. (McDonnell 1986)

JOHN ESPOSITO: I had written an anthology film and I was looking to sort of get it to anyone. There was a horror convention, believe it or not, where a special effects / makeup artist, Tom Savini, who is also a director and actor, was appearing. He was onstage and he was saying he was looking for material to direct. I literally went on the autograph line and asked him if I could send him the script. (St. John 2014)

GEORGE DEMICK: John Esposito had given Tom a script called THE TELL-TALE TAVERN, which is a really great anthology idea. I don't think anyone will ever make it because there's some shit in there where you go, "Oh, that's overstepping some lines." Like chopping up kids and stacking them like tinder. But Tom said, "Why don't you give him a call and see if he'll write the script?" So I called John, he came down, we had a meeting and made a deal. He ended up writing the script. [...] My initial idea was way different than what John Esposito did. My thought process was: Let's start a fire and let's get them down in the sub-basement within the first ten, fifteen, twenty minutes. And then just make it ALIENS, with giant rats and mutated bats flying all over and these people just trying to survive the onslaught. John brought in such a different viewpoint. [His version had] more characterization, more depth than what I wanted to do. (2021 phone interview with the author)

JOHN ESPOSITO: I looked for a theme I wanted to comment on. It was a real American horror story, which is what King does best. I grabbed that angle and ran with it as fast as I could, because I only had a week. (Stephen Jones: *Creepshows* 2002)

GRAVEYARD SHIFT (First Draft—March 30, 1986)

The short story "Graveyard Shift" consists of ten time-stamped scenes, charting a week in the life of several men who have been tasked with cleaning out the basement of a textile mill in the fictional town of Gates Falls, Maine. The central conflict is a power struggle between the mill's gruff foreman, Warwick, and an unhinged, college-age drifter named Hall. In the first scene, set at 2 a.m. on Friday, Warwick invites Hall to join his 36-man cleaning crew over the upcoming 4th of July weekend. Hall's usual gig is working a stationary cotton picker machine while fending off rats using a sling shot and empty soda cans. He figures the cleanup job can't be worse than that.

At 11 p.m. on Monday, Warwick addresses his crew as they prepare to go to work. Three hours later, Hall is toiling away alongside a whiny, obese fellow named Wisconsky, in a dark, dingy hellhole. Stephen King sets the scene as follows: "The bulbs couldn't banish the twelve-year darkness; it could only push it back a little and cast a sickly yellow glow over the whole mess. The place looked like the shattered nave of a desecrated church, with its high ceiling and mammoth discarded machinery that they would never be able to move, its wet walls overgrown with patches of yellow moss…." In King's story, the setting is the monster.

Two hours later, the cleanup crew breaks for lunch and Hall learns that a co-worker went home after being bitten by a rat. Three hours later, Hall and Wisconsky leave the mill together, then Hall falls asleep in his apartment and "dreams of rats." By 1 a.m. on

Wednesday, they are back at work. A fellow named Carmichael suffers a rat attack and another fellow named Cy Ippeston protests the inhumane working conditions at the mill. Warwick fires Ippeston, whose co-workers wither under the foreman's gaze. Work resumes.

At 2 a.m. on Thursday, Hall realizes he hasn't seen any rats lately and theorizes that they must have escaped into a sub-basement nest. At 3:30 a.m., his suspicions are confirmed by the discovery of a trap door into the sub-basement. Hall taunts Warwick with the discovery, threatening to tell local health authorities about the infestation, so the foreman promptly orders Hall to investigate the sub-basement himself. Hall, being somewhat unhinged (although it's not clear why), goes … but he makes Warwick and Wisconsky come with him.

Down below, they find a second trap door into a *sub*-sub-basement. They also find a rusty lock on the underside of the trap door, which begs the obvious question: "Who locked it?" King offers an oblique answer via writing on the side of a huge wooden crate: "Elias Varney, 1841." Warwick notes that the mill wasn't built until 1897 and the characters wisely leave the crate alone (fodder for a different story) but continue exploring the underground labyrinth, eventually bringing the struggle between labor and management to a head.

Once the pioneers realize they have somehow traveled beyond the outer walls of the mill, Warwick gets nervous and tries to turn back—but Hall won't let him. Wisconsky escapes, but Hall urges the foreman on, by force when necessary. The two men stumble into a nest of bats, mutated rats, and a moldy human skull. Hall relishes his newfound authority over Warwick, right up until the moment they encounter what King calls "the *magna mater*," a calf-size queen rat "whose progeny might someday develop wings." She eats Warwick, leaving Hall to be devoured by hungry bats. He dies laughing insanely.

King's story is effectively grim but it doesn't have much else to offer. The challenge for screenwriter John Esposito was not only expanding the plot of the ten-scene story but also creating characterizations that would give the story depth. Maintaining Hall as the central character, the screenwriter set out to explain why King's hero is so unhinged. In the short story, King introduces Hall as a graduate of Berkeley College who has been drifting through New England, working odd jobs; he has no romantic attachments and no legal obligations. Esposito's First Draft, dated March 30, 1986, sets up Julian Hall as a hyper-sensitive artist haunted by visions of a mysterious woman. In some ways, he seems like a younger, less effete version of Vincent Price's characters in Roger Corman's early Poe-pictures, HOUSE OF USHER and THE PIT AND THE PENDULUM. In the first scene, Hall "wakes up" to the sight of a mystery woman (he knows her but we don't) making breakfast for him. She stirs a mixer bowl full of blood, violently slopping it onto him—and awakening him for a second time. In the second scene, Hall finds himself in an empty bedroom. He looks down at a bloody wound on his arm—a gruesome reminder of a recent suicide attempt. Nearby is a pastel portrait of the Bachman Textile Mill, his future workplace.

In a subsequent scene, Hall waits for an interview with Warwick, the foreman at the mill. The interview scene is essentially directed on the page, with the screenwriter's text drawing attention to details that will convey the grittiness of the setting: close-ups of dripping sweat on Hall's body, thick smoke hanging in the air in front of him, and a clock ticking away the seconds of his life. Hall is thoroughly on edge when Warwick finally enters the room. As the foreman sizes him up, the drifter realizes that his suicide scar is bleeding again. He hears droplets of his own blood pounding on the floor "like thunder." A shot at the end of the scene clarifies that the wound was not actually bleeding; the tell-tale thunder existed only in his imagination. Warwick hires Hall to work the cotton picker.

Hall tours the facility and briefly meets Wisconsky—who, in this version of the tale, is a young woman. Suddenly, Hall's wound is bleeding again. This time, the blood turns out to be real, which shocks his future co-workers. They promptly brand him a "freak."

Two weeks later, Esposito's script picks up where King's short story begins; with Hall working the picker and picking off rats. Warwick pays him a visit but doesn't mention the cleaning crew (yet). Esposito takes more time to flesh out the main character. A subsequent scene in the local café pits Hall against his crude male co-workers, who gleefully serve him a plate of rat tartare. Hall doesn't react—he's obviously a guy who is used to repressing his emotions—but in the following scene he dreams of six "rat doctors" performing surgery on him.

Next, Esposito introduces a completely new character: a pistol-toting exterminator named Tucker Cleveland, who dresses like a hybrid of a Ghostbuster and Rambo. Cleveland rants about a horrific experience with rats in 'Nam—perhaps an homage to Robert Shaw's USS Indianapolis speech in JAWS? To punctuate the speech, Cleveland slices open Hall's belly and shoves his fist into the gaping wound. Hall looks down, sees that his belly is still intact, and realizes he's hallucinating again. Warwick interrupts the scene with an invitation to join the 4th of July cleanup crew.

Hall returns to his apartment, where he's working on a portrait of his dream woman covered by rats. A wider shot reveals it's one of many such paintings.

Back at work, Hall gets into an argument with Warwick and imagines the foreman hanging from the ceiling like an old punching bag. Soon after, Warwick takes him down to the sub-basement, which the screenwriter compares to the set of an old AIP / Edgar Allan Poe movie. (HOUSE OF USHER, THE PIT AND THE PENDULUM, THE HAUNTED PALACE...) The duo find a fully clothed skeleton with a rat living in its skull, then vermin swarm Warwick as Hall flees the scene. Later, in the café, Hall's male co-workers propose leaving Warwick for dead in the basement over the holiday weekend. *Little do they know.*

Meanwhile, someone has slashed the tires on Hall's car, forcing him to walk home. Wisconsky picks him up on the side of the road, but their dialogue is brief and awkward. When he arrives at his apartment, Hall finds Warwick—alive—engaging in a rat-infested orgy with the mystery woman. In the script's most shocking scene, the foreman feeds the woman a live rat, then retrieves the rat from between her legs. Hall dispels the horrific dream imagery by opening the blinds to let the daylight in. Instead, the scene culminates with a baseball smashing through the window in front of him. Hall looks out and sees a group of guilty children running away.

That night, Warwick blackmails Tucker Cleveland on behalf of the mill's owner—a "not very patient" fellow named Bachman. The exterminator goes to work and Warwick goes to pick on Hall. The foreman doesn't say a word at first, so Hall doesn't trust his eyes. *Did he really leave Warwick for dead in the basement or did he imagine that? Has Warwick returned from the dead?* Warwick leaves quietly, then Hall has a brief exchange with his co-worker Ippeston, who says he saw Warwick as well. Hall, unsure of what to believe, goes home "sick."

In the next scene, Warwick hears a Beach Boys tune ("Surf City") playing loudly in

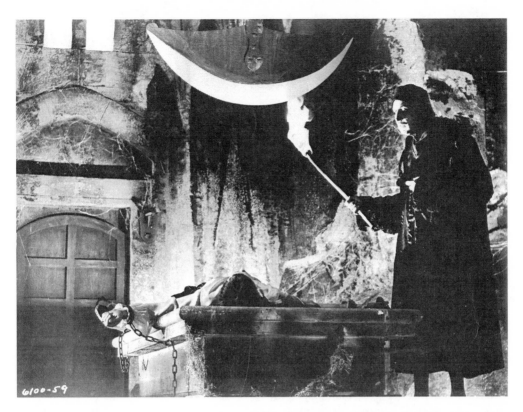

Vincent Price tortures a guest in the basement of THE PIT AND THE PENDULUM (AIP, 1962).

the sub-basement. He descends and sees rats surfing on flood waters. Brogan and Danson, two members of the cleanup crew, are wielding the fire hose that created the flood. The 4th of July "festivities" have begun.

This is essentially the mid-point of Esposito's screenplay (page 53 of 110). So far, the screen story has consisted almost entirely of embellishments of King's scant tale. The next scene replicates the second scene in the source story, with Warwick addressing a six-man (plus one woman) cleanup crew. The screenwriter stipulates that the basement looks different than the AIP-inspired setting Hall saw earlier, which indicates that Hall imagined the earlier scene and Warwick's death-by-rats. The skeleton crew goes to work, their first "day" on the job culminating with a rat-attack on Carmichael. This scene plays out as in King's story.

The script then returns to Hall's apartment, where Hall and Wisconsky observe real 4th of July festivities in the streets below. In dialogue, the screenwriter finally unravels the mystery of Hall's painted lady; she is his dead wife. Wisconsky changes the subject, addressing an equally important mystery: why they are both still in Gates Falls, working dead-end jobs. Wisconsky answers her own question by explaining how she fled her childhood home (Castle Rock), stubbornly married the wrong guy, and fell into Warwick's rat trap where she has been exploited in every possible way. She wants to leave but says she won't give the foreman the satisfaction of making her quit. The backdrop to her monologue is an ironic blast of fireworks, celebrating freedom.

On page 71 of the 110-page script, the cleanup crew discovers the sub-basement. Hall threatens to blackmail Warwick by telling local authorities about the infestation and then Warwick threatens to reveal Hall's "secret" to the rest of the crew. Hall responds by rolling up his sleeves to display his suicide scars. Warwick backs off for the time being, but in the next scene he reasserts his power by putting the screws to Tucker Cleveland. (Once again, Warwick invokes the name Bachman, this time mentioning that the mill owner's wife is named Tabby.) Then he fires Hall, saying Bachman told him to. After casting a weary look of defeat at Wisconsky, Hall leaves the mill and returns to his apartment.

In the third and final act of Esposito's First Draft, the main character is relegated to an offscreen presence while Warwick and the crew once again descend into the sub-basement. There, the foreman and his merry misogynists taunt Wisconsky with the hidden truth about her new boyfriend: he has been in and out of mental hospitals for years, suffering from an inability to distinguish dreams from reality. All his life, Warwick explains to Wisconsky, Hall has been haunted by dead people; first his parents, who were killed in an unspecified tragedy, and then his wife. Enraged by the foreman's callousness, Wisconsky decks Warwick. He hits her back, then the other goons pile on and accidentally kill her. Like the sleazeballs they are, they dispose of her body in the sub-sub-basement.

Meanwhile, in his apartment, Hall hears a knock at the door. The screenwriter specifies that the visitor uses the same distinctive eight-beat knock that Wisconsky used in her earlier visit to the apartment. Hall doesn't open the door because he doesn't have to. Like Hall, we know it's Wisconsky. Unlike Hall, we know that Wisconsky is dead.

Back at the mill, the wetwork weasels decide they need to cover their tracks better, so they descend into the sub-sub-basement to erase any evidence of Wisconsky's body. There, they encounter…. Hall. He tells them about his recent visit from Wisconsky and explains that she told him there were mutated monsters living beneath the mill. Brandishing a pistol, Hall persuades the killers—including Warwick—to find out for themselves. Once the goons descend, Hall locks the door behind them. In the darkness below, the mill workers find King's crate ("Elias Varney, 1841") as well as a giant rat's nest and the partial remains of Tucker Cleveland. In an amusing aside, the characters invoke the name of Ripley, the gung-ho heroine from ALIENS. Like the Marines in ALIENS, the supporting characters in GRAVEYARD SHIFT get picked off one by one, as they encounter mutated bats, bipedal rats, and a vaguely described bat-human hybrid. The story has no heroic Ripley.

Warwick becomes the last man standing against the *magna mater* and experiences a glimmer of hope when he finds that Hall has intentionally left behind a pistol. Ironically, the foreman uses it to attempt suicide—only to learn that the gun has no bullets. The screenplay concludes with a scene of the Bachman Mill on fire, collapsing into the earth as it burns. A casual observer notes that the presumptive arsonist's car (established in the earlier scene where Hall saw that someone has slashed his tires) is absent from the parking lot. A final shot shows Hall—the psychotic dispenser of karmic justice—driving into the sunrise.

Development Hell (Oral History)

With Esposito's First Draft in hand, George Demick partnered with a Los Angeles–based producer and flew out to Hollywood to meet with potential investors. They began with Charles Band, who was reportedly eager to have a Stephen King project.

GEORGE DEMICK: Through contacts of mine, I get a meeting with Charlie Band at Full Moon Entertainment. He comes in and he looks like death warmed over. He had, like, a 103-degree fever. He was *sick*. But he wanted Stephen King. [My producing partner] proceeded to be incredibly rude to him. She wouldn't even tell him any of the ideas we had for the movie, so the meeting was a complete and utter bust—because she was saying, "We're going to Paramount, we're going to Universal, we're going to all these places." Charlie Band was furious when we left. (2021 phone interview with the author)

Demick and his producing partner quickly discovered that other studio heads were less enthusiastic about making a Stephen King movie.

GEORGE DEMICK: MAXIMUM OVERDRIVE opened up the weekend I got out [to L.A.], and that was like the fifth or sixth Stephen King movie that had died at the box office. So, *none* of the studios were like "Oh, you got Stephen King!" [laughs] I remember we had a meeting at one studio and, I swear to God, it was like every story you had ever heard about meeting with executives in Hollywood. I remember FATAL ATTRACTION was big at that time, and during the meeting, the executive looks across the desk and goes, "Is there any way to make it more like FATAL ATTRACTION?" I'm like, "It's about giant rats and mutated bats. How the hell...?" (2021 phone interview with the author)

After more than a year of unsuccessfully shopping the project around Hollywood, Demick fired the L.A.-based producer and hired a new collaborator.

GEORGE DEMICK: Greg Nicotero contacted me and said, "Hey, I've got this new producing partner and we would kind of like to get on board with GRAVEYARD SHIFT." They got a deal with New World Pictures and we got $60,000 to $65,000 for signing with them. I was in debt for legal bills, option rights, paying for the script, so I didn't see a dime—but it got me out of debt. At that point, we had a script and Tom Savini was attached to direct. (2021 phone interview with the author)

TOM SAVINI: I've signed a deal with New World Pictures to direct two films; the first one is a Stephen King short story, GRAVEYARD SHIFT. When reviewing the script, I took out everything I couldn't personally believe in. We had a character become a Dream Walker, which means he dreams even in a waking state. In that kind of position, you can show anything you want because the audience knows it's part of somebody's hallucinations, illusions. (Daniel 1988)

GEORGE DEMICK: Tom had all these great visual ideas. I remember one of the visions was a dream where this vagina has teeth and starts trying to pull him in. I was stunned. (2021 interview with the author)

JOHN ESPOSITO: The *vagina dentata* sequence never actually made it into a script. Tom pitched it as the opening to the New World exec at our first meeting. Let's just say *she* wasn't amused. In 2010, we resurrected it for a segment of an anthology film, THE THEATRE BIZARRE, directed by Savini and written by me. [...] The big concern from Demick and Savini was Hall's obvious absence from the final act in the sub-cellar. What was I thinking?! I did another treatment and a new draft. New World wanted ALIENS and, at their behest, we ended up giving Wisconsky a child—I shit you not!— her very own Newt rummaging around the sub-cellar. From what I remember, it was pretty awful. (2021 correspondence with the author)

GEORGE DEMICK: We were two months away from preproduction when New World went bankrupt. At that point, the [annual cost of] the option [on Stephen King's short story] was a huge jump. The first year had been next to nothing. The following year was $5,000 and I had to get people to invest in that without crowd-funding because we didn't have stuff like that back then. The third year, it jumped up to like $15,000 or $20,000. I was like, *I'm not up to that. It was a nice shot.* So I kind of gave the rights back to Steve. (2021 interview with the author)

By the fall of 1988, Stephen King had licensed the "Graveyard Shift" story rights to William J. Dunn of Augusta, Maine. Dunn had served as the filming locations manager for CREEPSHOW 2 and PET SEMATARY, and also helped to create the Maine Film Commission. He was eager to get a new Stephen King movie set up in the author's home state.

WILLIAM J. DUNN: I met Ralph [Singleton] when we were both involved with the PET SEMATARY project. He was associate producer, I was location manager, and we became fast friends. I already had GRAVEYARD SHIFT in my pocket and eventually I approached him about directing it. (Labbe: "Oh" 1990)

RALPH SINGLETON: I read the short story and I talked to Bill and I said, "Let's do more research on this. Maybe this is a possibility." [...] And in his research, he found that this young guy had written a screenplay. (Singleton: "Working" 2020)

RALPH SINGLETON: I wasn't that interested in doing a film based on a short story, but Esposito's initial script was so well-done and the situation so inviting that I had to say yes. (Labbe: "Ratman" 1990)

GEORGE DEMICK: Bill Dunn contacts me and he goes, "Hey, I got the rights to 'Graveyard Shift' from Steve. We really want to option your script." I'm like, "Well, it's just sitting in a box in the closet..." [...] I remember I signed the contract on a Thursday. On Friday [April 21, 1989], fuckin' PET SEMATARY opens. On Monday, they had the deal with Paramount. (2021 phone interview with the author)

RALPH SINGLETON: I went to the president of marketing at Paramount and I said, "How would you like to have the next Stephen King picture at Halloween?" That was like throwing raw meat at a wild dog. (Singleton: "Working" 2020)

Ralph Singleton spent the following months working with John Esposito on a new draft of the script.

JOHN ESPOSITO: We've made some adjustments—mostly cutting down on what our budget just can't handle. I'd originally thrown in a lot of supernatural elements that proved superfluous. Now, it's about two-thirds reality and one-third supernatural. (Labbe: "Oh" 1990)

GRAVEYARD SHIFT (Second Draft—April 30, 1990)

Four years after delivering his First Draft of GRAVEYARD SHIFT, John Esposito completed a 102-page Second Draft. The revised story is tighter and incorporates a major re-think of the main character as well as the story's monster(s). Julian Hall is now John Hall, a more traditional all-American hero. (One character refers to him as "Uncle Sam.") Instead of resembling an unhinged Vincent Price character, he is now more like David Banner in THE INCREDIBLE HULK or John Nada in THEY LIVE: a strong, silent, idealistic working man. In short, more of a romantic leading man in a Hollywood film. No suicide scars, no crazy hallucinations, and his creepy, rat-obsessed drawings have been replaced by loving portraits of his late wife.

The screenwriter also gave Jane Wisconsky a slight makeover. She remains scrappy but she's more of an open-hearted idealist—the kind of girl who wears daddy's flag pin to work, and knows how to soothe a stray puppy dog like John Hall. In the pivotal 4th of July fireworks scene, she encourages Hall to let go of the past and embrace the present—meaning her. He does and the new lovers *almost* agree to put the town of Gates Falls in their rearview mirror forever. Their inability to do so turns the tale of romance into a bleak tragedy. Despite all odds, the leads retain their idealism; at one point, they even save the life of their contemptible boss Warwick because, as Wisconsky says, that's the type of people they are … right up until Wisconsky gets killed by the mutant creature in the sub-basement. At that point, Hall loses his cool. When Warwick's life is again threatened by the creature, Hall lets him die. The hero then squares off against his real nemesis.

At some point during the development of the shooting script, director Ralph Singleton decided that GRAVEYARD SHIFT didn't have a strong enough monster. He described his thought process in a 1990 interview: "We asked ourselves, what are two things that frighten people? Rats and bats, right? So, we molded both phobias into one and came up with a 'bat-rat'" (Labbe: "Ratman" 1990). To be fair, the bat-rat idea was present in Stephen King's short story, in a brief line suggesting that the *"magna mater"* living in the sub-basement might one day spawn progeny with wings. In Esposito's Second Draft, King's prediction is realized.

The bat-rat makes its presence known early in the revised script, in a completely new scene built around John Hall's predecessor. While working the cotton picker machine, the cheerful family man Jason Reed gets attacked and devoured. The script specifies that we (the movie-going audience) won't actually see the monster; we'll only see the bloody remains of Jason Reed. From that point forward, the script closely follows the visual style of the film ALIEN, revealing its monster only in fragments: a giant wing envelops a worker named Stevenson; something sucks Tucker Cleveland through the floor of an underground crypt; a giant shadow kills a minor character named Nardello. Only when the mill workers descend into the sub-sub-basement does the alien queen finally show herself.

In the script's final fight between bat-rat and hero, the screenwriter suggests that the bat-rat is not the most dangerous monster in the mill. Singleton explains, "The monster of the film isn't [the bat-rat], it's the picker. It's a man-made horror. It operates blindly, making no distinction between flesh or wool or whatever" (Labbe: "Ratman" 1990). Indeed, John Hall uses the indiscriminate "monster" to kill the biological monster; the mechanical teeth chew her up and spit her out—just as the mill does with its blue-collar workers.

An early scene in this revised draft sets up the ironic ending. Esposito proposes an opening shot—set sometime well before the central action in the script—that reveals an old cemetery hiding beneath the ruins of the abandoned mill. The camera then travels inside the mill and surveys the dusty ruins, before cutting to a present-day shot of the revitalized mill featuring a sign advertising its grand re-opening. The new opening sequence might have been inspired by PET SEMATARY, which opens with a similar traveling shot of a cemetery. The sequence was ultimately eliminated from the shooting script but the subtext of mill-as-undead-monster remains. In the final script, Jason Reed cuts his hand on the picker, making the picker seem complicit in his demise. That death scene is quickly followed by a darkly humorous shot of a mill worker hanging a "Help Wanted" sign. The subtext is clear: Humans are nothing but grist for this mill.

In a 1990 promotional interview, Stephen King described GRAVEYARD SHIFT as "a Marxist horror story" about "an intense class struggle" between "the proletariat and the overclass that exists on the sweat of the proletariat's brow" (Nutman: "King" 1990). Esposito's final shooting script amplifies the blue-collar American nightmare of King's story in some very pointed ways. For whatever reason, many of those amplifications didn't end up in the film. Wisconsky's flag pin, for example, is absent. Also missing is the 4th of July fireworks scene in Hall's apartment, which brought some intelligence and tonal levity to a mostly crude and bleak story. One wonders if the filmmakers decided that the scene—in which the two heroes plan their escape from the American nightmare while celebratory fireworks fill the air—was too obvious or too hokey.

Regardless, the overall tone of the final film is more oppressive than that of the Second Draft of the script—because the final film obliterates the glimmer of hope that the heroes might escape their plight. In comparison, the First Draft suggested a kind of mental escape from the same spirit-crushing reality, via the main character's mad visions. The fantastic dream imagery associated with those visions could have provided a sense of otherworldly escape for some moviegoers—the way the surrealistic imagery of HELLRAISER counterbalances that film's bleakness, or the way the ultra-stylized, comic-book imagery of CREEPSHOW encourages that film's audience to "have fun" being scared. Stephen King has suggested that such moments can be transcendent, providing cathartic relief to viewers.

There are still a few moments of levity in the film. John Esposito's original idea for a scene of carnivorous rats surfing through the flooded basement to the tune of a Beach Boys song survived to the final cut. The screenwriter's character Cleveland Tucker also survived and became larger-than-life thanks to the performance of character actor Brad Dourif. An exaggerated performance by actor Stephen Macht similarly infuses the War-wick character with a certain *joie de vivre*. In the final act of the film, these two characters almost seem to merge into one, as Warwick goes Section Eight in the dungeon.

Despite the world gone mad, John Hall manages to hold himself together long enough to dispatch the bat-rat but his demeanor in the final scene of the film suggests he might spend the rest of his life battling monsters in his mind. (Perhaps the Dream Walker's struggle to separate reality and fantasy could be fodder for a sequel?) The film ends not with a time clock and a flag pin, but with a return to the humorous shot of a "Help Wanted" sign hanging outside the mill.

Reflections on the Film (Oral History)

RALPH SINGLETON: I remember having one screening just with Stephen King. [...] Stephen King looked at me and said, "Well, Ralph, it's gonna do great video." (Singleton: "Filmmaking" 2020)

STEPHEN KING: There are things about it I like a lot. Brad Dourif gives a bang-up performance as the exterminator. [...] There's also this scene where they're flooding the mill and all these rats are flowing out on this muddy water, and they're floating on bits of board and shingles and the Beach Boys are singing "Surfin' Safari." It's funny. (Nutman: "King" 1990)

Although the film placed #1 at the box office on Halloween weekend in 1990, reviewers were harsh. Several—including San Francisco Chronicle's *Peter Stack and* TV Guide's

Derek Armstrong—declared GRAVEYARD SHIFT the worst Stephen King movie made to date. Even the most enthusiastic reviewers carefully couched their compliments.

JANET MASLIN (movie reviewer for *The New York Times*): Made as an unabashed B-movie, GRAVEYARD SHIFT has an offbeat, well-chosen cast of unfamiliar-looking actors, and they help to give the film its gritty edge. […] The early scenes that allow the actors a little color are more fun than the all-basement episodes, which are visually monotonous. (Maslin 1990)

KEVIN THOMAS (movie reviewer for *The Los Angeles Times*): This picture, which looks far, far better than it is, is so clunky that you can't be sure just how funny writer John Esposito, in adapting an early King short story, and director Ralph S. Singleton intended it to be. […] It plays like a crude burlesque, so numbskull that the over-the-top performances of Stephen Macht, affecting a terrible phony New England accent as the mill's Simon Legree foreman, and Brad Dourif as a spacey rat exterminator are actually welcome. (Thomas 1990)

SCOTT VON DOVIAK (author of *Stephen King Films FAQ*): The background is populated with authentically rough-and-ready rural Mainers; there are no Beverly Hills bodies on display here. The production design of the mill's interior is appropriately dank and cavernous: With its dark clutter of ancient machinery, half-flooded nooks and crannies, and walls seething with rats, it's a nightmarish setting … for some other movie. (Von Doviak 2000)

MARK BROWNING (author of *Stephen King on the Big Screen*): The confused notion of monstrosity, the blatant borrowing of generic elements, which feels more like wholesale theft than creative allusion, (particularly from ALIEN where Ridley Scott integrates an economic caste system within his character dynamics) and the consequent confusion over a political subtext all weaken the film. (Browning 2009)

STEPHEN KING: The story ["Graveyard Shift"] was gruesome, fast, and fun. It later became a film which was gruesome and fast, but unfortunately not much fun. (King: "Introduction [*Carrie*]" 1999)

Like MAXIMUM OVERDRIVE, GRAVEYARD SHIFT has, in recent years, acquired a handful of fans who are pulling the film's reputation out of the sub-sub-basement.

JOHN KENNETH MUIR (author of *Horror Films of the 1990s*): GRAVEYARD SHIFT is not particularly skilled in the way that it generates shrieks and howls, but it is commendably hardcore, excessively gory, and truly disgusting. With rats crawling everywhere, with frequent shots of rising temperature gauges, and with close-ups of sweaty actors in foul conditions, the film generates a true and horrifying sense of place. There's also a nifty third-act surprise in the disposition of the leading lady, and some dynamic performances, specifically from Macht and Dourif. (Muir: *1990s* 2011)

BRETT GALLMAN (movie reviewer for *Oh, the Horror!*): Director Ralph Singleton finds the perfect sweet spot between treating the material with dead seriousness and making a complete joke about it, so GRAVEYARD SHIFT has a wry sense of fun without being cheeky about it. He knows he's making schlock and indulges it just so. […] Few King adaptations feel this gleefully unrestrained and go straight for the throat like this one, and it sees its commitment to monster movie madness through to the end. (Gallman 2017)

CODY HAMMAN (movie reviewer for JoBlo.com): Can't a man make a fun monster movie? There are far worse King films and this has been unfairly grouped in for too long. No more. GRAVEYARD SHIFT has an amazing antagonist, a cool monster, some great looking set pieces. It deserves a retrial. (Hamman 2017)

GEORGE DEMICK: Recently, [bestselling horror author] Brian Keene was like, "Dude, you need to watch it again. Don't think about what you were going to do. It is the movie it is." I watched it again with fresh eyes—and it's a nice, fun 80s monster movie. (2021 interview with the author)

An Interview with John Esposito (2021)

JOSEPH MADDREY: I understand you attended the School of Visual Arts in New York. Is that where you wrote your first screenplay?

JOHN ESPOSITO: No. I attempted a few screenplays on my own as a teenager. Back in the day there weren't many resources. As far back as grammar school, I was interested in filmmaking. I was obsessed with movies. I ran Super-8 movies and later 16mm movies in my bedroom and I would read the novelizations but I couldn't find any professional scripts to study. The sole book on the market was Syd Field's *Screenplay*. That became my Bible.

When I was fourteen, I told my mother "I'm gonna write a script someday." She finally said, "Stop talking about it and just do it." So I wrote a script. It was terrible, of course, but I did make it to the end. I didn't have anything to base it on—except the theatrical plays we read in school—so I formatted it like a stage play. Later, I took screenwriting courses, the Robert McKee seminar, you name it. And to this day, I still check out new screenwriting books. But, basically, I'm a self-taught screenwriter.

MADDREY: When you were at SVA, was your goal to become a filmmaker?

ESPOSITO: Yes. And at the time, it seemed like the only way to break into the industry was with a script. I hadn't thought of myself as a writer—and it took me years to finally accept "I'm a writer." The script I wrote as a teenager generated some interest from an agent, so I thought maybe this is how I could break in.

At first I tried my hand at writing comedies. Because I loved horror films so much, I thought that they would be the step up [from comedies]. Isn't that hilarious? I resisted writing a horror film because I had an elevated opinion of the genre. Eventually, I wrote an anthology and managed to get it to Tom Savini, who was on stage at a convention saying he was looking for material to direct. I approached him for an autograph. I was terrified, didn't say a word. I had a friend from high school with me and he said, "Ask him if he'll read your script." I got back in line and said, "Mr. Savini, would you consider reading my script?" He said sure and jotted down his address so I mailed him the script. Every day after that, I'd ask my mother, "Did Tom call?" One day I got home and there was a note on the kitchen table that said "Tom called." He optioned the script and that led directly to GRAVEYARD SHIFT.

MADDREY: Was that THE TELL-TALE TAVERN?

ESPOSITO: Yes. Wow, you've done some research. He wanted to direct that and it was one of the most exciting moments of my life.

MADDREY: Tell me about the script. Based on the title, I'm assuming Edgar Allan Poe was a big influence. Also, your CREEPSHOW episodes [2019–2021] give me the impression that

you're a well-versed horror geek who likes to acknowledge the classic tradition of horror sto-
ries and put your own spin on familiar tales, so I'm wondering if that's what you were trying
to do with THE TELL-TALE TAVERN.

ESPOSITO: Absolutely. When I started writing it, CREEPSHOW—the movie—
was still in the air, but I'd also been a fan of E.C. Comics. (The reprints, of course. I'm
not *that* old.) I also loved the Amicus films, so those were in my head too. I had written a few short stories and decided to try my hand at a horror script, thinking maybe I
could incorporate some of my (unpublished) tales into an anthology. It was definitely
Poe-inspired, as most of my things were.

I was trying to get noticed. I knew I had at least one edgy story in there. The second
one. When I finally spoke to Tom, he said, "After I read that second story, I put the script
down and said I need to option this." That was an amazing moment because, as a struggling writer, you experience so much rejection. To have someone like Tom Savini tell
you he was moved by your work was tremendous.

MADDREY: And at that time, Tom Savini's name was even bigger than the directors. He
was the one on the cover of all the horror magazines.

ESPOSITO: He really was a horror superstar. He had just come off of DAY OF THE
DEAD and, from that point until the following year, with every project that came his
way as a potential directing gig, I got put on the script. I had come out of nowhere and
suddenly I was working on scripts for Tom. After the TELL-TALE TAVERN call, he was
approached to direct some direct-to-video movies and the producers flew me to Pittsburgh for a meeting. I was like "Oh my god, I'm going to Pittsburgh!"—the way most
people react when they're going to Hollywood.

MADDREY: Sure. Pittsburgh was the horror fan's Mecca in the 80s. The home of George
Romero!

ESPOSITO: I got to stay at Tom's house and I met his young assistant, Greg Nicotero. We hit it off and have been best of friends ever since. I also met Mike Gornick,
Romero's cinematographer and later the director of CREEPSHOW 2, who was a huge
influence and another guardian angel. He helped on GRAVEYARD SHIFT. And then I
met George Demick.

MADDREY: And George Demick hired you to work on GRAVEYARD SHIFT?

ESPOSITO: Savini called and said there's a producer who has the rights to a Stephen
King story and would I be interested in adapting it? I said "of course." I was thrilled, and
also intimidated. I was a major King fanatic. Still am. This was almost too much to process.
Demick called and explained that he had the rights to "Graveyard Shift." I think he might
have toyed with a draft himself, but it wasn't quite getting there and Tom had been talking
up TELL-TALE TAVERN, saying "Why don't you talk to this writer?" George asked, "Can
you get me a treatment?" I said, "Yeah, when do you need it by?" He said, "Can I get it in a
week?" [laughs] At the time, I didn't know enough to say "Can I have two weeks?"

MADDREY: He was probably staring down the deadline for his option on the short story.

ESPOSITO: You're absolutely right. George and I became very good friends and I
eventually learned the entire backstory but in the beginning it was very much "Yes, Mr.
Demick, anything you need, Mr. Demick." So I tore through the treatment. I call it my
piss and vinegar draft. And George and Tom liked what they saw. They gave notes and
we proceeded from there.

MADDREY: When I talked to George Demick, he said his original idea was to do GRAVE-YARD SHIFT as an ALIENS-style action movie. Get the characters into the basement as soon as possible and then the story would be about them trying to survive. He was impressed that you came in and fleshed out the characters and made it more of a traditional, slow-build horror movie.

ESPOSITO: That's nice to hear. You never know what the right direction is or what might have been.

MADDREY: "Graveyard Shift" is a very short short story, so you had a lot of expanding to do. What was your thought process on how to do that?

ESPOSITO: When it comes to adaptations, you generally go in to the short story and highlight things to put into the script. The story as it appears in *Night Shift* is only 18 pages long, so I really couldn't afford to lose anything. It had all the trappings of a modern Gothic. The mill was its own character—Castle Dracula with a time clock. And the story presented Hall and Warwick as somewhat of a hero and a villain. And of course the social commentary was already in place. I wanted to maintain as much fidelity to the short story as I possibly could. In a way, I was trying to write a feature that felt like a short story, concentrating more on tone than plot mechanics, if that makes sense.

The short story begins with Warwick offering Hall a job on the graveyard shift. I thought that felt like a natural break into Act 2, so I began reverse-engineering the script from there. Who is Hall? He's a drifter. A college boy. He comes into town, gets the job. And I added a supernatural element because it seemed like all of the King properties that had made it to the screen included characters with "a gift." A clairvoyance. My thought was that it couldn't be movie about a haunted mill—that felt a bit like *The Shining*—so maybe we could make it about a haunted character. Hall became my Man with No Name, who blows into town with a secret past and a dark gift.

The moment he and Warwick meet, they are at odds. Hall represents something Warwick doesn't have and that's freedom. He is a drifter; no ties, he can move from town to town. He's a threat to Warwick's tyranny. So it's a chess match. In the early drafts, Hall starts having visions and I was hoping to have [viewers] ask "Well, are these visions real or is he insane?" It felt true to the short story, where the main character essentially goes nuts.

After I turned in the first draft, I was so anxious I couldn't sleep. What if I'd taken it too far? But I got a great reaction from Savini and George Demick and Greg Nicotero and Mike Gornick. At the time, they were the team. They gave more notes and we continued from there.

MADDREY: I love the scene in the first draft where Wisconsky knocks on Hall's door. You've already established that she's dead but Hall doesn't know it yet, so her visit answers the question of whether Hall is crazy or not. Suddenly we know he's not hallucinating; he's actually seeing ghosts. It's a great payoff.

ESPOSITO: That was the big turning point in the script. Savini called it a "mind-fuck movie"—he's into that sort of thing—but the question had come up: Are these just dream sequences or is Hall actually having psychic visions? And if he's actually seeing something, can that be the impetus for why they go down into the sub-basement? Now, in that first draft, Hall does not go into the sub-basement with the crew. At the time, I had him force his co-workers down at gunpoint, which led to the third act. Everybody was like, "You can't do that. The main character has to be down there with them!" That was my first mistake.

MADDREY: *I'm curious about what inspired the visionary sequences. Your first draft was written at a very distinct time in horror movie history, right after films like A NIGHTMARE ON ELM STREET and HOUSE had kicked off the "rubber reality" subgenre. There were a lot of films being made during that time that had fantastic imagery but didn't make much logical sense. Were any of those films an inspiration on GRAVEYARD SHIFT?*

ESPOSITO: Part of it stemmed from the fact that this was going to be Tom Savini's directorial debut so we wanted to showcase the effects. Obviously, Tom is much more than an effects guy—he's a very visual storyteller, so I wanted to accentuate those elements. Even though I'd only known him for a short time, I felt the best way to get some outrageous visuals in the film would be through dream sequences or a character's "visions"—because Tom isn't a "rubber reality" kind of guy. He insists the environment feel real, so I hoped it would be a good way to get those types of visuals into the film and still satisfy Tom's storytelling sensibilities. In the original draft, I'd been saving most of the graphic horror for the sub-basement, so it needed to have something else happening to get us to that point.

Also, at the time, George Demick and I assumed the film was going to be *ultra* low-budget, so I kept the settings as confined as possible. Again, trying to retain the minimalistic plot of the short story: "a stranger comes to town and takes a job in this old mill, overrun by rats." I'm a major fan of ALIEN, a movie with a minimalistic plot. You've got these seedy blue-collar workers trying to survive against an unstoppable monster. Of course, I'm not Dan O'Bannon, but you get the idea.

MADDREY: *What you're saying reminds me a lot of Roger Corman's HOUSE OF USHER movie....*

ESPOSITO: It's 100 percent Roger Corman as well. I was looking at those classic AIP Poe adaptations, where the scripts expanded upon a single set piece, and the screenwriters—whether it was Richard Matheson or Charles Beaumont—built everything around it. I always loved the set up: a stranger arrives at the Gothic mansion and knocks on the door and Vincent Price answers.

MADDREY: *In this case, the guy knocking on the door is the Vincent Price character too, because Hall starts hallucinating and he's hyper-sensitive to his environment, which becomes the monster. I remember Corman saying that when he pitched HOUSE OF USHER, his investors asked, "Where's the monster?" and he had to tell them, "The house is the monster."*

ESPOSITO: Yes! Absolutely. I can't take credit for that. I mean, it's all there in the short story.... The Mill is clearly what Stephen King calls "The Bad Place." Years later, I'd talk to people who'd say "I can't believe you adapted an 18-page story into a feature script." But all the elements were there. It had a terrific setting and a Machiavellian villain and the social commentary about the working class being abused. It was all there in the short story.

MADDREY: *But you tuned in to that. In the first draft, you describe the heat of the mill and the claustrophobia of the place. In the first scene with Warwick, Hall is sweating. You call for close-ups of his sweat. There's smoke hovering in the air. The coffee has turned into this thick black sludge. You knew it was important to have those details in the script, to establish the setting as a character. You were directing on the page, which shows you understood the medium you were writing for.*

ESPOSITO: Thanks. It's so nice to even talk about it in a positive light, because for thirty-plus years I've been ducking GRAVEYARD SHIFT. It's been the gift that keeps on giving. Every time a new King movie is released, you get that list of 10 Worst Stephen King Movies and there it is! No one had anything too positive to say, so it's nice to have a serious discussion—because we did take it seriously. Critics assumed, "Oh, people will make anything with Stephen King's name on it"—and that's partially true from a commercial standpoint. But as filmmakers, we were sincere. We didn't just throw something out there. We put a lot of heart into the project and genuinely hoped it would be something an audience would enjoy. Whether or not the movie succeeds is a separate issue but it wasn't conceived as a mere cash grab. It was made with care. Don't get me wrong, it was always supposed to be a "trashy" B-movie. I say that with love. Actually, one of my big complaints about the movie is that it may not be trashy *enough*.

MADDREY: I've noticed that critics who say good things about GRAVEYARD SHIFT usually praise the same things—the exaggerated, unrealistic qualities of the film, the things that define it as a genre movie. For example, Stephen Macht going over the top as Warwick. And Brad Dourif chewing the scenery. I think that's what you mean when you say the movie is "trashy"....
ESPOSITO: It's sort of that. Right.

MADDREY: I think the production design also heightens the sense of nightmare overtaking reality. Everything is so dark and oppressive. And gooey. I imagine some of that was inspired by ALIEN, all those glistening shots of the monster ... but a lot the details are specified in the first draft of your script. That tactile, sensory quality of the place and the monster is there on the page.
ESPOSITO: Again, I would love to take credit for that—I was just trying to remain true to the tone and the spirit of the short story. It has a very strong sense of place and it was important to retain that. So thank you, because it's gratifying to hear that it came across.

The crew that Ralph Singleton put together was top notch. I have to add that our production designer—the late Gary Wissner, who was a friend of mine and who sadly passed away in 2001—was a genius. I have no doubt that he would have been one of the greats had he lived. He was also very passionate. Gary and I were the same age—he had recently moved up from an art director to a production designer—so we were both sort of green. I was on location in Maine and he would ask me questions about the script and how I envisioned it. Designers don't normally consult with the writer but we didn't know any better. We had a great rapport. I would show him old Universal monster movies—because he wasn't really an aficionado—and he'd gush over the Expressionist sets. The credit for the final film's look goes to Gary, along with [cinematographer] Peter Stein, because he really did a remarkable job. And by the way, he did it in very little time. The schedule was insane.

MADDREY: The production design is another thing that a lot of the positive reviews comment on. I think horror fans, in particular, like how nasty this movie looks. At least, horror fans of a particular stripe. There's a guy named Simon Brown who wrote a book a few years ago called Screening Stephen King. *He made the argument that there were two different types of Stephen King movie in the 1980s. There was the A-list, mainstream type—which included movies like THE DEAD ZONE and CUJO and CHRISTINE—and then there was* the off-brand stuff like CREEPSHOW and CHILDREN OF THE CORN and MAXIMUM OVERDRIVE. Which type is more authentic to Stephen King is debatable, but there's a distinct tonal difference between them. I feel like GRAVEYARD SHIFT suffers from an identity crisis. You set out to make a "trashy" B-movie, and the characterization of Hall a bit of a lunatic fits that type of narrative. But in the final film, he's a more traditional romantic lead … which goes back to what you were saying earlier, that maybe the final film wasn't trashy enough. The original concept was more off-brand, a little more ballsy, than the film.

ESPOSITO: Most people consider GRAVEYARD SHIFT a gross, trashy, B-movie. I'm always like, "No, we didn't quite get there." We could have sunk further. [laughs] Honestly, when we were shooting the film, I didn't know where it would land tonally. I had originally added the Exterminator to give the script some levity. I was trying to find a balance. At the time the first draft was written, there were films like SILVER BULLET that I thought toed the line between light and dark very well. Or FRIGHT NIGHT [1985], which delivered its horror straight but still had a lightness to it. I wanted GRAVEYARD SHIFT to be entertaining, not just a dark, brooding thing, so I was trying to locate that balance.

During the first table read of the script, I felt the black humor coming through. People were laughing in all the right places and I thought "We might have something here." But it didn't quite manifest on screen. Not the way I had envisioned it.

MADDREY: I think the film is maybe too unremitting for viewers who aren't hardcore horror fans, but there are still some moments of levity. Stephen King said that one of his favorite scenes was the "Surf City" scene—which was in your script from the very beginning.

ESPOSITO: Right, yeah, that's always been in there. By the way, speaking of King, it's always been one of the great hurts that I disappointed Stephen King. Although he was very supportive of the script, it kills me. Because I wanted to do right by him.

MADDREY: I'd argue that you did do right by him—by putting his character into a 1980s version of a Corman-Poe movie. In On Writing, Stephen King wrote he loved those movies when he was growing up. He called them "Poepictures." In fact, one of the first "books" he ever wrote was a novelization of THE PIT AND THE PENDULUM, which he sold to the other kids at his school. I think you expanded the source story in a way that was true to his interests and instincts, at least as a young writer. Of course, your initial version of the screen story—with that unhinged main character—didn't end up getting made. I think that's why King has said what he has said—that the film adaptation is gruesome and fast but not much fun. When some of the more comedic elements and surreal visuals got stripped out, some of the fun did, too.

ESPOSITO: I agree, although I don't know what that film [based on the first draft] would have been like. It's impossible to say. So many moments were lost because of the schedule. Ralph Singleton—who I have nothing but great things to say about—had promised Paramount a film for October and we were still shooting in August. It was crazy. It needed re-shoots. PET SEMATARY, which is a film he worked on, required a major amount of re-shoots. I guess most people don't know that. All I'm saying is, our film could have used the same help.

Ralph is a terrific person and a smart filmmaker so I'm not blaming him, but there were certain things that, from my perspective, cost us in the end. Now, having worked in the genre for years, I know that when the schedule and the budget are tight, the first thing [producers] go after are the effects sequences—because that's what costs money and takes time. Suddenly, the good parts are gone and the elaborate set pieces are lessened and you want to say, "But that's what people are coming to see the movie for. You can't take that stuff out." But it happens.

MADDREY: *In this case, some of the character-based scenes also got stripped out. In the shooting script, there's a pivotal scene set in Hall's apartment on the 4th of July, where he and Wisconsky talk about why they didn't stand up to Warwick and why they don't just leave town. It sets up the third act as a tragedy because they ultimately choose not to do the thing that would have saved them. The scene also articulates the theme of the movie, about American blue-collar workers being chewed up and spit out. But that scene is not in the film.*

ESPOSITO: There was a stronger cut of the movie that had that scene in it. I'm not saying we had SHAWSHANK, but it was a longer cut than the theatrical release, assembled in Maine. Later, they brought me out to L.A. for a test screening on the Paramount lot and it went terribly. The audience eviscerated the movie. I'm not saying that [the test audience] didn't hit on some legitimate problems, but a lot of their comments were really off the mark. For example, they rejected some of the musical cues—but it was a temp score. Big changes were made based on those types of notes. It was very frustrating.

When you work on a project for so long, it becomes a part of you. You fight the fight. There are arguments and meetings and discussions over every line of dialogue. And then, all of a sudden, a focus group of basically ten kids from the San Fernando Valley is granted the power to re-cut your movie after a single test screening. That was tough. The executives listened to whatever they said, and that [4th of July] scene left the movie. At that point, we were very close to the release date so no additional test screenings took place. Paramount said, "Cut it down to a 90-minute monster movie." The problem was, in my opinion, we didn't have enough really good monster footage to sustain it.

MADDREY: *Horror stories have a certain rhythm. It's all about building tension and relieving tension and then re-building tension. When you start pulling scenes, you can lose that rhythm—assuming it's there to begin with.*

ESPOSITO: Right. It wasn't a completely different movie, but those nuances made a difference.

MADDREY: *When did Stephen King first see the film?*

ESPOSITO: I was there when he saw an early cut at Paramount. He was supportive at the time. Later, we did a press conference in Maine, for the premiere. He showed up and did the full dog and pony show and he was terrific. The crowd ate it up. Then we all went in and watched the movie and he sat there with his son Joe and a bucket of popcorn and gave me a shout out. But truthfully, when I saw the final cut in the theater, I was traumatized. It didn't work for me. They had a second screening that same night and I wound up—stupidly—hiding out in my hotel room because I couldn't watch it again. Later, producer Bill Dunn found me and asked, "Where were you? Steve was looking for you." Apparently, King had stayed for both screenings and I still feel terrible about that decision. That weekend, I went back home to New York and King called and said, "Don't look at the reviews. Just watch the box office and have fun." He was incredibly sweet and supportive.

MADDREY: *The film did well in the opening weekend, but the reviews probably killed it down the line.*

ESPOSITO: The reviews were terrible. I mean, we're talking *cruel*. It was a really rough time because I was singled out as the architect of this cinematic disaster. I'd received a lot of compliments on the script over the years and I assumed I was on my way to a career in film. Then, from one day to the next, the script was terrible and "I was terrible." I had almost no interest in continuing after that. And being a genre guy, I knew the fans were unhappy. It was a brutal period in my life.

I'll tell you a funny story. They didn't do a press screening of the film, so the reviews didn't come out until Saturday morning. My niece called all thrilled and was like, "Uncle John, Uncle John, your name's in the paper." I said, "Oh really, what does it say?" And she very innocently read the part of the review where it said "First-time writer John Esposito wouldn't know a character if it bit him" or something like that. She was all excited and I was like, "Sweetheart, that's not really a good thing."

MADDREY: Let's talk about the characters. Obviously, you inherited Hall and Warwick but you invented the Exterminator from whole cloth—and that's one element of the film that everybody seems to like.

ESPOSITO: One of my favorite things in GRAVEYARD SHIFT was the Exterminator's speech, which stayed the same throughout the years. I tweaked it a bit, but it's almost intact from the first draft. And yeah, any positive reviews we got were for Brad Dourif as the Exterminator. Of course, his performance is brilliant. He went in and knocked it out of the park. What's funny is that the same people trashing the script would compliment Dourif's speech, as if he'd made it up himself. That gave me some solace because the dialogue was mine. So maybe I wasn't *so* terrible. [laughs]

MADDREY: It's easy to say "That's a great performance from Brad Dourif." I mean, who doesn't love Brad Dourif? But the character works exactly the way you intended him to work. He's cartoonish. He provides levity. He has that great monologue about the rats in Vietnam, which reminded me of Robert Shaw's speech about the Indianapolis *in JAWS—but exaggerated for comic effect.*

ESPOSITO: I remember watching him do the speech on set and thinking he was amazing. He delivers on every front. Another complaint is that the Exterminator isn't in the movie enough—because when he's onscreen, you're invested in that character.

I thought it would be fun for Hall to have visitors, to have these weird characters show up in the picker department. The first thing that came to mind was, "Well, the mill has a vermin infestation…. They'd need an exterminator." I also wanted the character to reflect the times. He provided another bit of Americana. I grew up post–Watergate, post–Vietnam. America was taking some shots. Then we entered the Reagan era and I figured, "This guy is a disgruntled Vietnam vet." There were all these stories about the rats in Vietnam so it fit. But the perfect casting—which was Brad Dourif—took it to another level.

MADDREY: He obviously understood how to play the character and I think that's because of how you described him in the script: "part Ghostbuster, part Rambo."

ESPOSITO: Right. And then he has a scene with Stephen Macht, so you have two of them [chewing the scenery]. "Let's see who's gonna one-up the other guy."

MADDREY: I admit I don't know Stephen Macht from anything else, but I couldn't read any draft of your script without hearing his voice in my head. His Maine accent is so compelling.

ESPOSITO: The accent was completely his idea. Stephen wanted to do that. He

Exterminator Tucker Cleveland (Brad Dourif) chews the scenery in GRAVEYARD SHIFT (Paramount, 1990).

played a supporting character on the TV show CAGNEY & LACEY, which Ralph Singleton was a producer on. When we were prepping, Ralph suggested a few names for the role and Stephen Macht was one of them and he is a really world-class actor. He has the chops. Also, my mother used to watch CAGNEY & LACEY and she had a crush on him, so I was like, "Stephen Macht—I know who that is!" Anyway, he's a great person and a renowned acting instructor as well. We met on location and hit it off.

When we did the first cast read-through, he played Warwick without the accent. He just read the part and he was terrific. I hadn't heard any of my scripts read aloud before, and people were digging it so I thought, "This could be really good." Then he showed up for the first day on set with the accent. I know he had spoken to Ralph about it and he had been working with a dialect coach—but the cast was shocked. I later realized that that had been his intention all along. He *became* Mr. Warwick. He would not fraternize with the rest of the cast. He acted like an asshole, which he is not, but he did it to help the project.

The crime of it was, his accent, whether you like it or not, was consistent [during the shoot] but we got a note from Paramount—they were watching dailies and weren't sure about it and so he was forced to tone it down, but he had already shot several scenes by then. Sometimes he gets criticized for [the inconsistency of his accent] but it really wasn't his fault. They made him change it during production.

At first I wasn't sure what to make of the accent but I grew to appreciate it. And now I realize—after reading what Stanley Kubrick has said about Jack Nicholson [in THE SHINING], that sometimes being "interesting" is better than being "realistic"—Stephen Macht made the right choice. He is endlessly interesting in the role.

MADDREY: *I agree, and he and Brad Dourif have that in common. They are quite a contrast to your romantic leads.*

ESPOSITO: Yes. The Hall character was dramatically stripped down. He was always supposed to be the strong silent type, but he was never conceived as a traditional hero. We got notes that would say, "Well, here, let's give him a hero moment." For example, the scene where Hall prevents Warwick from slapping one of the workers. We gave him bits like that. But the script didn't follow through on the original concept of the character and so I think David Andrews [who plays Hall in the film] got shortchanged.

Once we removed certain elements, such as Hall's supernatural abilities and his mysterious past, it became a problem for the script—because Hall became a *reactive* character. He lost his drive, his forward momentum. I think that's one of the failings people feel with the film. I know it's one of the things I wish I could have corrected.

MADDREY: *I wonder if you're a fan of THE INCREDIBLE HULK TV series.*

ESPOSITO: Yes!

MADDREY: *I ask because, watching the movie, I kept thinking that Hall is a lot like Bill Bixby in THE INCREDIBLE HULK. He's the mild-mannered drifter who doesn't allow himself to get angry. But sooner or later, you want him to see him turn into the Hulk!*

ESPOSITO: Well, that's just it! When I saw the Clint Eastwood film, UNFORGIVEN, I was like, "That's what I intended for GRAVEYARD SHIFT." It was about a guy who keeps saying, very quietly, "I'm not like that anymore. I don't do this." Then all of a sudden, he's put to the test and, *oh my god,* his violent impulses are unleashed.

MADDREY: *But instead of Hall going crazy at the end of the film, Warwick goes crazy.*

ESPOSITO: Exactly. [laughs]

MADDREY: *I guess somebody had to go crazy, so Stephen Macht said, "I'm going for it."*

ESPOSITO: And he was the guy for it! I remember when we were shooting the climax, the scene where Warwick attacks the creature. We had a bunch of options. One of the things they could do, effects-wise, was suspend the creature from the ceiling like a bat, so they decided to shoot it like that. I got a call from Stephen Macht to come down to set. When I got there, he was pacing back and forth, completely in character. He said to me, "I need a good line to say to the creature!" There wasn't anything in the script so I was trying to come up with something and he kept shaking his head, "No, no, no! I'm Captain Ahab! I need something like 'We're going to hell's heart together'!" So that's where the line came from. They removed the word "heart" in post. It was just a little *too* Captain Ahab. But Stephen understood what he was doing and made sure they shot it in a way where you couldn't remove the entire line even if you wanted to. [laughs]

A downside is that it took the moment away from Hall. In the draft, I had Hall watch Warwick die. Warwick asks for help and Hall says, "Sorry, Mr. Foreman, I'm on break." Then he walks away as Warwick gets eaten. That was the ending. In the film, Hall isn't even in the scene. I felt like it was an easy thing for us to get and, in my opinion, it diminishes the climax.

MADDREY: *I'm curious about the re-development process, when you were working with Bill Dunn and Ralph Singleton on the script. What were the changes they asked for?*

ESPOSITO: When Bill Dunn first contacted me, he said, "I have a Hollywood producer. I can't tell you his name yet, but he's really interested in your script and he wants a couple of changes before we move forward." It was a free option period. I said, "Okay, I'll do it." They wanted a traditional ending with Hall defeating the monster and leaving the sub-cellar and all that stuff. I worked up something and sent it off. I honestly didn't think anything was going to come of it. Then one day he called back and said, "This producer wants to meet you. He wants to fly you out to Hollywood." And that's exactly what they did. They flew me to L.A.—it was the dream I had when I was a kid—and I drove through the gates of Paramount. Ralph was working on HARLEM NIGHTS, a big Eddie Murphy movie. I was led to his office and he stood up at his desk and shook my hand and said, "You are a good writer." I felt like I'd been vindicated.

Then the real work began. [laughs] It was like, "We want to change every word of this script." [laughs] But that's the development process. I don't know how many drafts I wrote over the next six months. In the beginning, we were working from the original concept, so the supernatural elements were still there. But the studio wasn't biting. We were basically developing it through them even though it was not a traditional [development deal]. You could tell what they wanted—STEPHEN KING'S ALIEN. Finally, I wrote a new treatment based on the development I'd done with Ralph and company, which is basically the movie that ended up getting made. At that point, they gave me three weeks. They said, "Go back to New York and write a draft based on this treatment." I wrote it and that's what got us the greenlight. Also, Ralph had made them an offer they couldn't refuse, which was "I can get this in theaters by October." That's how it happened and then it was a mad rush.

MADDREY: *I'm surprised you had to start over with a completely new treatment because a lot of stuff from the early draft still exists in the final script. The big difference is that Hall and Wisconsky characters become more traditional romantic leads. I can imagine the execs saying, "Oh no, the hero can't be crazy ... and him and the female lead need to actually hook up ... and share their feelings more...."*

ESPOSITO: You were in those meetings, weren't you? Yes. That's exactly what it was. It was a learning process for me. I had to come out of thinking we were doing a small, dark indie movie that George Romero might have made. Now I was playing in a different sandbox. The budget at the time was $10.5 million. I couldn't believe it. *This is insane! Where did this come from?*

Ralph put together an amazing team of Hollywood professionals—and they didn't work on these kinds of movies. Horror wasn't their thing, so there were a lot of moments in development where I would tell people, "We can't really do that because it's been done to death [in older horror movies]." One of the things that came out of the development period was the cemetery that the mill is built on. Someone said, "Well, you know, in PET SEMATARY they had the Indian burial ground. Maybe we could do something like that." I said, "Well, it's been done in POLTERGEIST and then PET SEMATARY...." Eventually, it became "What if we put an actual cemetery *next* to the mill?" They wanted a literal graveyard in GRAVEYARD SHIFT, so that's where that came from.

That inspired me to go full-on E.C. Comics, so I wrote a sequence inside the monster's lair where there are stalagmites growing up through coffins and bodies—but we weren't able to build that. And the crew that had come off of all these mainstream Hollywood movies thought it was too weird. The visual consultant was a man named Harold Michelson, who was an industry legend, one of the all-time greats. He had worked extensively with Hitchcock. I shared a trailer with him and he appreciated that I was such a film buff, so during our martini lunches he would tell me stories about working on THE BIRDS and show me the original storyboards he drew for THE GRADUATE. He was the production designer on STAR TREK: THE MOTION PICTURE, and was nominated for an Oscar for that. I adored that man.

Our creature effects artist, Gordon Smith, had done some incredible work on films like PLATOON and JACOB'S LADDER, and I don't think he really liked the material. In an early production meeting, the script still had all of the different creatures in it, and I remember him pitching the idea of "Wouldn't it be more interesting if we had one great creature instead?" I didn't love the idea and I was vocal about it, but my words fell on deaf ears because "You're new. This could be STEPHEN KING'S ALIEN." So we started dropping effects.

Once we were on location, [the giant rat-bat monster] arrived. It was a beautiful piece, but it did not move. I got slammed in reviews for having characters basically run into it, as opposed to being stalked, but those scenes grew out of necessity. I think that hurt the film as well.

MADDREY: One of the critics that said positive things about the film at the time of its release was Joe Bob Briggs. He wrote a review in the Orlando Sentinel *in which he gleefully described the monster's lair as a nightmarish version of* Alice's Adventures in Wonderland. *When I read that review recently, I was reminded of a book [Eaten Alive at a Chainsaw Massacre by John Kenneth Muir] comparing Tobe Hooper's films to* Alice's Adventures in Wonderland, *because a lot of Hooper's films sort of descend into madness in the third act.*

ESPOSITO: That's a perfect comparison because that's exactly what I was trying to do.

MADDREY: But then Paramount steered you back to the traditional Hollywood ending, where the hero ascends and vanquishes the monster?

ESPOSITO: That's right, but I didn't have enough of a traditional hero in the story for it to work. We were patching in moments so it was like "okay, here's another hero moment" but it didn't fit in with the character we had established.

Going back to Tobe Hooper…. A film I happen to admire quite a bit is TEXAS CHAINSAW MASSACRE 2, which does exactly what you're talking about. You're suddenly plunged into a hellish nightmare world inside an underground amusement park in the last act. GRAVEYARD SHIFT was like that in my head. I thought if we could pull off that experience, where, for most of the movie, our setting is somewhat grounded in reality and then we enter a surreal environment, we might have something special.

We started getting notes from Paramount during production, saying that they wanted more kill sequences, so new scenes [featuring the monster] were added throughout the script. The problem with that is, once you know there's a creature hiding in the shadows, the ordinary drama no longer plays. It's like, "I don't really care about this woman beating up a car because a giant rat-monster is devouring workers." We had an opening sequence conceived along the lines of PSYCHO, with a character we think of as the lead getting force fed into the picker [by the monster]. But after that, it's hard to play that other movie. Once you know there's a creature, the other stuff becomes tedious. The audience asks "Why are we going back to this when there's something much more interesting going on?"

I also remember one of the notes we got saying, "Heroes don't smoke in the 90s." We somehow got away with it, but there was a debate. "You can't have Hall smoking." I explained that it was in there because we needed a visual representation of the heat. It was part of the environment. Another note was about a scene where Warwick fires one of the workers. The moment grew out of the short story. But [the execs] were very adamant that Hall should stand up to Warwick or not appear in the scene at all, because heroes shouldn't be complacent. I said, "But you've gotta understand the blue-collar origin of this story and this town. Nobody wants to lose their job, so no one's sticking up for anyone but themselves. That's one of the core themes of the movie." We kept it in—and I always felt that scene at least tries something different. And, there was a scene after that where [Hall says] he regrets it. I thought that was more interesting.

MADDREY: What happened to the scene where he articulates his regret? That scene, to me, was crucial to the story.

ESPOSITO: I don't disagree … but I also want to be careful not to come across as a whining writer who claims he always knew better. That's just not true. I made a lot of mistakes and there were things I wanted to do that may have worked or may not have worked. For example, they wanted the Wisconsky character to live. They wanted Hall and Wisconsky to leave town together at the end and I said I couldn't do that. The short story is so bleak that I felt like I had to keep her death in there [in order to remain true to the tone of the short story]. Hall comes to town, an enigma, and we set up that his wife had died mysteriously, with Wisconsky's death the mirror image of that tragedy.

I got on the phone with Ralph and I said—this was the first time I said something like this—I said, "Ralph, I can't write that. I won't write that. It feels wrong to me. Someone else can write it but not me." We ended the call and about an hour later, he called back and said, "You know what? You were so adamant that I'm going to stick with it." Now ultimately, I think a lot of people don't like the fact that she dies, so maybe I was wrong. [laughs] But I'm stickin' to it!

MADDREY: After you've made so many other changes, it's a question of whether Wisconsky's death still fits the version of the story you're telling—which has been distorted from the original story you were trying to tell.

ESPOSITO: "Distorted" is a great word. There comes a point where you have to be reminded of the things you originally intended. It's easy to forget.

MADDREY: I remember talking to one of the showrunners of the TV series MILLENNIUM and they told me they used to hold "tone meetings"—because it's so easy to lose track of the tone.

ESPOSITO: That's right. In the end, GRAVEYARD SHIFT felt like a different movie than the script. And I'm not saying that's such a bad thing. But when I saw it, it was not the movie I pictured—yet there were still things I really appreciated about it. It was hard to gauge it objectively.

MADDREY: What happened to the final scene in the script where Hall punches out of work and we see that he's carrying Wisconsky's flag pin?

ESPOSITO: The scene was shot but it was taken out after the test screening. This is what happened: There was a temp song laid in over the scene and the audience laughed. I forget what it was, but it was a pop song. I think the executives misinterpreted the laughter; they thought the audience was laughing at the scene, not the song, and they made us take it out. There's no reason it shouldn't be in the movie. There was also a nice crane shot of Hall leaving town—a really nice image, shot at magic hour. It looked fantastic. That's gone too.

MADDREY: That also explains the song that plays over the end credits in the film. It's definitely not a pop song. Actually, it sort of reminds me of the end credits of HOWLING II....
    ESPOSITO: Yes! But we didn't have Sybil Danning. [laughs] Maybe we needed that. [laughs]

MADDREY: I want to be the first person to suggest that you should write a sequel to GRAVEYARD SHIFT. Since Hall doesn't lose his cool until the end of the first movie, you could take your original concept of Hall as a traumatized, hallucinating drifter and make that the sequel. Or maybe a TV series, like THE INCREDIBLE HULK, where he visits a new town in every episode....
    ESPOSITO: [laughs] You might be the only one who would watch it, but I love it.

THE LAWNMOWER MAN Lawsuit

In the summer of 1992, Stephen King took legal measures to protect his name brand from Hollywood filmmakers. Following the release of THE LAWNMOWER MAN, which was initially sold as STEPHEN KING'S THE LAWNMOWER MAN, he filed a lawsuit seeking damages for irreparable harm related to the use of his name in conjunction with the film and requested that his name be removed completely from the film. Ultimately, the author's possessory credit—the use of his name above the title—was stripped from advertisements for the film but a "based on" credit was retained in the film itself. Although the film became a commercial success, making roughly $32 million at the box office (against a $10 million production budget), Stephen King's public repudiation of the film helped to give THE LAWNMOWER MAN a somewhat negative reputation.
    Ironically, producer Steven A. Lane said he originally set out to "break the jinx" of films related to Stephen King's *Night Shift* collection. No doubt remembering the mediocre-to-poor box office returns of CHILDREN OF THE CORN, CAT'S EYE, MAXIMUM OVERDRIVE, and GRAVEYARD SHIFT, he told an interviewer in the spring of 1991 that his company Allied Vision was mounting adaptations of "The Lawnmower Man" and "The Mangler" that would be "completely different from what people have come to expect from an adaptation" (Shapiro: "Monster" 1991).
    In the case of THE LAWNMOWER MAN, that meant hiring Brett Leonard, who had previously written and directed the low-budget horror movie THE DEAD PIT (1989), to significantly "expand" King's story. According to Leonard, the producers wanted to make a film "about a serial killer that ground women up for fertilizer" but the writer/director balked at the idea and instead proposed merging King's title with his pre-existing spec script CYBERGOD. Partly inspired by the Daniel Keyes short story "Flowers for Algernon," and partly by films like 2001: A SPACE ODYSSEY (1968), TRON (1982), and THE FLY (1986), CYBERGOD was a cautionary tale about a scientist that uses cutting-edge Virtual Reality technology to transform a mentally-challenged young man into a brilliant monster. The writer/director explains, "We basically used the idea [from King's short story] that [the Lawnmower Man] had telekinetic powers" but "we shifted that to be that he had telekinetic powers created by

Dr. Angelo experimenting on him with Virtual Reality brain stimulation sequences" (Griffith 2017).

A First Draft Revised version of THE LAWNMOWER MAN script, dated 1990 and attributed to Brett Leonard and Gimel Everett, includes a title page clarifying that the work was merely "suggested by a short story by Stephen King." An undated production draft amplifies the claim, giving King a possessory credit on the title page. The latter, 113-page script includes a scene in which Leonard's "lawnmower man," a rube named Jobe Smith, uses "cyber-kinetic" power to drive a lawnmower into the living room of his slobbish employer Harold Parkette. In his description of the scene, Leonard appropriates phrases directly from a similar scene

"Cybergod" Jobe Smith is *not* Stephen King's title character in THE LAWNMOWER MAN (New Line, 1992).

in King's short story. In a subsequent scene, police respond to the bloody crime scene and—as in King's short story—make a horrifying observation about the location of Harold's remains. Leonard and Everett's screenplay also makes references to The Shop, a secret government agency that figures prominently in King's novels *Firestarter* and *The Tommyknockers*, as well as in his novellas *The Mist* and *The Langoliers*, and the original TV miniseries GOLDEN YEARS. These details represent the specifics of King's influence on the story.

The allusions to The Shop indicate that the screenwriters were aware of King's larger body of work and suggest that they were particularly drawn to King's science fiction stories. With that in mind, it is perhaps worthwhile to contemplate some thematic connections between the author's fiction and the screenplay that exploits his name. First, Jobe Smith is arguably similar to several mentally-challenged King characters who display supernatural powers—beginning with Tom Cullen in *The Stand*. King has also created multiple characters that display powers of mind over matter—most notably, Carrie White. Separately, King has written many stories over the years expressing his concerns about the dangers of technological advancement without moral checks. To be sure, it is a well-worn subject for sci-fi literature, going back to Mary Shelley's *Frankenstein*, but King made it his own in a host of stories—including "Trucks," *The Stand*, and *The Tommyknockers*. In a 1984 interview, he said, "Our technology has outraced our morality. And I don't think it's possible to stick the devil back in the box. Every day, when I wake up and turn on the news, I wait for someone to say that Paris was obliterated last night ... by a gadget" (Winter 1986). In his work as a filmmaker, Brett Leonard has tackled the same theme. In a 1995 interview, Leonard reflected, "I like to track where the technology is now and where it's going to be around the corner. It's important as a storyteller to tell cautionary tales right now ... before it's too late" (Shapiro: "Virtual" 1995).

Stephen King himself might have appreciated some of these commonalities. When he first saw the film on March 3, 1992, three days before the film was theatrically released, the author wrote to his agent that he thought THE LAWNMOWER MAN was "an extraordinary piece of work, at least visually," and that "the core of my story, such as it is, is in the movie." Although he said he still intended to publicly disassociate himself from the film, he decided to "step back and shut up" about the misappropriation of his brand name (*Stephen King v. Innovation Books*, 976 F.2d 824, 2d Cir. 1992). By May 28, however, he had changed his mind. According to the legal case history, King "testified to the obvious point that his name and artistic reputation are his major assets, and offered into evidence certain unfavorable reviews of the movie [which] tended to discuss the movie in possessory terms and portray the work as a kind of failure on the part of King personally—persuasive evidence of the type of damage and confusion caused by the possessory credit."

In subsequent years, the author has colorfully restated his case on multiple occasions. In a 1992 interview for the *Los Angeles Times*, he said, "The movie had nothing to do with what I wrote. It's like taking a Mercedes hood ornament and putting it on a Chevrolet and selling it as a Mercedes" (Marx 1992). In a 1995 interview for *Fangoria* magazine, he called THE LAWNMOWER MAN "the biggest ripoff that you could imagine, because there's nothing of me in there" (Newton: "Virtual" 1995). King was equally vocal in his opposition to a LAWNMOWER MAN sequel when LAWNMOWER MAN 2: BEYOND CYBERSPACE made its way to the screen in 1996. For the record, Brett Leonard had nothing to do with that one; the screen story—about the continuing adventures of cyber-god Jobe Smith—was originated by ROBOCOP creator Michael Miner. In the meantime, the filmmakers at Allied Vision set out to produce another ill-fated man-machine mashup.

Development Hell (Oral History)

According to a 1986 interview with Milton Subotsky, Dino De Laurentiis originally optioned "The Lawnmower Man," "The Mangler," and "Trucks" for one year before deciding that he only wanted to adapt "Trucks." The movie mogul couldn't come up with workable scripts for the other two properties.

BILL PHILLIPS [screenwriter of CHRISTINE]: I had a meeting with Dino De Laurentiis, where we discussed my adapting [...] "The Mangler," about a laundry machine that "walked" down the street and killed people. I passed. I didn't want to become the "strange inanimate object-killer adapter." (Gambin 2019)

Once the story rights reverted back to Subotsky, his estate sold "The Lawnmower Man" and "The Mangler" to Allied Vision. In the spring of 1991, the company tapped Kevin S. Tenney—director of WITCHBOARD (1986), NIGHT OF THE DEMONS (1988), and THE CELLAR (1988)—to adapt "The Mangler." Then THE LAWNMOWER MAN happened.

STEPHEN DAVID BROOKS [screenwriter of THE MANGLER]: My understanding is Stephen King wouldn't let [Allied Vision] make THE MANGLER. So the rights were acquired by this legendary, infamous producer named Harry Alan Towers. [...] And he hired Tobe [Hooper]. (Bromley 2019)

Over the course of four decades in the film industry, Harry Alan Towers had written and produced dozens of independent feature films, including the FU MANCHU series starring Christopher Lee (1965–1969), 99 WOMEN (1969), and JUSTINE (a.k.a. EUGE-NIE, 1970). More recently, he had also produced TOBE HOOPER'S NIGHT TERRORS (1993).

HARRY ALAN TOWERS: [Allied Vision] had just released a Stephen King subject THE LAWNMOWER MAN and was being sued by Stephen King. [...] I was aware that my partner, [Allied Vision chairman] Ed Simons, owned another early work of Stephen King, "The Mangler," and that whilst he was involved in litigation with Stephen King, it would be difficult to launch. I had another associate, Anant Singh, who was anxious to make films in South Africa. [...] Anant bought the rights to THE MANGLER from Ed, and I co-wrote with Tobe Hooper a new screenplay. (Towers 2013)

HARRY ALAN TOWERS: I read the story and conceived the idea that you can't in this day and age make a movie where a mangler machine is the only physical sign of evil. [...] We had to introduce an essential character: the man who owns the laundry. So we now had the evil genius behind the whole horrid affair, and I took the story to a first draft screenplay which I then sent to Robert Englund. (Koetting 1996)

ROBERT ENGLUND: This was a no-brainer: in all the years I'd been doing horror, I'd never done a Stephen King project, and I'll always jump at a chance to work with Tobe, so I was in. (Englund 2009)

STEPHEN DAVID BROOKS: Apparently, Harry had taken a crack at the screenplay before me, and [Stephen King's Blue Ribbon Laundry] turned into a Chinese laundry, where everybody working there was like a 17-year-old Chinese girl. For some reason, Stephen King rejected that script. And it ended up with me by default. [...] I remember it being a five-page short story, all told in flashback, with no third act. And I'm reading this going, *How the hell are we going to turn this into a screenplay?* I did not see the movie at first, all right. So I go in and I sort of told Tobe my pitch. I don't remember what I said. And he goes, "Oh, man, that's far out. I'm gonna call Stephen King." (Bromley 2019)

TOBE HOOPER: Had I proposed to turn the Mangler into a Virtual Reality machine [*a la* THE LAWNMOWER MAN], I know he would have been very displeased. So when I contacted Stephen, I said, "If I'm true to your story and its mythological background, may I pursue getting the rights and making the film?" King said sure. (Shapiro: "Clothes" 1995)

STEPHEN DAVID BROOKS: The next morning, I get a call at 10 a.m., meaning Tobe was up all night because he didn't wake up early. He said he's been talking to Stephen King, he liked the pitch, and they're going to give me $1,500 and ten days to write the first draft, [and] that Stephen King will have script approval. [...] Robert's character, Gartley, is only mentioned in the short story, so that was the other thing. In the ten days of writing the first draft, I had to create a character for Robert Englund and then work him through. Robert wanted to wear leg braces, so, okay, we had to write the leg braces in. (Bromley 2019)

ROBERT ENGLUND: In 1947, [Orson] Welles wrote, directed, and starred in a classic film noir with Rita Hayworth called THE LADY FROM SHANGHAI, in which one of the supporting players had polio and was forced to wear cumbersome leg braces and walk with dual arm-fitted crutches. I borrowed those elements, then added a dash of Harry Truman's can-do personality, and, presto, I'd fleshed out Stephen King's quick character sketch. (Englund 2009)

STEPHEN DAVID BROOKS: We also had to add an ending, because in King's story the machine just gets out and that's it. (Shapiro: "Clothes" 1995)

Brooks delivered his first full draft of the script to Tobe Hooper on February 12, 1993. After that, the writer and director worked together on revisions.

STEPHEN DAVID BROOKS: I went to Tobe's house every day. Well, every evening. We worked from like 5 in the evening till 10 in the morning, because those were "Tobe hours." And, I mean, every single day, seven days a week, we were working on it. He would just focus on a line, a word, and we'd slug through it and get through it. (Bromley 2019)

TOBE HOOPER: Stephen King got to see all the drafts. He gave his approval on many of the things we were trying to do even though he was busy working on THE STAND. It was great because I would get these yes's and no's. So we continued to work it out. (Mauceri 1995)

THE MANGLER (Rewrite—June 9, 1993)

No screenwriter is credited on the title page of the June 9, 1993, rewrite of THE MANGLER but the script is a product of collaboration between Stephen David Brooks and Tobe Hooper, incorporating at least one detail from an earlier draft by Harry Alan Towers. Scenes taken from Stephen King's short story retain much of the author's dialogue, while new scenes flesh out existing characters, introduce new characters, and develop a backstory that sets up a new climax.

The screen story begins with the inciting incident that King's story only alluded to: the death of elderly Adelle Frawley at the Blue Ribbon Laundry. The scripted sequence introduces several supporting characters—including 16-year-old Sherry Oulette, 18-year-old Lin Sue, 75-year-old William Gartley, and Gartley's foreman George Stanner—as well as the Mangler itself. All of the characters except Lin Sue appeared in King's story but their roles are expanded in the script. The opening sequence also highlights two important props from King's short story: an antique ice-box and a bottle of antacid pills. In the source story, the ice-box existed only in a brief anecdote. In the screenplay, it comes into direct contact with the Mangler and absorbs the machine's curse, giving rise to a sub-story. Mrs. Frawley's antacid pills—which, according to Stephen King, contain a secret ingredient for demon-conjuring—also come into direct contact with the Mangler in the opening sequence. In the short story, the connection between the pills and the Mangler is revealed late in the tale, as a narrative aside. In the June 9 script, the screenwriters foreshadow the revelation.

The action begins when a pair of bumbling delivery men (Herb Diment and his not-so-bright partner Aaron Rodriguez—the former a King character, the latter a new creation) accidentally crash the ice-box into the Mangler, causing Sherry Oulette to cut her hand and bleed into the machine. Her blood awakens—or, as it turns out, reawakens—the machine's appetite for destruction. A few moments later, Mrs. Frawley drops her pills onto the Mangler's conveyer belt and ill-advisedly tries to retrieve them from the machine's hungry maw. Although it is not initially clear how or why, these two minor accidents lead directly to the onscreen death of Mrs. Frawley—a gruesome scenario that promises to shock the most hardened horror fan. The sequence ends with an establishing shot of the film's main villain, Blue Ribbon owner William Gartley, who observes the gory demise of Mrs. Frawley "in a state of ecstasy."

In a scene of parallel action outside the factory, the delivery men collide with police officer John Hunton, accidentally dropping the ice-box on him. As soon as Hunton gets back to his feet, he realizes that his wristwatch is broken. A moment later, he receives a phone call about the horrible accident at the Blue Ribbon Laundry and rushes to the scene. On the way, he pops antacids like candy—a detail that suggests some kind of connection between him and Mrs. Frawley.

When Hunton arrives at the Laundry, he talks to foreman George Stanner, who hands him Mrs. Frawley's bloody watch. Unlike Hunton's fragile timepiece, the old woman's Timex is still ticking. Screenwriter Stephen David Brooks says the exchange was meant to establish the darkly humorous tone of the film by slyly referencing "those old John Cameron Swayze commercials about a Timex watch, where they said, 'Takes a licking and keeps on ticking.'" (Booth 2018). Brooks says this was the first of many dark jokes that he and Hooper added to King's story because they knew they couldn't approach THE MANGLER as a traditional horror film. He explains, "The first thing we realized was the key to any horror film is a great monster. And a great monster is one that can attack at any time. We had a monster that was bolted to the ground, so that was problem number one: it's not a cinematic movie monster. We could have it get up and leave—I mean, spoiler alert, it gets up and leaves at the end of the short story and that's the end of it—but we couldn't have it just get up and leave *early on* because Stephen King had script approval. We had to follow the basic timeline of the short story." Their solution was simple: "Tobe decided—he said, 'Let's just have fun with it'" (Bromley 2019).

The director injected his own macabre humor into King's sober-sided story, but he did not want to turn THE MANGLER into a comedy. In a 1995 interview, Hooper said he felt that the biggest challenge of adapting "The Mangler" was trying to "ground" the outrageous events in Stephen King's short story. He knew that a tale about a demonically-possessed laundry machine could easily turn into a farce, so he tried to balance the surreal horror with realistic characters. He was, instinctively, following King's own recipe for creating effective horror fiction by combining ordinary people and extraordinary circumstances. In a 2003 interview, the author explained, "You cannot scare anyone unless you first get the audience to care about these make-believe characters. [...] Once this happens, it is possible to frighten the audience by putting the character in frightening situations" (Magistrale 2003).

Brooks remembers that he and Hooper focused obsessively on characterization, scrutinizing every action and every line of dialogue: "You need to start the beginning of each scene and go, 'All right, this character here, what do they want? How are they gonna get it? What's their plan? [...] You go through it character by character, moment by moment, and you start to refashion it so that it makes logical sense" (Booth 2018). To make the story more believable, the screenwriters decided to emphasize the main character's "agenda of disbelief." Moreso than the character in King's source story, the screen version of Officer John Hunton refuses to entertain the idea of a demonically-possessed laundry machine. In the June 9 script, he says he believes in God, country, and the law—in that order; everything else is bullshit.

As in King's story, the main character's foil is Mark Jackson, an eccentric college professor who proposes that the right ingredients and the right circumstances have turned the Mangler into a supernatural monster. Of course, Jackson doesn't jump to that conclusion right away. When Hunton pays him a visit after his long, bloody day at work, Jackson offers a sympathetic ear and acts as a sounding board. In both versions of the scene, Hunton closes his eyes and conjures a horrific image of Mrs. Frawley's remains, folded and steaming on the ass-end of the Mangler. In scripted dialogue, Hunton compares the experience of seeing her remains to a bad dream. In a twist that is new to the screen story, he then confesses that he's been having a lot of bad dreams lately and reminds his friend that today is the one-year anniversary of his wife's death. He solemnly remembers how she was killed in a car accident that he himself feels responsible for.

The most significant changes that Hooper and Brooks made to King's story are the embellishment of the William Gartley character (nothing more than a name in the short story) and the creation of an elaborate town history and mythology that explains Gartley's crippled appearance and cruel behavior. In an early scene in the June 9 script, safety inspector Roger Martin tells Hunton that the Mangler first appeared in Riker's Valley around 1931 and that, since then, it has never needed any sort of repairs. In a subsequent scene, Gartley says his father acquired the machine as part of a capital modernization plan. Years later, that plan remains in effect, with local workers—mostly, young women—providing the grist for Gartley's mill. The script indicates that the machine has been doing the devil's work for a very long time.

Following the tragic death of Mrs. Frawley, the Mangler steam-burns several workers, including Sherry Oulette and Annette Gillian. Once again, Gartley appears aroused by the bloodletting—and promptly begins to sexually exploit his female employee, Lin Sue. According to Stephen David Brooks' commentary on a 2018 Blu-Ray release of THE MANGLER, the Lin Sue character was a "leftover" from an earlier draft of the script by Harry Alan Towers, in which the laundry was populated by young female characters. This anecdote suggests Towers may have imagined THE MANGLER as primarily a story about the exploitation of women. The June 9 script retains that theme, although it's not quite as blatantly presented.

Critic Tony Magistrale credits director Tobe Hooper with the innovation, writing, "King's primary source material completely avoids the acute gender subtext present in the film, which suggests that Tobe Hooper—who both directed and wrote the movie's screenplay—envisioned THE MANGLER as something more ambitious than merely the story of a demonically possessed industrial machine." He goes on to suggest that the film's "misogynistic subtext poses a far more interesting explanation for the machine's particular choice of victims" (Magistrale: *Hollywood's* 2003). In King's story, the accidental introduction of virgin's blood into the machine is responsible for the demonic infestation of the Mangler. In Hooper's story, the machine has been feasting on a steady diet of virgins for decades.

As the screen story continues, Hunton gets called to the scene of yet another accident—this time, at the local dump, where someone has found a dead dog inside the haunted ice-box. At this point in the story, Hunton doesn't know that the ice-box came from the Blue Ribbon Laundry, so he doesn't make much of the incident. He goes home and dreams about the car accident that killed his wife, only to be awakened by a late-night phone call from William Gartley, who cryptically warns him not to delve too deep in the investigation of Mrs. Frawley's death. When the officer bites back, Gartley delivers a diatribe about the "business" of cleansing evil and the importance of the Mangler to the Riker's Valley community.

Delving deeper into the mystery, Hunton visits Annette Gillian at the hospital and learns that all of the recent troubles with the Mangler began when Sherry Oulette bled into the machine—which supports Mark Jackson's supernatural explanation. Following a very awkward conversation with Sherry (who, in this version of the tale, reacts aggressively to being questioned about whether or not she's a virgin), Hunton and Jackson return to the city dump and find that the haunted ice-box has suffocated an 11-year-old boy named Barry. Finally, Hunton makes the connection between the Mangler and the ice-box, and asks his friend about the possibility of an exorcism. The dialogue is taken mostly from King's short story but the dialogue scene ends on a different note: Hunton theorizing that Gartley intentionally summoned the demon inside the Mangler.

Hunton goes to the morgue to find Mrs. Frawley's body and bumps into a man who seems to know all the mysteries of Riker's Valley. The Pictureman, a 90-year-old crime scene photographer, is completely original to the screen story. He tells the officer that he is dying and ready to unburden a lifetime's worth of dirty secrets. For now, however, the detective thinks he has more pressing business to attend to.

First, Hunton breaks into the Blue Ribbon Laundry to conduct an off-the-books investigation of the Mangler. After a close encounter with the machine that leaves his coat in tatters, he goes to the dump and has an equally violent encounter with the evil ice-box. Firmly convinced that he is dealing with supernatural forces, Hunton returns to the Blue Ribbon and confronts Stanner and Gartley. The latter delivers a portentous speech about the true nature of power and declares his machine to be the beating heart of their idyllic community. After Hunton leaves, Stanner reminds Gartley that the Mangler is responsible for the death of Gartley's own daughter, as well as the "accident" that crippled Gartley himself. (The details remain vague.) The old man's response is matter-of-fact: "We all have to make sacrifices." When Stanner indicates that he's no longer willing to tow the party line—making human sacrifices to a bloodthirsty demon in exchange for wealth and power—Gartley warns him that "The Machine" (the phrase suggests a social / political monster as much as a physical one) won't appreciate his newfound independence. Stanner will have to learn this lesson the hard way. In the meantime, Gartley makes a phone call to the local sheriff—another devotee—in order to stymie Hunton's investigation.

At home, Hunton dreams about 11-year-old Barry getting "mangled," then wakes up to news that he has been suspended from his job at the sheriff's office. At this point, it is clear that Gartley is pulling all the strings in town. As if more evidence of his power is needed, the Mangler fulfills Gartley's earlier threat by attacking George Stanner. The scene plays out as in King's short story; Sherry tries and fails to turn off the machine and Herb Diment eventually chops off the foreman's arm with a fire-ax. Later, Roger Martin tells Hunton that Stanner died anyway. The third death in 24 hours motivates Hunton and Jackson to prepare in earnest for an exorcism of the Mangler.

First, they go back to see The Pictureman, who confirms (from his death gurney) that Gartley is managing a demon—and not alone. He explains that all of the powerful men in town have sacrificed family members in exchange for money and power, as well as the general social stability of their perfect town. Hunton and Jackson also find the photographer's scrapbook, which illustrates that all of the sacrificial lambs have been 16-year-old girls. Hunton surmises that Gartley's niece, 16-year-old Sherry Oulette, is next in line.

At the same time, Lin Sue tries to summon Sherry back to the Blue Laundry—without much luck. Gartley, realizing that the monster must be fed in a timely manner, sacrifices Lin Sue to the Mangler in order to gain physical strength for himself, so he can retrieve Sherry on his own. Meanwhile, Hunton and Jackson rehearse the rites of exorcism—over coffee at Denny's. They eventually arrive at the Blue Ribbon Laundry in time to rescue Sherry, and the Mangler claims a replacement victim: Gartley himself. The old man curses the disloyal demon with his dying breath and the heroes perform an exorcism that appears to dispel the evil.

As in King's story, however, the heroes quickly realize they have made a mistake. Hunton offers his friend some fast-acting relief for heartburn, then Jackson reads the ingredients label and realizes that the demon inside the Mangler has been conjured using belladonna. As a result, this demon is way out of their league. The bolted-down monster promptly escapes its concrete moorings, transforms into a "metallic centipede," kills Jackson, then chases Hunton and Sherry into the bowels of the Blue Ribbon Laundry. Much like the sub-basement of the Bachman Mill in GRAVEYARD SHIFT, the basement of the Blue Ribbon is startlingly vast, boasting hellish dimensions and décor. The screenwriters describe a spiral staircase descending into a seemingly bottomless pit, like some surreal combination of Alice's Wonderland and Dante's Inferno. Luckily, the Mangler is not as surefooted as the heroes; they are able to evade the metallic centipede as it falls into the pit—although it takes one of Sherry's fingers with it on the way down.

Hunton and Sherry then manage to escape the subterranean nightmare through a street-level sewer grate. The officer drops her at the hospital and returns to his apartment, where he finds a piece of mail from the Pictureman. Through his letter, the weary whistleblower posthumously reveals one more crucial detail about the power brokers in Riker's Valley. Instead of using secret handshakes or wearing matching rings, members of the cabal recognize each other due a common physical attribute: missing fingers. (Maybe they took some inspiration from Quitters, Incorporated?) Thoroughly disgusted with a society that willfully breeds monsters, Hunton visits his wife's grave and explains that he's going to flee the town and its evil politics. He makes one last stop on his way out—and when he arrives at the Blue Ribbon Laundry, he is horrified to see that the place is back in business and the Mangler is operating as usual … under the watchful eye of Sherry Oulette. She waves goodbye to Hunton and he sees that she is missing a finger.

On a commentary track for the 2018 Blu-Ray release of THE MANGLER, Stephen David Brooks reflects, "The whole backstory of the people in the town and the missing body parts, that was all Tobe." The screenwriter says the filmmaker was consciously reiterating a theme that appeared in many of his films—"the small town that looks idyllic and everything should be wonderful and everybody should be happy but there's a deep dark secret." Actor Daniel Matmor, who played the role of Mark Jackson, asserts that "the whole film is about greed" and that Tobe Hooper "wanted it to be an attack on capitalism" (Budrewicz 2020). By filtering King's story through his own sensibilities, the director created a distinctly American gothic tale about the sins of the fathers being visited on their children. THE MANGLER suggests that, in the end, *everyone* who lives in a society that allows unrestrained capitalism will get trapped in The Machine.

THE MANGLER (June 17, 1993, Final Draft)

Script changes made between June 9 and the June 17 shooting script are relatively minor, reducing the page count by six pages and adding some nuance—and horror—to the story. The final draft features Gartley and Lin Sue more prominently, and Lin Sue plays a more active role in the later part of the script, becoming Gartley's henchwoman instead of his victim.

When Hunton investigates the dead boy in the ice-box, the ice-box attacks him and he fights back with a mallet. As Pictureman looks on, the officer purges the demonic spirit from the ice-box—forcing Hunton to question his own rigid belief system. Afterward, Hunton confronts Gartley for the first and only time. The villain's dialogue has been heavily revised, making him seem confident and haughty while Hunton becomes increasingly crude and belligerent. Stanner becomes a bit bolder in his reproach of Gartley and the Pictureman's final encounter with Hunton becomes more poignant. Interestingly, Hunton also notices that the photographer is missing a finger.

In general, dialogue revisions provide greater clarity about the town's dirty secret, although it's still not entirely clear why Gartley has to sacrifice his niece after previously sacrificing his daughter—or why he himself had to give more than a finger to the machine. (Maybe because he wanted to be the top dog in town? The bigger the sacrifice…) New dialogue indicates that the dirty launderer is "running out of time"—maybe because the unanticipated accident involving Sherry's blood and Mrs. Frawley's death have made the Mangler greedy?

A revised climax introduces a physical struggle between Lin Sue and Sherry Oulette. Although Lin Sue is Gartley's intended successor and Sherry the intended sacrifice, the script reveals that the Mangler is not a discriminating eater. After Sherry pushes her nemesis into the machine, and Hunton also pushes Gartley into the fold,

Bill Gartley (Robert Englund) and Lin Sue (Lisa Morris) prepare to feed Sherry Oulette (Vanessa Pike) to the machine in THE MANGLER (New Line, 1995).

Sherry becomes the demon's new familiar. The Mangler pulls itself out of the concrete and chases her into Hell, claiming her soul by collecting her finger. In the final draft of the script, however, we don't actually see Sherry lose the finger in the basement battle for survival. In the final scene, Sherry's wave plays as a bigger reveal. Prior to that, Hunton observed that Sherry's hospital attendant, a doctor named Ramos, was missing a finger—which helps explain how Sherry got turned; the whole town is in on the conspiracy. Now that Sherry is one of the boys (so to speak), Hunton leaves town without even bothering to visit his wife's grave.

Reflections on the Film (Oral History)

TOBE HOOPER: I like it and Stephen [King] likes it. Now let's see what the audience thinks. (Shapiro: "Clothes" 1995)

THE MANGLER was released into theaters on March 3, 1995. The film made just over $1 million in its opening weekend and slunk away from theaters a week later with a total take under $2 million—which was less than the total box office receipts for CHILDREN OF THE CORN 2 or LAWNMOWER MAN 2, and much less than THE MANGLER'S production budget. Scathing reviews didn't help.

RICHARD HARRINGTON (movie reviewer for The Washington Post): THE MANGLER is ludicrous from start to finish: Its plot lines dangle, its effects fail to dazzle, and the acting and directing are uniformly bad. (Harrington 1995)

DAVID KRONKE (movie reviewer for The Los Angeles Times): Narrative coherence is mangled more than anything else. [...] Hooper could have made at least a token attempt to create one interesting or sympathetic character and shot more than one take per scene—even by horror standards, the acting here is lame. (Kronke 1995)

MARC SAVLOV (movie reviewer for The Austin Chronicle): It's all set design and blood effects, and while that may have been just fine during the early to mid–Eighties splatter movie boom, it's just plain boring now. (Savlov 1995)

MICHAEL GINGOLD (in The Motion Picture Guide: 1996 Annual): The best part of the movie is the fetid, oppressive atmosphere Hooper works up inside the sweatshop that evocatively serves as an industrial hell. The Mangler itself is an imposing creation, and its gory activities [...] pack an occasional chill. (Gingold 1996)

JOHN KENNETH MUIR (in his 2002 book Eaten Alive at a Chainsaw Massacre: The Films of Tobe Hooper): The very idea of a possessed laundry machine is inherently ridiculous, but Hooper who found humor in the macabre (and sometimes ridiculous) incidents of THE TEXAS CHAINSAW MASSACRE and POLTERGEIST is completely somber and straightforward here. [...] You can't laugh while you're gagging. (Muir: Eaten 2002)

STEPHEN KING: THE MANGLER is energetic and colorful, but it's also a mess with Robert (Freddy Krueger) Englund stalking through it for reasons which remain unclear to me even now. [...] The movie's visuals are surreal and the sets are eye-popping, but somewhere along the way (maybe in the copious amounts of steam generated by the film's mechanical star), the story got lost. (King: Stephen 2009)

STEPHEN HUNTER: The film for the most part offers [...] solid, well-crafted, professional scares, lots of gore and an overall aura of menace. [...] Horror fans may enjoy, as I did, the novelty of the situation. (Hunter 1995)

SIMON BROWN (in his book 2018 *Screening Stephen King*): THE MANGLER represents the apotheosis of this particular type of low-budget King film, totally distinct from the bigger-budget mainstream product and, through the Unrated edition, aimed more at horror fans watching at home than multiplex cinemagoers. (Brown: *Screening* 2018)

CARL H. SEDERHOLM (in his 2021 essay "Feeding the Industrial Monster: A Critical Reconsideration of Tobe Hooper's THE MANGLER"): Not only does the film resonate with the kinds of thematic interests that Hooper explored in such films as TEXAS CHAINSAW, POLTERGEIST, and SALEM'S LOT, but it also raises significant questions about American labor conditions, the working classes, and the religious overtones of certain capitalist practices. Ultimately, Hooper's film addresses the overall price of power—and specifically how that price is exacted from the laboring classes, a theme that should resonate even more strongly with viewers living in an age of online corporations and their glittering promises of instant gratification via ever-faster delivery. (Sederholm 2021)

CLAYTON DILLARD (in his 2021 essay "Get Back to Work!: Critiquing the Hollywood-Industrial Complex in THE MANGLER"): THE MANGLER further evinces Hooper's unfashionable artistic interests, including the film's use of a decidedly expressionistic *mise-en-scene* and Robert Englund's depiction of Bill Gartley as a vampiric relic whose pinstriped suits offer one of numerous visual allusions to the iconography of villainous industrialists in classical Hollywood cinema. Taken as a whole, these elements formulate an implicit refusal on Hooper's part to acquiesce to the broader aesthetic trends of the 1990s. (Dillard 2021)

SCOUT TAFOYA (in his 2021 book *Cinemaphagy: On the Psychedelic Classical Form of Tobe Hooper*): THE MANGLER wasn't released when people were looking for scapegoats for their woes, so it's possible no one felt the urge to forgive its over-the-top theatrics. THE MANGLER is elementally always going to be relevant—its tone and images are more a matter of taste. (Tafoya 2021)

An Interview with Stephen David Brooks (2021)

JOSEPH MADDREY: You started your filmmaking career as a Visual Effects assistant eventually rising to Visual Effects Supervisor and went on to become a writer/director. When did you first decide to pursue writing?

STEPHEN DAVID BROOKS: I was always writing. I was writing shorts when I was in high school and I wrote my first feature screenplay when I was in film school at UCLA. After that, I was writing several scripts a year. But my route to Tobe [Hooper], who was the first one to hire me as a writer, was a circuitous one.

In the early '80s, I started working for a guy named Robbie Lantz, who was a big-time talent agent. He helped launch the careers of Jeremy Irons and Sam Neill and Rutger Hauer. I was his office PA and I met all those guys. I also met and became friends with Bette Davis, who gave me some great advice. She asked me, "What do you want to do?" I said, "I want to be a writer and director." And she goes, "Why are you working for an agency? You have to quit. Go pursue writing and directing." So I quit.

Through a connection, I ended up becoming a production assistant on commercials because I wanted to get production experience. Then I got into a car accident. Suddenly,

I could no longer pick up bagels at 4 a.m. for the shoot because I had to go to physical therapy every day from 8 to 9. I was really messed up. It was a bad car accident. But when I was a PA, I had given out my resume all over town.

At one point, I had been working on a commercial at Apogee, which was John Dykstra's visual effects company in Van Nuys. The Apogee facility was the original location for Industrial Light & Magic, ILM, and that's where the first STAR WARS movie effects were done. I gave out my resume to some people there. Later, when I couldn't work as a p.a., I got a call from John Swallow at Apogee and he goes, "We need a driver. Can you start tomorrow?" I said, "Yeah, but can I start at 9 a.m.? I have to go to physical therapy…" "No problem." So I started working at Apogee.

I was a driver, running errands, stuff like that, but I would hang out on the stage at night. At that time, they were finishing up LIFEFORCE (1985), which was the first time I ever saw Tobe. I didn't meet him until years later but I went on the stage while they were finishing that movie, on my own time, and I learned how to set a C-stand, set a light, load a motion-control camera. I was a photographer so I already knew lenses and exposures and stuff like that. Then after LIFEFORCE, Apogee got INVADERS FROM MARS (1986), another Tobe movie.

They had a new motion control system called Lynx Robotics that nobody knew how to use. They had laid off all the camera people [after LIFEFORCE wrapped] but I was there as a driver, so I shot some tests for them. I was the only person on the planet— other than Paul Johnson, who programmed the software—who knew the new motion control system, so Bob Shepherd at Apogee got me in the camera union. I became a motion-control camera assistant on INVADERS FROM MARS. Once again, I got to hang out with Tobe on set. He still didn't know who I was, but I was always around him.

After that, a company in Toronto named Light & Motion bought two Lynx Robotics systems and wanted to get their camera people trained. Since I was one of the only people who knew the system, Paul Johnson got me a job teaching them Lynx Robotics motion control. Six months later, the same company got a contract to do the visual effects for the Michael Anderson movie MILLENNIUM [1989]. Bob Ryan, the guy who ran Light & Motion, called me and said, "Stephen, can you come up and help us put things together?" I said, "I'll do it, but you have to give me an Associate Visual Effects Supervisor credit." He said fine, so I went from being a camera assistant to a Visual Effects Supervisor in the course of about a year and a half. It was insane.

Long story short: We made the movie. I shot a bunch of second unit pyro stuff. The movie was about plane crashes, so I did a bunch of inserts with stuff blowing up, fireballs, that kind of thing. Then I came back to Apogee with a reel. Not too long after that, John Dykstra—who was a real mentor to me—called me into his office and said, "Tobe Hooper needs a Visual Effects Supervisor for a new movie and I can't do it." He was busy on another show. "So I'm going to send you up to meet Tobe and talk about it."

I went up to Tobe's Beverly Hills house and met him. I remember he was sitting in the living room and he had the Leatherface mask from CHAINSAW 2 on the shelf behind him, staring at me. I showed him my reel and he goes, "Oh, man, that's far out." I didn't even know that the movie was going to be called SPONTANEOUS COMBUSTION … but my reel was all fire stuff, so he hired me.

All of the sudden, I'm a Visual Effects Supervisor working very closely with Tobe. He let me direct second unit on that movie. At first, I was finishing up scenes that he didn't have time to finish because he had to go to the next location. Later, he gave me entire sequences to direct with the main cast. Suddenly, I was directing Brad Dourif and Melinda Dillon!

I continued to work as a Visual Effects Supervisor for a while. I had met Harrison Ellenshaw in Canada and he asked me to help him finish DICK TRACY (1990), so I did that. Then I went to Disney and supervised a movie called WILDER NAPALM (1993), which was Vince Gilligan's first screenplay. While I'm at Disney—this is around 1992—I get a call on the stage and the receptionist says, "Tobe Hooper's on the line for you." I go to the phone and he says, "Hey, man, have you ever written horror?" I had given Tobe a couple of scripts after SPONTANEOUS COMBUSTION, but I don't think he ever read them. I had never written horror in my life but I said, "Yeah, of course." He goes, "Pick up a copy of Stephen King's *Night Shift*. Read 'The Mangler.' Come see me." So I went into Harrison's office and said, "Harrison, I've got to take the afternoon off." I explained why. He goes, "Okay, go ahead." I didn't think anything of it at the time. I just thought, *This is weird*. I didn't realize that this was a life-changing moment. [laughs]

MADDREY: *But that's how things happen in Hollywood.*

BROOKS: Right. So I picked up *Night Shift* and I drove over to Tobe's house. I remember sitting outside, reading "The Mangler," and going, *How the hell do you turn this into a movie?* It's all told in flashback. I remember it being five pages, although I think it actually may have been 12 to 20 pages. But it definitely wasn't a full movie, so I'm going, *I don't know*. And I literally don't remember what I said to Tobe.

MADDREY: *The King story starts with Hunton arriving at the Blue Ribbon Laundry to investigate Mrs. Frawley's death. The inciting incident has already happened—"off camera," so to speak—but the whole story stems from that incident. I'm assuming you must have pitched the idea of starting with Mrs. Frawley's death, since that's how the movie begins.*

BROOKS: That's probably what I did. I literally don't remember. I just remember I was sitting in the same seat I'd been sitting in when I interviewed for SPONTANE-OUS COMBUSTION. Same seat, with Leatherface staring at me. I do remember saying, "We need to make this story more linear." Because the short story was all told in flash-back. Whatever else I said…. Let me put it this way: All my good pitches have been like when an actor performs a scene and they're really in the moment. When they're done, they don't know what they did. My pitches are like that. I don't know what I did. I just remember saying "Let's make it linear." And Tobe goes, "That's far out. I'm gonna call Steve King. I'll talk to you tomorrow."

I get a call at 10 a.m. the next morning. Tobe says, "Steve King loved your pitch. We're gonna pay you 1,500 bucks. Can you write a draft in ten days?" I said, "Sure." I almost killed myself writing that script in ten days. I don't know how I did it. It was obviously very different from the final draft—because you can't write a good screen-play in ten days—but I sent it to Tobe and he sent it to Stephen King. I realized later that the script was my audition. After that, Tobe said, "Stephen King loved your draft. Good thing, as he has script approval. Now we're gonna make a deal and we'll start writing the script together." They paid me more money and then Tobe and I started revising, page by page.

At the time, Stephen King was in his cabin in the woods of Maine somewhere, writing a novel. While he was there, the only way to get in touch with him was via fax machine and the only one who knew the number was his agent. So we would write pages, I would print them, Tobe would fax them to Stephen King's agent, the agent would fax them to Stephen King, and then Tobe would get either a phone call or faxed notes back from the agent. That's how we wrote the script.

MADDREY: I understand Harry Alan Towers had written an earlier draft that Stephen King didn't approve. What do you remember about that one?

BROOKS: I found out once I got the job that a lot of people in Hollywood—including some well-known writers—had taken a crack at this script. Stephen King had rejected all of them. Harry Alan Towers, who was one of the producers on the film, wrote a draft set in a Chinese laundry with all these scantily-clad young Asian women. Tobe described the script to me, but I never saw that draft. The only thing left of that draft is the character of Lin Sue, who was "L-i-n S-o-o" in Harry's draft and "L-i-n S-u-e" in ours.

MADDREY: I'd like to talk through some of the specifics of your draft, starting with the opening sequence, which is extremely gory. I have heard people like Wes Craven and John Carpenter say that one of the things a horror director has to do, right up front, is make the audience wonder how far the director is willing to go. Is that something you and Tobe talked about when you were conceiving that opening sequence?

BROOKS: Yes. Also, Tobe is also really big into symbolism. I've read reviews [of THE MANGLER] saying, "This is Tobe's commentary on the state of capitalism and how it abuses workers," and that's absolutely correct. He articulated that. He said, "We want to show this oppressive machinery"—the "machinery" being, physically, the Mangler, and also, symbolically, the state of capitalism at the time. I mean, Tobe's an old hippie, right? He viewed THE TEXAS CHAINSAW MASSACRE as an anti–Vietnam film. He always talked about that. So the idea of the opening sequence of THE MANGLER was to feature the steam, the overwhelming sound, the giant chains grinding—to show how this type of workplace grinds people up, physically and spiritually.

MADDREY: I've been reading a new book of essays on Tobe Hooper's films [American Twilight: The Cinema of Tobe Hooper] and there's an essay on THE MANGLER that points out a key detail in the set design—a sign on the wall of the Blue Ribbon Laundry that says "Labor Makes You Free," which is a paraphrase of a message that was posted on the gates of Nazi concentration camps....

BROOKS: Yes, that was intentional. From the concentration camps: "Work will set you free." I don't remember if Dave Barkham, the production designer, thought of that or if it was Tobe. I think it was Dave Barkham. But that was intentional. There's very little that was accidental with Tobe. He was very deliberate as a director.

MADDREY: Another essay in the same book points out that all the power-brokers in THE MANGLER are men and all the victims are women. That's not the case in Stephen King's short story so I assume that was something you and Tobe added deliberately.

BROOKS: Yes, it was.

MADDREY: Did that come out of the Harry Alan Towers draft, where all the workers were young women...?

BROOKS: Like I said, I never saw Harry's script. I only heard Tobe's description of it. What Tobe said was "it's a Chinese laundry" and he described all these young, scantily-clad women. I go, "Yeah, okay. I can see why Stephen King rejected that." Nothing in our script was from Harry's draft. [The exploitation theme] was our idea and it's an old idea. The rich oppress the poor and men oppress women. It's been going on for a very long time. Tobe didn't want to beat the audience over the head with it; it's just part of the story.

MADDREY: I'm curious about some of the other changes from King's story. In the short story, John Hunton has a wife and a daughter. Why did you and Tobe decide to add the backstory about Hunton's wife dying in a car accident?

BROOKS: Well, there are time constraints in a movie, right? You're always worried about page count. We thought about expanding the story of Hunton and his family, but that didn't help the story move along. It would sort of stop the story dead. So the brother-in-law, who I don't think was in the short story.... I think we came up with the brother-in-law....

MADDREY: Mark Jackson was in the short story, but he was just a friend. You made him Hunton's brother-in-law.

BROOKS: Right. And we had Hunton driving the car [when his wife was killed]. The idea is that you want to give a character a ghost. A well-designed character has a ghost, something that haunts them, something that they did, that happened before the movie started, but it still affects them now. That's why Hunton doesn't just want to solve this puzzle as a cop; he also wants to save the women working in the Laundry because he couldn't save his wife. That's the reason for that. And then we needed someone to explain the supernatural stuff, so that character became the brother-in-law—because it ties back to the wife and it connects everything nicely. Stephen King approved those changes.

MADDREY: There were several dream sequences in the draft I read, including one where Hunton remembers the final moments before the car accident that killed his wife. Why didn't the dream sequences make it into the film?

BROOKS: Time and budget. The only dreams in the film are quick shots of the machine and I shot all of that. I don't think it hurts to just *know* that Hunton's wife is dead; there was no point in showing the accident. Also, we had the only left-hand-drive Jeep in South Africa—they drive on the other side of the street there, so they use right-hand-drive cars—so we couldn't afford to wreck a car. [laughs] That was the main reason. In fact, there's a scene where Ted [Levine, the actor playing John Hunton] kicks the door of the Jeep and dents it, and we were like, "Oh, we don't have another Jeep. We have to keep shooting scenes with this one." We ended up shooting the Jeep from the other side for the rest of the movie because of that dented door.

MADDREY: John Hunton is a much gruffer character in the film than in King's story—partly because he's dealing with the loss of his wife and partly because you cast Buffalo Bill [actor Ted Levine, who played serial killer Jame Gumb in SILENCE OF THE LAMBS] in the role. In the film, he's constantly yelling, saying outrageous things like "you miserable piece of dog fuck"—which, I notice, is not in the script. Was it always the plan to make the character so angry or did that come about during the filming?

BROOKS: That was actually a phrase I used to use all the time—"miserable piece of dog fuck." That was my reaction to a bad PDF printer at Buena Vista Visual Effects on the Disney lot when I was a VFX Supervisor there, so that's where it came from. To answer your question: Hunton was always the hard-boiled, bitter cop, which is an archetype that audiences know. The hard-boiled cop who's seen it all, but dammit he's gonna get the bad guy, no matter what.

The casting of Ted Levine was really interesting. At that point, SILENCE OF THE LAMBS was still fresh in everybody's mind. Tobe and his girlfriend were in a hotel somewhere and SILENCE OF THE LAMBS was on TV and she said, "What about that guy as John Hunton?" And Tobe goes, "Oh, man, that's far out."

I remember when I met Ted for the first time in South Africa. I was in the hotel and I heard his voice in the lobby—he's got that distinctive voice—and I introduced myself. I remember he was really grateful for the role. All he'd gotten since SILENCE OF THE LAMBS were offers to play insane serial killers, so the offer to play a cop was like a gift for him. He played Hunton as sort of a city cop in a country setting. He's so out of place in Riker's Valley. He even dresses like a New York cop rather than a small-town sheriff.

And then he has to make this huge transition into somebody who believes in the supernatural. Until he sees that machine come alive, he doesn't believe it. But once he sees it, he's like, "Okay, I believe it now. Run." [laughs] The idea was to make him so hard-boiled and so tough that it's impossible to convince him until the right moment—so he functions as a surrogate for audience members who may not buy this stuff.

MADDREY: One thing that I think makes Hunton sympathetic is his friendship with Mark Jackson, who is so completely different from him. Hunton is a very pragmatic guy and a die-hard skeptic, whereas Jackson is this eccentric hippie intellectual. But Hunton never disparages his friend. They live in different worlds but they're still friends.

BROOKS: Right, well, again, it's his brother-in-law, so Mark reminds him of his wife. And it's a small town so it's not like Hunton can avoid him. [laughs] I mean, they live next door to each other. The reason they live next door, by the way, is because there was only one block of houses [in the filming location of Johannesburg] that looked vaguely American that didn't have a massive wall around it.

MADDREY: I love the set decoration in Mark's backyard, with all the Christmas lights and wind chimes....

BROOKS: Tobe wanted it to look magical so that it would be a stark contrast to the Blue Ribbon Laundry. Also, that was sort of Mark's personality. Mark was the kind of guy that would have all these lights and wind chimes.

MADDREY: In the script, you describe the décor and you specifically mention the wind chimes, along with metal sculptures and a mobile of witches being burned at the stake, but the script doesn't specify the lights and colors.

BROOKS: I always believe that if someone says the movie plays just like the script reads, then the director, the actors, the art department, the cinematographers didn't do their jobs. The movie should be better. It should be more vivid, it should be clearer, it should be more dramatic, funnier, whatever. When it comes to life, it needs to be more than what's on the page.

MADDREY: I think it's impressive that you and Tobe, as screenwriters, were already thinking about how the set decoration would help define the characters. That's a strength of the writing.

BROOKS: Well, thank you. I learned a lot about writing from Tobe. He didn't actually *write* anything, but he had great ideas for the script. Whenever I work on a shooting script today, I still use his method of starting at the first line and working your way through the script, figuring out what's working and what's not.

MADDREY: Let's talk about Bill Gartley. He's a character who is completely new to the screen story. Stephen King mentions the name but you and Tobe invented the character.

BROOKS: The creation of Bill Gartley is 100 percent Tobe and Robert Englund. All I did was transcribe their ideas. Tobe would go, "Oh, man, he's going to wear leg braces and have a bad eye…." And I'd say, "Okay." [laughs] And Robert was totally into it. He loves playing in makeup. Loves it. So that role was custom made for Robert. I mean, I came up with some of the dialogue—"Hells bells, Adelle!" and "There's no free lunch," that dialogue was mine—but the character was totally Tobe and Robert's.

MADDREY: I assume the goal was to create a larger-than-life villain. Sort of like the opening sequence, with all the gore. "Go big or go home."

BROOKS: Yes!

MADDREY: I remember some of the contemporary reviews compared him to Dr. Strangelove and Lionel Barrymore's evil banker in IT'S A WONDERFUL LIFE (1946).

BROOKS: The Dr. Strangelove analogy is spot-on because Tobe and Robert had both talked about that. They even talked about the character being in a wheelchair but Robert said, "No, I want leg braces so I can stand up and walk." But they definitely talked about Dr. Strangelove.

MADDREY: Like a lot of people, I know Robert Englund primarily as Freddy Krueger, but he's done a lot of smaller films in which he has completely transformed himself through makeup and wardrobe, to the point where he becomes unrecognizable. Have you seen DANCE MACABRE?

BROOKS: No.

MADDREY: He plays an elderly female ballet instructor in Russia.

BROOKS: Ha! Was that a Harry Alan Towers movie?

MADDREY: Yes! He made four Harry Alan Towers movies: THE PHANTOM OF THE OPERA (1989), DANCE MACABRE (1992), NIGHT TERRORS (1993), and THE MANGLER. So there's this quartet of batshit-crazy horror movies where he just goes for broke.

BROOKS: Robert loves acting. He loves chewing the scenery. He didn't mind making himself look silly. And he loved makeup. I've never met an actor who loved makeup so much. Lovely guy. Just the nicest guy in the world.

MADDREY: Gartley gets top billing but I have to say that my favorite character in THE MANGLER is The Pictureman.

BROOKS: Ah. Let me tell you about Pictureman. We couldn't find a 100-year-old actor in South Africa, so one day Tobe parades in this skinny guy with jet-black hair who must have been in his 30s at the time. That was Jeremy Crutchley, who was a huge star in South Africa but—because of the boycott—nobody knew him outside of South Africa. Tobe goes, "Hey, man, what do you think? Pictureman?" I looked at him and said, "I think he's gonna need some makeup." So we got Scott Wheeler, who's a great makeup artist, to do the makeup. I remember watching Jeremy act [in THE MANGLER] and saying, "One day you're going to star in a movie for me." And in 2015, he starred in my second feature FLYTRAP.

MADDREY: His performance in FLYTRAP is great. It's such a spare film and he does so much with so little. What I love about Pictureman is that the character adds so much sadness and humanity to the film.

BROOKS: The scene with him and Hunton is heartbreaking. And then Tobe had to add the final beat, with [Pictureman] throwing up into the camera. Such a Tobe moment. [laughs]

I remember the prop department found one of those old cameras with the flash bulbs and Jeremy took it home and spent two weeks learning how to shoot and reload it. He practiced that, so he'd look like a guy who had been using the camera for 100 years.

MADDREY: *It makes him seem like a guy who wandered in out of an old film noir movie, which connects him to Hunton's hardboiled detective.*

BROOKS: He's the one who took all those old photos in the scrapbook. I don't know if we articulated that in the film or not.

MADDREY: *That's the assumption I made—that he's been documenting the sacrifices for decades. So he's aware of what's been going on there for a long time, but he hasn't done any-thing about it and now he's filled with remorse. A lot of that stuff isn't explicit in the dialogue but I think Jeremy Crutchley's performance suggests it.*

BROOKS: Jeremy's brilliant.

MADDREY: *Another difference I noticed between the script and the film is that, in the script, Gartley sacrifices Lin Sue, but in the film she becomes his accomplice. Gartley grooms her as his replacement and she helps him prepare Sherry for sacrifice. Then Sherry kills Lin Sue and becomes the new boss. So you have these two female characters who start out as potential victims and end up becoming victimizers. It's a great twist.*

BROOKS: The idea with that last scene was that Tobe wanted Hunton to walk in thinking he'd saved the day and then realize that nothing had changed. That whole scene was set up for Hunton's benefit, really.

MADDREY: *Where did the detail about the missing fingers come from?*

BROOKS: That was Tobe's idea. If you do something wrong in the Yakuza, the Jap-anese mafia, they cut your finger off. That's how you can tell someone is in the Yakuza—they're missing a finger, or a part of the finger.

MADDREY: *I want to ask a more general question about adapting Stephen King. Whenever anyone sets out to adapt King, they always talk about wanting to be faithful to his voice—but, in this case, you were adapting an early short story that was written before Stephen King was "Stephen King." His* Night Shift *stories have a much darker tone—and bleaker endings—than most of the novels he wrote in the '80s. Did you feel like there was any con-flict between being true to the tone of "The Mangler" short story and being true to the sensi-bilities of Stephen King in the '80s and '90s?*

BROOKS: In a short story, you can be bleak from beginning to end. In a movie, you have to give the story some place to go. With THE MANGLER, the tone starts out really bleak. An old woman gets crushed to death. Then it lightens up a bit when Mark Jackson appears. You have to let it ebb and flow. It's like a wave; the story has peaks and valleys.

In terms of Stephen King, it had to feel like what he would do if he was making the movie—but he didn't comment on tone as much as he did on plot and character. This is jumping way ahead but when the movie was done, Tobe flew to Portland, Maine, to screen the movie for Stephen. Apparently, Stephen—as he was watching the movie—kept saying, "Was that me?" He hadn't read the story in thirty years or more, so he didn't know what was [from his short story] and what was ours. And Tobe would go, "No, man, that was us." "Oh. Damn." Then again: "*Was that me?*" "*No, man, that was us.*" The fact that he thought [our ideas] were his ideas made me feel like we did our job.

MADDREY: I imagine Stephen King must have appreciated the macabre humor you added to his story. It seems like he and Tobe have a similar sense of humor.

    BROOKS: Most people don't know this if they haven't met Tobe but he was hysterically funny. After I met him and worked with him, I went back and looked at THE TEXAS CHAINSAW MASSACRE and found it hilarious. When Grandpa is using the hammer to hit Sally, that's Tobe's humor. We put the same humor in THE MANGLER. There's the scene where Hunton is handed this Timex watch that's cracked and still ticking. At that time in America, in 1993, most adults remembered the old Timex ads where they'd run over a watch with a steamroller, then pick it up and say "Takes a licking and keeps on ticking." That was the joke—but it got cut out of the movie at the last minute.

    An executive somewhere—I forget who—was looking at the movie for distribution and he said, "Why is this watch still ticking? This needs to be explained or you have to cut it out of the movie." They got nervous and cut it out of the movie. Somewhere, I have a VHS tape of the edit with the Timex watch scene—and that's the version we showed at film festivals. And people laughed. They got it. But the scene was cut. And what happened is, because there's no obvious joke five minutes in, people didn't get the rest of the humor in the movie. When Hunton vomits after seeing Mrs. Frawley's mangled body, it just plays as gross. But with the humor that [should have] led up to it, it played as funny. Tobe Hooper funny.

MADDREY: I've heard you talk about that scene before, so when I was reading the script I was looking for other examples of Tobe humor. One of the things that struck me as funny was the two delivery men who bump the ice-box into the Mangler, then drop it on Hunton. They're so inept. It's like Abbott & Costello meet The Mangler.

    BROOKS: That's classic Tobe humor. He called those guys "the two idiots." When he was directing the actors, he'd go, "The two idiots need to move camera right."

MADDREY: My favorite bit of comedy is where Hunton and Jackson are rehearsing the rites of exorcism at a Denny's restaurant and the waitress comes over, waits for them to finish, then says, "Regular or decaf?" It's a great comic moment—but in the film, they have that conversation on the side of a road and the gag isn't there.

    BROOKS: I think the reason we changed it was because we couldn't find a Denny's in South Africa. We had to turn it into something else that fit into the schedule.

MADDREY: It occurs to me that the absence of that joke might hurt the real exorcism scene. You obviously have to play the real exorcism scene for suspense—and playing the "rehearsal" for laughs might have kept audiences from laughing nervously at the real exorcism. It's like saying to the audience "Okay, go ahead and laugh now. Get it out of your system...."

    BROOKS: I agree. But that's the nature of filmmaking. We all have to make sacrifices. Sometimes we have to sacrifice our best scenes.

MADDREY: How did you and Tobe come up with the new ending? In King's story, the Mangler pulls itself out of the ground and runs amok, but you guys invented a completely new sequence in which the machine chases the heroes down into the bowels of Hell.

    BROOKS: That was Tobe. We really struggled with how to end it. We knew the Mangler had to get up and leave. We knew it had to chase Sherry. We had a lot of possible endings and none of them worked. Until we came up with the idea that the machine bites Sherry's finger. That's sort of what made our ending click. And yes, it's supposed to be going down to the gates of Hell. Which kind of takes the movie in a new direction—it becomes an effects movie—but that was the idea.

MADDREY: That sequence reminds me of INVADERS FROM MARS and THE TEXAS CHAINSAW MASSACRE PART 2, which both have a similar descent sequence at the end. It also reminds me of POLTERGEIST, because both stories appear to end with the cleansing ritual / exorcism ... but then all hell breaks loose.

BROOKS: I mean, all horror movies have the double ending....

MADDREY: But in this case the double ending isn't just a coda. It's more like a fourth act.

BROOKS: Yes. The double ending is Sherry missing a finger. The exorcism not working is about the characters getting in over their heads, trying to fix a situation, making it worse, and raising the stakes. In screenwriting in general—not just in horror stories—you want to raise the stakes. You want to have the characters make mistakes—because humans make mistakes. So they go in to perform the exorcism and Mark believes it's going to work. Hunton never believes it, so when it doesn't work, it's up to him to fix it. He's the real hero of the story. But then he fails to save the woman—because it's a horror movie and horror movies can have an ironic ending.

MADDREY: I know you took your lumps from critics when THE MANGLER was released in 1995. How do you feel about the film all these years later?

BROOKS: I gotta tell you, I went to movie jail after THE MANGLER came out. As did Tobe. It wasn't until Tobe got me the job writing SPIDERS (2000) for Boaz Davidson that I got out of movie jail. A few weeks ago, there was an announcement in *Deadline* magazine about my new movie with Linda Perry. In the article, they mentioned that Stephen King selected me to write THE MANGLER. So now, because it's become kind of a cult movie, I've been exonerated from movie jail and I'm back among the living. [laughs]

I mean, look, I've seen THE MANGLER listed as the worst Stephen King adaptation ever. But I'm also seeing reviews where people are going back and reevaluating it. People are discovering THE MANGLER for what it is and there's an audience for it. When Shout! Factory put out the Blu-Ray a few years ago, I went, "People are getting it now!" It's a flawed movie but it's very Tobe. I find it fascinating that it's taking on a new life. Tobe would have been really happy about that.

MADDREY: I know you recently turned a pilot screenplay into a novel (Jack Be Dead: Revelation). *Did that change the way you think about adapting a short story or novel into screenplay?*

BROOKS: No, because that's actually easier. All the ideas that you don't have time to put into a screenplay you can put into a novel. Novels are more about the language, how you write. Part of the joy of reading the novel is the musical nature of the prose. Where a screenplay is short and direct; it's about getting a fast read. [Screenwriters] do enjoy the language sometimes but usually you just want people to get through the script without stopping. I think the best compliment you can get on a script is "I read it in one sitting."

MADDREY: When you write a script, do you try to emotionally engage a reader the same way that a novel or a short story does? I ask because it occurs to me that most people don't read screenplays as finished pieces but rather as blueprints for a film. So, with a horror movie for example, is the goal of your script to scare the reader or is your goal to make a reader understand how a film based on the script might scare them?

BROOKS: I have this thing that I call the theory of drafts. I see most people make the mistake—and this is a mistake that's taught in film schools and in screenwriting books—that when you're writing the script, you're writing the movie. You're not. You want people to think it's the movie but what you're really doing is writing a script for financiers, actors, and to attach a director if you don't have a director. You're writing a script to get people interested in making the movie.

What I will do in spec scripts is I'll include a little bit more exposition than I would in the shooting draft. I will simplify certain things so that it reads easier. Even if the way you write the scene won't play scary on the screen, you have to get past a certain group of people. You have to get past producers. You have to get past financiers. Nowadays, you have to get past sales agents. You have to get past that first group of people in order to make the movie. So you're writing for them. That's your audience. Not the audience in the theater.

That's why I put a little bit more exposition into a script. On the screen, an audience will go with a mystery. An audience will think "Oh, why did he do that?" and wait for you to answer that question later. If you give it to an executive sitting behind a desk, they're going to go, "Why did he do that?" and stop reading. You don't want that. You want them to read it all the way through. So I will explain things [early] in the script. Once there's money and we're going to shoot it, I'll change the script so the film plays better.

MADDREY: Any final thoughts about adapting Stephen King? Would you do it again, if given the chance?

I did write an early draft of THE MIST, when Tobe was going to direct THE MIST. But that was pretty much a fully-formed story. That was a pretty easy adaptation. But Tobe ended up not doing it. Frank Darabont did it and it was a whole different thing.

I think the mistake a lot of different writers make [when they're adapting a pre-existing story] is to say "I have to make it mine." No. If you're adapting someone—particularly Stephen King, a well-known novelist, but even if it's just a first-time novelist—you have to think about "what was the original intent?" There are some things you can do in a novel that you can't do cinematically, so you have to make changes there. And you might change the location of a scene to make it more interesting—but the scene itself should be the same. You have to start with the original intent of the novel and go from there.

Reborn?

Since the death of Tobe Hooper in 2017, THE MANGLER has become ripe for critical reevaluation as a neglected work by a neglected *auteur*. In 2001, however, the film was still mostly remembered as the most commercially disappointing—and arguably the most critically reviled—Stephen King adaptation to date. One wonders, then, why anyone would have wanted to make a sequel to it. Writer/director Michael Hamilton-Wright and producer Glen Tedham, who had previously worked together on the sci-fi adventure RETROACTIVE (1997) and the erotic thriller DANGEROUS ATTRACTION (2000), had their reasons—but those reasons apparently didn't have anything to do with the plot of the original film.

THE MANGLER 2 is a standalone story revolving around a computer virus that infects the security system at an elite private school. As soon as the Mangler 2.0 goes viral, THE MANGLER 2 follows the standard slasher movie formula, knocking off clueless teenagers in creative ways. On a commentary track for the DVD, Hamilton-Wright claims that the script was written in eight days and tailored to a specific filming location—an abandoned military base outside of Vancouver—but he says almost nothing about following THE MANGLER or Stephen King. In early 2002, the sequel-in-name-only was released directly to home video, where it languished just as its predecessor had languished in theaters.

Not content to let sleeping dogs lie, THE MANGLER 2 producer Barry Barnholtz (who also had a hand in SOMETIMES THEY COME BACK ... AGAIN) decided that the world needed another sequel to THE MANGLER. He acquired the franchise rights and hired filmmakers Matt Cunningham and Erik Gardner, who had previously collaborated on the comedy-horror film DECAMPITATED (1998), to write and direct THE MANGLER REBORN (2005). Cunningham remembers, "We said okay, read the original story and really tried to pull stuff out of there that we thought was good. You know, King is very vague in the story but at the same time he's kind of telling you 'it could be this, it could be that, this is how the machine could've been possessed.' So we kind of tried to play with that a little bit" (Fallon: "The Arrow" 2005).

The filmmaking duo conceived a franchise reboot about a repair man named Hadley Watson—named after the Hadley-Watson Model 6 Speed Ironer and Folder in King's original story—who gathers some fragments of the Mangler machine and welds them together. The reconfigured Mangler promptly eats him, spits him out, and compels him to murder people and drink their blood. According to a commentary track on the DVD release of the film, Cunningham and Gardner thought of THE MANGLER REBORN as a "modern vampire tale" and an homage to THE LITTLE SHOP OF HORRORS (1960). Elsewhere, they have cited the horror films KAIRO (2001) and HAUTE TENSION (2003) as influences (Fallon: "The Arrow" 2005). Unfortunately, aside from its oblique connection to Stephen King and Tobe Hooper, THE MANGLER REBORN is forgettable.

Where does this leave THE MANGLER? In 2018, *Bloody Disgusting* journalist Zachary Leeman suggested that the franchise is "practically begging to be revived," arguing that Stephen King's "looney concept [...] could really ignite a fire in the right artist's belly" (Leeman 2018). He nominates BONE TOMAHAWK and BRAWL IN CELL BLOCK 99 writer/director S. Craig Zahler for the job. But don't hold your breath.

PART SIX

21st-Century Adaptations

NIGHTMARES & DREAMSCAPES: "BATTLEGROUND" (2006)

In the years after Stephen King wrote his treatment for a proposed NIGHT SHIFT TV series, his published short stories became highly coveted fodder for small-screen adaptations. Following the 1982 release of CREEPSHOW, King collaborators George Romero and Richard Rubinstein developed the anthology TV series TALES FROM THE DARKSIDE (1984–1988) for CBS, and the first season boasted an adaptation of King's short story "The Word Processor of the Gods" (first published in *Playboy* magazine and subsequently collected in *Skeleton Crew*) by novelist Michael McDowell. Soon after, Harlan Ellison adapted the *Skeleton Crew* short story "Gramma" for the inaugural season of CBS's rebooted THE TWILIGHT ZONE (1985–1989). Following CREEPSHOW 2 (1987) and TALES FROM THE DARKSIDE: THE MOVIE (1990), Haskell Barkin adapted the *Nightmares & Dreamscapes* story "The Moving Finger" as the final episode of Richard Rubinstein's Sci-Fi Channel series MONSTERS (1988–1991). Finally, Brad Wright's adaptation of "The Revelations of 'Becka Paulson"—a short story that was first published in *Rolling Stone* magazine, and later incorporated into King's novel *The Tommyknockers*— aired during the third season of Showtime's THE OUTER LIMITS (1995–2002).

It was not until 2005, however, that the idea of a King-centric anthology series finally came to fruition. Michael Wright, TNT's Vice President of Movies and Miniseries, remembers that his network was doing particularly well with the limited series format in 2003 and 2004. Contemporary projects included the counterterrorism drama THE GRID, the Steven Spielberg-produced historical drama INTO THE WEST, and the new SALEM'S LOT miniseries starring Rob Lowe. The success of SALEM'S LOT prompted Wright and executive producer Bill Haber to mine King's oeuvre for new material. In the end, they decided to pursue the rights to adapt multiple short stories. Haber says the goal was to create "eight completely separate movies, not connected at all except the title and coming from Stephen King stories, each with different creative people" (Haber 2007). Although the title, NIGHTMARES & DREAMSCAPES, suggests that all eight stories came from King's 1993 collection of the same name, in fact only five stories appeared in that volume. Two other stories, "The Road Virus Heads North" and "Autopsy Room Four," appeared in King's 2002 collection *Everything's Eventual*, while "Battleground" came from *Night Shift*.

The oldest story was the most ambitious and the producers turned to a veteran TV writer to adapt "Battleground." Richard Christian Matheson, son of novelist and screenwriter Richard Matheson, had been writing episodic television since the late '70s, on series including QUINCY, M.E. (1979), THE INCREDIBLE HULK (1978–1979), and THE A-TEAM (1983–1984). He adapted one of his father's short stories for NBC's AMAZING STORIES (1986), an E.C. Comics tale for HBO's TALES FROM THE CRYPT (1991), a Dean R. Koontz novel (for the TV movie SOLE SURVIVOR, 2000), another of his father's stories for the first season of Showtime's MASTERS OF HORROR (2005), and an Ambrose Bierce short story for the second season (2006). By the time TNT came calling, Matheson had also spent some time contemplating the challenges of adapting Stephen King.

In a 1989 interview with Stephen J. Spignesi, he opined that most adaptations of King's novels were "very disappointing." The problem, he theorized, was maintaining the author's elaborate characterizations: "You can't take five, six, seven, eight hundred pages of detailed characterization and jam it into a hundred pages. How do you do it? There's just no way … and with King, so much of the fun is in his characters." He conceded that a few adaptations of King's *shorter* stories had turned out okay but maintained that, in most cases, "something" still "went wrong" (Spignesi: "His" 1991). The assignment to adapt "Battleground" challenged him to beat the odds.

One of the first creative decisions Matheson made was to re-tell King's short story without writing any dialogue. Despite telling Spignesi that "dialogue is the clearest and most immediate way you can get characterization across," he sensed that the BATTLE-GROUND screen story would be more compelling if all of the emphasis was on action (Spignesi: "His" 1991). Remembering that his father had used the same technique in a successful episode of the original THE TWILIGHT ZONE series ("The Invaders"), the younger Matheson set out to repeat that feat of daring: "Experimentally, I cut it all, conveyed exposition via silent details, and was immediately struck by the effect. Shed of spoken language, I felt the script lured more enigmatically" (Matheson 2012). Brian Henson, who directed the episode, agrees: "By removing all the dialogue, he was forcing the audience to watch much more closely than they would normally be comfortable doing. No one was telling the audience what the characters had chosen to do, instead you had to watch their actions to follow their thoughts" (Henson 2012).

The challenge was to tell the story entirely through nuances of acting, art direction and sound design. Luckily, King's source story was narratively simple enough to allow for that minimalistic approach. Matheson reflects, "Most of what is bad, in my experience, and I've written probably 750 to a thousand scripts, is the exposition. That's what kills you. So the more you can get your story across without exposition, the better it will usually be. […] You need a story that has a sort of strange inevitability to it, so you can kind of follow it. But with 'Battleground,' it fit perfectly. The only thing I needed to do with 'Battleground' was extend it" (Rausch: *Perspectives* 2019)

The screenwriter expanded King's tale by starting earlier and adding an additional character. Similar to King's 1978 NIGHT SHIFT treatment, Matheson's teleplay begins with Renshaw murdering toymaker Hans Morris. In King's adaptation, the hitman used a car bomb. In Matheson's version, the killer is more methodical and the murder more intimate; Renshaw sneaks into the Morris Toy Company late at night, incapacitates two security guards, and confronts his victim face-to-face before shooting him. Director Brian Henson says he and Matheson wanted the confrontation to define both characters. By giving Hans Morris a poignant final moment to admire his toys, the filmmakers sought to make him seem more sympathetic. By showing Renshaw's desire to get up close and personal with his victim, they sought to establish the main character as a sociopath. Reliable serial killer that he is, Renshaw takes a "trophy"—a ballerina figurine—from the crime scene. In the process, he notices a framed photo of his victim's mother, featuring a distinctive handwritten message. With this scene, Matheson has provided a wealth of exposition.

The screenwriter added another new scene in which Renshaw interacts with a woman on an airplane, as well as a scene in which he overpowers a juvenile delinquent in the airport bathroom. The latter scene did not make it into the TV show—according to the director, it was "redundant"—but the former did (Henson 2012). In the airplane scene, the woman soundlessly asks Renshaw for a piece of gum. (He can't hear her because he's wearing earbuds—a detail that reinforces his sociopathic disconnection from other people.) When he reaches for his bag, the nosy woman catches a glimpse of the ballerina figurine. As he hands her the gum, he glares hard at her. According to the script, the look speaks volumes and the woman "*instantly knows she wasn't supposed to see that.*"

This simple character note—italicized like the inner thoughts of characters in Stephen King's prose fiction—tells the filmmakers and the actress what they need to convey to the audience without words. Throughout the script, Matheson attributes many private thoughts to Renshaw's character in the same style, frequently repeating character-defining phrases from Stephen King's short story.

After Renshaw returns home to his San Francisco high-rise apartment, the plot unfolds as in King's source story but with some significant modifications. One new detail contrasts King's penchant for visual storytelling with Matheson's emphasis on sound design. In the short story, Renshaw enters the elevator, closes his eyes and lets "the job replay itself on the dark screen of his mind." King's phrase seems to call for a cinematic flashback. In the teleplay, however, Renshaw enters the elevator, removes his earbuds and grimaces as the sound of Muzak fills his ears. The script specifies that the killer prefers Miles Davis and acid jazz to elevator jazz.

When Renshaw enters his apartment, the décor—minimal furniture, meticulously arranged—further illuminates his character. Only Robert DeNiro's OCD bank robber in the film HEAT (1994) can boast a more Spartan living environment. Renshaw carefully places the ballerina figurine in a very full trophy case. In the TV show, one of the trophies is the Zuni warrior doll from the anthology film TRILOGY OF TERROR (1975), scripted by Richard Matheson. Oblivious to this geeky hint of things to come, Renshaw takes a shower, checks his email, and nods off.

He is awakened by

If looks could kill: William Hurt plays hitman John Renshaw in the first episode of NIGHTMARES & DREAMSCAPES (TNT, 2006).

the sound of a doorbell—and security camera footage of a young woman delivering a nondescript brown package to his doorstep. In King's story, Renshaw received the package as soon as he entered the lobby of his apartment building. Matheson's delay puts a greater emphasis on the mystery object. Another subtle change: in King's story, Renshaw instinctively assumes the package is a bomb; in Matheson's adaptation, he has a specific reason for making that assumption. He recognizes a "telltale scribble" on the package—the same scribble he saw earlier on the photo of Hans Morris's mother. This subtle change allows the story to unfold with greater narrative clarity. No doubt Renshaw would appreciate the efficiency.

Interestingly, the scene was a source of some confusion for director Brian Henson. King's story specifies that the package is postmarked five days before the date Renshaw receives it. How, the director wondered, did Hans Morris's mother know the address of her son's murderer before he was murdered? Henson posed his question to Stephen King. Although the author had addressed the same question in his own adaptation of the short story—by explaining that the toy maker's mother was a witch—King told Henson not to "over think" things (Henson 2012). The filmmaker decided to simply remove the postmark.

At this point, the screen story enters a new mode in which every moment is milked for suspense. Renshaw opens the package—slowly, methodically—and views his unlikely gift: a footlocker filled with tiny plastic soldiers, helicopters, and weapons. In King's story, the Lilliputian army attacks Renshaw immediately but Matheson continues to draw out the scene. Renshaw crosses the room to get a drink and, while his back is turned, hears the footlocker fall off a kitchen counter and crash to the floor. He looks closer and sees that the box is now empty; the soldiers have infiltrated his apartment. As the scene progresses, lights go out one by one and Renshaw tracks the sound of tiny footsteps until one of the soldiers appears and stabs him in the foot with a miniature bayonet. Then the special effects-driven battle begins.

Matheson's teleplay details the action shot by shot, using King's plot as a framework while augmenting it with his own details and unspoken dialogue (*"What the fuck is going on?"*). In one new beat, the hitman strafes his living room couch with machine gun fire, then flips the couch and sees tiny, wounded soldiers retreating and regrouping. The surreal image is enough to make anyone (maybe the viewer?) laugh, but Renshaw doesn't laugh; he's still under fire. Helicopters attack and Renshaw retreats to the bathroom, where—in another humorous addition to King's story—he flushes one of the choppers down the toilet, adding a hairdryer to electrocute the survivors. As in the source story, the soldiers slide a note under the bathroom door, requesting Renshaw's surrender. He remains defiant so they turn the bathroom door into Swiss cheese, forcing him to climb out a window onto a narrow ledge surrounding the high-rise apartment.

A few years after writing "Battleground," Stephen King created a similar scene as the centerpiece of his short story "The Ledge." Perhaps he felt that he had missed an opportunity to milk the "Battleground" scene for more suspense? Matheson seizes the opportunity, and even visualizes a beat that King avoided. In the short story, Renshaw worries that one of the helicopters will fly through the open bathroom window and shoot him off the ledge—but it doesn't happen. In the screen story, a helicopter does fly through the window and attack him on the ledge. Renshaw barely manages to shoot it down before he takes a dive. In both versions, he eventually makes his way to the veranda outside his living room and prepares to make one last stand.

In the short story, the climactic battle is brief; Renshaw bolts for the front door of his apartment. Before he gets there, the entire apartment explodes. According to the short story writer: The hitman "never knew what hit him." A couple on the street below discovers an explanation: a printed label indicating that the footlocker included a scale-model thermonuclear bomb. Matheson had his own ideas for the final battle. Realizing that he needed to fill an hour's worth of screen time—and that extending Renshaw's standoff with the small soldiers would likely become repetitive and dull—he decided to add a completely new character: "a vicious jungle-fighter I named the Savage Commando; a toy as soulless as Renshaw" (Matheson 2012).

In Matheson's screenplay, Renshaw wins the battle against the soldiers and helicopters—only to learn that the war is far from over. In a new third act, the hitman slips into his indoor pool for a celebratory swim. There, he gets knifed by the Savage Commando. Although he manages to escape his apartment, the Savage Commando pursues Renshaw into the elevator and delivers more knife wounds. The hitman escapes through the roof of the elevator and hitches a ride on a second elevator car—but the Savage Commando isn't far behind. In a last-ditch effort, Renshaw plays possum, buying himself an opportunity to trap the Savage Commando between a pair of closing elevator doors. The pint-sized opponent loses his head … but then Renshaw hears a warning bell and sees a flashing red light, indicating that he the Commando has triggered a time bomb. Renshaw chuckles knowingly—maybe even a bit admiringly. As in the short story, a close-up shot of a packaging label (in the kitchen trash can, rather than on the street below) delivers King's final gag. Matheson ends the story with a playful image of Hans Morris's ballerina figurine, dancing.

Richard Christian Matheson's screen story is more suspenseful and more humorous than Stephen King's source story. Since BATTLEGROUND served as the first episode of NIGHTMARES & DREAMSCAPES, it was a welcome harbinger of things to come. Touting the series before its premiere, producer Jeffrey M. Hayes promised that it would demonstrate King's range as a storyteller: "We are not doing a horror show *per se*. We are doing Stephen King short stories, and within that realm there are a number of horrific elements, but there are also twisted tales and TWILIGHT ZONE types and just a real mix of different kinds of storytelling, which is one of the great things about Stephen King's writing" (Helms 2006). It was an admirable attempt to reintroduce the author to a 21st-century audience.

An Interview with Richard Christian Matheson (2021)

JOSEPH MADDREY: Your writing career is amazing to me—because you are so prolific and you work in so many different genres and so many different mediums. I was trying to figure out when you might have written your first adapted screenplay. Was it "Miss Stardust"?
     RICHARD CHRISTIAN MATHESON: You're right, it was. I was working with my friend, Tom Szollosi, at the time. We wrote two AMAZING STORIES and I wrote one of my own.

MADDREY: By the time you worked on that show, you must have written dozens of episodic television shows.
     MATHESON: Yes. I lose track. Hundreds of episodes.

MADDREY: Having written so many original screenplays, was there anything about writing your first adapted screenplay that surprised you? Did you find it easier or harder than writing something original?

MATHESON: It was fairly easy … my father's short story is great and led the way.

Over the years, I've adapted H.G. Wells (*The Time Machine*), Roger Zelazny (*The Chronicles of Amber*), Whitley Strieber (*Majestic*), Dean Koontz (*Sole Survivor*) and Stephen King. As a prose writer, I'm tuned to not diluting or re-inventing their original text. Given realities of production, I do my best to assure the script reflects their voice and vision.

I know screenwriters and producers who regard the original text like tear-down real-estate. I go the other way. With "Battleground," staying true to Steve's story was also fairly easy because it's great. For reasons of length, I added the "Savage Commando," and the vote was to have Renshaw, a highly paid pro, living in a penthouse. I wrote the script minus dialogue but there wasn't a lot in Steve's short story, so it worked out.

MADDREY: I remember an interview you did years ago in which you talked about how hard it was for screenwriters to successfully adapt Stephen King's novels to the screen. You said you thought it was a little easier to get the short stories right.

MATHESON: Steve is brilliant with character. Details. Dialogue. Psychology. Contradiction. It's all real, lands right, cuts deep. For me, his novels are a challenge to adapt to two-hour film length, depending purely on the scope of story and number of characters. With a limited series, a popular form these days, obviously that changes; there's time to introduce more characters, explore their details and impact.

For example, when I adapted Dean's *Sole Survivor* as a four-hour mini-series, to do the novel justice, with all characters, it became clear we'd need an eight-hour. Dean was a producer on the project and the first to suggest cutting characters to streamline.

*MADDREY: When you published your first short story collection [*Scars and Other Distinguishing Marks, *1987], Stephen King wrote a foreword in which he paid you a huge compliment. He said there are two kinds of short stories—stories of narration and stories of style. He said he mostly writes stories of narration but he marveled that you can write both. I'm wondering if you agree that his short stories are mostly stories of narration, because it seems to me that so much of his style is related to his characterizations, to the way he presents the thoughts of characters in his stories.*

MATHESON: Interesting. I love magic realism; tend to read stylists like Martin Amis, Isabel Allende, Nabokov, Margaret Atwood, Ray Bradbury, F. Scott Fitzgerald, Jorge Luis Borges, James Wolcott, Lorrie Moore, Tanith Lee, and Don DeLillo. I aspire to such writing. That Steve said I'd achieved any degree of it, all those years ago, when *Scars* was published, will stun me to my dying day. I do differ with him regarding his own style which I find consistently remarkable; far more than narrative in approach. The lyricism and sway of his sentences; really something.

Though my stories are short, I don't seek brevity, but trance. The alchemical braid of words is a passion and preoccupation.

MADDREY: There's a part of me that thinks style is wasted on a script because not many people read scripts. Most people think of scripts as a stepping stone to a movie and the movie is the finished product. But I recognize that you can win people over by writing a stylish script—and that if you don't do that, the script might not sell and the movie might never get made.

MATHESON: Completely right. It's also just more fun. I see scripts as rhythmic and, as a drummer, am guided by tempo; pause, groove. And emptiness; a thing under-rated. My scripts all have shot descriptions that use few words, try to paint images. For example, in my novel *Created By*, I referred to Hollywood agents as "Armani Hammer-heads." An image more than a thought. Used in scripts, it makes reading them a more visual experience, engaging directors, actors, producers; the key people that get a film going. I've written, co-written and sold sixteen spec feature scripts and each took that approach. Evoke; don't instruct.

MADDREY: *In interviews, you've said that dialogue is one of your specialties as a screen-writer, so I'm curious why you decided to attempt "Battleground" without dialogue. Was that a situation where you decided to challenge yourself? "Let's see if I can pull this off...." Or was there something specific about the source story that made you want to tell it that way?*

MATHESON: Actually, neither. Exposition is my nemesis—in anything. Even con-versation. It herds information, footnoting, suffocating. Flow stiffens. Scripts are highly susceptible to its navigations as they try to not lose the audience. Whether telling your story as a half-hour, one-hour, two-hour, or ten-hour, the hourglass tempts clunky exposition.

To avoid it, there are approaches and tricks. For example, I prefer dialogue where characters don't say what they really mean, since it's usually obvious given context and performance. The contrast is also more psychologically telling than dialogue servicing plot points, which is just Play-Doh writing.

I suspect the audience values working a bit to understand ... interpret, find mean-ing. My father always said in a good piece of writing, the reader does half the work. In a good film or TV series, the audience does the same. Left un-clobbered by exposition, they'll intuit implication; subtext.

Keeping all that in mind, "Battleground" was a blessing as it could all be conveyed visually; my choice to write it minus dialogue didn't seem to confuse but add tension. In the script, I used a few devices to sneak in story; the CNN crawl at the airport, for exam-ple. I didn't know if the producers and TNT would buy into no dialogue ... but they loved it.

Our "Battleground" Executive Producer, the legendary Bill Haber, one of the founders of powerhouse agency CAA, is a connoisseur of the offbeat. He was excited about this approach to "Battleground," as was our director, Brian Henson, who made spectacular magic, along with William Hurt.

MADDREY: *When you've got an actor of that caliber, you know he'll be able to tell a story with a look.*

MATHESON: In some ways, maybe we're all fatigued by dialogue; whether clever, confessional, plot-centric. Much is needless, especially for good actors that get things across with nuance. That said, there are fine actors who would have been very good as Renshaw but thrown by no dialogue. Hurt was undaunted.

MADDREY: *This reminds me of something actor Lance Henriksen once told me. When he's playing a powerful character, he tries to trim his lines because he believes that truly powerful people don't talk about their power. They don't have to. Everybody can tell they're powerful.*

MATHESON: He's completely right. It's a revelation how little you need. Again, the strongest writing is seduction not explanation. Acting, too. Bad acting is termed "indicative" which says it all; a behavioral variation of being expository.

MADDREY: I think a good storyteller is someone who can engage the viewer's emotions— which doesn't necessarily require narrative clarity. I'm a David Lynch fan and I loved TWIN PEAKS: THE RETURN because I was so emotionally engaged in every scene. I was constantly confused, but I was actively trying to figure things out because I was emotionally engaged.

MATHESON: What I experience with David Lynch's work is dread. I'm engaged because I don't know everything, drawn down the pathological rabbit hole. For lesser directors, that kind of provocation and vagary fails. Lynch walks a burning tightrope. He's another example of things explained diluting. He doesn't fall for that.

MADDREY: He lets the audience do half of the work. That's what impressionism does.

MATHESON: That's it. That's the word.

MADDREY: I think this is a related question—but also kind of a random question. When I read your script for "Battleground," I noticed that you specified that Renshaw likes Miles Davis and acid jazz. In your mind, what does that reveal about the character?

MATHESON: I felt the intricate, alert patterns of jazz were in synch with his psyche. Both adrenal; an espresso soundtrack for a hyper-vigilant man.

MADDREY: Another thing I noticed is how you repurposed Stephen King's style of characterization. In his prose stories, he often italicizes the first-person thoughts of his characters. What a lot of adapters do is import those thoughts into dialogue, but you imported them into the scene descriptions instead—and kept the italics. As if to say to the actors, "Here's what you have to get across without saying it...."

MATHESON: Exactly. It's a stage direction and helps the actor meld with the character's state-of-mind. In my scripts, I try to make them contradictory. Not straight-ahead direction. I want to give an actor two different things to feel. A duality. Unresolved conflicts. Even paradox. It adds to the approach of not having characters say exactly what they mean. Fine actors like Lance Henriksen or William Hurt know how to juxtapose. Look vulnerable and deadly. Arrogant and doomed. All of it.

MADDREY: A director friend once told me that whenever there's a scene where an actor has to cry on camera, he'll tell them to act as if they're trying not to cry.

MATHESON: Yes. Or if drunk, try to hide it, not play it. Authentic is the goal. I also write comedy series and films, and characters saying the opposite of what they mean is part of the technique. Applied to drama, equally effective. I also often have characters speak in metaphors; another way to indirectly say what they mean using a striking image. Too much can be a gimmick. But too much of anything can be. Used sparingly, they're fluorescent.

MADDREY: It's all about the context.

MATHESON: Always. You can change the context; re-shape expectation. Not just twists but revealed truth. Another scriptwriting tip is to avoid starting a dialogue scene at the beginning. And avoid waiting until the end to exit the scene. Intros and outros are pudgy bookends most of the time. I like to drop in, drop out. Your director friend is right about tension through contradiction. Things relevant, yet non-linear, attract the ear, stir edge.

MADDREY: In "Battleground," you also do a lot of juxtaposing through visuals. You describe the décor of Renshaw's apartment as being very minimal, very neatly arranged—which makes it ironic when the whole place gets turned upside down and blown apart.

MATHESON: In my intro for the "Battleground" book I compiled/edited, I referred to Renshaw's upscale apartment as looking "embalmed by order, overdue for ruin." He was just asking for it.

MADDREY: That sets up why Renshaw is the perfect person to go through this experience—because he's a guy who's sort of OCD and who wants to control every aspect of his life.

MATHESON: Renshaw savors tailored clothing, a penthouse of stark elegance, a flawless hit. He's more than just orderly; has elevated esthetics, trophies from his "jobs" elegantly displayed under glass. The ballerina's delicacy struck his arctic marrow. But when someone challenges him, he goes jungle. Though it really pisses him off when his art and décor are strafed and cannon-balled by the puny dogfaces, he'll sacrifice his impeccable pad; fight to the death. Priorities.

MADDREY: And none of that is in the Stephen King short story. You also added a beat where you make the toy soldiers sympathetic. When Renshaw turns over the couch, we see them regrouping and actually helping each other. They are behaving humanely while Renshaw is going jungle....

MATHESON: They only know this is their mission and they must lay down their lives for one another. Lethal simplicity on both sides: victory at any cost.

MADDREY: It's fascinating to hear you say that because I was thinking mainly in terms of the effect on the audience and you're talking about getting inside the heads of the soldiers.

MATHESON: Right. They're true soldiers and Renshaw respects that; among the few things, in life, he may. It takes one to know one. Their scale is initially a joke to him but he quickly sees their loyalty to their own ranks. Fearless commitment. And when he refuses to surrender, their dedication to killing him.

MADDREY: I realized that at the end of the episode, when Renshaw sees that the Savage Commando has triggered a time bomb. There's a look on William Hurt's face that says "oh shit" but also ... "touché." He's impressed.

MATHESON: Absolutely. He realizes he's been checkmated and is about to die ... relishing the irony, admiring their expertise.

MADDREY: The more we talk about it, the more I realize how many nuances there are in the screen story that aren't in the short story. There's a lot of humor and a lot of suspense that's just not there in the source material. For example, in the short story, when Renshaw opens the box, he gets attacked right away. In the screen story, the soldiers get loose in the apartment and start stalking Renshaw, but he doesn't realize immediately what's going on. You play that scene for suspense.

MATHESON: I did slip-in dead-pan humor; irresistible. A lethal hit man versus toy soldiers; comical on the face of it. But soon too deadly to remain that. Ripe for under-cutting his hubris. The suspense blended filling an hour and not breaking the spell. Length dictates many creative choices and Brian and I absolutely agreed about the gradual reveal.

MADDREY: You used a brilliant phrase once to define suspense. You said it's all about "how you conceal and when you reveal."

MATHESON: There's a French axiom: "*To know is nothing. To imagine is everything.*" Its application is the very definition of suspense. Still, you'd be surprised how many film and TV production executives you run into, as a screenwriter, who *just have to know*. Plot. Motive. Everything. They're smart, quick-minded. But almost none are writers and don't feel at ease with unknowns; their controlling instincts, it seems, thwarted. It isn't just being commercial. It's personal. They feel they know how to tell a story and, often fatally, figure the audience will agree. But the audience doesn't need to know everything and usually resents it.

In short stories, novels or scripts, my goal is to provide the dots, let others find connection; however they perceive it.

MADDREY: It seems to me that writers like you—and Stephen King—have spent so much time writing stories that you are immersed in the craft. At a certain point, storytelling becomes instinctive. Whereas a less experienced writer might have to create an outline and spend a lot of time planning things out, you guys can just sit down and just start writing without a plan and manage to produce something that looks like it was planned out. Which is kind of miraculous.

MATHESON: It comes from a variety of things. One is learning to spot clichés and tropes; guillotine them. I worked for six years, as a writer-producer, with the immensely gifted Stephen J. Cannell who was inclined to say about storytelling and plotting "…just do the next most interesting thing." I'd remind him, "Steve, that presupposes a writer knows what's interesting." In my experience, some do. Not all.

Stephen King has it in spades. As did my father. A writer that many enjoy always has an instinct for what's interesting to others. How? A mystery. Many writers who are talented are cursed by having little or no feel for what interests others. You could write a TWILIGHT ZONE about it. Irresistible instinct and style are the rare and ultimate armory.

MADDREY: It's like the post-apocalyptic episode ["Time Enough at Last"] about the guy who finally has all the time in the world to read books—but his glasses break and he can't see the pages.

MATHESON: In this case, the glasses are the writer's sense of what's interesting. He's blind to what's of zero appeal to others.

MADDREY: When you adapt a story that works on the page and already resonates with a certain audience, are you more methodical about the way you re-tell it? Do you make an outline and analyze it in terms of plot and characters and themes and tone?

MATHESON: I do all of that, but in no particular order.

MADDREY: You said you wrote "Battleground" in less than a week, so I'm assuming all of this experience gives you the ability to dive into writing a script without having to do too much pre-planning.

MATHESON: Yes. Same thing happened with BIG DRIVER [the 2014 TV movie based on Stephen King's novella] after Bill Haber and I met with Lifetime, who were hot to go into production. Having a Stephen King project was a major first for them; even a potential re-brand re: more prestigious stuff.

They asked how soon I could write a story and script, and I said working on a treatment, for them to approve, would take a couple of weeks. I suggested, instead, I go right to script and they give me notes on that.

They agreed and, as with "Battleground," I wrote the script fast—in a week or so. Happily, they were thrilled; had few notes; cast Maria Bello, Ann Dowd, Olympia Dukakis, Joan Jett; hired director Mikael Salomon (who also directed SOLE SURVIVOR) and raced into production.

MADDREY: Did you know that Stephen King also wrote a script for "Battleground," back in 1978?
MATHESON: No, I didn't. What happened?

MADDREY: He was pitching a NIGHT SHIFT anthology TV series and he wrote a two-hour pilot that adapted three of the short stories from that collection, one of which was "Battleground." One thing that jumped out at me in his script was a detail about the toy maker's mother that is not in the short story. I had read that Brian Henson was confused about how the package containing the toy soldiers was postmarked five days before the toy maker's murder—so Brian asked Stephen how the mother could have known that her son was going to be murdered by this guy. And Stephen said, "Don't overthink it."
MATHESON: Logic is not always an entertainment value.

MADDREY: But Stephen King had already thought about it, because in his '78 script, the mother is a witch.
MATHESON: Interesting. Makes sense.

MADDREY: You once made a comment in an interview that you thought it was hard to pin down Stephen King's worldview simply by looking at his work. The Night Shift *stories, for example, are much more nihilistic than the later novels. There's not as much of the humanistic perspective. This makes me wonder about what people always say when they're adapting Stephen King—that they are trying to be true to "the spirit" of Stephen King. Do you think an adapter can actually be faithful to the "spirit" of Stephen King? Or can they only be faithful to an individual story?*
MATHESON: Tough question. Prodigious as Steve is, his spirit is arguably everywhere in his work. But, for me, not easy to define. He's many things as a writer. Spiritual. Philosophical. Terrifying. Funny. Political. Tender. I do think he has a genius for resonant irony; every idea, twist, character, scare, redemption. He rarely does what you think he will. It's never coy swerves … it's revelation. And his choices, in every way, have something to say. For me, that's his voice. His spirit.

MADDREY: I think you're right that his sense of humor is key. A lot of people talk about the need for humor in horror, but it's only a certain type of humor that works—that doesn't trivialize the horror. Irony can function as a sort of coping mechanism for particularly grim horror.
MATHESON: It's detachment. A funhouse-mirror of reversed meaning. For example, the emcee's monologues in [the MASTERS OF HORROR episode] "Dance of the Dead"—talking about ghastly things, as if speaking of things practical. Detached. Reversed. Humor, amid horror, can puncture tension … or be a warning of worse things to come. But always, essentially, at remove; detached. Like impieties from a jaded god.

I've written short stories where, in a well-reasoned voice, I'm presenting something aberrant or insane. I love writing the calm logic of madness, persuasively presented as reasonable. Done right, it turns meanings inside-out.

MADDREY: And that's a real skill. It's not something every writer can pull off.
MATHESON: It can be tricky. When we first started talking, you mentioned my

writing in different forms and genres; the range. Blending comedy and drama in my writing always opened doors for me in film and TV. Not set-up-punch line comedy … but a sideways POV oddly phrased. I see writing comedy and drama dialogue as very similar.

MADDREY: Did I hear that you're working on a new Stephen King adaptation right now?
    MATHESON: I'm producing and writing a limited series.

MADDREY: Can you talk about it?
    MATHESON: Not yet. Wish I could because I'm excited about it. Steve's agent, Rand Holston, let me know Steve said I could choose whatever I wanted from his available stuff, to write for film or TV. I knew he'd been pleased with my work with various of his adaptations, and a feature re-write I'd done for THE SUN DOG [unproduced as of 2022], but the offer was a big honor. I pored through the trove and there were, of course, many things I loved. What I finally chose and developed, I sold to Sony as a six-hour limited series. Suspense, not horror.

MADDREY: You and King seem to have a real kinship.
    MATHESON: I wish I knew Steve better but I guess we're both pretty private. We also don't live close and, aside from playing drums in his band, The Rock Bottom Remainders, for an amazing Miami gig, we've never hung-out. We did ride, just us two, to the after-party in a limo, talking about the gig, life and writing … unforgettable.

    He's always been very complimentary about my work, starting with his *Scars* Introduction. At a Stoker Awards banquet, he called my writing brilliant which kinda made my decade.

    Thinking about adapting Steve's work, I do feel we share a sensibility about humor and dark stories. Whenever I see him interviewed, despite his profound talent for creating horror and fear, he's funny; a fount of mischief. Actually, thinking back: when we rehearsed in Miami for our gig, I remember how hilarious Steve and Dave Barry were and just laughing our asses off.

    It was the same with my father, who was wickedly funny. There was always tons of irreverent laughter in our house and, when I was a kid, his writer pals would come over and they'd be up all night, talking stories and ideas, joking around. I'd fall asleep to the sound of their laughter and imaginations whirring, like wondrous Sandmen.

    So, for me … humor and horror are right at home.

CREEPSHOW: "GRAY MATTER" (2020)

    The original CREEPSHOW film was not the box office hit that Stephen King, George Romero and Richard Rubinstein hoped for, but it certainly cast a long shadow—inspiring at least three TV series and three more films. The first series was Laurel Entertainment's TALES FROM THE DARKSIDE (1983–1988), which probably would have been named CREEPSHOW if Laurel—rather than Warner Brothers—had owned the title. The Laurel series featured stories written by Romero ("Trick or Treat," "The Devil's Advocate," "The Circus," and "Baker's Dozen") as well as Stephen King ("The Word Processor of the Gods" and "Sorry, Right Number"). After the cancellation of TALES, Rubinstein launched an even more horror-centric anthology series called MONSTERS (1988–1991), which included an adaptation of King's short story "The Moving Finger."

King also provided story ideas for CREEPSHOW 2 and Romero wrote the original screenplay for that film. A 1984 Second Draft of the script incorporated two original tales ("Old Chief Wood'nhead" and "Pinfall"), two adaptations of previously published short stories ("The Raft" and "The Cat from Hell"), and a fairly elaborate wraparound story. In a 1987 interview, King referenced a newer version of the script that featured an original story called "The Hitchhiker" in place of "The Cat from Hell." Ultimately, "The Cat from Hell" segment became part of TALES FROM THE DARKSIDE: THE MOVIE (1990) and the "Pinhead" segment was completely discarded. In 2016, the latter tale was finally presented in comic book form—by artist Jason Mayoh—for Arrow Video's limited-edition Blu-Ray release of CREEPSHOW 2.

Around 2005, Richard Rubinstein tapped the writer/director team of Ana Clavell and James Glenn Dudelson—who had recently collaborated on the ill-advised sequel DAY OF THE DEAD 2: CONTAGION (2005) for Rubinstein—to resurrect the CREEPSHOW franchise. CREEPSHOW 3 was released direct-to-video in 2006. Fans of the original film were not pleased with the results, leading some to declare that TALES FROM THE DARKSIDE: THE MOVIE is the *real* CREEPSHOW 3. It would have been a sad note to end on but thankfully The Creep still has some life left in his old bones.

In 2015, the AMC network launched its streaming service Shudder and execs began looking for horror franchises to adopt. According to Shudder's general manager Craig Engler, a production and management company known as The Cartel approached him about distributing a new anthology series called CREEPSHOW, indicating that Greg Nicotero had already expressed interest in reviving the title (Porch 2019). Nicotero was coming off of his success as a producer on AMC's wildly popular series THE WALKING DEAD (2013–2022) and CREEPSHOW seemed like a return to his filmmaking roots. He remembers, "I grew up in Pittsburgh where I met George Romero when I was around 15 years old and he invited me to the set of this movie that he was making called CREEPSHOW. It was the first movie set I had ever been on … and it changed my life that day" (McGrew 2019). As Creative Executive of the new CREEPSHOW series, he says his goal was to extend—not re-create—King and Romero's original experiment: "I'm not rebooting anything, or like, 'Oh, we're going to upgrade it and retell it.' It's really like you're picking up another issue of *Creepshow* and these are the stories" (Hall 2019). Like the original filmmakers, Nicotero promised "the most fun you'll ever have being scared."

Unfortunately, CREEPSHOW director George Romero had passed away one year earlier—but the producer wasted no time reaching out to Romero's collaborator. As soon as the show was greenlit, he remembers, "I reached out [to Stephen King] and said, 'Hey, we're doing CREEPSHOW.' I can't imagine CREEPSHOW without a Stephen King story." And King wrote me back within two hours and was like, "I got the perfect story'" (Anderson 2020). The author suggested "Survivor Type," a gruesome tale from his *Skeleton Crew* collection. Nicotero says he adapted the story himself but quickly realized that budgetary restrictions would prevent him from making the episode the way he wanted to. He reached out again to King and asked for the rights to an alternative story: "Gray Matter" from *Night Shift*.

As it turned out, "Survivor Type" wasn't the only Season One story that had to be scrapped due to budgetary limitations. Philip de Blasi and Byron Willinger had written an original script that had impressed Nicotero but seemed unproduceable—so the showrunner remembered the writing duo when he had to switch out King's stories. The combination of de Blasi and Willinger with King's source story seemed like a natural fit; both screenwriters were lifelong fans of the novelist and King had practically pre-approved them by praising their 2018 action film THE COMMUTER. On January 13, 2018, King tweeted, "Don't be misled by the booger-splat on Rotten Tomatoes. THE COMMUTER is smart, involving, and suspenseful. Hitchcock crossed with Agatha Christie." For de Blasi and Willinger, the new challenge was crossing the undead spirit of George Romero with Stephen King.

The short story "Gray Matter" is set in a dive bar in Bangor, Maine—where an unidentified narrator, along with bartender Henry Parmalee and a trio of "old duffers," is riding out a fierce January snowstorm. Things turn dark when teenager Timmy Grenadine shows up to buy beer for his father, using dollar bills covered in a mysterious gray slime. Suspicious, Henry pulls the boy aside and asks him if something is wrong. The short story's limited first-person point of view means that we, the reader, don't know what Timmy has told Henry until later. All we know is that Henry, the narrator, and one of the old-timers (Bertie Conners) go to check on Richie Grenadine—and Henry brings a gun.

On the way to Richie's house, Henry relays Timmy's account of his father's rapid descent into alcoholism, following a debilitating injury at work last October. For weeks, Richie has done nothing but sit in the dark and drink and rely on Timmy to make beer runs. One day, Richie says, he returned home and found his father wrapped in a blanket, like a caterpillar in a chrysalis. All he could see was his father's hand—except, the narrator stipulates, Timmy said it "*didn't look like a hand at all. Just a grey lump.*" When the boy started to call a doctor, his father pulled down the blanket—revealing a face "buried in gray jelly." King's short story detours into the unnamed narrator's recollection of a local man named George Kelso, who told him about a terrifying encounter with "a spider as big as a good-sized dog" in the sewers beneath Bangor. The anecdote serves as a reminder to the reader that "there are more things in heaven and earth."

The trio eventually arrives outside of Richie Grenadine's apartment building and Henry shares the horrifying conclusion of Timmy's story, which indicates that Richie has turned into a giant, cat-eating slug. The old duffers ascend to the third floor—ominously observing that none of the other tenants seem to be home—and knock on Richie's door. An inhuman voice responds and the narrator suddenly remembers recent news reports about a pair of young girls and a wino who have gone missing. The door bursts open and "a huge grey wave" of man-shaped jelly attacks Henry. The monster appears to self-replicate as it feeds. The narrator and Bertie make it back to the bar, where the narrator calculates the number of replications that would be required for the monster to completely absorb the human race. At the end of the tale, he seems to be anticipating that apocalyptic future.

When Philip de Blasi and Byron Willinger set out to adapt the story to the screen, they chose to focus on the relationship between Richie and Timmy Grenadine. On a 2020 Blu-Ray commentary track for the episode, Greg Nicotero remembers, "They really keyed in on what this story is about—which is alcoholism and the co-dependency between the boy and his father." Instead of telling the story from the perspective of one of the barflies, the screen version allows Timmy to tell his own tale—which, according to de Blasi, builds suspense around the question of "how honest a narrator Timmy becomes in describing his relationship with his father" (Trumbore: "CREEPSHOW" 2019).

When Timmy first arrives at the bar—in the midst of a Class 4 hurricane (a budgetary concession, because rain was easier to simulate than snow)—he finds three people there: police Chief Conners, the Chief's friend Doc, and Dixie Parmalee. The final episode uses set decoration and background audio to tease the events ahead: a series of flyers about missing pets and missing kids, plus a radio broadcast about the ballooning world population. A series of inside jokes also ground the story in Stephen King's fictional universe—beginning with Timmy's yellow rain slicker and building up to Chief's account of George Kelso's encounter with a giant spider in the sewers. De Blasi explains, "This little story about George Kelso, it's creating tone, it's creating expectation that something horrific is out there. And it creates the verisimilitude that we're in a universe where the impossible, the evil, can happen" (Trumbore: "CREEP-SHOW" 2019).

Once the adults are properly spooked, Chief and Doc leave to check on Richie. Timmy stays behind with Dixie Parmalee, who in this version of the tale is something of a surrogate mother. Dialogue reveals that she took on that role after the recent death of Timmy's mother—a detail that essentially replaces Richie's injury at work and casts the father character in a different light, making him and his enabling son more sympathetic in the screen story. Nicotero explains, "The unique aspect of the story is it really is about the relationship between the son and the father. And his father not knowing any other way to deal with his grief other than through alcohol. And the little boy really doesn't know what else to do. So he ends up enabling his dad" (Trumbore: "Greg" 2019). In their end, that dual emotional surrender costs lives.

The second half of the screen story intercuts Timmy's halting confession to Dixie with Chief and Doc's encounter with Richie. As Timmy describes the events of the past few months (which are illustrated via cinematic flashbacks), we—and Dixie—slowly come to the realization that the boy has knowingly sent Chief and Doc to their deaths. When the two men arrive at Richie's apartment house, the show shifts into traditional horror movie mode; begging the question "What's behind the door?" It's at this point, de Blasi says, that the spirit of CREEPSHOW really comes alive: the "unpredictabil-ity" conjures "primal emotions" and the "fun" of being scared (Trumbore: "CREEP-SHOW" 2019). In his Blu-Ray commentary, Nicotero remembers that the original script started with the climactic scene—"we see them screaming in panic and struggling"—then flashed back to Timmy's arrival at the bar. The filmmakers ultimately decided to tell the screen story more linearly, hoping to give the narrative "more momentum." The final show extends the climactic sequence in the apartment house by adding a beat in which Chief and Doc discover two dead girls (the Grady twins?) in the bathtub before coming face to face with a ten-foot Blob-man.

The appearance of the show-stopping monster gives special effects wizard-turned-producer/director Greg Nicotero an opportunity to shine. King's "gray matter" has mor-phed into a creature resembling the shape-shifting alien in director John Carpenter's THE THING (1982)—which is an appropriate visualization for King's ending about a self-replicating monster that can wipe out humanity in a matter of days. King's origi-nal story may have been partly inspired by John W. Campbell's short story "Who Goes There?"—the inspiration for Carpenter's THE THING—although it probably owes just as much to Jack Finney's novel *The Body Snatchers*, in which aliens initially attempt to invade earth by replicating the slime at the bottom of a can of peaches. Perhaps King thought, *If the aliens invaded our beer, we'd be in real trouble.*

In de Blasi and Willinger's adaptation, only Doc escapes and makes his way back to the bar where he tells Dixie and Timmy what happened. As Dixie runs mathematical calculations to predict the fate of humanity, the screen story delivers one last scare: the monster attacks from above, pulling Doc up through the ceiling. The decision to end the pilot episode of the new CREEPSHOW series on a visceral shock rather than a note of dread captures the tone of the original CREEPSHOW film—George Romero and Stephen King's funky, flat-out, unapologetic approach to horror.

An Interview with Philip de Blasi and Byron Willinger (2021)

JOSEPH MADDREY: I guess you guys are used to being interviewed as a writing team?

BYRON WILLINGER: Yes, it's true. We've been a team for a long time. Going back to preschool!

MADDREY: Wow.

WILLINGER: Yeah, we used to make stories and movies back in elementary school. We've known each other forever.

MADDREY: So this was always the plan—to make movies together?

WILLINGER: Yeah, basically. Right, Phil? We used to make movies with our little 8mm cameras.

PHILIP DE BLASI: As you always said, we were ahead of the superhero curve because we made The Hulk and Superman before anyone else. I mean, we had a limited number of actors—Byron and I mostly....

WILLINGER: I enjoyed our versions better because they weren't so CG heavy. They had more charm.

MADDREY: Sounds like CREEPSHOW was a good fit for you since it uses practical effects.

WILLINGER: I love practical effects! My fourteen-year-old kid and I watch John Carpenter's THE THING all the time. It is one of our favorite movies.

MADDREY: Those are still top-of-the-line effects.

WILLINGER: I still enjoy that stuff more than modern computer effects.

MADDREY: I understand you're both from New York. Did you guys go to film school there?

WILLINGER: I went to NYU, to Tisch. Phil went to Ithaca College, which is in upstate New York.

DE BLASI: Yeah, I was an English major there, but then I did some NYU Film after.

MADDREY: Was THE COMMUTER (2018) your first big break as screenwriters?

WILLINGER: We had sold a few scripts before that. We had sold scripts to 20th Century–Fox, Sony, New Line—in the early 2000s. That was when the spec script market was really robust. And THE COMMUTER, we wrote that a long time ago. When did we write that?

DE BLASI: 2008.

WILLINGER: And it just kind of bounced around to different producers over the years. Eventually, it found its way into [actor] Liam [Neeson]'s hands, and he happened to be riding that same train line when he read the draft. That's a train line Phil and I used to take, back and forth to each other's places. We actually wrote the script in L.A. but I think it was in our heads before [we moved from New York to L.A.]—the idea of turning that train line into a story. Because we'd ride it every day and we'd see the same faces. It's like an insular little world, so we always thought, *Hmmm, could there be a little mystery involving all these people that we see every day?*

DE BLASI: Out of mundane boredom comes an action movie. That's what happened.

MADDREY: How did you first get involved with CREEPSHOW?

DE BLASI: It was purely serendipitous. We would go to this café—18th Street Coffee House in Santa Monica—a lot of writers hang out there—and we actually just bumped into a guy named Jordan Kizwani, who had the rights to CREEPSHOW. We became friends and then he suggested we pitch on the CREEPSHOW TV series, so we came up with a few ideas. Showrunner Greg Nicotero gravitated toward this one idea called "Two for the Road," which is kind of like DUEL meets "The Raft" segment in CREEPSHOW 2, about a goo creature on a moving vehicle. It was a fun piece, but because of budgetary reasons they couldn't pull the trigger.

WILLINGER: It was a car chase. The whole episode was two cars chasing each other, which Greg really loved, because he liked DUEL so much. He thought he could do it, but it was just too expensive.

DE BLASI: Then Greg's other pilot episode for CREEPSHOW was also too expensive.

WILLINGER: That was Stephen King's "Survivor Type."

DE BLASI: Right. So they needed a new pilot. Because Greg had his hands full, he wanted us to do the new pilot. And they found "Gray Matter."

WILLINGER: They really wanted a Stephen King episode to start the series—because it is CREEPSHOW—but his episode fell apart within a few weeks of production. So he called us and said, "Uhhhhh, we asked Stephen. He gave us 'Gray Matter.' Can you come up with something over the weekend?" [laughs] We had two days to come up with a take on the story. But we were thrilled. We were excited about the challenge to take on a Stephen King story.

MADDREY: Were you fans of the original CREEPSHOW movie?

WILLINGER: Yes, of course! I always loved the one with Ted Danson ["Something to Tide You Over"]—because I used to watch CHEERS when I was little. Then I saw [CREEPSHOW] on late night cable and I was like, "Oh my god! Sam Malone's buried on a beach!" And the guy that put him there is the doctor from AIRPLANE! So I loved it.

MADDREY: I know Greg has talked about wanting to maintain the tone of the original film, which was summed up by that great tag line: "The most fun you'll ever have being scared." I'm curious what that meant for you guys—because to me it suggests a very delicate balance between horror and humor.

WILLINGER: The funny thing is our original story, which we sold to them, had more humor. I think it was a little more of that balance.

DE BLASI: It had that humorous-horror bite.

WILLINGER: This story ["Gray Matter"] was bleaker. It's not as humorous. I mean, it's about alcoholism.

DE BLASI: It remains darkly humorous because of what the father becomes—that goo monster. And it's caused by contaminated beer. That idea is inherently humorous, but the way we told the story is, I think, more horrific than funny.

WILLINGER: Well, the epilogue is kind of humorous. The idea is taken from the original story, where the creature is going to multiply exponentially. It's kind of an absurd jump from "dad's turned into a creature" to "it's now taking over the whole world." So that, I thought, was funny. Otherwise it's a pretty dark story.

MADDREY: *You brought up watching THE THING with your son and the ending of "Gray Matter" reminds me a lot of THE THING, but of course the short story was written years before John Carpenter made THE THING.*
> WILLINGER: Way before. But there was the Howard Hawks version too.

MADDREY: *I wondered if you guys had thought about that version because the whole setup of that movie is the question of "what's behind the door?" When are we going to see the monster? And it's the same thing in your episode of CREEPSHOW, which is a slow build to "what's behind the door" when Chief and Doc get to the apartment building.*
> WILLINGER: That was our approach.

MADDREY: *But then in the Blu-Ray commentary, Greg said you originally thought about starting with the big reveal and flashing back? What was the thought process there?*
> WILLINGER: The reveal of what is behind the door was never intended for the opening. We always wanted to save the creature until the end. What we had proposed was revealing some of the epilogue where "Adrienne [Barbeau, who plays Dixie Parmalee]" is calculating the rate the creature is multiplying and Giancarlo [Esposito, who plays "Doc"] is yelling that they have to get out of there. But we definitely did not want to give away the creature in the beginning. We just wanted to set up a dramatic question that pays off with the epilogue. Our concern was that if we saved the idea of multiplying until the end, it might feel a little rushed and out of left field. It's a big idea to shoe-horn in.
> In the original story the idea of it multiplying is only hinted at. I don't believe the story *shows* it. Phil and I kind of gravitated away from that. Actually, we were willing to lose that idea altogether. Greg really wanted to keep it, though, as it was a big part of the original story. And the way he executed it, I think, ultimately added to the absurdity and gave it that fun CREEPSHOW tone.
> In the original story, Henry Parmalee is the shop owner. He takes the boy, Timmy, in the back and Timmy tells him the story offscreen. Then, he goes on a journey and he's retelling the story Timmy just told him. There's a couple of reasons we changed it. For production reasons, we couldn't have the actors do a lot of exterior scenes where they're walking and telling a story. On CREEPSHOW, they're very limited by budget and locations, so that was the first thing that tied our hands. Then we thought, *Wouldn't it be more interesting if we cross-cut to build tension, and we see the boy tell the story [while the others investigate]?* That was really our focus.
> DE BLASI: The other big thing we had to figure out was who are the main characters and what's the central relationship. Who are we really invested in? In the original story, it's these three guys walking to Timmy's apartment but there's nothing really dramatic going on, so we were like, *What are we caring about here?* So we gravitated toward the son and the son's relationship to his father, and how he was aiding the father by getting this alcohol, and [witnessing] how the father was slowly transforming. That's what gave us the gravity of the piece—that relationship. Otherwise, it was too thin. We didn't have anything we were invested in with the characters. It was just guys talking about a story *en route* to a house. That's not compelling enough.
> WILLINGER: The original story—which I love—is about what the father became,

how alcoholism destroys him, and the idea of it multiplying as it consumes everything around him. [King] has the boy character in the beginning but then he's out of the story right away. We thought, *What if the reveal of the monster is also the reveal of how far the boy will go to feed his father's addiction?* I mean, he led them there. It started with giving his father beer and now he's feeding him these old men from the bar. The story became about enabling. We liked the idea that the boy becomes a monster as well through his actions. That's the devastation of enabling an addiction. That was something we could run with.

MADDREY: You gave the story some narrative momentum by doing that—adding character arcs which the source story does not have. I think the source story is more of a tone poem. The bleakness is the point of it.

DE BLASI: And the mediums are different, right? Film is not a short story and that's fine. They shouldn't be; they don't have to be. But you hit it exactly right: *While the characters are traveling, where are they going emotionally?* That's slightly different.

MADDREY: Was the decision to replace Henry Parmalee with Dixie Parmalee based on the idea of casting actress Adrienne Barbeau?

WILLINGER: Originally, we were going to have the three men in the story [including Henry]. They simply cut it down to two for budget reasons, but we did write a draft with all three guys. Once we shifted the focus to the boy and we decided it would be more interesting to hear the boy telling the story—which seems like a very Stephen King thing to do—we thought it would be more interesting if he was talking to this woman. I think she was his former teacher.

This was all done really quickly! Remember, we wrote the script in three or four days, then we did rewrites, then we found out we were going to set, and then—oh!—we got Adrienne Barbeau. [laughs] Greg may have had her in his mind but it didn't affect our writing. We just had that idea and then he surprised us with Adrienne Barbeau. Which was great!

MADDREY: Earlier you were talking about how projects can stay in development for years and years, so it must have been sort of refreshing to have this one move so fast.

WILLINGER: That was great! I think it was like three weeks from "hey, we've got a story for you" to "we're on a set." I wish they all happened that way.

DE BLASI: In creating the Dixie character, we wanted a mother surrogate. It's all about hinting at what kind of relationship this is. We allude to the idea that she was a math tutor to Timmy. We thought it would be that much more horrible that this motherly woman is helping him and trying to help him get over his psychological issue, and then at the end—"Oh by the way, I fed your husband and the other guys to my dad."

MADDREY: The "Chief" and "Doc" characters were new as well....

WILLINGER: Those names were just for shorthand.

DE BLASI: I think there was at least a "Doc" in the short story, if I recall.

WILLINGER: The characters had [proper] names in the story. I think we just used "Chief" and "Doc" for shorthand because we needed to define them economically.

MADDREY: That makes sense. One guy is going in as a medical professional, to help Timmy's father, and the other guy carries a gun. You've covered all your bases there.

WILLINGER: Right. And Henry Parmalee, sadly, got axed from the script.

DE BLASI: He had no function anymore.

WILLINGER: Also, there was no budget. They were like, "You can only have two guys. You can't have three guys."

DE BLASI: That's right. Now that you remind me of that, that's why [Dixie] would have been truly horrified [by Timmy's story], because it was her husband that was being fed to the monster. Henry was long-deceased in the filmed version, but that was not the original intent. It was "I just fed your husband, with the other two dudes, to their death."

MADDREY: Another death probably required a bigger special effects budget too.

DE BLASI: I just remember Greg said, "Lose it. It's redundant next to the other guys getting killed." He asked us to cut the cast down.

WILLINGER: These things are shot in three and a half days, so there are a lot of budgetary considerations.

DE BLASI: In the original story, there's a blizzard moving in. Now it's a hurricane, with some fans off to the side [of the camera].

MADDREY: Blizzards are expensive.

WILLINGER: Also because they're shooting in Georgia, it became a hurricane.

MADDREY: Do you remember your discussions about the very last scene, where Doc is pulled up through the ceiling? About why that was the right way to end the story?

WILLINGER: I think that was all Greg.

DE BLASI: That was definitely all Greg. We always intended the creature to have a tentacle pop in at the end. We didn't know exactly how he was going to do that. That was something Greg had in his head.

WILLINGER: That whole epilogue scene was challenging because there was a lot that had to be crammed into those last moments. And Greg really wanted it because he wanted to stay true to the original story, the idea that it would multiply.

DE BLASI: In the original story, if I recall, the guy is in a bar and he's drinking and he's like, "We don't have long." It's a very low-key, the-world-is-over ending.

MADDREY: It's the end of John Carpenter's THE THING. "Why don't we wait here for a little while and see what happens." The reason I asked about the last scene is because I think it's interesting how you've negotiated the tone of the episode. The Stephen King short story ends on that note of dread—it's open-ended—but your screen story ends with one last scare.

WILLINGER: I think that really comes from Greg because he knows the tone of these things better than anybody. He knows it better than we do, so he really wanted that over-the-top, hard cut to [the monster]. There's no subtlety in CREEPSHOW when it comes to the endings, right? So that's what he went for. And we didn't know what that shot was going to look like. When we were watching them film it, Giancarlo Esposito was coming up to me and looking at outtakes on my phone, trying to figure out what it was going to look like as well.

MADDREY: With three and a half day shoots, thank God you had great actors like that, who could deliver in the moment.

WILLINGER: We were thrilled. We got to set and saw Tobin [Bell, who plays Chief]—who we'd kind of met in passing—and then Giancarlo, who we both love. He's had such an incredible career. I was just watching TRADING PLACES (1983) and there's Giancarlo Esposito in the prison cell. He's been in everything. Forget Kevin Bacon; it should be "Six Degrees of Giancarlo Esposito."

MADDREY: He's also in MAXIMUM OVERDRIVE. He's the guy that gets electrocuted by the arcade game.

WILLINGER: It's amazing. So it was really fun and the actors were really great. They were engaging us on the set, coming up and talking to us about their characters and their motivations, breaking down dialogue with us. That was a thrill.

DE BLASI: I remember Adrienne wanted to know if her character realizes that Timmy was murdering them.

WILLINGER: She asked if her character knew. We said, "Yeah, for sure. Your character is putting it all together." She said, "Okay, it's important that I know that." And I think she really delivered on the expression.

DE BLASI: Her expression, for me, sells the whole thing. Her horrified expression seems so genuine in the end, when she puts it together.

WILLINGER: She was really good. She also looked over some of the dialogue and said, "Let's work on this line and that line." So we were writing [dialogue] on the set for her.

DE BLASI: It's such a different character from who she was in "The Crate" [in the 1982 film CREEPSHOW]. She has real acting chops and it was great to see that.

MADDREY: Are you both horror guys? Have you written any other horror scripts?

DE BLASI: We did. Our first breakthrough spec sale—way back in ancient times—was a haunted prison script. Very Stephen King. Very THE SHINING. Very SHAW-SHANK. That bounced around a little bit. Didn't get made obviously or you would know about it.

WILLINGER: It was sold to 20th Century–Fox when [producer] Arnold Kopelson was a big deal. He'd done SEVEN and PLATOON. You know, it was our first sale and here we were going to "The Nakatomi Tower" [the Fox Plaza in Los Angeles, where DIE HARD was filmed] to meet Arnold Kopelson. Unfortunately, it didn't get made. It's bounced around over the years—but, many years later, we still get calls from people, saying, "What ever happened to that script?"

MADDREY: Have you written many adapted screenplays or do you mostly write originals?

DE BLASI: I would say mostly original....

WILLINGER: *Paradise Lost*....

DE BLASI: Oh yeah. That's the biggest one, when we adapted Milton's poem. We sold that to Legendary Pictures in, I think, 2009...?

WILLINGER: Something like that. It blurs now, but we—on spec—we had taken Milton's *Paradise Lost* and adapted it on our own. It was a three-hour, huge, epic fantasy movie. And it almost got made. It had Alex Proyas directing and Bradley Cooper was going to star in it. It was weeks away from production. It was rewritten by a few people. I have to say—you don't like to be rewritten, but when you see Lawrence Kasdan's name next to yours, that was kind of exciting. And we were weeks away from production when, unfortunately, it all kind of fell apart.

MADDREY: Do you find adapted screenplays to be easier, harder, more rewarding...? How does it compare to writing an original screenplay for you?

DE BLASI: I think adapting is easier. I think when you have something on the page to start with, the gears start turning and you can see different ways into the material that gets you excited.

WILLINGER: And you're a little more removed from it, so you can look at it more objectively—about what works for you and what doesn't and how you can shape it. Whereas an original, you're starting from the dreaded blank page.

DE BLASI: Right, with an original there's so many ways to tell the story, so many ways to explore it. Everything is rewriting but I think, when it's an original, it's *really* rewriting. It's finding the ideal version, the most economical version of what you're trying to say. Sometimes you think you're trying to say something thematic and then you go, "Wait a minute, this is really what it should be about...."

WILLINGER: That happens to Phil and I a lot. We'll be working on an original script and we'll think we know what it is and then you look at it five, six, seven, eight drafts later and it's a very different movie than what we originally came up with. But hopefully it's for the better. It's just part of that process where you're lost in the woods for a while. At least when you have source material, you have something to fall back on, to kind of guide you. Your job is to tell the best version.

MADDREY: *Because there are so many Stephen King properties being adapted these days— plus forty-five years' worth of older adaptations—did you worry at all about trying to be true to some popular conception of what a Stephen King adaptation should be?*

WILLINGER: I don't think we had enough time to think about that.

MADDREY: *[laughs] Fair enough.*

WILLINGER: I think it was literally Greg on a Thursday saying "Get me a story by Monday." So we were just like, "Oh, let's do it."

DE BLASI: Well, we wanted it to be creepy and scary. That's for sure. We wanted to live up to that, which he does so well. That was our only bar. Is it disturbing and creepy? Yeah. I mean, fun, but ... it has to be horror. That was important.

MADDREY: *I think you succeeded in not only making a good Stephen King adaptation but also recreating the tone of the original CREEPSHOW which balanced horror with humor. You included a lot of Stephen King "Easter eggs" in your story, which is something that a lot of King adaptations do—they make tongue-in-cheek references to the larger Stephen King Universe. Sometimes that sort of thing can be distracting, but I think the nudge-nudge, wink-wink quality of inside jokes works well in something like CREEPSHOW. It reminds the audience that you're having fun, so they should be having fun too.*

WILLINGER: Greg wanted a lot of Easter eggs. Definitely. That was a mandate: Let's get Easter eggs in there.

MADDREY: *So some of them were yours and some were his...?*

DE BLASI: I don't recall him doing his own, like, secretive stuff.

WILLINGER: No, we had some. The Grady twins in the newspaper was us. I think Greg put Cujo on the wall. I think that was a surprise when I saw it. Timmy's yellow raincoat, that was Greg. That wasn't in the script. I'm trying to remember them all. I would say it was about half and half. But I think Greg would come up with stuff on the set. I think in Timmy's room, isn't there a Plymouth Fury in the background? We certainly weren't as focused on the Easter eggs as Greg. He's more of an encyclopedia of King than we are. I've read a lot of King, but ... there's a lot of King to read. [laughs] But even the original story had elements [of other King stories]. Remember they talked about the guy who saw the thing in the sewers? A lot of people thought that was a reference to *IT*? Although the book hadn't come out yet....

MADDREY: Right, "Gray Matter" was written years before he wrote that novel.

WILLINGER: We really wanted to include that little speech [from the short story] and we got a studio note that said "cut this stuff." We said, "You can't cut that! That's Stephen King's dialogue and it's a reference to *IT*!" Greg didn't want to cut it but some executive did.

DE BLASI: Yeah, I love that line about how there are things in the corners of this world that will drive a man insane. At the end, they're all insane. This is something so inexplicable and so horrible in our world that you can't look.

WILLINGER: The funny thing is it ended up being a line in the trailer for the show. And we fought to preserve that line.

DE BLASI: Also, in Universal's CREEPSHOW maze [at the studio's Halloween Horror Nights experience in 2019], that line played over and over. Good thing we fought for that line! [laughs]

WILLINGER: When the studio notes came back and said "cut this line," we just said "That's not our line, that's Stephen King's." That stopped them. "Okay, you can keep the line." [laughs] I'm always of the belief that, if you're adapting something, you should try to preserve the best moments from that author. Why throw it out?

MADDREY: Did King have to approve the script? Do you know?

WILLINGER: I don't think he had to approve the script, but when they first came to us, Greg said that he approved of us. He liked our film THE COMMUTER, so they knew he liked us. And I like to believe he approved the script. [laughs]

MADDREY: Do you think you'll write another episode of CREEPSHOW?

WILLINGER: We're trying to put together some ideas now for a hopeful Season Four. We'd love to. We had a great time.

CHAPELWAITE (2021)

In 1989, King biographer George Beahm indicated that every single short story from the *Night Shift* collection had been optioned for adaptation into a feature film—except one. "Jerusalem's Lot" might have been ignored by filmmakers because it is a pastiche of earlier horror stories (most notably, Poe's "The Fall of the House of Usher" and Lovecraft's "The Rats in the Walls"), lacking King's distinctive voice. Alternatively, filmmakers might have avoided it because the story is a period piece and therefore potentially more expensive to recreate onscreen. Yet another possibility: maybe no one felt confident that they could transform the author's fragmented, epistolary narrative—which spans centuries, introduces a multitude of barely-developed characters, and relies heavily on nebulous descriptions of an ever-morphing threat—into a coherent film.

Whatever the case, "Jerusalem's Lot" remained buried until 2020, when executive producer Michael Wright, president of MGM Scripted Television, began looking for a gothic horror project to air on the studio's new streaming service Epix. He called on producer Donald De Line for advice and De Line knew exactly who to ask. "I have an old friend," the producer remembered, "who represents Stephen King. So I went over to his office and said, 'What undiscovered treasures of Mr. King's might there be?' and he handed me the short story ['Jerusalem's Lot']. I went home and read it and fell in love with it" (Blem 2021). Wright was also impressed and decided to introduce De Line to

Peter Filardi, who had adapted King's novel *'Salem's Lot* into a TNT miniseries when Wright was the head of that network.

Filardi remembers he and his brother Jason had recently pitched a "horror western idea" to Epix when they learned about the King project in development. The duo read the short story and jumped at the chance to adapt it as a ten-hour limited series—although they realized that they were confronting a major challenge. As writer-producers, they would need to significantly expand and clarify a rather choppy short story, while remaining true to an authorial voice that was itself a mishmash of Edgar Allan Poe, H.P. Lovecraft, and Stephen King. That would mean inventing new characters and new plot-lines while embellishing existing ones.

In Stephen King's short story, the protagonist Charles Boone writes a series of let-ters—dated October 1850—to his friend "Bones" from Chapelwaite, a manse in Cum-berland County, Maine, that Charles recently inherited from his late cousin Stephen. In his letters, Charles writes that he suffered from "brain fever" following the death of his wife Sarah, but he hopes that his time at Chapelwaite will be restorative—and maybe inspire him to write the great American novel. Almost immediately, his hopes are dashed; the house appears "sinister" to him and Mrs. Cloris, a cleaning lady from the nearby town of Preacher's Corners, warns him that "no Boone has ever been happy there." Charles learns about an uncle (Randolph) who committed suicide there after his daughter (Marcella) fell to her death on the cellar stairs. He also hears eerie rum-ors about devil-worshippers in the nearby woods. A local logger named Thompson tells Charles about an abandoned village in the woods called Jerusalem's Lot.

Haunting laughter behind the walls of Chapelwaite leads Charles to a map, which in turn leads him to Jerusalem's Lot. He travels there with his manservant Calvin McCann and finds the place vacant but perfectly preserved. At the center of the aban-doned town is a church that Charles declares "spiritually noxious." Inside, he discovers a hideous painting of Madonna and child, an inverted cross, and an ancient text entitled *De Vermis Mysteriis (The Mysteries of the Worm)*.

Afterward, strange things begin to happen in the town of Preacher's Corners, including the rise of a blood-colored moon, "flocks of whippoorwills which roost in the cemeteries," the birth of an eyeless child (to a woman named Barbara Brown), and the discovery of "a flat, pressed trail five feet wide in the woods beyond Chapelwaite *where all had withered and gone white.*" As the mysteries deepen, Charles learns that his ances-tor Philip Boone was the first to discover the "hell-book" in Jerusalem's Lot and that he reportedly "trafficked with the unholy." Later, he encounters the living corpses of his Uncle Randolph and cousin Marcella in the basement and senses the ominous threat of "blood calling to blood." Charles concludes that his arrival at Chapelwaite has "wak-ened a Force which has slept in the tenebrous village of 'Salem's Lot for half a century, a Force which has slain my ancestors and taken them in unholy bondage as *nosferatu*—the Undead."

Next, Charles discovers the 1789 diary of his ancestor Philip Boone, who provides a historical account of the settlement of Jerusalem's Lot in 1710 by his half-mad ances-tor James Boon. The diary indicates that the original Boon's worship of "faceless pow-ers [that] exist beyond the rim of the Universe" has cursed Chapelwaite and the Boone family bloodline. Convinced that he too is cursed, Charles returns to Jerusalem's Lot and tries to burn the church, in hope of destroying the evil there and ending the curse. Instead, his actions summon a "monster worm" buried beneath the building. Charles burns the "hell-book" and banishes the conqueror worm—but his final letter to Bones indicates that the evil has not been completely vanquished. There are, he writes, four more copies of *De Vermis Mysteriis* in the world. Furthermore, he senses that he himself, as the last living Boone, has become a "gateway" for evil. By committing suicide, he hopes to end the family curse. King ends his short story with one more missive, written by Charles's heir James Robert Boone, at the time of his inheritance of Chapelwaite on October 2, 1971.

It is perhaps worth noting that the short story "Jerusalem's Lot" ends four years before the novel '*Salem's Lot*—which was, in its manuscript form, titled *Jerusalem's Lot*—begins with the arrival of novelist Ben Mears in his soon-to-be-vampire-infested hometown. The similarities between the two titles and the stories themselves invites comparison—but the CHAPELWAITE screenwriters insist they did not consciously set out to connect the two tales. Instead, they infused "Jerusalem's Lot" with some of their own inspirations—beginning with a re-invention of the main character Charles Boone.

Peter Filardi, who grew up in the coastal town of Mystic, Connecticut, explains that he and his brother drew on local lore about the 19th-century whaling industry in the Mystic seaport: "Our Charles Boone is a whaling captain who inherited this mansion and has come back. The Quakers saw whaling as a holy mission of sorts, a religious mission. It was going out into the great unknown to slay a Leviathan, bringing back lamp oil to light homes at night, to push back against the shadows—and also the metaphoric shadows of fear and superstition and prejudice" (Bennett 2021). Elsewhere, the writer adds, the main character became "a little bit of a modern Prometheus-type character, bringing a new sensibility into this very dark and shadowy world of Preacher's Corners, Maine" (Sheppard 2021).

Upon his arrival in the town of Preacher's Corners, the screen story's Charles Boone faces the challenge of protecting his family from multiple forms of darkness—including the perceived darkness within himself. As in King's story, Charles's wife Sara has died recently. Instead of suffering from "brain fever," however, the whaling captain has been suffering from vivid nightmares related to a violent childhood attack on him by his own father. In the screen story, he also has three new reasons to investigate the rumors of a family curse and clear his family name—because he wants to protect his mixed-race children: Honor, Loa, and Tane.

Peter Filardi explains that the purpose of making Charles Boone a "family man" was to "raise the stakes" in the story (Timpone 2021). The change also sets up a new theme—about battling the "metaphoric shadows" of prejudice—as Jason Filardi explains: "Boone is a whaling captain and these guys would get on a ship, leave New England, and go around the world for four years at a time. Oftentimes, they'd stop at these islands and fall in love with Polynesian women and start a family. [...] He fell in love with this interesting woman and had these children and now he has to take these children to small-town Maine where they don't see people like this too often" (Stone 2021). Another new supporting character named Able Stewart—a young black man who works for Charles and befriends Honor—faces the same challenge in lily-white colonial Maine.

Producer Donald De Line says the filmmakers' main effort at "modernizing" the short story was tapping into the timeless theme about fearing and persecuting otherness—a central tenant of Stephen King's fiction and of modern horror fiction in general. De Line credits the Filardi brothers with bringing this issue into "greater focus" by framing the question of otherness in terms of race, religion, and vampirism (Stone

Charles Boone (Adrien Brody), "a modern Prometheus," with (from left) his children Tane (Ian Ho), Honor (Jennifer Ens), and Loa (Sirena Gulamgaus) in CHAPELWAITE (Epix, 2021).

2021). He might easily have added sexism to the list. In much the same way that the Boone children represent the perceived threat of racial otherness, other new characters confront the dangers of religious persecution, sexism and vampirism.

In Preacher's Corners, a large segment of the religious community—led by former (but still influential) minister Samuel Gallup—denounces the Boones as cursed outsiders, hampering Charles's attempts to build a business and his children's attempts to get an education. Only Martin Burroughs, the current minister and Gallup's more liberal son-in-law, welcomes and supports them—partly, it seems, because Martin is harboring his own dark secret. As the story progresses, it becomes clear that the town minister has fathered a child out of wedlock with a young woman named Faith Pringle. Like the character of Barbara Brown in King's source story, Faith gives birth to an eyeless child—a situation that the religious community interprets as a dark omen. No one in town knows that the child's father is the local minister, so the promiscuous young woman is shunned like Hester Prynne in *The Scarlet Letter*. As a result, Martin Burroughs experiences a crisis of faith while witnessing the town's treatment of Faith.

Another new character in the screen story, Rebecca Morgan, represents the challenge of being a well-educated, headstrong woman in 19th-century rural Maine. In the screen story, Rebecca is an aspiring novelist—like Charles Boone in King's short story— and she initially regards the Boone family as inspiration for a gothic novel. Over time, however, she recognizes her kinship with these other outsiders and becomes part of their family. The new characters of Loa Boone and a mysterious young woman dubbed "Apple Girl" align the otherness of being a strong-willed woman with being a monster; both eventually join the vampire "family."

Peter Filardi says the ten-episode series CHAPELWAITE was carefully structured to present an "ever-changing face of terror"—escalating from "personal horror, a person's fear of themselves or what's within them," to "interpersonal horror, as Boone takes on the antagonists around him," to Lovecraftian "cosmic horror" (Timpone 2021). The screenwriters decided early on that they did not want to end their story as King did, with the physical manifestation of a monstrous worm. Instead, they imagined the Worm as a metaphor for primal fears of the type embodied in Lovecraft's pre–Christian Elder Gods. In CHAPELWAITE, as in "Jerusalem's Lot," the servants of these "faceless powers [that] exist beyond the rim of the Universe" are *nosferatu,* or vampires.

Unlike the vampires in *'Salem's Lot,* which possess the townsfolk in order to feed on them, the vampires in CHAPELWAITE have a loftier goal. Led by a mysterious elder named Jakub, who commands the pulpit of the not-so-abandoned church in Jerusalem's Lot, the coven is devoted to magically resurrecting the Elder Gods, establishing permanent night, and destroying humanity. Only those humans who serve as guards and familiars (and walking blood banks) will get to become vampires in the apocalyptic future that Charles Boone foresees in his darkest fever dreams. The crisis at the end of CHAPELWAITE is a battle between Us and Them—forcing the human characters to set aside their differences and fight a common enemy.

The filmmakers depict the common enemy not as romantic Hollywood vampires but as "barnyard vampires, more like vermin" (Timpone 2021). At the same time, the screenwriters grant several of the monsters nuanced motives and distinctly human personalities. In Filardi's 2004 adaptation SALEM'S LOT, there were some narrative discrepancies regarding the effects of vampirism; at least one character (Mike Ryerson) appeared to retain his moral faculties after becoming a vampire, but it was not clear how or why. In CHAPELWAITE, the screenwriters overtly explain—via a pivotal line of dialogue—that vampires can choose to hold onto as much of their humanity as they wish to hold onto. This explanation invites viewers to compare and contrast the most carefully-developed vampire characters—Philip Boone, Stephen Boone, Mary Dennison, and eventually Loa Boone and the mysterious "Apple Girl"—with the human characters, whose actions demonstrate the same ability to choose whether or not they behave like humans. The conclusion of the limited series complicates and undermines easy assumptions about the distinctions between Us and Them, turning even the main protagonist into a walking contradiction—a human vampire.

According to Peter Filardi, the expansion of King's source story—accomplished with screenwriting help from veteran TV scribes Scott Kosar (who worked on A&E's BATES MOTEL and Netflix's THE HAUNTING OF HILL HOUSE) and Declan De Barra (Marvel's THE IRON FIST and Netflix's THE WITCHER)—was vetted and approved by Stephen King himself. With scripts in hand, the Filardis assumed the roles of co-showrunners, allowing them to oversee every aspect of translating their scripts to the screen. One goal, according to Peter, was to emphasize *naturalistic* visuals in order to make their supernatural story believable; to that end, the showrunners encouraged their crew to emulate the spare décor, desaturated colors, and minimal camerawork in films like THE ASSASSINATION OF JESSE JAMES BY THE COWARD ROBERT FORD (2007) and THE WITCH (2015). The result was an old-fashioned, slow-building folk horror film in ten parts.

CHAPELWAITE premiered on the Epix television network on August 22, 2021, and concluded on October 31, 2021—roughly one half-century after Stephen King's fictional character James Robert Boone arrived for the first time at his cursed family estate. The ending of the TV series begs the question of where the Boone family (and its curse) goes from here—and perhaps whether or not there are more copies of *De Vermis Mysteriis* in existence. When questioned about the possibility of a second season of CHAPEL-WAITE in the fall of 2021, Peter Filardi said, "We would definitely bring Charles Boone back, if he would have us." Jason Filardi added that the ongoing story could track the now-immortal character "20 years, 50 years, 70s years" into the future (Timpone 2021).

Some Stephen King fans have suggested that the screenwriters could formally connect their CHAPELWAITE story to *'Salem's Lot*, and/or mount an official adaptation of the *Night Shift* short story "One for the Road," King's own mini-sequel to *'Salem's Lot*. Certainly, that would establish Peter Filardi as the consummate adaptor of King's vampire trilogy—but the screenwriter has expressed reservations about making so obvious a connection between the stories. In a September 2021 interview, he said, "I personally would be reluctant to just bump it up to present day, even though you might be able to. I think there's room out there for a television show set in the past, a period piece that still has the ability to scare the shit out of you" (Sheppard 2021). In February 2022, Epix announced that CHAPELWAITE Season Two was already in development.

Endless *Night*

As of 2022, only a few of Stephen King's *Night Shift* stories are still awaiting big-budget, commercial film or television adaptations—but all of the stories have been translated to a new medium at one point or another. Some stories have been adapted multiple times by so-called "dollar baby" filmmakers. In his 1989 book *The Complete Stephen King Encyclopedia*, Stephen J. Spignesi brought attention to a 1987 adaptation of "The Lawnmower Man" by screenwriter Michael De Luca (future exec of New Line Cinema, MGM, and Warner Bros.) and director James Gonis, as well as an adaptation of "The Last Rung on the Ladder" written and directed by Jim Cole and Daniel Thron. Later, King fans discovered an animated 1987 adaptation of "Battleground" by Soviet Ukrainian filmmaker Mikhail Titov and a 1989 adaptation of the *Skeleton Crew* story "Cain Rose Up" by writer/director David C. Spillers.

After a lull in the early 1990s, King ushered his "dollar deal" into the public consciousness in 1996, when he described it in an introduction to Frank Darabont's screenplay for THE SHAWSHANK REDEMPTION. Since then, over a hundred non-commercial King adaptations have been produced. Writer/director Andrew Newman's adaptation of "The Man Who Loved Flowers" kicked off the new wave, but Jay Holben's impressionistic short film PARANOID (2000) was the game-changer. The author liked the latter film so much that he allowed the filmmaker to release it online in 2002 and the film inspired a new generation of "dollar deal" filmmakers.

The 21st-century proliferation of dollar baby films has inspired a series of public screenings of the most successful ones—starting at a pair of short film festivals in 2004 and 2005 at the author's alma mater UMO. The festivals were organized by James Renner, who made an adaptation of King's tale "All That You Love Will Be Carried Away" in 2004, starring film critic Joe Bob Briggs. Subsequent festivals were organized by filmmaker Shawn L. Lealos, who adapted the *Night Shift* story "I Know What You Need" in 2005; journalist Anthony Northrup; and novelist Bryan Higby. Lealos and Northrup have also written books about the Dollar Baby phenomenon; Lealos' *Dollar Deal: The Story of the Stephen King Dollar Baby Filmmakers* (2015) is the more incisive, Northrup's *Stephen King Dollar Baby: The Book* (2021) the more comprehensive. Higby maintains an up-to-the-minute website (stephenkingmovies.com) containing a wealth of additional information—including details about more than a dozen retellings (each) of "The Man Who Loved Flowers," "One for the Road," and "I Am the Doorway."

Although there is no shortage of material available through Stephen King's dollar baby program, the *Night Shift* collection offers only a few remaining titles. In 2021, writer/director Lee Metzger turned "Strawberry Spring" into an 8-episode audio drama for the iHeart podcast network, knocking that title off the list. Also, BLACK SWAN screenwriter Mark Heyman is penning a script for a feature film adaptation of "The Boogeyman," to be directed by DASHCAM director Rob Savage. The promotional logline for THE BOOGEYMAN indicates that the film will deviate significantly from the source material and revolve around "a teenage girl and her little brother" as they "struggle to get their grieving father" to recognize "a sadistic presence in their house" (Fleming: "20th" 2021).

According to Stephen King's official website in late 2022, only four *Night Shift* stories ("The Last Rung on the Ladder," "The Man Who Loved Flowers," "One for the Road," and "The Woman in the Room") are currently available to license through the dollar baby program—which suggests that "Night Surf," "I Am the Doorway," and "I Know What You Need" have already been optioned for the Hollywood treatment. In the meantime, it seems safe to assume that the birth rate for new dollar babies will continue to rise—as filmmakers around the world keeping trying to capture the spirit of Stephen King.

This survey of four decades of *Night Shift* adaptations begs the question: What exactly is the "spirit" of Stephen King that filmmakers have been trying to capture? Like the man himself, it seems the definition has changed over time. Today's hugely influential novelist is not exactly the same person who wrote the early short stories that appear in *Night Shift*. Neither are the filmmakers who translated those stories to the screen exactly the same people they were when they adapted Stephen King. To some extent, stories are products of particular places and times—and of particular sensibilities. Times change and sensibilities change, allowing for the possibility of reinterpretation and re-imagination. As long as a story endures, those possibilities may be endless.

Bibliography

Abraham, Edward, and Valerie Abraham. BEWARE THE GREEN GOD. Based on Stories by Stephen King. Film script, undated (69 pages).

Abraham, Edward, and Valerie Abraham. THE MACHINES. Based on Stories by Stephen King. Film script, undated (91 pages).

Albarella, Tony. "Leading the Charge: An Interview with Michael Wright, TNT Executive Vice President and Head of Programming." *Stephen King's Battleground: A Commemoration of the Emmy-Winning Television Adaptation.* Ed. Richard Christian Matheson. Gauntlet, 2012.

Anderson, Kyle. "Greg Nicotero on the Bloody Madness of CREEPSHOW Season 1." Nerdist. com. June 1, 2020.

Anonymous [Bruce Clavette?]. "Former UMO student presents THE BOOGEYMAN." *Maine Campus.* November 17, 1982.

Anonymous. "Future Film Forecast." *Famous Monsters of Filmland* #164. June 1980.

Anonymous. "Termination of Transfers and Licenses Under 17 U.S.C. 203." U.S. Copyright Office. [2021]

Argent, Daniel, and Erik Bauer. "Frank Darabont on THE SHAWSHANK REDEMPTION." *Creative Screenwriting.* April 22, 2016.

Armstrong, Stephen B., ed. *Roger Corman's New World Pictures, 1970–1983: An Oral History.* BearManor, 2020.

Associated Press. "Hilly cornfields cancel Iowa role in movie." *Des Moines Register.* July 5, 1980.

Associated Press. "Stephen King trying to sell 'moron movie.'" *Nashua Telegraph.* August 3, 1986.

Base, Ron. "Stephen King makes the worst Stephen King movie ever made." *Toronto Star.* July 25, 1986.

Beahm, George. *The Stephen King Companion.* Andrews McMeel, 1989.

Beahm, George. *The Stephen King Story.* Andrews McMeel, 1991.

Beeler, Michael. "CHILDREN OF THE CORN." *Cinefantastique* Vol. 30, No. 4. August 1998.

Beeler, Michael. "SOMETIMES THEY COME BACK 2." *Cinefantastique* Vol. 29, No. 9. May 1996.

Bennett, Tara. "CHAPELWAITE Showrunners Adapt King's 'Jerusalem's Lot' into a Gothic Horror Series." Syfy.com. August 19, 2021.

Berrong, Trish. "Stephen King: Making his directorial debut with MAXIMUM OVERDRIVE." *Austin Daily Texan.* July 17, 1986.

Biodrowski, Steve. "David Price's Sequel Rites." *Gorezone* #21. Spring 1992.

Blem, Tiffany. "Interview with the Creators of CHAPELWAITE, Peter Filardi, Jason Filardi and Donald De Line." Pophorror.com. August 23, 2021.

Bloch, Robert. *Once Around the Bloch: An Unauthorized Autobiography.* Tor, 1993.

Blue, Tyson. "King Goes into Overdrive." *Twilight Zone* Vol. 5, No. 6. January 1986.

Booth, Paul (interviewer). "Talking Pictures: Tobe Hooper's THE MANGLER Interview with Stephen David Brooks." *Talking Pictures with Paul Booth.* December 15, 2018. Podcast.

Borchers, Donald P. "*The Shining* and Being True to Stephen King." https://www.youtube.com/channel/UCdD-5KRbMdKfKgAwAXv7MmA. August 14, 2016. Video.

Borchers, Donald P. "The SyFy Channel—Part 3." https://www.youtube.com/channel/UCdD-5KRbMdKfKgAwAXv7MmA. August 14, 2016. Video.

Borseti, Francesco. *It Came from the 80s!: Interviews with 124 Cult Filmmakers.* McFarland, 2016.

Briggs, Joe Bob. *Joe Bob Goes to the Drive-In.* Delacorte, 1987.

Briggs, Joe Bob. "Road Warriors on the Loose: MAXIMUM OVERDRIVE Idles Through Second Half." *The Orlando Sentinel.* August 10, 1986.

Brinn, David. "Making Things Up, Without a Hitch." *The Jerusalem Post.* January 11, 2015.

Bromley, Patrick. "FTM Bonus: Tobe Hooper Tribute with Stephen David Brooks." FThisMovie. net. January 25, 2019.

[Brooks, Stephen]. THE MANGLER. Based Upon the Short Story by Stephen King. Rewrite. Filmscript, June 9, 1993.

Brooks, Stephen. THE MANGLER. Based Upon the Short Story by Stephen King. Final Draft. Filmscript, June 17, 1993.

Brooks, Stephen David. Commentary. THE MANGLER. Shout Factory, 2018. Video.

Brosnan, John. "Milton Subotsky." *Starburst* Winter Special #2. 1988/1989.

Brown, Simon. *Creepshow (Devil's Advocates)*. Auteur, 2019.

Brown, Simon. *Screening Stephen King: Adaptation and the Horror Genre in Film and Television*. UT Press, 2018.

Browning, Mark. *Stephen King on the Big Screen*. Intellect, 2009.

Budrewicz, Matty. "The Matmor Chronicles: A Look Back at NIGHT TERRORS (1993) & THE MANGLER (1995)." TheSchlockPit.com. January 9, 2020.

Burke, David. "Q-C Finally Can See Itself in CHILDREN OF THE CORN This Week." QCTimes.com. September 20, 2009.

Cadigan, Pat, Marty Ketchum, and Arnie Fenner. "Has Success Spoiled Stephen King? Naaah!" *Shayol* Vol. 1, No. 6. Winter 1982.

Callaghan, Caroline. "Peter Duffell and the House That Dripped Blood." BritishFantasySociety.org. February 16, 2009.

Canby, Vincent. "CHILDREN OF THE CORN, based on King Story." *New York Times*. March 16, 1984.

Chaka, Chris. "MAXIMUM OVERDRIVE (1986)." VHSRevival.com. May 22, 2019.

Childs, Mike, and Alan Jones. "DOMINIQUE." *Cinefantastique* Vol. 6–7, No. 4–1. Spring 1978.

Chute, David. "King of the Night." *Take One*. January 1979.

Clavette, Bruce. "Boogeyman adapted into movie." *Maine Campus*. November 10, 1982.

Collings, Michael R. *The Films of Stephen King*. Starmont, 1986.

Conner, Jeff. *Stephen King Goes to Hollywood*. Plume, 1987.

Counts, Kyle. "New World, Stephen King Collaboration is a New Low for Both." *Cinefantastique* Vol. 14, No. 4/5. September 1984.

Crawley, Tony. "CREEPSHOW." *Starburst* #44. April 1982.

Crawley, Tony. "The King/George Conversations." *Starburst* #54. February 1983.

Crawley, Tony. "Media Macabre." *Halls of Horror* #29. 1984.

Crow, Thomas. "Screaming FOR MORE." *Fangoria* #174. July 1998.

Crow, Thomas. "Terror on a Budget." *Fangoria* #159. January 1997.

Daniel, Dennis. "Savini Speaks." *Deep Red* #3. June 1988.

Dawidziak, Mark. "SOMETIMES THEY COME BACK." *Cinefantastique* Vol. 21, No. 6. June 1991.

Dillard, Clayton. "Get Back to Work!: Critiquing the Hollywood-Industrial Complex in THE MANGLER." *American Twilight: The Cinema of Tobe Hooper*. UT Press, 2021.

Ebert, Roger. "Children of the Corn." *Chicago Sun Times*. March 12, 1984.

Emery, Robert J. *The Directors: Take Four*. Big Show, 2003.

Englund, Robert, and Alan Goldsher. *Hollywood Monster: A Walk Down Elm Street with the Man of Your Dreams*. Simon & Schuster, 2009.

Esposito, John. GRAVEYARD SHIFT. Based on the Story by Stephen King. First Draft. Filmscript, March 30, 1986.

Esposito, John. GRAVEYARD SHIFT. Based on the Story by Stephen King. New Version. Fourth Draft. Filmscript, May 30, 1990.

Etchison, Dennis. "Foreword." *Reign of Fear: The Fiction and the Films of Stephen King*. Ed. Don Herron. Underwood-Miller, 1988.

Everitt, David. "Stephen King's CHILDREN OF THE CORN." *Fangoria* #35. April 1984.

Everitt, David. "To Direct a Cat." *Fangoria* #43. March 1985.

Fallon, John. "The Arrow Interviews Matt Cunningham and Erik Gardner." Joblo.com. February 9, 2005.

Fallon, John. "MAXIMUM OVERDRIVE." Arrowinthehead.com. December 15, 2001.

Farren, Mick. "Stephen King." *Interview* Vol. 16, No. 2. February 1986.

Felsher, Michael (producer). "Field of Nightmares." Red Shirt Productions, 2017. Video.

Felsher, Michael (producer). "Stephen King on a Shoestring." Red Shirt Productions, 2009. Video.

Fleming, Mike, Jr. "Stephen King on What Hollywood Owes Authors When Their Books Become Films: Q&A." Deadline.com. February 2, 2016.

Fleming, Mike, Jr. "20th / Hulu Conjure THE BOOGEYMAN from Stephen King Short; Rob Savage Directs & 21 Laps Produces." Deadline.com. November 1, 2021.

Fletcher, Jo. "The Limits of Fear." *Knave* Vol. 19, No. 5. May 1987.

Folkart, Burt A. "Richard Irving; Director and TV Pioneer." *Los Angeles Times*. December 27, 1990.

Ford, Luke. "Profile: Joel Soisson." Lukeford.net. Interview conducted on April 11, 2002.

Freff. "The Dark Beyond the Door: Walking (Nervously) into Stephen King's World." *Tomb of Dracula* Nos. 4 & 5. 1980.

Gagne, Paul R. "CREEPSHOW." *Cinefantastique* Vol. 13, No. 1. September-October 1982.

Gagne, Paul R. "Five Jolting Tales of Horror from Stephen King & George Romero." *Cinefantastique* Vol. 12, No. 2. April 1982.

Gagne, Paul R. "Interview with Stephen King." 1989. *Feast of Fear: Conversations with Stephen King*. Ed. Tim Underwood and Chuck Miller. Grand Central, 1993.

Gagne, Paul R. "Stephen King." *Cinefantastique* Vol. 10, No. 1. Summer 1980.

Gagne, Paul R. *The Zombies That Ate Pittsburgh*. Dodd, 1987.

Gallman, Brett. "Graveyard Shift (1990)." Oh-the-horror.com. October 26, 2017.

Gambin, Lee. *Hell Hath No Fury Like Her: The Making of CHRISTINE*. BearManor, 2019.

Garrido, Oscar ,and Bernd Lautenslager. "Jeffrey C. Schiro; April 23, 2006." StephenKingShortMovies.com. April 23, 2006.

Garris, Mick (interviewer). *Post Mortem with Mick Garris* Episode #93. October 28, 2020. Podcast.

Gingold, Michael. *The Motion Picture Guide: 1996 Annual (The Films of 1995)*. Bowker, 1996.

Gire, Dann. "A minimum of logic chokes MAXIMUM OVERDRIVE." *The [Chicago] Daily Herald*. July 31, 1986.

Goldman, William. *Which Lie Die I Tell?: More Adventures in the Screen Trade*. Random House, 2000.

Goldsmith, George. CHILDREN OF THE CORN. Based on the Short Story by Stephen King. Second Revision. Film script, August 5, 1983.

Goldstein, Dan. "Showtime." *B'nai B'rith Messenger*. February 6, 1976.

Goldstein, Patrick. "MAXIMUM OVERDRIVE Spins Its Wheels." *Los Angeles Times*. July 28, 1986

Grant, Charles L. "I Like to Go for the Jugular." *Twilight Zone* Vol. 1, No. 1. April 1981.

Grant, Charles L. "Interview with Stephen King." *Monsterland* No. 5. May/June 1985.

Grater, Tom. "Kurt Wimmer Wraps CHILDREN OF THE CORN Reboot in Australia After Cast & Crew Isolate Together During Lockdown Shoot." Deadline.com. June 12, 2020.

Griffith, Daniel (director). "Cybergod: Creating THE LAWNMOWER MAN." Ballyhoo, 2017. Video.

Gross, Edward. "Stephen King Takes a Vacation, Part 2." *Fangoria* #58. October 1986.

Grosso, Chris. "Dimension Films Can Go F*ck Themselves—An Interview with Doug Bradley." *The Indie Spiritualist*. October 30, 2010.

Groth, Gary. "Zombies, Homunculi, and (Swamp) Things That Go Bump in the Night: An Interview with Bernie Wrightson." *The Comics Journal* #76. October 1982.

Haber, Bill. "Under the Radar." *Stephen King's Battleground: A Commemoration of the Emmy-Winning Television Adaptation*. Ed. Richard Christian Matheson. Gauntlet, 2012.

Hall, Jacob. "CREEPSHOW Producer Greg Nicotero on Resurrecting a Horror Legend with Practical Effects and a Small Budget." Slashfilm.com. September 4, 2019.

Hamilton-Wright, Michael. Commentary. THE MANGLER 2. LionsGate, 2002. Video.

Hamman, Cody. "The F*cking Black Sheep: Stephen King's GRAVEYARD SHIFT." Joblo.com. September 13, 2017. Video.

Harrington, Richard. "THE MANGLER." *The Washington Post*. March 6, 1995.

Harris, Blake. "How Did This Get Made? MAXIMUM OVERDRIVE (An Oral History)." Slashfilm.com. September 18, 2015.

Harris, Kathryn. "Real Cliffhanger: Will New World Be the Next Financial Horror in Hollywood?" *Los Angeles Times*. March 6, 1988.

Hatlen, Burton. "Stephen King and the American Dream: Alienation, Competition, and Community in Rage and The Long Walk." *Reign of Fear: The Fiction and the Films of Stephen King*. Ed. Don Herron. Underwood-Miller, 1988.

Helms, Michael. "NIGHTMARES & DREAMSCAPES." *Fangoria* #254. June 2006.

Henson, Brian. "In the Trenches." *Stephen King's Battleground: A Commemoration of the Emmy-Winning Television Adaptation*. Ed. Richard Christian Matheson. Gauntlet, 2012.

Herndon, Ben. "New Adventures in the Scream Trade: A Non-Stop King Takes on TV." *Twilight Zone* Vol. 5, No. 5. December 1985.

Hewitt, Tim. "CAT'S EYE." *Cinefantastique* Vol. 15, No. 2. May 1985.

Hewitt, Tim. "OVERDRIVE." *Cinefantastique* Vol. 16, No. 1. March 1986.

Hewitt, Tim. "Stephen King's SILVER BULLET." *Cinefantastique* Vol. 15, No. 5. January 1986.

Holwill, Naomi, and Jim Kunz (directors). THE LIFE, LEGEND AND LEGACY OF DONALD P. BORCHERS. 2016. High Rising Productions. Video.

Horsting, Jessie. "CUJO." *Fantastic Films* #36. November 1983.

Horsting, Jessie. "Interview with Stephen King." 1986. *Feast of Fear: Conversations with Stephen King*. Ed. Tim Underwood and Chuck Miller. Warner, 1989.

Horsting, Jessie. *Stephen King at the Movies*. Starlog, 1986.

Horsting, Jessie. "Stephen King Gets Behind the Wheel." *Fangoria* #56. August 1986.

Hughes, Dave. "A Hope in Hell." *Fangoria* #147. October 1995.

Hunter, Stephen. "Only horror fans are likely to be impressed with THE MANGLER." *The Baltimore Sun*. March 7, 1995.

Jones, Alan. "CHILDREN OF THE CORN." *Starburst* #72. August 1984.

Jones, Alan. "The Subotsky-King Connection." *Cinefantastique* Vol. 16, No. 4. October 1986.

Jones, Alan, and Phil Edwards. "Tales from the Crypt." *Starburst* #38. October 1981.

Jones, Stephen. *Creepshows: The Illustrated Stephen King Movie Guide*. Billboard, 2002.

Jones, Stephen. "The Night Shifter." *Fantasy Media* Vol. 1 No. 1. March 1979.

King, Stephen. "The Crate." *Shivers VII*. Cemetery Dance, 2013.

King, Stephen. *Danse Macabre [Revised Edition]*. 1981. Gallery, 2010.

King, Stephen. "An Evening at the Billerica Library." 1983. *Secret Windows: Essays and Fiction on the Craft of Writing*. Book of the Month Club, 2000.

King, Stephen. "Foreword." *Night Shift*. Doubleday, 1977.

King, Stephen. "Foreword." *Silver Bullet*. Signet, 1985.

King, Stephen. "The Horror Writer and the Ten Bears." 1973. *Secret Windows: Essays and Fiction on the Craft of Writing*. Book of the Month Club, 2000.

King, Stephen. "Inside LISEY'S STORY: An Exclusive Apple TV+ Interview with Stephen King." *Lisey's Story*. Scribner's, 2021.

King, Stephen. "Introduction." *The Arbor House Treasury of Horror and the Supernatural*. Arbor House, 1981.

King, Stephen. "Introduction." *Carrie*. Pocket, 1999.

King, Stephen. "Introduction [to 'The Glass Floor']." *Weird Tales* #298. Fall 1990.

King, Stephen. "King's Garbage Truck: A Blessed (?) Event Announced to the University of Maine at Orono!" *Maine Campus*. May 14, 1970.

King, Stephen. *Night Shift*. Doubleday, 1977.

King, Stephen. "A Novelist's Perspective on Bangor." *Black Magic & Music*. The Bangor Historical Society, 1983.

King, Stephen. "On *The Shining* and Other Perpetrations." *Whispers* Vol. 5, No. 1–2. August 1982.

King, Stephen. *On Writing: A Memoir of the Craft*. Scribner's, 2000.

King, Stephen. "Opinion." *The Maine Campus*. November 16, 1967.

King, Stephen. "Rita Hayworth and the Darabont Redemption." *The Shawshank Redemption: The Shooting Script*. Newmarket, 1996.

King, Stephen. *Stephen King Goes to the Movies*. Pocket, 2009.

King, Stephen. "Weeds." *Shivers VII*. Cemetery Dance, 2013.

King, Stephen. "Yellow-Bellies." *The Maine Campus*. April 27, 1967.

King, Stephen. CAT'S EYE. Film script, May 14, 1984.

King, Stephen. CHILDREN OF THE CORN. 2nd Draft. Film script, undated (104 pages).

King, Stephen. CHILDREN OF THE CORN. Revised 6/80. Film script, June 1980.

King, Stephen. CREEPSHOW. 1st Draft. Film script, 1979.

King, Stephen. MAXIMUM OVERDRIVE. Film script, May 29, 1985.

King. Stephen. NIGHT SHIFT. 2nd Draft. Treatment/Synopsis, undated (21 pages). Sy Salkowitz Papers, 1956–1982. Box 115, Folder 5. Wisconsin Center for Film and Theater Research.

King, Stephen. OVERDRIVE. Film script, May 22, 1985.

King, Stephen. TRUCKS. First Draft. Film script, February 8, 1985.

Knight, Chris. "The Amicus Empire." *Cinefantastique* Vol. 2, No. 4. Summer 1973.

Koetting, Christopher. "Making Book for Fear, Part 2." *Fangoria* #152. May 1996.

Kronke, David. "MANGLER a Tale of a Hungry Machine." *Los Angeles Times*. March 6, 1995.

Labbe, Rodney A. "Oh, Rats! It's GRAVEYARD SHIFT." *Fangoria* #98. October 1990.

Labbe, Rodney A. "Ratman." *Fangoria* #99. December 1990.

Larson, Randall D. [Interview with Robert Bloch.] *Fandom Unlimited* #1. October 1971.

Lealos, Shawn S. *Dollar Deal: The Story of the Stephen King Dollar Baby Filmmakers*. Self-published, 2015.

Leeman, Zachary. "10 Horror Franchises That Are Practically Begging to Be Revived." Bloodydisgusting.com. July 5, 2018.

Leicht, Aine (producer). BRIAN TAGGERT: THE B-MOVIE KID. Shout Factory. Video, 2014.

Lilja, Hans-Ake. "Interview: Frank Darabont." *Lilja's Library: The World of Stephen King*. Cemetery Dance, 2010.

Lloyd, Ann. *The Films of Stephen King*. St. Martin's, 1993.

Lofficier, Randy. "Stephen King Talks About *Christine*." *Twilight Zone* Vol. 3, No. 6. February 1984.

Longhetti, Chloe-Lee. "The show must go on! Police are called to the set of Hollywood movie filming in Sydney over concern the crew is flouting social distancing rules." *Daily Mail Online*. April 3, 2020.

Magistrale, Tony. *Hollywood's Stephen King*. Palgrave, 2003.

Magistrale, Tony. *Landscape of Fear: Stephen King's American Gothic*. Popular Press, 1988.

Magistrale, Tony. "The Writer Defines Himself: An Interview with Stephen King." *Stephen King: The Second Decade, Danse Macabre to The Dark Half*. Twayne, 1992.

Martin, Bob. "KNIGHTRIDERS." *Fangoria* #12. April 1981.

Martin, Perry (director). HARVESTING HORROR: CHILDREN OF THE CORN. Anchor Bay, 2004. Video.

Martin, R.H. "Stephen King on OVERDRIVE and PET SEMATARY." *Fangoria* #48. October 1985.

Marx, Andy. "King's Kingdom: We Get It All the Way Up to the Mercedes Part." *Los Angeles Times*. June 14, 1992.

Maslin, Janet. "Review/Film: Underground Horror." *New York Times*. October 27, 1990.

Matheson, Richard Christian. "BATTLEGROUND." *Stephen King's Battleground: A Commemoration of the Emmy-Winning Television Adaptation*. Ed. Richard Christian Matheson. Gauntlet, 2012.

Matheson, Richard Christian. "Introduction." *Stephen King's Battleground: A Commemoration of the Emmy-Winning Television Adaptation*. Ed. Richard Christian Matheson. Gauntlet, 2012.

Mauceri, Joe. "THE MANGLER." *Shivers* #17. May 1995.

McDonnell, David. "Have Chainsaw, Will Travel." *Fangoria* #56. August 1986.

McGrew, Shannon. "Interview: Talking CREEPSHOW with Greg Nicotero." Nightmarishconjurings.com. September 25, 2019.

McLoughlin, Tom. "The Curse of STEPHEN KING'S SOMETIMES THEY COME BACK." *Stephen King—Dollar Baby: The Book*. Ed. Anthony Northrup. BearManor, 2021.

Modderno, Craig. "Topic: Horrors!" *USA Today*. May 10, 1985.

Muir, John Kenneth. *Eaten Alive at a Chainsaw Massacre: The Films of Tobe Hooper*. McFarland, 2002.

Muir, John Kenneth. *Horror Films of the 1980s*. McFarland, 2007.

Muir, John Kenneth. *Horror Films of the 1990s.* McFarland, 2011.

Munster, Bill. "Stephen King: A 1981 Interview." 1981. *Feast of Fear: Conversations with Stephen King.* Ed. Tim Underwood and Chuck Miller. Warner, 1989.

Nevison, Henry [interviewer]. "I Sleep with the Light On." *UMO Magazine.* 1982. Video.

Newton, Steve. "The BORDELLO Fellows." *Fangoria* #156. September 1996.

Newton, Steve. "Virtual Unreality." *Fangoria* #141. April 1995.

Nicotero, Gregory. Commentary. CREEPSHOW, SEASON ONE. AMC, 2020. Video.

Norden, Eric. "Playboy Interview: Stephen King." *Playboy.* June 1983.

Northrup, Tony. "Jeff Schiro—Interview." ThroughtheBlackHole.com. July 21, 2014.

Nutman, Philip. "King Talks, Part One." *Fangoria* #99. December 1990.

Nutman, Philip. "The Vault of Subotsky!" *Fangoria* #32. January 1984.

Palmer, Randy. "The British Terror of Freddie Francis." *Fangoria* #30. October 1983.

Parales, John. "Film: By Stephen King, MAXIMUM OVERDRIVE." *New York Times.* July 25, 1986

Paul, Zachary. "Doug Bradley Speaks (Again) About HELLRAISER: JUDGMENT." Halloweenlove.com. February 9, 2017.

Peck, Abe. "Stephen King's Court of Horror." *Rolling Stone College Papers.* Winter 1980.

Petkovich, Anthony. "The Kid from Hancock Park: An Interview with Screenwriter Brian Taggert." *Shock Cinema* #57. November 2019.

Pirani, Adam, and Alan McKenzie. "A Starburst Interview with Stephen King." *Starburst* #61. September 1983.

Platt, Charles. "Stephen King." *Dream Makers: The Uncommon People Who Write Science Fiction.* Berkley, 1980.

Porch, Scott. "Shudder GM Craig Engler on the Runaway Success of CREEPSHOW." Decider.com. October 31, 2019.

Rausch, Andrew J. *Fifty Filmmakers: Conversations with Directors from Roger Avery to Steven Zaillian.* BearManor, 2008.

Rausch, Andrew J. *Perspectives on Stephen King: Conversations with Authors, Experts and Collaborators.* BearManor, 2019.

Rogak, Lisa. *Haunted Heart: The Life and Times of Stephen King.* Griffin, 2009.

Rosenthal, Mark, and Lawrence Konner. SOMETIMES THEY COME BACK. Fourth Draft. Filmscript, August 31, 1990. Cinematic Arts Library. University of Southern California.

Ryan, Danielle. "CHAPELWAITE Showrunners Share What It's Like to Play in the Stephen King Sandbox." Slashfilm.com. August 18, 2021.

St. John, M.A. "Digital Hotspot: WALKING DEAD Web Series writer John Esposito." Streamzcurator.tumblr.com. 2014.

Savlov, Marc. "THE MANGLER." *The Austin Chronicle.* March 10, 1995

Sayers, Dorothy L. *The Mind of the Maker.* Harcourt, 1941.

Schauer, Bradley. "Dimension Films and the Exploitation Tradition in Contemporary Hollywood." *Quarterly Review of Film and Video* Vol. 26. September 25, 2009.

Schiro, Jeff. THE BOOGEYMAN. Film script, undated (22 pages).

Sechrest, Jason. "Keys to the Kingdom: The Bill Thompson Interview (Part Two). Suntup.press. November 13, 2018.

Sederholm, Carl H. "Feeding the Industrial Monster: A Critical Reconsideration of Tobe Hooper's THE MANGLER." *American Twilight: The Cinema of Tobe Hooper.* UT Press, 2021.

Seger, Linda. *The Art of Adaptation: Turning Fact and Fiction into Film.* Owl, 1992.

Shapiro, Marc. "THE MANGLER: Clothes Encounter of the Gory Kind." *Fangoria* #141. April 1995.

Shapiro, Marc. "Master of Cathode Carnage." *Fangoria* #101. April 1991.

Shapiro, Marc. "Monster Invasion." *Fangoria* #103. June 1991.

Shapiro, Marc. "Virtual Virtuoso." *Starlog* #218. September 1995.

Sheppard, Richard (host). "Episode 18: CHAPELWAITE Special with Peter Filardi." *The Constant Reader Podcast.* Sept. 9, 2021.

Singleton, Ralph S. Interview. "Filmmaking in Stephen King Country: Ralph Singleton on GRAVEYARD SHIFT." Shout Factory, 2020. Video.

Singleton, Ralph S. Interview. "Working the Night Shift: Ralph Singleton on GRAVEYARD SHIFT." Shout Factory, 2020. Video.

Spignesi, Stephen J. "His Father's Son: An Interview with Richard Christian Matheson." *The Complete Stephen King Encyclopedia: The Definitive Guide to the Works of America's Master of Horror.* Contemporary, 1991.

Spignesi, Stephen J. "A Talk with Stephen King's True First Collaborator: An Interview with Chris Chesley." *The Complete Stephen King Encyclopedia: The Definitive Guide to the Works of America's Master of Horror.* Contemporary, 1991.

Stewart, Bhob. "FLIX." *Heavy Metal* Vol. 3, No. 9. January 1980.

Stewart, Bhob. "FLIX." *Heavy Metal* Vol. 3, No. 10. February 1980.

Stewart, Bhob. "FLIX." *Heavy Metal* Vol. 3, No. 11. March 1980.

Stone, Sam. "CHAPELWAITE Creators Discuss Whaling & Adding Multiracial Children to Stephen King's Story." CBR.com. Aug. 20, 2021.

Strauss, Robert. "Interview with Stephen King." 1986. *Feast of Fear: Conversations with Stephen King.* Ed. Tim Underwood and Chuck Miller. Warner, 1989.

Stroby, W.C. "Cinema Cats and Dogs, Part One." *Fangoria* #113. June 1992.

Subotsky, Milton. "The Work of the Film

Producer." *Screen* Vol. 10, No. 6. November/December 1969.

Subotsky, Milton (interviewee). "Two's a Company." *Film Night*. BBC. July 29, 1972.

Swires, Steve. "George Romero: Master of the Living Dead." *Starlog* #21. April 1979.

Swires, Steve. "Roy Ward Baker: Life After Hammer, Part 2." *Fangoria* #117. October 1992.

Tafoya, Scott. *Cinemaphagy: On the Psychedelic Classical Form of Tobe Hooper*. Miniver, 2021.

Teitelbaum, Sheldon. "Tales from the Crypt: The Comics." *Cinefantastique* Vol. 20, No. 3. January 1990.

Thomas, Kevin. "Movie Review: GRAVEYARD Deserves an Early Burial." *Los Angeles Times*. October 29, 1990.

Thomases, Martha, and John Robert Tebbel. "Interview with Stephen King." *High Times*. January 1981.

Tilley, Doug. "Interview with BURNING DEAD Director George Demick." Nobudgetpodcast.com. 2014. Podcast.

Timpone, Tony. "Siblings Jason and Peter Filardi on Creating CHAPELWAITE." GruesomeMagazine.com. August 30, 2021.

Towers, Harry Alan. *Mr. Towers of London: A Life in Show Business*. BearManor, 2013.

Trembath, Ron. "TWS Week of Horror Day 8: John Frankin (Interview)." *Trainwreck'd Society*. October 30, 2016.

Truffaut, François. *Hitchcock (Revised Edition)*. Simon & Schuster, 1985.

Trumbore, Dave. "CREEPSHOW Writers on Adapting Stephen King's 'Gray Matter' and Keeping It Fun." Collider.com. Sept. 26, 2019.

Trumbore, Dave. "Greg Nicotero on CREEPSHOW, Collaboration, Stephen King, and Keeping Things Praactical." Collider.com. Sept. 26, 2019.

United States District Court, Central District of California. *Donald P. Borchers, Plaintiff, v.*

The Weinstein Company, LLC d/b/a Dimension Films; Miramax, LLC; The Walt Disney Company; and DOES 1 through 50, inclusive, Defendants. Complaint for Declaratory Relief. Filed August 24, 2017.

Van Hise, James, ed. *Enterprise Incidents Presents Stephen King*. New Media, 1984.

Von Doviak, Scott. *Stephen King Films FAQ: All That's Left to Know About the King of Horror on Film*. Applause, 2014.

Waddell, Calum (director). BACK TO THE 80s: AN INTERVIEW WITH DONALD P. BORCHERS. High Rising Productions, 2011. Video.

Warren, Bill. "King of All Media." *Fangoria* #163. June 1997.

Warren, Bill. "The Movies and Mr. King." *Fear Itself: The Horror Fiction of Stephen King*. Ed. Chuck Miller and Tim Underwood. 1982.

Warren, Bill. "The Movies and Mr. King, Part 2." *Reign of Fear: The Fiction and Films of Stephen King*. Ed. Don Herron. 1988.

Whittington, James. "Exclusive Interview with Legendary Director Kevin Common." HorrorChannel.co.uk. August 7, 2012.

Wiater, Stanley. "Stephen King: The MAXIMUM OVERDRIVE Interview." 1986. *Feast of Fear: Conversations with Stephen King*. Ed. Tim Underwood and Chuck Miller. Warner, 1989.

Wiater, Stanley, and Roger Anker. "Horror Partners." *Fangoria* #42. February 1985.

Winter, Douglas E. *Stephen King: The Art of Darkness (Expanded and Updated)*. New American Library, 1986.

Wood, Gary. "Stephen King and Hollywood." *Cinefantastique* Vol. 21, No. 4. February 1991.

Wood, Gary. "To Direct, or Not to Direct." *Cinefantastique* Vol. 21, No. 4. February 1991.

Wood, Rocky. *Stephen King: Uncollected, Unpublished (Revised and Expanded)*. Cemetery Dance, 2010.

Index